Party Lines, Prayers, And Privies

The Indomitable Three

Sarah	1875 – 1940
Esther	1897 – 1996
Helen	1918 – 2003

A Historical Novel

Family is forever -
Judy Steffen Lambert

Judy Steffen Lambert

First Edition Design Publishing
Sarasota, Florida USA

Party Lines, Prayers, And Privies

ISBN 978-1506-910-26-0 PBK
ISBN 978-1506-910-27-7 EBK

LCCN 2021906960

April 2021

Published and Distributed by
First Edition Design Publishing, Inc.
P.O. Box 17646, Sarasota, FL 34276-3217
www.firsteditiondesignpublishing.com

DISCLAIMER

Party Lines, Prayers, and Privies is a historical novel as I imagine the lives of three women: Sarah, Esther, and Helen. To the best of my ability, it is based on family stories and extensive research—others may have different versions. Occasionally I have taken liberty with historical details, characters, and dates to enhance the flow of the story. Every effort has been made to make the content authentic to mind and nondefamatory. The author and publisher cannot be held personally liable.

To my daughters, Lisa and Stephanie, who breathe the spirit of
The Three in the kindness and integrity of their lives
and
My grandchildren: Maya, Charlotte, and Wyatt, whose torches
even now sparkle brightly

LINEAGE

Lucinda Zumbrun	Uriah Long
1841	1833

Lucinda and Uriah married and had 7 children; **Sarah** was the youngest

Jacob	Ira	Henry	Perry	Juda	William	**Sarah**
1862	1864	1866	1867	1869	1871	1875 Married **Judson Swihart** 1873

(Sarah and Judson Swihart's Children)

Edith	**Esther**	Ruth	Carl	Clara	Floyd	Noble	Ruby	Merle	Don
1896	1897 Married **Earl Phillips** 1896	1899	1901	1902	1908	1912	1913	1915	1919

(Esther and Earl Phillips' Children)

Helen	Erdene	Rosemary	James	Louise
1918 Married **Walter Steffen** 1919	1923	1924	1929	1931

(Helen and Walter Steffen's Children)

Janice	Judy	Nancy	Susan	Randall	Steven
1942	1943	1945	1948	1954	1956

Prologue 1980

I would rather do anything in the world than the dreaded task before me. It was springtime, and while I usually enjoyed the three-hour trip through lush, prosperous Indiana farmland; today I was apprehensive driving north to Grandma Esther's home.

I simply adored her. She was the eighty-three-year-old revered paragon of my mother's family. A small woman with curly white hair, she possessed a gentle sweetness that only comes with age. The essence of propriety, she dressed each day in a "Sunday" outfit, always with a brooch at the neckline, face powder for make-up and black lace-up shoes with two-inch heels. She wore a dress-up hat when she went calling, a part of her daily routine. The family agreed there was nothing better than her thumbprint molasses cookies. She was a woman steeped in the Christian faith of the Brethren Church. She said the most beautiful prayers because she meant the words from her heart and lived the faith that gave meaning to her life.

I arrived at her home having buttressed my resolve and murmured my own prayers. She welcomed me with warm hugs and kisses. Oh, the security to be in her loving arms, safe from all that had been tearing my life apart. Her kindness brought another barrage of tears, bringing dismay to her face as I knelt on the floor by her chair. "Oh, Judy, what has happened to you? I'm so sorry" she said as she lovingly placed her hands on my face.

I had to just say it. "I told Wayne I'm filing for divorce. We'll tell the girls next week and separate at the end of the school year. I know this is wrong, but I have to do this, Grandma."

In the society of the 1970's, divorce was not uncommon. But in my little town and particularly in our Church of the Brethren, divorce was anathema. I had grown up in a cocoon of love and acceptance where no one in our extended family had a "broken marriage". It was not part of our world and now I would be tainting her with this evil.

"I'm so sorry. I never meant this to happen. In fact, I determined I never would give up on a marriage, but I can't fix this." We were both crying, our joined hands wet with tears. I didn't think I could stand it if she were critical or begged me to reconsider. I certainly didn't want to contaminate her mind with the sad turn my life had taken.

"Oh, Judy, I've known you all your life and I know the good, loving person you are. I know this isn't what you want. I don't know what's been happening to you and I never want to know. I'm sad you have to go through this with your little girls."

"This is part of the reason I have to get a divorce, Grandma. I have to be an example for my girls, to stand up for what is right."

What Grandma said next imprinted in my mind. "Judy, I love you. Nothing you do will change that. I'm sad knowing you will be going through difficult times." Her eyes moved to the collage of old family photos on her living room wall and, with a look of certainty she said, "I know you'll be okay. Look at the women in our family, their struggles through the years. My mother, Sarah, never had a childhood after her mother died. My babies were so sickly, and I thought I wanted to die after my baby boy died. And look how Helen, your mother accomplished so much despite her handicap. Why, someone could write a book about these hard times—they have molded our backbone. You've inherited this strength, Judy. I promise you won't just survive, you'll become a better woman. You know I will pray every day for your family."

My heart was full on my return home. I had seen uncommon love and wisdom in my grandma's being. I knew after that visit, my girls and I would indeed make it, because we have a heritage of resolute courage from generations of women. I began that day to hear the voices of my great-grandmother Sarah, grandma Esther, and mother Helen. Their struggles to overcome hardship were a part of me that was an invaluable gift to my daughters. I must tell their stories. Listen, my dears, to their voices.

CHAPTER 1

Lucinda, April 1884

A muffled cry pierced the night on a small Indiana farmstead. The sound shocked her awake: she heard a scream. Her sleepy eight-year-old mind remembered the happenings earlier in the day and she was troubled. Things had seemed normal walking home from school, being teased by big sister Juda: "Sarah got caught talking before the bell today. Her new name is Miss Windbag!"

Brother Will ran past, grabbing her hat from her head. "Miss Windbag, the wind blew your hat off." He ran ahead, laughing and throwing her hat in the air. She could never keep up with ten-year-old Will, who kept growing out of his overalls. He barged into their two-room log cabin, then stopped short when he noticed Papa fixing harness at the wood slab table. Papa never came up from the field in the middle of the day.

"Quiet, Will. Mama doesn't feel well. She's in bed." Standing, Papa stretched, running his hands through his frizzy salt-and-pepper hair. "You and Sarah do the milking tonight, Will. Juda, after you finish your chores, boil up some potatoes for supper. Mrs. Hazen will be coming to be with Mama."

Turning toward the bedroom, Sarah asked, "Can I tell Mama I got perfect on my spelling test?"

"No Sarah, she needs to rest. It may be a long night," Papa replied.

Sarah changed to work clothes and walked to the barn. She was glad she had Sol to milk, though she didn't like that she swung her manure-clumped tail around her neck while she milked. She liked doing chores with Will because he made her laugh. This time she teased *him*, "Susana told me at school today she thinks you're good looking. She says because of your dark skin and black hair you look like an Indian."

Will laughed, tapping his hand to his mouth, "O-E-O-E-O-E, get my tomahawk!"

"Susana takes a shine to you," she taunted.

As Will and Sarah walked back from the barn, Mrs. Hazen came in her buggy. She had a bustling, no-nonsense personality and was the one sent for when neighbors got sick. Though she was older, she was Mama's best friend.

Papa and Mrs. Hazen were with Mama while we ate our supper. We heard her muffled moaning. Mrs. Hazen spoke gently, "There, there, Lucinda." Soon Mama called out, sounding angry. Papa came out of the bedroom, pacing while he ate his potatoes and bread. "Where is he?" he muttered, striding from the fireplace to the bench across the room. He fanned his fingers back through his hair and pawed at his beard.

Will kept reaching across the table to poke Sarah's hand. Papa yelled, "Leave her alone, Will. Can't you just eat?" Will looked miserable as he took his plate to the dishpan on the cupboard.

Papa opened the bedroom door, "I'm going to get Dr. Ott. He should have been here two hours ago."

Mrs. Hazen agreed. "That's good. Things aren't moving here."

"Juda, have everyone in bed by nine o'clock," Papa called as he grabbed his coat and hat while running out the door. Sarah dried the pottery dishes then swept the rough wood floor. Will brought in wood for the fire. It was April, but still cold and drafty in the cabin. Sarah practiced her letters while Will and Juda did schoolwork. They were quiet and uneasy, listening to Mama moan and cry.

"Is Mama bad sick? Why is Papa getting the doctor?" Sarah asked.

Juda stood up. "Let's wash and get into our bedclothes. Then I'll tell you a secret."

They climbed the ladder into their attic bedroom, taking their brick foot warmers. Sarah loved Juda's secrets. Last time she told Mama's secret that there was Indian blood in the Zumbrun family. Since then, she and Will teased about being Indian, but they didn't want anyone to know and call them a Redskin.

The three sat on the straw tick mattress that Juda and Sarah shared. Juda undid Sarah's braids and brushed her dark, wavy hair. "Have you noticed Mama's tummy has grown big and round? She has a baby in her tummy. It's time for the baby to come. This is painful and someone must help the baby be born. Mrs. Hazen knows how to do that. Sometimes doctors need to help too. Sarah, I'm so excited! We'll get to take care of the baby. We can hold it and rock the cradle. Will, you can change the baby's diaper," she laughed.

"PeeUuu!" Will held his nose. "Babies are women's work. I'll teach him how to fish."

"Let's say our prayers now. Ask God to keep Mama safe and maybe when we wake up, we'll hear a baby crying," Juda said as she knelt beside the mattress. After prayers, Sarah and Juda cuddled together and fell asleep.

These memories of the day were interrupted by another scream as Sarah's mind returned to the present. She could hear Mrs. Hazen moving about and speaking softly. For several minutes she listened to the sounds below. Unable to sleep, she slipped from Juda's arms, tip-toed to the attic opening and peeked down. Through the soft kerosene light, she watched Mrs. Hazen hurry from the bedroom, check a large pot in the fireplace, put out towels and clean rags, and carry her case into the bedroom.

She heard noise outside, then Papa burst in the door with old Doctor Ott, who staggered to his knees, dropping his bag and scattering his instruments. His hat and glasses went flying and he crawled around trying to collect his things.

"Thank goodness, you're here," said Mrs. Hazen as she bent to assist Dr. Ott. Looking at him, she said, "The baby is breech. I haven't been able to turn it. Lucinda is pert near out of it from such a long labor. Did you bring the new gadget, the forceps? She's hardly aware. I don't think she'll be able to push."

Doctor Ott crawled over to the bench, attempting to pull himself up. He was holding his head as Papa reached and shook him. "You've got to do something, doctor. The baby's in trouble. Get up now; you need to help her!"

Mrs. Hazen grasped the doctor's arm. She sniffed, then looked disgustedly at Papa. "Uriah, he's drunk. He'll be no use to us. Lucinda will die if we don't do something NOW."

As she spoke, Mama wailed desperately. Doctor Ott's head snapped at the sound, and he tottered into the bedroom with Papa and Mrs. Hazen rushing behind.

Sarah's body was numb. She couldn't believe what she saw. As her eyes lifted to the attic, she noticed Juda and Will were peeking out the opening too. The three were frozen with dread, not saying a word. Mrs. Hazen rushed in and out of the bedroom carrying the steaming pot and the things she had gathered. Glancing at Juda, Sarah saw her eyes were closed and her mouth was moving silently. Sarah whispered her own prayer, "Dear God, take the hurt away from Mama. Make her all better."

Juda quietly led them back to bed, her arms shaky. Mama became quiet, her sounds more like a mewling kitten. Finally, everything was quiet, too quiet. Sarah reached for Juda's hand.

When she woke, she didn't hear the usual bustling sounds downstairs. Each of the children went to a corner to dress—to be alone with their thoughts. Sarah put on the long dress and apron Mama had stitched from a feed sack. It was still cold enough for her to need brown underwear and long stockings. Will didn't tease this morning, running around and hiding her stockings. When Juda braided her hair, Sarah saw tears sliding down her cheek.

After climbing down the attic ladder, she noticed the bedroom door was closed. Papa was just now stoking the fire at the hearth. No Mama. No cornmeal mush bubbling in the pot. In her heart everything felt wrong. As they walked outside to do chores, Will took her hand, not saying a word. She went to the privy, fed the chickens, and gave mash to the calves while Will milked.

Returning to the cabin, Sarah washed her face in a dishpan of cold water before sitting at the table. Papa washed his face, bent over the dishpan, washing again and again, like the cold water was soothing. Juda, her eyes swollen and red, brought us bowls of warm milk with bread and butter. Because Papa couldn't hear well, he spoke loudly as he said the morning prayer:

> Our Father in Heaven, we thank You for this new day. We are grateful for the blessings You have bestowed upon us: our warm home; food to eat; and land for sowing and reaping. Dear God, be near to us this day as we walk through the valley of the shadow of death. In Jesus name we pray. Amen.

As Papa finished his prayer, Will sobbed. He jumped up from the table and climbed the ladder to the attic, tears running down his face. Then Sarah cried, standing to leave with Will. Juda put her arms around her and wiped her tears with a hanky, "Leave him be, Sarah. He wants to be alone. Let's have some bread and milk."

Papa, Juda, and Sarah tried to eat the bread soup. Sarah spooned a little warm milk. Papa and Juda drank their coffee. Without Mama it didn't feel like their family. After a while, Will came down and sat at his place. It was an uneasy quiet.

Papa lowered his head to his hands. "Children..."

Sarah stood up. "No!" She looked at Papa, "Don't say it."

"Come here, Sarah," he held out his arms. His voice seemed to blare, "Children, Mama died last night and went to Heaven. We were going to have a baby, but something was wrong. While you were asleep, the doctor came but nothing could be done." He jumped from the table, pacing the small room, his hands clasped behind his head, "If only I'd brought the doctor earlier. I didn't know until it was too late...."

For a time, all you could hear was quiet crying and sniffles. There was no question now. Mama was gone. Will laid his head in his arms. Juda covered her face with her hanky.

"But Papa, where is our baby?" Sarah cried.

"There is no baby, Sarah," Papa said sadly.

With a heaving sigh, Papa said, "Now we must go on. We need to be strong and dry our tears. Mama wouldn't want us to cry. This is God's will, and we must be thankful that Mama is in a happier place where every tear will be dry." Sarah went to sit on Juda's lap; she rocked her like when she was a baby.

Speaking to himself, Papa said, "Mrs. Hazen will come in the morning to prepare Mama."

Then with resolve, "Juda, you will be the Mother now. Wash Mama's church dress and clean her shoes. John Hazen and I will make a coffin and prepare the grave. I'll go to Blue River and see if Reverend Hill can have a service for Mama tomorrow afternoon."

"Do Uncle William and Aunt Caroline know about Mama?" asked Juda.

"Oh dear God," Papa said, shaking his head. "My mind is muddled. Ride the donkey to Uncle William's. He was Mama's favorite brother. I wonder if Aunt Caroline will be surprised. Last month when she saw Mama, she knew something was wrong because of the brown spot that came on Mama's face."

Papa sat on the bench beside Sarah. "You muck Boss and Sol's stall and put the manure on the garden." Shaking his head, he muttered, "But who will do the garden now anyway? Don't forget to gather the eggs and feed the calves this evening." Papa put his hand on Juda's shoulder, "Things will be different without Mama. We're all going to have to do our share. When it's time for planting, you, Will, and Sarah will all need to quit school. We'll need you at home to help get seeds in the ground."

Juda drew in a sharp breath, "Papa." This was the worst possible news. All three children loved school. Most girls quit school at age twelve, but Miss Banks had told Mama Juda was especially gifted and should get special instruction. Mama agreed, believing school the most important thing, even for a girl. Leaving school would break Juda's heart; Sarah and Will didn't want to quit either.

"We have much to do today. We're all sad and it will be easy for us to feel sorry for ourselves. The Bible says, 'let not your heart be troubled and heavy laden'. We remember Mama being cheerful and singing as she worked. That's the way she would want us to carry on. Let's get busy now."

Juda heated water to wash clothes while Sarah chipped soap and pushed the arm on the rocking washer to slush about the clothes. Even though Papa said not to be sad, Juda and Sarah hardly talked, and then they only whispered with quavering voices.

There were so many things Sarah didn't understand. "What does it mean to die, Juda?" she asked, handing her a shirt by the corners.

Grasping the shirt and pegging it to the clothesline Juda said thoughtfully, "I learned in school that your heart stops beating, and you don't breathe anymore. Nothing in your body works. Then you die."

"Does it hurt to die?"

The next shirt dropped back into the basket as Juda bent to hold herself, remembering Mama's screams, "Yes Sarah, I think it hurt Mama to die," she said in anguish.

"I know Mama is in Heaven but where is Heaven? Will we ever see her again?"

Juda straightened up, stomping her foot and yelling, "I don't know! I don't know! I don't know! Nobody tells me anything either," she cried. She grabbed Sarah in her arms as they settled to the cold hard ground, rocking and crying, wondering what would happen to them without a mother. When Juda could speak again she said, "Sarah, I know Mama was going to have a baby and something was wrong with the baby when it was being born. Mama and the baby both died. Remember Aunt Nellie died when she had a baby? I think mothers get sick with babies sometimes. I know Mama went to Heaven 'cause she was a good person and she was saved by the blood of the lamb. Heaven is a special place in the sky where people go when they die. You never come back from Heaven, so we'll never see Mama again."

It felt good to cry with Juda and let their sadness be real. There was still a lot Sarah didn't understand but she knew Juda would tell her what she knew. Sitting on the ground, crying with Juda, felt like a relief to her.

"Sarah, Mama isn't with us anymore, but we can still love her and remember her. We should never forget that she loved us. I'll remember how she sang to us and combed our hair. She would kiss the top of your head and call you Sarah Cake. She didn't make me eat dandelion greens 'cause she knew I didn't like them. Always remember Sarah, that Mama loved you very much and where she is in Heaven, she still loves you even if she can't be with you. I think Mama would say to me, 'Juda, you take care of Sarah and help her not to be scared'. That's what I'll do, Sarah. I promise you."

It was quiet while the two rocked and thought about losing Mama. "I make a promise to take care of you too, Juda," Sarah said with eight-year-old pride.

That afternoon Juda rode the donkey to Aunt Caroline's. Papa and Mr. Hazen were working in the shed. Sarah had finished her jobs and was poking around the fire. She thought how everything had changed in one day—would things ever be the same? Why was the bedroom door still closed? No one had told her not to go inside. Was Mama still there? Could she see her...talk to her? She slowly opened the door and peeked in. There was Mama, as if she were asleep. She had on a clean nightgown and a blanket covering to her chest. Her long black hair was spread on the pillow.

"Mama?" She crept to the bed and reached to touch her face. It was cold and hard, not warm like Mama. She didn't reach to hold Sarah. Her eyes were closed; she didn't see Sarah. She wasn't like Mama. "Mama?" Sarah said timidly. Her combs, the ones that looked like pearl, held her hair back. Sarah reached and took a comb from her hair. "Bye, Mama. I'll remember you, just like Juda said," and she backed out of the room and closed the door.

CHAPTER 2

Sarah

Life went out of the cabin when Mama died. It was as if the cold windy day of her burial settled in and never left. The four of them rattled about the next morning, not used to so much togetherness with nothing to do. Mid-morning Mr. and Mrs. Hazen arrived with Susan, Frances, and George. Papa and Mr. Hazen went to the barn to finish the coffin. Mrs. Hazen put a big pot of soup simmering on the fire. Soon Aunt Caroline, Uncle William, Chloe, Donald, and Jesse came. Mrs. Hazen ran to Aunt Caroline. The two sobbing women held each other, swaying in their embrace. Ordinarily, with so many childhood friends visiting, the children would have had a heyday, but they just didn't know how to be on this occasion. Instead of normal bantering, the children were confused and afraid. Death was too new and real.

Mrs. Hazen and Aunt Caroline heated water and went to the bedroom to bathe Mama. Sarah worried they would discover Mama's missing comb, but both women seemed sadly preoccupied. They said nothing coming from the bedroom. What a relief. Sarah decided she would tell no one about this treasure she had from Mama.

"Get out of the way...move aside." Papa called out as the cabin door opened. He and John carried the coffin into the bedroom and closed the door.

Sarah glanced at Juda, their eyes frantic. "No...I can't be here." They ran toward the cabin door, fearful of seeing Mama leave the cabin in a coffin. They ran like thunder across the yard into the barn. Soon Will and the other children joined them, running pell-mell, falling in a tangled heap in the haymow, sobs unloosed. Finally they sat up, unwound, wiped their faces on their sleeves, and sat in silence until Aunt Caroline called them for dinner.

In the afternoon they rode in buggies to the simple log cabin that was the Blue River Dunkard Brethren Church. On the back of their wagon, they brought Mama in the coffin. There were a lot of neighbors already at church. The men carried Mama's coffin inside, placing it on a table at the front. The congregation sat on wood slab benches arranged with a center aisle, men and boys on the right, women and girls on the left. Sarah didn't like being in front where everyone could see her red eyes. Usually everyone visited before church, but today, even with all these people, it was quiet. The homemade dress of their friends and neighbors was drab. The men wore black gabardine suits with a stand-up collar. The women wore large black shawls over a long dark dress with a starched black bonnet covering their hair. These were the neighbors, friends, and family who loved Lucinda. A lady began to sing in a clear soprano voice, and everyone joined in:

> When peace like a river attendeth my way.
> When sorrow like sea billows roll.
> Whatever my lot, God has taught me to say
> It is well, it is well…with my soul.

Reverend Hill, like the other men, was a farmer who was chosen to be minister in a drawing of lots. He looked stern with his glasses at the end of his nose and he yelled when he preached. Today he appeared somber in his black suit as he strode to the pulpit and arranged his papers. His eyes rose, nodding to Lucinda's family, then taking in the congregation. He read from the Bible:

> For everything there is a time and a season: a time to be born and a time to die, a time to plant and a time to reap, a time to kill and a time to heal, a time to tear down and a time to build, a time to weep and a time to laugh, a time to mourn and a time to dance.

He paused, taking off his glasses and looking around. "For those who loved Lucinda, it may seem God got this wrong. This shouldn't be Lucinda's season. She is too young. She has a young family who need her." His voice raised as his finger pointed to Heaven, "But God has a plan for Lucinda's life that is His perfect plan. While we may not understand now, God knows best."

Sarah began to cry. Reverend Hill was right about one thing: she didn't understand why he would say Mama dying could be best. Maybe it was best for God, but it wasn't best for her.

Papa lifted her into his lap, encircled, like in a safe nest. She knew Papa would take care of her.

She heard Reverend Hill's closing remarks. "We know Lucinda has been born again and is saved by grace. We know she is in Heaven at the right hand of God. Whoever is here today who has not accepted Christ as your savior, Lucinda would beg you to confess your sins now." Lowering his voice to a threat, "Tomorrow may be too late. Death may come in the morning."

He stepped from the pulpit, leading the mourners in a rousing hymn: "When the Roll Is Called Up Yonder, I'll Be There." As the hymn concluded, the family walked by Mama's coffin. Sarah was too short to see Mama, but she didn't care. She knew it wasn't her real Mama. She remembered her real Mama as she touched the comb in her pocket.

CHAPTER 3

Spring - Summer 1884

Everyone said it was the wettest spring in Whitley County in ten years. When Papa tried to plant, the horses kicked up clumps of mud and the plow kept getting stuck. The only good thing was that Juda and Sarah got to go to school. Some days they went to Mrs. Hazen's after school so she could teach Juda to cook. These were good days, because Sarah got to play with the Hazen's daughter, Susan, and they had a good supper.

In June the rain finally stopped. Papa was eager to get in the fields—work started at sun-up. Papa hitched Belle to a single share plow. Some of the bigger tree stumps were left in the field, so plowing was difficult. Will and Sarah worked on their hands and knees. Will set the corn marker, moving it along the furrow while Sarah dropped five corn kernels at each intersection of the marker grid to get precise spacing. Then Juda hoed the dirt over the corn, leveling the furrow. It was hard work. Early chatter gave way to grunts and groans as their unused muscles started to complain. The sun was hot, and the mud mixed with sweat. They worked until afternoon before Papa came to break for dinner.

"How is it going?" he asked as he watched Will set the corn marker. "Will! What are you doing?" he yelled. "You're holding the marker sideways, not longways. Damn it Will, tell me you haven't done the whole field this way."

Will's eyes filled with tears. The children had never heard Papa swear. "Papa, I'm sorry. I didn't know I was doing it wrong."

"Juda, I can't believe all the times you've helped plant corn, you don't know how to line up the corn marker."

"Mama always helped before. She told us how to do it. I thought I remembered."

Red-faced, Papa grabbed Juda's arm, "You've planted twice too much corn. It'll be too crowded to grow. Now we'll run out of corn seed. I can't believe you've made such a mess of things." Angrily, he turned to walk to the cabin, removing his hat and wiping his face on his sleeve. The children followed at a distance, feeling the weight of their error.

They ate deer stew in silence. Sarah was certain she would get spanked too, though it wasn't her fault. Would Papa use his hand or the razor strop? Papa got up from the table. "The only thing we can do is wait till the corn comes up, thin it out and transplant it. Your punishment is many hours of extra work. I just hope Mr. Tanner doesn't see it," he growled, stomping out the door.

Sure enough, a few days later, a fancy buggy came into the yard. Noticing that it was Mr. Tanner, the man who owned the farm, Will said, "I'm glad he came before the corn is up." As he walked out to Papa, Mr. Tanner glanced in disapproval at the children, planting corn on *his* farm.

"Hello Uriah. I see you're still planting corn. If we're going to have a crop this year, that corn needs to be in by next week. I've heard after all this spring rain, it's going to be a dry summer. If so, this late corn will scorch." When Papa explained what Mr. Tanner already knew, that the field was low and the water didn't drain, he was ignored. Mr. Tanner knew Papa couldn't hear and he purposely spoke softly, so Papa had to ask him to repeat.

"I'm going to keep checking on you, Uriah. Maybe you need to think about getting some decent help," he glanced at the children.

They worked from sunrise until dark, day after day, planting corn then transplanting the incorrectly planted seedlings. After corn planting, they used a scythe to cut alfalfa, taking it to the barn in the wagon, and forking it into the hay mow. They were no longer children, they were field hands, moving by rote, focusing on the job. Their only thought was to rush the minutes until day's end when they could fall on their mattress in a dead sleep.

Juda took seriously her promise to care for Will and Sarah. "You've raked enough hay for today, Sarah. I can gather it. Go to the cabin and get a can of water and take it to Papa in the other field."

"My hand hurts, Juda," she whined, holding out her hand with drainage on the rag bandage.

Juda removed the rag and startled with alarm when she saw the infected blister draining pus. "Sarah, this looks bad. When you take water to Papa tell him to look at your hand. It's infected."

With no sign of rain to soak the hay on the ground, Papa let them stop early. After looking at Sarah's hand, he said, "We need to clean Sarah's infected blister. Let's all go down to the creek and go swimming."

"Yippee!" Skinnying down to their underwear, they took off across the field to the little creek, jumping in, screaming at the cold, swimming and splashing, diving and racing. Oh, the joy of it. Even Papa entered in the fun, flipping them into the water and catching them as they jumped off the side. Yes, they *were* still children; they hadn't forgotten how to play.

Sarah was off by herself trying to catch tadpoles, thinking of all the times Mama had brought them to the creek, when she felt Mama's presence as surely as if she'd touched her. She saw her gentle smile and heard her voice: "I'm sorry I left you, Sarah. I didn't want to. You're being a good girl. I'm proud of you" ... and she was gone, just as quickly as she came. "Oh...Oh"...she reached, but there was nothing. She knew what happened was strange and couldn't be explained; it was Mama's gift that no one could take away.

"Sarah, come here" Papa called. He took her sore hand and rubbed it with lye soap. It was cold, so it didn't hurt much. They all took a bath in the creek, then as the sun was setting, they put on their clothes and slowly walked back to the cabin, not wanting the magic to end.

Papa told Sarah to leave the blister open to the air. It was such a happy night. They chattered and teased, just like old times. Before bedtime, Papa put a bacon fat poultice on her blister and told her not to work in the field tomorrow. This was the best day ever.

* * * * *

July brought a drought. The corn that was barely up became shriveled and yellow. One day Mr. Tanner came to talk to Papa, who was in the far field. They saw Papa extend his arms and shake his fists in the air. He dropped to his knees, his face in his hands. Mr. Tanner walked up behind him, gesturing, then walked away, leaving in his buggy. That night Sarah heard Papa crying.

A few weeks later, a man in a nice buggy with two horses came into the yard. The children followed Papa in from the field, surprised when he greeted the stocky man with dark hair and beard sprinkled with silver, heavy brows, and a closed, sculpted face devoid of expression. Though not a tall man, his formidable bearing and brusque speech suggested a chill detachment. His dusty clothes were store bought. Papa said, "Children, meet your Uncle Levi. He's Mama's older brother. How long have you been on the road, Levi?"

"It took about two and a half days. I have good horses and didn't want to overtire them. The road is in bad condition." Uncle Levi nodded to them, then turned to wipe down his horses.

"Uncle Levi will be staying the night. Will and Juda, see that the horses are cooled down, watered, and put in the barn stalls."

Company was always a treat. When Papa said Uncle William and Aunt Caroline's family would be bringing supper, the children were thrilled.

He said they could quit work early and take a bath before the rest of the company came. A bath? In the middle of the week? This was a celebration. Juda and Sarah were so excited they were silly, as they got down the galvanized tub and heated water. Juda washed Sarah's hair and put on a clean apron. She fixed her hair special too, prompting Sarah to notice how much she looked like Mama, now that she was tall and pulled back her long black hair.

Before supper, their cousins Chloe, Donald, and Jesse came. The six of them slid down the hay in the barn. They raced in when Aunt Caroline called for supper, and what a feast it was: roast beef, potatoes, bread, and fresh garden carrots, with apple pie for dessert. It was such a fun evening, the best time since Mama died. Sarah noticed Aunt Caroline had tears in her eyes after Uncle Levi's prayer. When it was time for them to go home, Aunt Caroline hugged them like she would never let go.

The next morning, Papa became serious as they finished breakfast. "I need to tell you children what is happening—why Uncle Levi is here. When Mr. Tanner came two weeks ago, he told me someone else is renting this farm; we have to find other work. Will, you're old enough to stay with me. Juda and Sarah, Uncle Levi will take you with him. He's taking you as a favor, so I hope you can be helpful to him. I can't manage all three of you." He turned to Uncle Levi, "Juda and Sarah are good, hardworking girls. Their mother trained them well. These three have been through a lot lately and they've given it their all. Well, God moves in mysterious ways. You girls get a clean feed sack to pack your clothes."

Juda and Sarah looked down at their hands; they couldn't look at Papa. Sarah held her breath so she wouldn't cry in front of Uncle Levi. Everything was crashing again. She couldn't believe the words she heard.

In a tear-filled voice, Juda said, "Papa, if you let us stay with you, I promise I'll take care of Will and Sarah. I'm almost grown. I'm a good worker and they'll help too. Please Papa, Sarah and I can't leave," she said desperately.

"I'm sorry Juda," Papa said. "None of this is what I wanted to happen. Jehovah is a cruel God. But we can't live on this farm any longer. Now girls, get your things together. You have a long trip and Uncle Levi wants to get started."

Uncle Levi. This whole time he just sat there, looking down without saying anything. *Couldn't he have thought of one kind word, something to make us less afraid? Mama had taught, "never say you hate someone".*

I hate Uncle Levi! Sarah thought to herself.

* * * * *

Juda, Sarah, and Will left the table and climbed the ladder to the attic. Away from Papa and Uncle Levi, their tears came freely. The three faced each other on Juda's mattress, trying to put meaning to Papa's words.

"Juda, what's going to happen to us?" Sarah asked in a bewildered voice.

"Oh Sarah, I don't know. I never thought our family could be broken up like this."

She grabbed Juda's hand, her voice timorous, "I'm afraid of Uncle Levi. I don't want to live with him."

"I don't want to stay with Papa either," Will countered. "I would rather go with you to Uncle Levi's. At least he has a nice buggy and good horses. Papa isn't the same since Mama died. He's always sad and angry."

"Yes, like when we messed up the corn planting," Sarah remembered.

"Maybe we could run away" Will said. "Maybe we could live with Aunt Caroline. Wouldn't it be fun to live with Chloe and Donald?" Their hearts lifted briefly at this possibility.

"They can't take us, or we would have gone with them yesterday. This is why Aunt Caroline was sad last night." Juda's voice was tinged with anger. "I think Papa has had this planned for a while. That's why Uncle Levi came: to take us home with him. I just can't believe Papa would do this. If Papa had died, I know Mama would never have broken up our family. She would have found a way."

"It seems so long since Mama was with us. Some days I can hardly remember her," Will said sadly.

"Oh no, Will. We *must* remember. The best thing I have is memories of Mama." Secretly in Sarah's mind she was glad she had Mama's comb to help her remember.

Juda clasped their hands together and said, "Sarah is right. We must remember all the good things Mama taught us: like being kind and saying our prayers, the happy times we had together, and all the special things about Mama. If we remember these things, even though she's in Heaven, she'll stay in our hearts. Then when we're grown up—and I'm nearly grown—Sarah and I will come and get you, Will."

"You're right Juda. In a few years I can be a hired hand and work for Uncle Levi." Will grabbed each of his sisters in a crushing hug. "This gives me something to hope for," he said tearfully. With a final look, he descended the ladder.

"Are you girls nearly ready? You certainly don't have much to pack," called Papa from downstairs.

Juda and Sarah gathered their few worn belongings in a feed sack. They got their hand-me-down winter coats and overshoes. Last, Sarah reached under the mattress to get Mama's comb. She wasn't quick enough; Juda saw her grab it. She gasped, her mouth forming a perfect circle. Then Juda reached into her sack and with a twinkle in her eye, pulled out Mama's other pearl comb.

Juda and Sarah sat behind Uncle Levi in the buggy. They were both in their own world, too distressed to talk or notice the countryside. Sarah had expected it would be sad to say goodbye to Papa and Will. All of them cried, even Uncle Levi had tears in his eyes. But Sarah hadn't thought about the sadness in saying goodbye to dear Sol and Boss who gave their milk and even let Sarah milk them. She would miss their beloved horse Bell, and Nellie the donkey, who were so calm and hardworking. She wondered what would happen to these dear gentle friends who couldn't understand what was happening to their family. Listening to the steady rhythm of the horses, she fell into an exhausted sleep.

In the afternoon, they stopped beside a stream where Uncle Levi watered the horses. He brought out a lunch bucket and spread roast beef and bread left from last night's feast. Sarah's heart jumped. That supper seemed to be in another world, so happy and unsuspecting they were. How could life change so much in less than one day? Uncle Levi sat by himself to eat his lunch.

As they were going to be living with him, Sarah was curious. "Uncle Levi sure doesn't talk. It's hard to believe he's Mama's brother."

"He seems strange to me," Juda said. "When he does talk, he doesn't look at you. I can't decide if he's shy or mean...he doesn't drive his horses hard," she said thoughtfully. "Possibly he's as uncomfortable with us as we are with him."

"Maybe he never had children so doesn't know how to treat us." As Sarah said this, Uncle Levi walked toward them, giving each a pink peppermint candy from his pocket. As he went to hitch up the horses, they grinned at each other. Candy had been rare in their lives, and they savored this treat. "Well, he understands children and candy," Juda laughed.

There were not many villages on this trip, and they met few travelers on the two-track road. Twice the horses went through a small river and the water came high on the wagon. It felt good to have cold water splashed on them, and Uncle Levi assured them the water wouldn't come over the wagon.

It was nearing sunset when Uncle Levi stopped beside a small stream. "It's time to rest the horses so we'll stop for the night. Go yonder and wash in the river."

Juda and Sarah sat on a rock by the river to wash off the dust, dangling their feet in the water.

"I wonder what work we'll do for Uncle Levi. I hope he lets me do housework and work in the garden. I don't want to do field work. Whatever we do, I'm sure he'll let you help me," Juda said.

"Do you think he has a wife? Maybe his wife died like Mama."

"I hope there will be more family than just you, me, and Uncle Levi," Juda replied.

"Do you think we'll have candy every day?" Sarah asked. "Uncle Levi's clothes are fine, this is a nice wagon, and he has candy."

"Oh no, Sarah. No one gets candy every day."

As it was getting dusk, the deer flies came in swarms. Juda and Sarah couldn't slap fast enough. Their supper was biscuits, dried beef and apples. They drank water from the stream. Uncle Levi built up the fire, then spread blankets under the wagon where Juda and Sarah slept. Deer flies were replaced by mosquitoes and they swatted as they said their prayers. Though Juda was soon snoring, Sarah was wide awake. Poking her head from under the wagon, she saw the stars, wondering about Will and wishing she was back sleeping in the attic with him and Juda. She heard many night noises. Uncle Levi told them they were safe from wild animals, but she noticed he fell asleep by the fire with his gun across his lap. The night was long before she fell asleep.

They woke with the rising sun, washed in the stream, and munched dry hard food. Uncle Levi said that mid-day they would be stopping in the village of Columbia City to get supplies for his home.

It was another hot day, with flies and mosquitoes adding to their dusty, bumpy misery. Uncle Levi stopped the horses and walked along the road, pulling up green plants. He brought them back to the wagon saying, "Wild onions rubbed on your skin will keep the mosquitoes away." He chopped them with his knife, and they rubbed them on their face and arms. Sarah and Juda giggled and pinched their noses, but it did seem the bugs were less bothersome.

They finally arrived in Columbia City. It was the biggest village the sisters had ever seen. Two story buildings lined the dirt street with hitching posts in front of the stores. The girls wanted to spend the afternoon peeking in windows, but had to rush to catch up with Uncle Levi. They noticed many of the townspeople had fine clothes, fancy hats, and store-bought shoes. Uncle Levi had several errands: the blacksmith checked and repaired the horses' shoes; he got bags of seed from the feed store; and they went to the grocery, where he got sacks of flour, sugar, and a bucket of lard. They were thrilled when he bought each of them a stick of candy. When Uncle Levi loaded everything in the wagon, there was hardly room for Juda and Sarah. They were just outside town when Uncle Levi turned the horses into the yard of a log cabin with a sign: Thorncreek Township School.

"We'll wait here," Uncle Levi said as he checked his timepiece. He climbed down from the wagon and led the horses to grass. It was hot in the direct sun and they waited a long time as Uncle Levi paced around the school. Finally, returning to the wagon, he said, "We're waiting for John Clement. He's meeting us here to take Juda to his home near Ft. Wayne to work as his hired girl. I promised your Papa I would find a good home for you, Juda. The Clements are good Christian folks with seven children. Mrs. Clement is having another baby shortly and needs full-time help. I'm sorry we can't keep both of you in my home, but it seems my wife can't have children and she wants the younger of you to raise. I just hope she can handle it. She has a nervous problem and two strangers in the house would get the best of her."

Uncle Levi walked ahead to the horses. He wanted to put space between himself and the girls' frantic distress. Now everything was clear to Juda. The pieces fit. Uncle Levi, even Papa, knew the horrific cruelty they would inflict when separating Juda and Sarah. They played out a hardhearted ruse, keeping the sisters ignorant, so they wouldn't have to deal with their grief. Their behavior was scarred with mistruth and dishonesty. They waited until the last minute to inform them they were severing the cord between the beloved older sister and the baby she had raised and cherished.

"Juda, a girl like you can hire out for a good wage. I'll allow you to send your wage to your father—he certainly can use it. I have the Clements' address and when your father gets resettled, I'll send his address so you can mail him your wages.

Now, I suggest you say your goodbyes so you're ready when John comes." Uncle Levi walked away quickly. He did not want to be near us.

Juda jumped off the wagon and ran after him. She grabbed his shirt, spinning him around, beating on his face and chest. He cowered in his guilt, taking the blows. "You cannot do this. You cannot leave an eight-year-old alone in the world with strangers. She has never been away from home. She is *AFRAID OF YOU*," she pushed her finger into his chest. She sobbed, her words incoherent. Then lifting her face, "I *beg* you, think what Sarah has been through these last months. She has lost her family and her home—everything she knows. Let us stay together till she gets used to you, then send me away. I'll work on your farm, I'll do anything." Her screaming turned to begging, her arms dropped to her sides as tears coursed down her face. "Uncle Levi, if you have any kindness, let Sarah and me stay together, at least for a while. When she was so afraid after Mama died, I promised I would take care of her. Just let me take care of her."

"You're only fourteen, Juda. The care of children is a decision for adults. This may not be perfect, but it will work. Sarah will be okay. I'll make a good home for her. It may be you can visit sometime," and he walked off to pump water for the horses.

Juda sunk to the ground, holding herself and rocking. Sarah got on her knees and put her arms around her. Even her young innocent mind knew they had lost...she would not live with Juda. She saw John Clements drive his wagon into the school yard.

Never in her memory had anyone acted with such passion and selflessness as Juda did the day she fought for Sarah. They'd been taught to honor their elders; they did what they were told; they didn't know they could have their own ideas, especially in disagreement; they would never yell or plead; these were behaviors they didn't know. But everything in their world changed when Mama died. They hadn't known fear and desperation, but for the last months this was all they knew, and it changed them.

Juda put her face close, her hands on Sarah's cheeks. "I'm so sorry I couldn't keep my promise to you Sarah. I don't know when I'll see you again. Remember me, Sarah, and I'll remember you.... Someday we'll be a family again. And Sarah, when everything is bad like it is today, you must always be strong. Don't let the hard times get you down. Mama wouldn't want us to stay sad. She would say, 'Sarah, pick yourself up, lift your chin and be strong'."

Her sobs wouldn't let Sarah say goodbye to Juda. But she wanted to be a big girl like Juda; she wanted to be strong like she said. They stood, had one last embrace, and she got into Uncle Levi's wagon and Juda got in John Clement's wagon. She waved till she couldn't see her anymore.

CHAPTER 4

Uncle Levi's House, September 1884

"Wake up, girly." Sarah jolted awake to see a giant standing over her—a giant's body with a youthful face. She screamed, trying to jump from the wagon.

He gently touched her face, "Don't be scared. You're plain tuckered out. Mr. Levi told me bring you to the house and take you to the Missus. I'm Benji. I live here."

Benji's smile was as bright as the morning sun. It was hard to be afraid of this strange man-boy. She openly stared at his large head with protruding ears, smooth chubby cheeks, and full pink lips. His brown hair was flecked with gray and had mostly receded, leaving fine straggles that were wildly untamed. He wore blue overalls that strained at every seam. The sleeves of his plaid long-sleeved shirt flapped halfway to his elbows. He wasn't just tall, every part of him was oversized.

Even as an eight-year-old, Sarah sensed something wasn't quite right—but not dangerous. Before Sarah could move, she was hoisted into the air in the crook of Benji's arm and galloped-bounced into the house. He jabbered nonsensically, pointing finger guns and yelling, "bam! bam! bam!" Then he cowered, shushing with his finger to his lips, saying in a stern tone, "Quiet for Missus Hannah. Lift your feet. No talking."

Passing the summer kitchen, Benji sailed over the steps, crashing into the back porch at the rear of the two-story white frame house. This house was fine, different than anything Sarah had known. Her mind flashed back to the small, shabby cabin in the clearing, in the other life where she belonged.

Benji became uncertain as he carried Sarah through the kitchen, lowering her to the floor. "Rosa, Mr. Levi says take the girl to the Missus," Benji said to the young girl who was peeling potatoes.

She lifted her chin, "You do it. I'm getting supper."

"Come on," Benji motioned, taking Sarah into a dining room that had smooth finished floors and walls that were flat and colorful, not logs and mortar. A fireplace had soft couches facing it and there was a large dining table covered with a blue cloth. He went to a door and knocked hesitantly.

"Come in, Benjamin," a voice replied. Sarah followed Benji into a room that reeked with the smell of camphor. The room was decorated with fancy store-bought furniture and a dark rug that looked like velvet. Sarah saw large paintings with little angels, making her feel she could walk right into the picture. Pillows and plush chairs were arranged beside a table. At the windows, satiny curtains with gold fringe hung all the way to the floor. She glanced at movement across the room, taking a minute to realize it was herself in a large mirror. She had seen just her face before, and without thinking, she waved, stuck out her tongue, and twirled on one leg. She sensed she was in unexplored country, a place past her understanding. Maybe she was in Heaven.

"Mr. Levi said bring you the girl," Benji muttered with eyes lowered, his feet pawing the rug.

"Stand still, Benji. You'll wear a hole in the carpet. And please lower your voice. I heard you coming all the way from the barn. You know I can't take your noise when I'm sick. It's like an ice pick through my brain," she complained. She stopped for breath from the overexertion of this brief speech.

Sarah tore her eyes from her reflection to follow the harping voice. Uncle Levi's much younger wife looked like a fragile queen sitting in the bed, propped with pillows. She was beautiful: peaches-and-cream skin with auburn hair that fell in waves, caught loosely in a blue silk scarf that matched her satin dressing gown. There was a rag plaster on her chest. Her eyes were hazel, the perfect complement to her coloring. Her eyes on Sarah were unwavering and curious.

Sarah had known farm women: women who worked in the field, planted garden, and mucked the barn. This refined lady looked like she'd never dirtied her hands. But beyond the beauty, the overriding aura was one of suffering. Her face told the story without words: dark eye sockets, pale grimace, and weariness as she held an ice pack to her head. The bedside table was covered with sickroom supplies: medicine bottles and vials, eye shades, and a spittoon.

"So, you're Lucinda's daughter. I'm Missus Hannah," she said, as she appraised Sarah holding her meager gunny sack of belongings. "Benjamin, take your leave and finish your chores," she waved him away. "Since you're living here as our daughter, there are some things you should know. Mr. Levi and I haven't been blessed with children, so we're doing our Christian duty, taking in children who need a good home." She settled against the pillows, catching her breath. She moved the ice pack to the back of her head while Sarah gawked, dumbstruck by the beauty of this frail lady and the luxury of her home.

"It's unfortunate that neither of us has high vitality. My husband has had nervous tendencies since serving in the War Between the States. He has melancholy and doesn't sleep well. Some days, he stays in his room. You'll do best to stay away from him and stay quiet. Neither he nor I can abide noise." Missus Hannah rested her head on the pillow and caught her breath. "Benjamin saved my husband's life. They were both injured during the war, and he has been living with us ever since. Benjamin is in his late forties, near my husband's age, but he acts like a twelve-year-old. He's an excellent farm hand, but he aggravates me and he eats us out of house and home. He won't hurt you." Again, she rested, closing her eyes. "Would you come and fan me, please? I'm too weary to move."

Sarah dropped her sack and walked to the bed. "Stand on this step beside the bed," Hannah motioned, handing Sarah the fan, then withdrawing it. "Oh, my dear! I can't tolerate your odor. Go back across the room," she said, waving her hand in front of her face. "Rosa will give you a bath tonight and get you clothes left by other girls who were your size. Throw away the stuff in your bag. Keep the shoes; shoes are expensive." In a daze, Sarah moved back beside her bag.

"My constitution is weak too. I was raised with culture and wealth. Now I'm stuck in this swampy, God-forsaken wilderness," she extended her arm to include the room. "I have a delicate nature; this place saps my vigor. Some days, like today, I'm bedridden."

"Besides Benjamin, who behaves like a young boy, the children we have now are Grace, George, Noble, and Rosa, who are a family. George and Noble hire out and Grace, who is sixteen, hires out part-time. She's my right hand; she runs the house. She prepares the meals for Rosa to cook." Missus Hannah was quiet as she rested her eyes and fanned herself. "Rosa is twelve or thirteen and will hire out in another year. Then you will step up."

She closed her eyes and spoke to herself, "It's impossible to run this house. I have to train all the little girls so when they become of age Mr. Levi can hire them out, though the young ones don't bring much. God does send blessings, though. By the time the boys are old enough to act feisty and eat so much, they're hired out for good money." She turned to Sarah, "I'm done with you for today. Go sit at the dining table until supper time and I'll have Rosa get you fixed up. Don't touch anything till you're clean. You'll sleep with Rosa and Grace in the girls' room."

As Sarah was leaving the room, she turned back. "Can Juda come here to live with me?" she asked in a tearful voice.

"Who is Juda?" Missus asked.

"She's my big sister and I was supposed to be with her," Sarah was crying full-out now.

"I'm sorry, Sarah. We don't have a place for another girl. There's just one bed in the girls' room. Rosa is your big sister now. You'll be okay. The first few days are always hard. Go along now, Sarah. Take this bag and have Rosa get ice from the basement."

Sarah sat at the big dining table, her head in her arms, feeling alone and dislocated, her head too full. She felt like a worn rag doll with stuffing popping from all the holes and tears—too much for a little girl to contain.

Because this large home was such a contrast to the log cabin familiar to Sarah, her curiosity was piqued, and she was soon peeking and poking around. The dining room walls weren't white-washed logs but smooth plaster, covered with decorative paper. Sarah touched her fingers along the carved scrolling of the darkly stained doors, woodwork, and fireplace mantle. Objects were not merely functional, but decorative: a cross-stitched "Home Sweet Home" print, quilted pillows on the two couches facing the fireplace, a hearthrug, fresh flowers in a vase on the mantle, painted wall sconces holding kerosene lanterns, and curtains at the windows. One door led to Missus Hannah's bedroom, another to steps upstairs, and the third to the parlor. Sarah slipped into the cool room, her eyes wide in amazement. The floor was a carpet of flowers, there were soft velvety draperies, an overstuffed couch, and chairs around a tea table. Finely crocheted needlework lay across the furniture. A large glass case held shelves of books.

"Oh-h!" it took Sarah's breath away. She'd seen a Bible and a few primers at school, but she couldn't believe anyone owned so many books.

"You'd better get out of the parlor or you'll get in trouble with Missus." Sarah jumped guiltily to see Rosa's head peering in the door. "Benji got stropped one time when he brought a chicken in here. You can help me in the kitchen." Sarah scuttled after Rosa to the kitchen. "I'll let you snip the beans."

Sarah relaxed a bit. It felt good to be with another girl and do a familiar job. As with the rest of the house, Sarah noticed the modern kitchen: a black stove beside the chimney had a pipe that went out through the wall. Potatoes were bubbling in a heavy pan sitting on the stove. Rosa opened a door on the front of the stove to a box where meat was cooking. Along the back wall, a cupboard had a deep sink in the corner. Near the ceiling above the sink was a large galvanized tank with a pipe that drained water to the sink. Pottery dishes were stacked on shelves above the cupboard. There was a shiny bucket with a water dipper.

Later Uncle Levi and Benji came into the kitchen. They stood at the sink, washing their hands and face. Benji's eyes swept to Sarah as he gave her a shy smile. Uncle Levi, who seemed not to notice her, went into Missus' bedroom. Sarah helped Rosa by carrying a tray of food to a table in front of a large window, where Missus and Uncle Levi sat for supper.

The children ate at a small table in the kitchen, filling their plates from pans. Away from adults, they acted as children. At least Sarah thought of Benji as a child, even if he almost filled the kitchen. He shoveled food into his mouth, eating two platefuls.

"I'm glad Grace gets home tonight," Rosa said. "Even though she prepares the food, I'm afraid I'll burn something. Missus gets after me when I mess up."

"You're lucky to be with your sister. Uncle Levi sent my sister to another family," Sarah said tearfully.

"We came here a long time ago, after our mother died. Mr. Levi didn't have any other children. I guess that's why they kept us together. George and Noble soon hired out, so I don't see them much. Rosa was thoughtful. "Grace and I will be your sisters, Sarah."

"Thank you. I still need Juda," Sarah said mournfully.

"Bam, Bam." Benji, having finished eating, jumped up, pointing his knife at Sarah. Rosa grabbed Benji's arm and pulled him to his seat. "Be quiet, Benji, you'll get us in trouble. You can't play war games in the house. You can help with the dishes. I'll let you wash. Maybe by sundown Grace will be home. You love Grace, don't you Benji?"

Rosa explained to Sarah, "Ever since Benji was hit in the head during the war, he thinks he's still at war, so that's what he wants to play. He knows he's not allowed to play in the house, but since you're new, he's testing to see if you'll play with him."

"I'm not allowed to play war, Benji, but I'll play another game," Sarah said.

"Will you play tickle my poker?" asked Benji.

"You know we only play that at bedtime, Benji," Rosa replied. "Put water in the dishpan and I'll get Missus' and Mr. Levi's dishes. Sarah, you can help dry."

"I like to wash dishes. The water is slippery. Sarah, will you sing with me? Do you know the alphabet song?" Benji asked.

"You can sing if you sing soft, Benji," said Rosa.

The three sang softly while they washed dishes: "A B C D E F G..."; "Are you sleeping? Are you sleeping? Brother John..."; "Jesus loves me, this I know".

"Here comes Grace," yelled Benji, running out the back porch, with Rosa and Sarah following.

"Gracie, Gracie," he called, as Grace stepped clumsily from the farmer's buggy. "I'm glad you're home." He lifted her as if she were a doll, though she was a plump sixteen-year-old.

"I'm happy to see you, too," Grace smiled brightly. "And who is this?" Grace knelt to Sarah's level, searching for Sarah's face as her eyes wandered about, unable to focus. Her face was pitted and pink with smallpox scars and her dark hair, parted in the middle, was pulled tightly in a bun.

"Her name is Sarah, and she is sad," Benji patted Sarah's head. "She misses her sister and she cried at supper."

"I told her we'll be her sisters," Rosa chimed in.

"That's a good idea, Rosa. We don't want Sarah to be sad. Welcome to our family," she said, patting Sarah. While many would have seen in Grace a miserly beauty, lacking in everything becoming, Sarah saw one to fill the hole left by Juda. Grace looked around as she entered the dining room. "Did supper turn out okay, Rosa? You tidied up good. I'm glad, 'cause I'd like to go to bed early."

"Mr. Levi finished his supper, but Missus didn't eat much. She's been in bed all day with a sick headache."

Just then, Mr. Levi came out of the bedroom. "Grace, Missus wants you to prepare her for bed. You might bring her a touch of brandy so she can sleep. Rosa, you empty the chamber pot. Benjamin, don't forget to herd the cattle from the field and take them to the loafing shed." Uncle Levi glanced at Sarah in surprise, as if he'd forgotten she was there. "I'm going to my room. You all need to stay quiet," he said, as he went upstairs.

Rosa took the chamber pot to the privy and returned to Missus' bedroom. She motioned to Sarah, "Come to the back porch. You're supposed to take a bath," she said, lifting the tub from its hook on the wall. Missus says to wash your hair, too. Rosa poured warm water into the tub, then added a tablespoon of lavender. "Missus never lets anyone use her bath soap. I think she likes you best because you're family," she remarked.

"When I went to her room today, she told me I was stinky. I made her sick. That's why she wants me to use it," Sarah said, luxuriating in the warm water.

"I don't think so," Rosa responded testily.

Grace came into the porch, "Um-m, it smells good in here. I wish I could take a bath. Here's clothes and a nightgown, Sarah. I went through your sack of things. Missus wants to get new clothes for you. I found this comb. Do you want it?"

Sarah jumped out of the tub, grabbing the comb from Grace, "It's mine. It's my treasure. It was Mama's comb. I must keep it safe."

"Of course. We'll find a good place for it. You're lucky. I don't have anything from my mother. I hardly remember her."

"Juda says we must think of Mama and remember how much she loved us."

"I'm sure she did." While toweling Sarah, she spoke to Rosa, "Benji has his pajamas on and is ready for you to do his bedtime cuddle."

"I get so tired of that," complained Rosa. "He makes such a mess."

"We all take turns helping Benji. I'll do it tomorrow night. Tell him not to make noise. Mr. Levi is in his room and needs quiet. Since we have water, you may take a bath too, Rosa. The water isn't very warm, but it will refresh you."

"Yeah, I'd like a bath," said Rosa, rushing upstairs.

"Do you like stories? Missus has a book of fables for children," Grace said, toweling Sarah's hair and helping her into an oversized, faded nightgown. "Rosa can read to us."

Grace took Sarah up the stairs and through a central room which had three doors: one to Mr. Levi's room, another to Benji's room, and the third to the girls' room. The central room had beds for boys to sleep. The girls' room had a big bed where the girls slept together, and a dresser for clothes. Sarah ran to the window. She had never been "high" on a second story. She laughed excitedly, "Look at the road down there. There's a brown chicken," Sarah laughed. "It looks like it has a dress over its wings."

"That's Benji's pet chicken, Queenie. He loves that chicken. He thinks it's human. It follows Benji while he does chores. Never make fun of Queenie. You'll hurt Benji's feelings. Missus Hannah wants to kill it, but she doesn't dare. I'm pretty sure Benji brings it into his bedroom sometimes. Missus would be mad as a hatter if she knew that."

Sarah pointed in the distance to the biggest water she'd ever seen, "What's that?"

"It's Crane Lake. It's swampy over there. You can't ever go there. It's not safe. Here, try these clothes to see if they fit. I think Missus wants you to have new clothes for school and church. Let me brush your hair, Sarah. It's so thick and wavy. I wish I had such pretty dark hair."

After a few moments Grace noticed Sarah crying silently, the tears running down her face. "Why are you crying?" Grace asked. "Am I brushing too hard?"

"I miss Juda and Will. She brushes my hair and tells bedtime stories. I don't think I can sleep without her," Sarah whimpered. "I don't even know where she is."

Grace gathered Sarah into her lap. "I know how you feel. I cried after my mother died when I moved to Mr. Levi's. I was scared too. It takes a while, but it gets better."

"Why are you holding her?" Rosa asked, coming into the bedroom.

"She's missing her family," Grace said.

"Well, she might as well get used to it. We're the only family she has now," Rosa snipped.

"Will you read the storybook, Grace?" Sarah asked.

"I can't read 'cause of my bad eyes. They didn't let me go to school very much. But Rosa can read a story," Grace said.

"I'll read about the tortoise and the hare. That's my favorite," Rosa said, reading fluently and with expression.

When the story was finished Sarah said, "I like that story too. You're a good reader, Rosa."

"Yes. I'm the smartest one in the seventh grade."

The girls were snuggled in bed when Sarah jumped from under the blanket and knelt beside the bed. "God take care of Mama in Heaven and help me not to forget her. Keep Papa and Will and Juda safe. Help them not to forget me. Help me be strong like Juda said." After a short pause, "Help me not to be afraid at Uncle Levi's house. Amen." Sarah climbed under the covers beside Rosa.

"What were you doing?" Rosa asked.

"Saying my bedtime prayer."

"Why do you do that?" Rosa asked.

Sarah was thoughtful, "Because my Mama and Juda taught me I should always pray before I go to sleep. Since Mama died, it's the way I talk to her."

"Elder Hyre always prays on Sunday and Mr. Levi prays when we have dinner together on Sunday. I didn't know children could pray. Can you show me how?" Rosa asked.

"I think Sarah can show both of us, but another time. We should sleep now. It's been a long day," Grace said.

Soon Grace and Rosa were asleep, breathing deeply. As tired as she was, everything felt strange and wrong. The bed was crowded. She was curled up close to Rosa, but she wasn't comfortable being this close to a stranger—and all the people in this house felt strange. She was the outsider. Tears ran down her cheeks, wetting her pillow. In her mind's eye she pictured Juda. She went over every feature: her eyes, her face, her smile. Then she moved behind her and brushed her hair. Sarah fell asleep brushing Juda's hair.

CHAPTER 5

School Days, Fall 1884

"Ouch, that hurts." Sarah complained as Missus Hannah pulled and tugged while braiding her hair. This was just another change for Sarah at Uncle Levi's house. In the log cabin, brushing and braiding hair was a twice daily interlude of camaraderie where the females chatted, touched, and complimented each other.

"Well, I'm sorry Sarah. This is the only way I know to braid. I got you a new ribbon. It's a bit large but it's all the rage for young girls." Sarah saw her reflection with the hideous "wings" on top of her head.

"I don't like it, Missus. Take it off," Sarah complained.

"I'll wear it. I like it," Rosa begged, coming into the room.

"Don't squander my good humor, Sarah. We have only one ribbon. Sarah will wear it today. Maybe you can wear it later, Rosa. By your leave, girls. I hear the bell. You mustn't be late the first day of school."

Sarah, wearing a new dress with dark stockings, grabbed her lunch tin and raced the short distance toward Little Lake School.

"Rosa, take the ribbon off my head. I'll fasten it in your hair. It'll look much nicer on you." Sarah begged.

Rosa ran ahead so Sarah would have to enter the school alone. "Keep your dumb ribbon. You look like a flying witch."

Mr. Young, standing at the door of the one-room brick schoolhouse, knelt as Sarah came up the steps. He was handsome, with a full head of dark hair, brown eyes, and aquiline nose. He exuded pride in his profession with his clean-cut appearance, his broadcloth suit, bow tie, and friendly demeanor. He had completed eighth grade and three months of Saturday classes at Teacher Institute. He took seriously the education of the twenty-three children in his charge.

"I'll bet you're Sarah Long, our new nine-year-old student," he said. "Welcome to Little Lake School. I'll work with you this morning to decide which grade you'll be in." Sarah entered the school, where older children stood in clusters and younger ones chased about. She sat at a board bench next to a long table. At each place was a small slate tablet. In front, behind the teacher's table was a picture of George Washington. The front wall had a large slate board and along one side was a large fireplace with low stools lined up. In one front corner was a tin bucket with ladle, the children's water for the day. The other corner had a paddle hanging from a hook. Job assignments were listed on the slate board: bring water, bring wood, clean hearth, sweep floor, clean blackboard, clean erasers. Mr. Young welcomed the children and gave job assignments. He asked Sarah to come to the front, where he introduced her. She felt so shy she could hardly speak. He assigned older children to work with young ones. Taking Sarah to his desk, she read, worked math problems, and demonstrated her penmanship. He seemed pleased with her progress. Sarah ate her lunch, a sandwich of mashed soup beans and butter. At recess she played with a girl named Louise, and before she knew it, her first day at Little Lake was over.

That night after supper, there was a knock at the door. Rosa came to Missus' room saying Mr. Levi had guests: Mr. Young, the teacher, and Mr. Markham, the school superintendent. Mr. Levi seated them at the dining room table. Missus Hannah motioned to Rosa, her finger to her lips, standing behind the nearly closed bedroom door.

"Mr. Zumbrun, we'd like to make some improvements to the school this year. We hope to ascertain your willingness to help," Mr. Markham said.

"When anyone wants money, I'm always the first place you come begging," Mr. Levi grumbled.

"We need two privies—one each for the boys and girls," Mr. Young stated. "The older girls complain about having to go into the woods. We've had a few incidents where some fellows have become a bit vulgar and indelicate, embarrassing the girls."

"Oh, twaddle," Mr. Levi interrupted. "Boys will be boys. It's typical school-yard antics. We've gotten along for how many years using the woods? Young girls today are getting too fancy-dancy."

"You make a point, Mr. Zumbrun," Mr. Young remarked. "The students *have* been going to the woods for several years. It's becoming unhygienic. It's quite disgusting out there, I know from experience. Our young ladies are becoming less countrified and more modest."

"Most of the other schools in the township have privies. We don't want it said we lag behind the other schools," Mr. Markham said.

Mr. Levi sat for a long moment, his head down. "I'll tell you what I'll do. I want the older boys to make the drawings, figure the math for the lumber, and deliver the supplies. Benji and I will supervise and help the boys build the first privy. They'll be able to do the second one without help. I'll pay for one. The rest of the parents can pay for the second. That settles that. I'm thinking you didn't come just about privies. What else are you begging for?"

"Thank you, Mr. Zumbrun. It's an excellent idea to make this an educational project. It's fair that other parents help, and I'm sure they will after your generous contribution," Mr. Young smiled.

"There is another request," Mr. Markham said. "We need a well at the school. Mr. Young brings a lard tin of water every day in his buggy, but it's hardly enough for twenty-three children. We need to dig a well at the school. I'd like to have a fundraiser to collect money. I think Mrs. Zumbrun would be the perfect person to chair the committee. Everyone knows her interest in educating our children and her generosity with Mr. Young's salary."

"Mrs. Zumbrun will be glad to chair your committee. It may take a while to raise the money. I suggest you assign an older student to come to our well beside the barn and carry water back to the school. It would be one less responsibility for you, Mr. Young."

"An excellent suggestion." Mr. Young smiled and stood to leave, shaking Mr. Levi's hand. "I'll have one of the boys come before school until we get money for a well."

Mr. Markham stood, shaking Mr. Levi's hand. "Express our thanks to Mrs. Zumbrun. We thank both of you for your long support of Little Lake School."

As the men left, Missus Hannah quietly closed her bedroom door. "Mr. Young is working out quite well," she mumbled to Rosa. "Maybe we'll get some civilization here in the hinterlands." After a thoughtful minute she said, "I know what we'll do to raise money. Mrs. Fisher with the Albion Temperance League said they had a box social. We've never done anything like that. I think it would bring a lot of money. Rosa, send Sarah in."

"Sarah, Mr. Young told me the other day you're reading at sixth grade level. That's as good as Rosa."

"Juda taught me to read. Why can't Grace read, Missus?" Sarah asked.

"She can't read because her eyes are crossed."

"She said she wants to learn. If she closes one eye she can see better. Why didn't she go to school?" Sarah asked.

"Sarah, Grace's station in life is to be a hired girl. She's a sweet girl and a good helper—I couldn't get along without her. She doesn't need schooling for what she will do. It would only frustrate her. It would be good of you to read to Grace sometimes, especially from the Bible. I'm sure Benjamin is ready for bed, Sarah. You can go up now and help him get to sleep. I know Grace gave you the rules: both of you keep your clothes on. You can't sleep all night with him. Once he's asleep, wash your hands and go to your room. Even though he's older, he has a young man's thoughts and feelings, so the games satisfy his needs. Benjamin asks so little; it seems the least we can do to help him get his rest. Don't let him stretch the rules because you're the youngest. Good night Sarah. Read a story before you go to sleep."

Sarah went to Benji's room, where he was in his long suit, lying in bed. "Hey Benji, you silly boy. Are you ready for me?" Sarah laughed, jumping on his bed, tousling his hair and pulling his ears. Sarah hopped about, crawling under the covers, only to be chased and caught. Benji pulled her up on his stomach and she jumped up and down. "Giddy-up horsy," Sarah called in a loud whisper, remembering Mr. Levi was in his room. "You can't buck me off!"

"You're just a baby cowboy," Benji teased. "I'll bounce you in the air and send you flying!" Sarah rolled and tussled, climbing around on the giant fluffy body. "Here Sarah, slide between my legs and lean forward like you're riding a horse. Yes, like this," he said, pulling her back and forth.

"Benji, your face is getting red," Sarah laughed.

"That's because you're a good horsy rider."

"Is it time to get the rag, Benji?"

"I got it. I want you to play tickle my poker now.... Oh, your hand is so soft, Sarah."

"Remember to be quiet, Benji."

Benji stiffened, catching his breath, "I remember. I'm a big cowboy! I'm big! I'm huge! Here I come...!" Benji relaxed. "Let me rest a minute, Sarah. That was a good ride. Will you cuddle with me for a little before you go?" Sarah lay sheltered in Benji's arms while he quieted. "Night, Night, Sarah. Don't let the bedbugs bite," he said in a sleepy voice. In a few minutes Benji's breathing was deep and steady. Sarah went downstairs to wash. She returned to the girls' room where Grace and Rosa were ready for bed.

"What story should we have tonight?" Rosa asked.

"I want to read *The Lion and the Mouse,*" Sarah replied.

CHAPTER 6

Christmas

Excitement was full to bursting as everyone practiced, baked, primped, and decorated for the Little Lake School Christmas party. Even the weather dressed for the occasion, gentling down a quiet dreamland of wet flaky snow, gliding the sleighs, trimming the trees, and cozying out the lamplight from windows in the night.

Mrs. Zumbrun's committee was in charge of the box social. She lay awake nights designing and filling a box that would be most ostentatious, and filled with unparalleled delicacies. She determined that her decorative box supper would take top bid, contributing the most money to the school improvement fund. The pleasurable tete-a-tete of a shared meal with a man other than her husband quickened her senses—an anticipated benefit.

Sarah sat at the dining table drooling at the decorated box. On the box top was a replica of Little Lake School made from gingerbread. No detail was overlooked, from the ice cream cone bell tower, Necco Wafer roof, windows and doors encircled with licorice, gumdrop trees with snowy icing, and gingerbread children playing in the snowy icing playground. Missus had spent hours baking and decorating the cake.

"Sarah, come to the kitchen. I'll take out your hair rags," Missus Hannah called. She looked beautiful in a burgundy dress with a matching bow dressing her hair. The high color in her cheeks was caused by her cough and breathlessness, but the shiny color on her lips was not usual for Dunkard women. Earlier in the day she had wrapped Sarah's hair around rags. Now she untied them, combing the hair around her finger to shape curls. Sarah looked in the mirror, "I don't look like me, Missus."

"You look pretty, Sarah. Don't run around tonight and mess up your hair. I want you to play with Margaret and Sadie from church. I know at school you befriend little Louise, but that's not appropriate tonight. Her mother isn't of our station, and you may mix with her out of kindness but not in social settings."

"But she's my best friend. I like her. Do I have to have curls *and* a big bow?"

Uncle Levi came into the kitchen. Generally, he was like a dark shadow in the house, only found in Missus' room at supper and in his bedroom after. His morose mood caused a dark pall that floated in his wake, causing the children to find shelter away from him.

"Mr. Levi, will you get me a restorative before we go, please?" Missus Hannah requested.

"Yes, of course. Why isn't Benjamin dressed yet?"

"Benjamin will stay home tonight. It's better that way. He doesn't have clothes to wear," she answered.

"I don't give a snap what he wears. Find something clean." Uncle Levi never showed anger with Missus, but he had raised his voice. Everything in the house got quiet.

"It isn't prudent to take Benjamin, Sir. He can't take the excitement. I've saved him a sack lunch with an orange, like all the children are getting. I'll have Grace come and check on him."

"Can't you see how cut up he is over this? Have Grace get him ready," Mr. Levi growled.

"Go Sarah," Missus Hannah's voice was shaking. "Get your coat and overshoes."

* * * * *

It snowed for two days before the Christmas party. Heavy snow covered the fields as farmers came in sleighs and wagons with sapling runners, leaving the roads and flying through the fields and over drifted fences. The cold invigorated people as they congregated at the school. High spirits were infectious as Rev. and Mrs. Ada Jones of the Baptist Church greeted Elder Hyre and Sister Minnie of the Dunkard Church.

"Good evening," Rev. Jones welcomed jovially. "I'd shake hands but I'm protecting this decorated box supper with my life."

"I understand," Sister Minnie said, "I got it this far without ruining it. I'd hate to spoil it now."

"How about you ladies deliver your boxes. Rev. Jones and I will get cocoa and find a quiet corner to warm up."

"Great idea. I hope no one slips demon rum in the drink like they did at last year's party. I've never had such a headache."

"I'll do judicious checking this year. Fool me once, shame on you. Fool me twice, shame on me," Rev. Jones stated.

"Lawsy me, Mrs. Ada, isn't it all beautiful, lit with the red lamplight? Someone has done a lot of work. Look at this beautiful tree with the strings of popcorn, paper chains, and pinecones. Someone was sure creative to drape the pine bough garlands from the corners to the bell at the center of the ceiling. I'll bet Hannah Zumbrun helped Mr. Young with this. I'm glad they don't have pagan Santa Claus decorations like they have downtown. It confuses children when they're not clear about the meaning of Christmas."

"Listen to the little ones singing. This sure gets me in the Christmas spirit," Sister Minnie said with awe in her voice. "Our Christmas is going to be meager. We were glad to get a little something made for each child. But they'll remember this party, alright—the decorations and especially the sack supper for the children. I heard they each get a block of maple sugar candy and an orange. I told Elder Hyre to bid on my box 'cause it's plain eatins' and I don't want anyone else to be disappointed."

"Mine is skimpy too. I'll tell Rev. Jones to bid on your box. Elder Hyre can bid on mine. That will settle that," Ada Jones said.

Rev. Jones and Elder Hyre returned, handing a steaming cup of cocoa to their wives. "You ladies are in for a treat. See on top of your cocoa: it's something new called a marshmallow. It's puffy sugar. Mrs. Hannah found them at a store in Ligonier. She bought one for everyone to have in their cocoa. They're spongy. Sweet like candy. What an extravagance."

"But I'm happy for the children. They get so little. They'll talk about this party for weeks," Ada Jones said, then gasped. "Oh, don't look now. There comes Lois Hudson with her little Louise. I never thought she'd have the nerve to show her face! Just watch her traipse in, looking like a tart. She has no shame."

"John and Ruby Hudson, her parents, are members of my church." Rev. Jones lowered his voice as the room suddenly became quiet. "They can't hold their heads up anymore. They have three daughters, and this Lois has been trouble for them since day one. She goes out and about with little Louise like she's normal, not a bastard. She'll continue in Little Lake School, it seems. I wonder what Mr. Young thinks about that?"

Noise in the room picked up as everyone whispered and gawked. Sister Minnie, leaning into the group of four, said in a hushed voice, "And our little Lizzie insists Louise is her best friend. She wants her to come play at our house."

Rev. Jones shook has finger, his voice ponderous, "This is what happens when the husband isn't the authoritative head of his household. For years I've counseled John Hudson to come down hard on Lois. After all, who's going to buy the cow when they can get the milk for nothing? They should have sent her away when they found out she was in the family way, and saved all of us the disgrace. We required her confession in front of the church, but she wasn't really repentant. That's what gripes me. I wish she wouldn't come to church, but she marches in Sunday morning with her nose in the air just like she did tonight. She acts like we should just accept her and Louise like they're one of us—we should get over it."

"In the Dunkard Church our procedure for confession requires the lady to name the person she sinned with. Then the gentleman must confess as well. Has Lois named the father?" asked Elder Hyre.

"Humph." Ada Jones frowned, "My husband has tried, but Lois refused to call out the father. She told Rev. Jones he should read the scripture about the woman at the well—that's how lippy *she* was. One time a few years ago I had business in the courthouse. I was looking out a window facing the jail. Sherriff Williams was in his buggy and he came up to Lois who was walking and followed along, talking to her. She kept her head down ignoring him, until she quickly turned back around, walked away from him, and went into the hardware store. You know what they say about his behavior with women prisoners—right there in the jail with his wife downstairs."

"Oh, my stars! Benjamin has the Carson's baby," shrieked Sister Minnie, jumping from her seat. Their eyes followed, aghast, as they observed the gentle giant who had picked up the small baby, throwing it higher and ever higher in the air. The baby was rigid, unable to catch its breath. The mother was frozen mid-step, her arms extended, her face warped with fear. There was instantaneous quiet, everyone holding their breath, afraid to move. Benjamin called: "Fly, baby! Come to Benji! Fly baby! Come to Benji!"

Mr. Levi, across the room, moved intently toward Benjamin, repeating, "Hold the baby, Benjamin. Don't throw the baby." Benjamin, feeling the hush and recognizing all eyes were on him, became uncertain. He finally held the baby who erupted in panicky screams, frightening Benjamin. Mr. Levi handed the baby to his tearful mother, apologizing profusely. Then he uncertainly knelt to comfort Benjamin who was bawling, sitting on the floor with his arms over his head, knowing he'd done something wrong—but not understanding. Sarah and Louise came running, hugging and standing on Benjamin's folded legs, encircling his neck: "Don't cry, Benji. It's okay," Sarah said.

"I want to go home," Benjamin sobbed in a plaintive voice. "It's too noisy here."

Grace came, taking Benjamin's hand, "It's okay. We'll go home now."

Mrs. Hannah, her face pink, the veins beating in her temples, brought Benjamin hot chocolate and his sack supper. "Give him a bit of brandy to help him settle," she whispered to Grace. "Once he's asleep, come back to the party. He'll be okay. Take the lantern from the wagon."

The reverends returned to their seats. "I'll be bound, that gave me a fright," Sister Minnie exclaimed. "Poor Mrs. Hannah. She does have her hands full with all the children Mr. Levi rounds up. She does so much for our community. I think she is poorly, may have lung fever."

"I met her on the road coming back from the medicine man. She must be worried if she's taking the Indian cures," Mrs. Ada said.

"I think the all-knowing Lord in His wisdom chose not to give Mr. Levi and Mrs. Hannah children—it was preordained; they were meant to be childless. I know they think they're doing the Lord's work by taking in those children. But as you can see, they're troubled. I wouldn't want that stunted man in my house with a bunch of young girls," Rev. Jones opined.

"They're a good Christian couple," stated Elder Hyre. "Mr. Levi and some of the children come to church most Sunday mornings. Mrs. Hannah comes when she can. They take to heart 'as you do it unto one of the least of these, you have done it unto Me'.... Now it's getting interesting: they're bidding on Lois Hudson's box. What if no one bids—that would be embarrassing. Maybe I'll open the bid just to get it started: twenty-five cents," called Elder Hyre.

"If no one else bids, you'll find yourself eating with her," Sister Minnie said.

"The bid is up to a dollar-fifty. I'll keep it interesting: two-dollars," called Elder Hyre.

"Remember you need to feed your family this week," Sister Minnie laughed.

"What men won't do to be with a pretty woman, a fallen one at that," Mrs. Jones complained.

Now there was fun in the air, friendly competition. All the slights paid Miss Lois the past six years were put to rest. Full of Christmas cheer, several men who previously looked askance, now hoped for the notoriety of having her as their supper partner. For her part, Miss Lois didn't know if she was being ridiculed, humiliated, or finally embraced. There was joy in the air, tears in the eyes, and old hurts appeased, when the auctioneer's voice called: "sold to Levi Zumbrun for six- dollars!" Whistles and catcalls filled the warm glowing room.

"We could have bought a good used plow for six-dollars," Mrs. Jones grumbled.

As they had discussed, the convivial reverends each bid on the other wife's box. When the time came they spread their meals and communed as friends.

The auctioneer's voice called, "The last box for bid: the ingenious gingerbread representation of Little Lake School created by Mrs. Hannah Zumbrun. I happen to know there are homemade French eclairs in this box. It's a work of art. Let's up the ante, folks. Let's dig a well for the school. How about one-dollar to open the bid."

Mr. Markham, the superintendent bid one-dollar. Mr. Zumbrun bid one-fifty.

"That poor guy," Elder Hyre chuckled, "He's buying it twice."

"Two-dollars," bid Mr. Young.

"Two-fifty," called Mr. Zumbrun.

"What's he going to do, make Mrs. Hannah eat with him and Miss Lois? I would like to be a fly on the wall for that one," snickered Mrs. Jones, "seeing how Mr. Zumbrun rarely talks."

"Three-dollars," bid Mr. Young, his face red, his eyes blinking a storm.

"Poor fella," Sister Minnie commiserated, "He's so in love with her."

"Oh, law! Do you think so?" Mrs. Jones popped out of her seat, her eyes wide. "Mr. Levi wouldn't be happy if he knew that."

"Oh, he probably knows," Sister Minnie said, "He also knows that, while she basks in the adoration, she's a woman of scruples. She wouldn't act on it."

"Well, I'll be hornswoggled. I didn't see that," Mrs. Ada said, shaking her head.

"Well just look: she's educated and well read. He's about the only other educated person around here. She has that coquetry that men love. They both want to improve the school, teach manners to us country folk. They're near the same age. She lives close to the school, so it's easy for her to help out. But she's a woman of fidelity and Mr. Levi knows that."

"SOLD! To Mr. Young for six-dollars." Mr. Young pumped his arms in the air, sweating and red-faced, unconcerned that a month's salary went for a gingerbread schoolhouse and a lavish supper.

He spoke to the group, "Now the children can enjoy the artistry of their schoolhouse, thanks to Mrs. Zumbrun. We'll display it in other schools. Thanks to all of you, we have more than enough money for the well. Indeed, this is a Merry Christmas. Let's open these meals and enjoy. Rev. Jones, would you bless our food, please?"

CHAPTER 7

Conversion

"In the twinkling of an eye, the trumpet will sound and God will take you home. Repent! I say again, repent your sins," Brother Culp pleaded, gesturing wildly. "Accept God's forgiveness. Soon, maybe tomorrow, the Son of Man will come in glory and all the angels with Him." His spit flew as he waved his arm and wiped his brow with his handkerchief. "All who repent will be gathered into the Kingdom of Heaven. The unrepentant will B U R N in the fires of Hell. Come now as we sing. His blood was shed, just for you. Say publicly now, Oh Lamb of God, I come. I accept you into my heart."

Revival meetings were a yearly occurrence at the Blue River Dunkard Church. Brother Culp, a charismatic guest preacher from Elkhart County, came recommended to bring converts and grow the congregation.

"Yes, we have a young child," Brother Culp celebrated. He stepped from the podium, taking ten-year-old Sarah's hand, seating her on the front bench of the church. "Jesus said, 'Even a small child shall lead them.'"

Church was dismissed with a prayer of gratitude for a child's soul saved. As was the practice, Elder Hyre met alone with the confessed sinner. "Praise the Lord, my child," he took Sarah's hands. "This is the most important decision you'll make in your life. I want to be certain you understand the step you're taking."

Sarah's voice was timorous, "I was going to run away instead, but I got scared and came back."

"Oh my dear, why would you run away?" Elder Hyre questioned her soberly.

"I need to find Juda. I need my family. I have prayed to God every night to let me live with Juda or my papa and Will. God isn't listening to me. I guess I'm too young."

"But God *does* hear you Sarah. He's telling you that you *are* with your family—Mrs. Hannah and Mr. Levi, Grace, Rosa, and Benjamin are your family."

"No, God is wrong. Missus Hannah and Uncle Levi are *not* my family. I *have* a family, and I want to live with them. If I can't, I want God to take me to Heaven to live with my mama," Sarah said with certainty. "The preacher said Jesus looks for every one of his lost sheep and will take them home to Heaven. Well, I've lost my family; I want God to take me to Heaven to be with my mama."

"But Sarah, Jesus will come for you in His own time. You're a young child. You're too young to go to Heaven," he said, patting her hand.

"Are you telling me there's no hope for me?" Sarah asked plaintively.

For once in his life Elder Hyre was speechless.

* * * * *

"You always have to be first. Missus Hannah said I was too young to go forward during revivals but you're younger than me. You have to be best, Miss Goody Two-shoes. It's not fair." Rosa lashed out at Sarah, pulling her braid as they stumbled and pushed on the walk home from school. "Ever since you came here it's Sarah, Sarah, Sarah."

"You could have gone forward to confess if you wanted to be first," Sarah tripped Rosa, causing her to fall. "I only went forward 'cause I wanted to go to Heaven and be with Mama. Now Elder Hyre says it doesn't work that way. I wish I'd never done it. Now I have to confess my sins and ask forgiveness from everyone I've sinned against. Do you really think I wanted this?"

Rosa got up and stuck her chin out, "You just want to wear a white prayer bonnet like Jane Wilson and the other big girls."

"I don't even *like* the bonnets, Rosa. Now will you forgive me for beating you in the spelling bee and bragging that I'm better? And forgive me for the time I left your coat outside and a mouse made a hole in the sleeve."

"No, I don't forgive you 'cause you're not true when you say sorry," Rosa snipped.

"Then you're going to Hell 'cause the Bible says you have to forgive." Sarah threatened, running ahead to the house.

"Is that you, Sarah? Come to my room," Missus Hannah called. Rosa pretended to gag.

"Yes, Missus," Sarah went beside her bed where she was propped with pillows, an ice bag held to her forehead.

"Tomorrow is your baptism at Big Cedar Lake. We need some discourse on the matter. I'm not reproaching you though it might have been more appropriate had you waited a few years. You're mature for a ten-year-old, but you must understand—this is a serious step." Missus Hannah coughed deeply, expectorating into a hanky.

"If you don't want me to be baptized that's okay with me. It doesn't mean what I thought. That preacher tricked me."

"The die has been cast and you'll go through with it. I venture to say most preachers have a touch of trickery in their words, though you'll not repeat my opinion on that."

"Yes, Missus."

"Being baptized means you become a member of the Dunkard Church and live by their teachings. Elder Hyre will take you into the water, not deep, and will put your head under the water three times: in the name of the Father, the Son, and the Holy Spirit. This type baptism is why we're called Dunkard Brethren. Personally, I much prefer the German Baptist name. You must hold your breath each time you go under water. Your nose is running, Sarah. Get a hanky out of my drawer. This would not be an auspicious time to get a chill. Do you feel sick?"

"Maybe a little," Sarah answered, blowing her nose.

"I think you're worried about tomorrow." She paused to catch her breath. "You've not been in a lake so it can be frightening. I want you to show what a brave girl you are, even though you're the youngest one being baptized. Show everyone how grown-up you are. Elder Hyre will not let your head stay under water. He'll keep you safe. It has already snowed so the water will be cold. I'll take a blanket to wrap you and we'll come right home."

"This is such a fuss. I wish I never went forward."

"That will be our secret, Sarah. It's good you want to live the Dunkard way of life: go to church, treat people kindly, try to get along peaceably with people, live simply and plainly so as not to be noticed. You can be a Christian example to Rosa. She has some things to learn in that regard."

"Rosa said I have to wear a lady's white bonnet."

"Dunkards believe ladies should cover their head when they pray. The Bible says we should pray at any time, without ceasing. We'll just have you wear a bonnet at church since you're so young. Sarah, let me feel your forehead, you look a little peaked."

Sarah felt Missus Hannah's cool hand on her forehead and basked in her uncommon attention. It was almost worth going through the baptism ordeal. She coughed hard and it wasn't even to get sympathy.

Saturday was chill and overcast. The leaves had fallen, the migrating birds gone south. The family crowded into the buggy and gathered with about thirty church members along the banks of the lake. The setting was cold and desolate, the lakeside muddy with dead leaves.

Baptism was the most important sacrament of the church as new members were brought into the fold. Current members committed to assist them to live in accord with church doctrine. Everyone was bundled and huddled together, their breath steaming out the words of the baptismal hymn:

> Lord Jesus, I long to be perfectly whole,
> I want Thee forever to live in my soul.
> Whiter than snow, yes whiter than snow
> Lord, wash me and I shall be whiter than snow.

Sarah walked down into the water, the sudden cold piercing her body, forcing a cough, as Elder Hyre took her hand. She knelt in the freezing water feeling the gravity of the moment. She wanted to be God's child, a kinder person. She didn't want to go to Hell. In a quiet voice she answered "yes" to each of Elder Hyre's questions: do you believe in God the Father, Son, and Holy Spirit? Do you confess your sins? Do you promise to live in accord with Christ's teachings as taught by the Dunkard Brethren Church? Elder Hyre dipped her three times forward, completely under water, symbolically washing her of sin. Sarah gasped, holding a hanky to her nose. Just that quick, it was over. Elder Hyre handed her to Missus Hannah who wrapped her in a blanket and took her to the buggy where there were warmed bricks.

"My dear, come on my lap, I'll keep you warm," Missus said, rocking Sarah like a baby. "I don't want you to catch your death." Sarah lay awkwardly snuggled against Missus, neither of them familiar with touching. Every sense was overflowing as she heard Missus' breathless words sung with the congregation: "Whiter than snow, yes whiter than snow; Lord wash me and I shall be whiter than snow...." Sarah felt sheltered, cleansed, and the peace of a new beginning.

* * * * *

It was the middle of the night. Rosa knocked on Missus Hannah's bedroom door. "Missus, Missus. Sarah is sick. I think she needs help."

She opened the door, "What is it, Rosa?"

"It's Sarah. She's coughing so hard she throws up. She can't get her breath."

"Oh, my goodness. I'd better check her." Rosa watched as Missus got into her robe and slippers, her hair frizzy in a long plait under her nightcap. As they ascended the stairs, Sarah coughed a harsh barking cough.

"We'd better bring her downstairs before she wakes Mr. Levi. He'll be in a foul mood if he doesn't get his sleep. Oh, I should never have let her be baptized and get a chill. God will smite me." She gently shook Sarah. "Wake up, Sarah. You need to come downstairs to my bedroom. Goodness me, you are burning up. Rosa, you get rags and a pan of cold water. In the morning we'll send Benjamin for Dr. Mathys.

"It's whooping cough," Dr. Mathys pronounced. "It's going around. She probably got it at school. It can run an easy course of a week, or she can die from it. There isn't much I can do. Her temperature is one-hundred-three degrees. When she feels hottest, put her in a tub of cool water. Otherwise just cool cloths. The big danger is pneumonia. Coughing can make her vomit as it did last night, and she can aspirate into her lungs. I don't hear any rales in her lungs this morning. She may be sick for weeks. It's contagious, Mrs. Zumbrun, and your lungs are already bad. Whooping cough could be the death knell for you."

"God's will be done," Missus said, rinsing the rag in cool water.

"Let Rosa take care of her, Mrs. Zumbrun. Her body is young and strong. Keep the mentholatum plaster on her chest. I'll leave some valerian to help her relax. Let me listen to your lungs while I'm here," he said, placing his stethoscope on her chest and back. "Your lungs are very congested. What does your sputum look like?"

"It's yellow. Brownish sometimes," she answered.

"Do you cough bright blood?"

"No, never blood. I think I can beat this consumption, Doctor."

"You're not a healthy woman, Mrs. Zumbrun. You must take care not to overtire," he warned as he prepared to leave.

Missus allowed Rosa to help with Sarah during the day. She stayed up during the long nights when Sarah's temperature went up and the violent spells of coughing intensified. Night after night for two weeks Sarah coughed in unremitting spasms. With the high fever, Sarah was in a semiconscious netherworld, hardly aware of her surroundings.

"What's the crackling noise in my chest? It makes it hard to get my breath," she asked.

"Dr. Mathys said some people get that when they get whooping cough," Missus answered.

"Am I going to die?"

"No, Sarah. I won't let you die. You're my child."

Sarah's voice was hardly audible as she gasped the words, "For a long time I've been asking God to let me be with Juda or Papa and Will. He didn't hear my prayers. So I asked God to take me to Heaven to be with Mama. This new family is not where I belong—I'm out of place here." With talking, Sarah went into another paroxysm of coughing. Missus, exhausted by her own congested cough, dried Sarah's eyes and wiped her mouth, holding her until she caught her breath.

"This *is* your home, Sarah. You're part of *our* family. We take care of you, give you everything you need. Why aren't you happy here?"

Sarah heaved to breathe, "I feel out of place. I'm an outsider in this family." She paused for a moment, "It's like a whole bowl of red apples except one is green. No matter how you look at it, one doesn't belong. My heart is with my real family." Another gasping pause, "I'm so tired of being sick, Missus. I want God to take me to Heaven."

"Don't say that. You can't give up, Sarah. When morning comes, we'll go to the Indian medicine man. He has special medicine for lungs. We'll bundle you in warm blankets. There has to be something to help you." And so, the night passed with gurgling chest sounds emanating from both Sarah and Missus.

The next morning Uncle Levi gathered five leghorn hens into a cage and carried Sarah into the bitter cold Indiana winter to the buggy, disapproval written over his face. Sarah was hardly aware and didn't remember the trip down the back roads to the Indian medicine man.

"Mr. Levi, have you noticed Sarah hasn't coughed since we left home? It's the first time in two weeks I haven't heard her cough. It seems a miracle," Missus said, as they drove to the Indian's cabin. The old Indian came out, smiling and waving at the Zumbruns. They had been friends for many years when they worked on farm projects together. He motioned for them to stay in the buggy.

"Your diseases come to my house," he explained.

Missus Hannah called to him, "Sarah has whooping cough for two weeks and now pneumonia. She's very sick with high fevers. She can't rest from the coughing."

The Indian went into his cabin and shortly returned with a bag of dried leaves, handing them to Missus Hannah. "Put one leaf in hot tea, morning and evening. Great amounts catarrhal drainage comes from her mouth. Is good. If doesn't come, she die. When she has bad coughing take her outdoors. Cold air will stop the cough."

As if on cue, Missus Hannah began her own coughing spasm, choking and gasping, then spitting into her hanky. "Oh," she gasped, staring fearfully at the hanky, then holding it for the medicine man to see: sputum with bright red blood. "The blood just started recently."

Mr. Levi glanced with understanding, his face crumbling. "No, No, it can't be," he put his face in his hands.

"Can this be whooping cough? I've been with Sarah," she wiped stains of blood from her lip.

The medicine man shook his head, "Not whooping cough."

"Is the lung fever getting worse?" she asked.

"It is galloping consumption." He looked sadly at her. "No medicine will make better. Twelve moons you pass to the other side."

Her shrinking body and gray pallor belied her determination, "Then there's much to get done," she gently nodded to Mr. Levi.

He got down from the buggy, opening the door of the cage, letting the chickens loose.

"Good egg producers," he promised, unloading a gunny sack of cracked corn. His eyes begged his friend, "Have you anything to heal Missus Hannah's lungs?"

The old Indian went back to his cabin and returned with a bag. "Will not cure. The tonic will send nourishment to the blood. Chew one every day. Return when these are gone." He stepped back, holding his arm aloft, "May the Great Spirit guide your path," he intoned as the buggy circled away.

"We'll find a doctor who can help you," Mr. Levi pulled her close. "I'm no good without you, my dear. I don't know how to be with people. I think you've sickened yourself in caring for the girl. Your constitution has never been strong. I blame her for this dread malady." he ranted.

"The sands of time run for all of us, my love. I've been lying low for some time. Pledge to me you won't hold Sarah to account. Maybe we should bring Grace home until my vitality is restored."

"I would give all I own for your health. I have no life without you." Mr. Levi's fragile equilibrium was shattered by the Indian's pronouncement. Missus Hannah realized she would become the resilient one in the family—this sore trial would be on her shoulders. Contrary to Elder Hyre's sermons about men being the head of the household, Mr. Levi would be unable to take this role in the future.

She did not yield easily to her disease. Everyone she knew who spit blood had the inexorable trajectory to incapacity and death. In the sleepless nights alone in her room she warred with God, her faith in jeopardy. Not because she had consumption and was dying—that fate wasn't unusual for women of her day. She railed because she was barren; her lifelong dream of motherhood an illusion. She and Mr. Levi had botched together a cadre of sham children, none of whom were right, none who loved them, none who would carry them in memory. The hurt engulfed her.

CHAPTER 8

Queenie

"Since when have you been first in the buggy on a Sunday morning? You must have spring fever, Benjamin," Grace remarked as they piled into the buggy for the ride to church. Missus had stayed abed, requiring Grace, who had moved back to the farm, to get dinner prepared. An additional challenge was preventing Benji, Rosa, and Sarah from diddling around.

Uncle Levi was pink-nosed and flustered as he drove the buggy alongside the recently built platform in front of the white frame church. "So high-toned and consequential...a waste of money...them and their popular airs," he muttered, grumbling into his beard. The platform with steps permitted the ladies to step from their buggy to the church entrance so their long skirts didn't drag through the mud as they walked into church. Mr. Levi was convinced it was one more unnecessary money grab.

Mr. Levi and Benjamin sat on benches on the men's side midway to the front. Grace, Rosa, and Sarah sat behind them and across the aisle with the women. The girls left their coats on over dark dresses and cotton stockings. Grace and Sarah wore white prayer bonnets.

Old hymns were sung in harmony. As there was just one hymnal, a leader sang one line of a song, the congregation following, until the hymn was finished. Eleven-year-old Sarah liked the singing, and her lovely childlike voice was noticed by the congregants. She got bored and easily distracted during the scripture reading, the long sermon, and when they knelt on their knees to pray, facing back toward the rough bench. Any man who wished could offer a prayer, and as many were prideful in extolling their piety and praise in flowery prose, prayers were interminable. Except for Mr. Levi—Sarah had never heard him pray in church. He saved praying for Sunday dinner when the food was getting cold.

Sarah was bored during the sermon, playing with her bonnet strings. Across the aisle, Benji's hushed snickers caught her attention. His eyes sparkled, his naughty smile beamed, and he was as antsy as a March hare. He lifted open his coat jacket and out popped Queenie's head!

Involuntarily Sarah exclaimed, "Gee whillikers!" her hand over her mouth as a tittering laugh tumbled out before she reddened and huddled into her coat.

Many people in front of her were startled, twenty pair of frowning eyes turned to look at her—their eyes steely and unforgiving.

"What are you doing?" Rosa hissed.

Sarah was shamed. Children were to be seen and not heard, especially in church. The fact that she was recently baptized and supposed to measure up to high standards was not in her favor. But Sarah's funny bone had been strummed. She glanced over at Benji who had a chicken foot sticking out between his coat buttons. Sarah convulsed in laughter, splitting her sides to hold in the guffaws while Benji sat waving the chicken foot as innocently as you please. People were stirring at the disturbance, looking and wondering quizzically what they were missing, while Sarah shook in her seat.

"You're really gonna git it when you get home," Rosa threatened, mad that she wasn't in on the joke.

At last the sermon was over and the congregation knelt for the prayers. About the time Sarah got her giggles under control, Queenie, dressed in a pinafore, wiggled herself out of Benji's coat, stepped along the raw wooden bench and promptly dropped a pile of shit. Benji's eyes widened, his expression horrified, which of course got Sarah going off again, tears running down her cheeks. Now heads were bobbing, noses wiggling and the man who was praying paused while he tried to sniff-snort whatever was amiss. Sarah got up from her knees and with her hand over her mouth loped out of church to the buggy. Not two minutes later came Benji, a bit more rotund, his coat buttoned up and a wicked smile on his face. The two stood by the buggy, bent over, hooting with laughter which slowed to sporadic chuckles, then subsided.

"Did you clean up the shit?"

"Of course, Sarah. At least pretty good."

"What did you use?"

"My shirttail."

"We're in big trouble, Benji."

"Yeah, we're in trouble alright. Mr. Levi will strop us."

"They might make me confess or even kick me out of church," she looked up at him, dissolving in gales of unrestrained laughter.

"I'm sorry I got you in trouble. It was my fault. What will you do if they kick you out?"

"Go to Hell, I guess. I doubt anyone gets two chances at baptism."

"We'll be in Hell together then, 'cause I ain't never been baptized."

"But you're old, Benji. You should have been baptized a long time ago. I'm surprised Elder Hyre hasn't been after you."

"They were after me awright. I'm just too scared to get in the water. Instead of getting dunked, I ran all the way home. Mr. Levi said don't worry about it."

"They might change their minds after this, Benji."

"No way. I'm not gittin' in a lake. Oh boy, here they come. Now we're in for it." Some of the children ran around playing, and soon men came to drive the buggies to the door.

"You children got out in a hurry," Uncle Levi said noncommittally as he guided the buggy to get Rosa and Grace.

"Yes'r," agreed Benji, sitting in front with Uncle Levi. Grace and Rosa were full of whispered questions: "What was so funny? Why did you run out?" They waited, expecting Mr. Levi's wrath to explode. But Mr. Levi had changed in recent weeks: he was more depressed and introspective, alone in the world of his mind. As they neared home Benji turned, grinning at Sarah—apparently Mr. Levi had missed the whole incident.

While the three girls were preparing dinner, Sarah told them every incredible detail about Queenie in a pinafore, hidden under Benji's coat, getting out and shitting on the bench. Now, in on the joke, they were appalled at Benji's disobedience and brazen behavior and in disbelief that apparently he got away with it.

Missus joined the family in the dining room for Sunday dinner. "You children have the collywobbles today. Why are you so wound up?"

The four children looked innocently at each other, then broke into hooting laughter, holding their sides in mirth. Benji, his hands over both ears, jumped up from his chair and ran toward the stairway, a dark stain spreading down his pant legs. The girls laughed till they cried and each time they regained control, one would start again.

"Mr. Levi, something must have happened at church. It would seem Benjamin is up to something."

"I don't know what it is, Missus Hannah. I was praying during much of the sermon—my eyes were closed."

"Well let's hope Elder Hyre knew you were praying, not sleeping," she said.

The chickens came home to roost on Thursday with the printing of the Albion New Era. The weekly paper was read verbatim by everyone in the county, including Missus Hannah. Mrs. Roe, the local reporter/gossip, gobble-chinned and wide-of-beam, was off-put by Mrs. Hannah's too colorful finery, so at every opportunity she was happy to spread a word about tawdry goings-on with the Zumbrun family. She had a tongue that would latch on to anyone, refusing retreat. It was never known who saw Benjamin in church with Queenie and reported it to Elder Hyre and Mrs. Roe—both who heartily assumed the burden of keeping rural children on the straight and narrow.

As usual Mr. Levi had supper in Mrs. Hannah's room and the children ate in the kitchen. Missus had left the paper on the table open to the incriminating item in the Albion newspaper:

> Those who take God in vain by bringing unwanted
> helpless farm animals to church then laughing at
> their antics are not welcome in the house of God.
> Mental incapacity is no excuse. It appears that recent
> baptismal vows were not taken to heart. Watch out!
> Your names are known.

Rosa read it aloud to Benji. "This is about *you*, written in the paper. You are so in trouble," Rosa taunted, thrilled that Sarah and Benji were finally getting their comeuppance, but again jealous of their notoriety at being in the paper. While names weren't mentioned, it would take precious little digging—a word here, a question there, and everyone in the county would know the story.

"Why was it wrong for Queenie to go to church? I dressed her nice and she didn't bother anyone." Benji asked.

"She bothered Sarah," Grace said. "Sarah laughed out loud and that upset people who were worshipping. You got Sarah in trouble, Benji."

"That's okay, Benji. I liked seeing Queenie in church. I've never laughed so hard," Sarah grinned.

There was a knock at the door. Grace opened it to Elder Hyre and Deacon Kelling. She announced the visitors to Mr. Levi and Missus Hannah who invited them into the parlor, closing the door. Sarah and Benji sat with eyes down, fear on their faces. It was dire to disappoint one's elders and be brought to task for wrongdoing. In school Sarah always obeyed the rules; she wanted to go unnoticed. Now the story was in the newspaper and the minister was making a call because she was a troublemaker. Her tears were close to the surface.

The parlor door opened and the children were ushered in. Missus whispered to Grace to get a kitchen chair with a towel in case Benji had another accident. Everyone looked at the floor.

Missus' voice was stern. "Tell us what happened at church on Sunday."

Rosa eagerly spoke up, "Sarah told Benji to dress Queenie in a pinafore and sneak her into church. Queenie dropped a poop right on the church bench."

"Rosa that is crude talk. Did you do that, Sarah?"

"I didn't tell him to do it. But when I saw Queenie under his coat, I laughed out loud, disturbing the worship."

Benji was crying, jumping around in his chair, "Don't make Sarah go to Hell. It was my fault. Sarah didn't know."

"Benjamin, quit crying. No one is going to Hell," Uncle Levi stormed.

"I do have a concern that Benjamin and Sarah do not have appropriate respect for the hallowed nature of God's house—this should be a place we enter with reverence and awe. As a new convert, Sarah should be filled with devotion. A more mature Christian would not have seen the humor, but been dismayed by Benjamin bringing his pet to church."

"I'm sorry. I wasn't expecting to see Queenie under his coat."

"It's not Sarah's fault," caterwauled Benji.

"Our service was disrupted. Some told me their prayers were disturbed. Benjamin and Sarah, I expect you to repent of the sin of not keeping God's house holy. We have a good example from scripture in the New Testament when Jesus cast out the money changers who were selling animals in the temple. Jesus said, 'you are corrupting God's house' and He put them out. Next Sunday you will both come up on the platform to confess your sin and ask the church members for forgiveness for disturbing their worship. Sarah, this is not an auspicious beginning for your life in God's kingdom. You need to pray daily for forgiveness and ask God for a pure heart and Christ-like attitude in your walk with our Savior. Benjamin, we will ban you from the Lord's house for four Sundays. We suggest you spend the time in prayer and supplication, beseeching a right spirit within you. Hopefully in the future, you will not be tempted by sinful pursuits. Mr. Levi, as head of the household you are responsible for Christian instruction of your children. A lesson based on Chronicles twenty-nine where we're warned to keep filthiness out of the house of the Lord, seems appropriate. Does anyone have any questions or comments?"

Benjamin and Sarah were wretched. His handkerchief was busy sopping up tears and noisy sniffles. Sarah was quiet, her face down, tears wiped with her shirtsleeve. To be disciplined by the preacher was shameful.

Elder Hyre was somber. "If not, we will close with a prayer:

> Our dear Heavenly Father. Since Adam, all have sinned and fallen short. These children too were tempted by Satan and have gone astray. They have not shown reverence in God's house or respect for God's people in worship. Help them see the error of their ways and come

> to you on bended knee for your forgiveness. As our Savior who died on the cross for our sins, we know you continue to love us and welcome us back to your fold. Help these children look to you for guidance and walk aright. In Jesus name we pray. Amen"

The mood was somber that night in the Zumbrun household. Everyone felt the full measure of wrongdoing and sin, either by doing the deed or by association. It was a matter of "waiting for the shoe to drop". Sarah was almost disappointed when nothing happened that night; she wanted to be done with the punishment. Neither did anything happen the next morning and she went to school as usual. As Sarah knew she would, Rosa told all the girls at school about the pastor's visit, suggesting Sarah was the ringleader of the episode. Sarah was glad her friend Louise didn't go to the Dunkard Church. She seemed disinterested in the whispered gossip and cool treatment by some of the girls.

When they got home from school Missus asked Sarah to bring in the wash hanging on the clothesline. The girls ironed and put clothes away while she got supper. Sarah relaxed a bit; she liked the mindless tedium of folding clothes and the orderly appearance of the crisply ironed dresses.

As usual Missus and Mr. Levi ate in her room and the children ate in the kitchen. Sarah dug in to her favorite meal: noodles, mashed potatoes, and fried chicken. As she gnawed on her chicken leg she realized what she was eating, and her heart dropped to her toes. She gasped, looking at Grace who had the same shattered expression. Benji as usual, was completely oblivious, focused on feeding his face.

"Benji, did you see Queenie tonight?" Sarah asked, holding her chicken aloft.

"No, I couldn't find her," Benji answered, then noticing Sarah and Grace's distress, realized what they were eating. "No-o-o! No-o-o!" Benji screamed, jumping up and running outdoors. The girls joined him in the henhouse where the chickens were roosted. Benji had totally lost control. He was screaming, grabbing chickens and twisting off their necks as fast as he could. The headless chickens were run-flopping around, spurting blood all over the chicken house, the chickens, and the children. It was absolute bloody, squawking, screaming pandemonium when Mr. Levi walked in. Roughly grabbing and shaking Sarah and Benji, smearing blood on their faces, he bellowed, "Did you learn your lesson? Did you learn your lesson?"

CHAPTER 9

Missus Hannah

The spring of Sarah's twelfth year brought unwonted changes in the Zumbrun home. Missus rarely left her room. Every breath felt like a mile-long race. She knew every cough with clotted blood rushed the sands of time through the hourglass of her days. Dr. Mathys believed he could cure her with Dr. King's expensive remedy for consumption. Missus had more faith in the old Indian who touched her shoulder saying, "Soon, my lady. Take these herbs when your spirit needs peace."

Mr. Levi could not accept that Missus Hannah was not getting better. In his eyes her strength was improving, and her cheeks were rosy. His fear was only evident in his all-consuming drive to improve his farm. He did the work of a man half his age. He had more tillable acreage than most farmers in the region. Land in Noble County was low, swampy, and wet, though fertile if drained. A visionary, he was one of the first farmers to dig trenches and lay tile on all tillable land. It was back-breaking work. He could not have done it without Benjamin, who had the strength of two men. He also brought Grace and Rosa's brother George, to work on the farm.

He paid little attention to care of the animals, planting, preserving food from the garden, and upkeep of the impressive homestead. Missus Hannah had taken pride in running a fine home, planting flowers, and preparing good meals. She was one of the leading ladies of Albion society. The last years she had increasing difficulty running the homestead. Rosa had been hired out so Grace and Sarah were worked like horses. Grace cared for Missus Hannah and did the housework and gardening. Sarah did the farm work: milked the cows, slopped the pigs, and tended the chickens. She began helping with field work—plowing and planting. Most days in spring and fall, work prevented school attendance. Though Missus Hannah was ill and needed constant care, Mr. Levi was too frugal to bring Rosa home to help. He worked until sunset then came to the house, washed, and went to Missus room where supper was served. This hour or two was the favorite time of day for each of them as they discussed farm and family activities.

After supper Mr. Levi walked across the room, his back to Missus. He was uncomfortable discussing this subject. "We need to change the situation with Grace and Benjamin. They should get married."

Missus' head snapped upward in surprise. "Sir, why ever would Grace want to marry Benjamin? I understand she'll be an old maid, but it's possible she could have a good life." Missus stopped to catch her breath and cough up phlegm. "We keep her so busy she never gets off the farm to meet other young people. Benjamin is fifty-some but like a twelve-year-old. He's unstable, Mr. Levi."

"Yes, he is—because his masculine needs aren't being satisfied. If he was married, his needs would be sated and he would settle down, be easier to handle. Grace acts like she likes Benjamin."

"She likes him as a child, not a husband. There's no advantage to Grace. She would be saddled with a huge, unappealing twelve-year-old man." She paused in thought, breathing shallowly. "She would have babies he couldn't help with."

"Certainly there's an advantage to Grace. You know she's as ugly as the butt end of a stick. No one will have her. I would build them a cabin on the farm where they could raise children. They would be more accepted by the community than they are now."

"Grace is a normal, smart girl. She has dreams. Maybe she could get her eyes fixed." She brooded, "Sometimes I think we have misused Grace." Missus dropped her eyes; it was not in her favor to appear vexed.

Mr. Levi concluded the conversation, "Benjamin needs to have normal relations with a woman. He has needs that aren't being met." Mr. Levi hoped Missus would agree to his plan, though her consent wasn't necessary.

After he left, Missus went into a paroxysm of coughing. Grace made her tea from the Indian's herbs, but she was restless and short of breath all evening.

* * * * *

She coughed. Oh! Red. Everywhere! She tried to catch the blood, but it gushed, gagging her. Grace turned at the sound, "Oh Missus," she paled, sure she would faint, but her feet moved, and she somehow followed, grabbing towels to sop the hemorrhage. The room was suffused with the tannic, metallic-smelling wetness.

"I'll get Mr. Levi! Send Benji for the doctor," Grace cried.

"No," Missus shook her head emphatically, still spitting blood.

"Get Sarah, now!" She weakly waved her away. She thought to herself: *it's January. I've had eleven moons. I needed more time.*

Immediately Grace and Sarah were beside the bed, aghast, panicking—so much blood that it puddled, it was everywhere! *She mustn't die before Uncle Levi gets here. It's running down the window. Oh God, help. Oh God, help.*

The blood was slowing, she could spit it into the towel. "Must talk. Listen careful." Her face was white, like the sheets before the blood. "Grace, do you want to marry Benji? Live here on farm?"

Grace gazed intently, feeling the urgency to understand, but not comprehending. *Why would she ask a crazy question like that? The blood is in her hair.* "Me! Marry Benji?" she screeched.

"Mr. Levi wants" she said.

Frantic tears. *Oh, the sickening smell. Clean her lips. Clean her hands. Dank, earthy. He'll hate us if she dies.* "No! No! Not Benji. How could I marry Benji?" she wailed.

"Then you must leave soon."

"Leave? Where would I go? I don't want to go." Grace was stressed senseless.

"Go or marry Benji. I'm sorry, Grace." Her eyes so kind, sad, determined. "Leave day after burial, Levi won't miss you then." She closed her eyes, her strength ebbing. Her hand pointed to the dresser. "In bag in top drawer." Sarah hurried, bringing the bag. Money. She gave it to Grace. "So sorry. I couldn't get more." Her eyes welled with tears of frustration. "Enough to get you to Ft. Wayne." A paper with a name and address. "The address of my friend. She is expecting you. She will help." She grabbed their hands, bloody tears painting her face. "Tell no one. Levi will look for you." She sat forward, another gush of bright blood, not as bad as the first, still shocking. "Sarah, you must help her. Take her to Columbia City. Is twelve miles. A big city, people won't recognize you." She rested on the pillows, living now on sheer determination. "Catch day coach to Ft. Wayne. Leaves at eleven o'clock in morning. Go day after funeral. Leave first light. Before they wake. Take Gus. Hitch to the small wagon."

This scene, this conversation—surreal. Suspended in time and space. Like being on a stage where one could walk off at any time. "I can't do it, Missus. I'm afraid. I've never been away from Albion." Grace whimpered.

"You can do it. You have to. I thought I'd have more time. Grace, get Mr. Levi now, hurry."

Grace hesitated, her eyes pleading, knowing this was the last time she would see Missus Hannah, but uncertain what to say or do. She turned and ran.

Missus tried to talk around oozing blood. She was becoming weaker. Sarah helped her move on her side so blood could drain from her mouth.

"Mr. Levi won't treat you well." She cried sadly, wiping her eyes with a bloody hand. "He doesn't know how," she whimpered. "War destroyed him. Benjamin too." Missus closed her eyes, her breathing rapid, making speech difficult.

"Missus, do you know where my Papa is? Or Juda?" Sarah begged.

"No. Never knew. Sorry. Wish I did better...." She wept.

At thirteen Sarah was too young, too traumatized by being alone with a dying woman, each of them sticky with blood. She held her hands, her tears mixing with Hannah's blood until Mr. Levi barged in, his look as cold as an Artic wind, "Get out of here. This is all your fault."

* * * * *

Early. The sun not yet up. Sarah and Grace stole out of the house with Grace's belongings. All-encompassing shivering fear—to go so far into the unknown. Grace, crying silently, clutched the blood-stained, hand-drawn map. Sarah wanted to comfort Grace, but felt drained of succor. Though Grace had been hired out much of the time Sarah was at Uncle Levi's, she had been the kindest, gentlest soul Sarah had known in the last four years. Of necessity, Grace was a hard worker: cooking, gardening, tending the animals, planting corn, and haying. All this she had patiently taught Sarah so that soon Sarah would be hired out.

"I'm afraid to go to Ft. Wayne, but I can't marry Benji. He's sweet, but he's not *right.* What if Mr. Levi catches us? What if we get lost? What if someone on the coach recognizes me?"

The roads were muddy paths with washboard potholes. Rainy drizzle caused the horses to sink to their bellies in the mud, requiring the girls to get out and push the wheels.

Both girls' last years had been in a home that was dysfunctional. Sarah went to school. She was bright and could read so her world enlarged. Grace was hired in a variety of homes and had been exposed to other families and social norms. But both were ill-prepared to find their way in a city, use money, or associate with strangers.

Sarah tried to show encouragement she didn't feel. "Missus Hannah wouldn't have planned this if she didn't think we could do it. I can't believe she would take up against Uncle Levi to help you, Grace." Sarah was thoughtful, "You know, he was hard on *her* too. But this is so unlike her... I think she must have loved you, Grace."

Grace's head jerked toward Sarah, her eyes wide. A shocking thought: "Love? I never thought of that."

"I wish you could write to me but if Uncle Levi saw your letter he'd come and get you," Sarah said. "I have Missus's friend's address. I'll write to you. George can mail a letter for me. Once you stop living at her friend's house, she can mail a letter for you. Grace, remember my sister, Juda Long. She may live near Ft. Wayne. If by chance you hear that name, please make contact with her."

The girls arrived early at the coach station. Aware that mud-spattered clothes would arouse suspicion, they stayed hidden from the crowd. At the last minute, Grace entered the coach. With tears streaming, Grace went north to the big city and Sarah returned to the farm.

The Zumbrun household had shrunk to Mr. Levi, Benji, George, and Sarah. Sarah confided to George the reason for Grace's secretive departure. Benji helped Sarah with outside work, assuming Mr. Levi had sent Grace to another farm. Everyone was in despair, particularly Uncle Levi. He buried himself in work and collapsed in his room at night. Sarah scrubbed Missus' room, never getting all the blood out of the carpet. After that, the room was rarely entered.

One evening about a week after Grace left, Sarah took Mr. Levi's supper tray to his room. "Sarah, you're old enough to hire out. There's a position opening in a few weeks. You should get prepared. Send Grace in now," he requested.

"I'm sorry, Mr. Levi. She's not here. She hasn't been here since after the funeral. We thought she was hired out at a farm."

He stood up, alarmed. This was his first inkling that something was amiss. Because the household was so loosely run with children working both at home and away, Sarah's story was plausible.

Mr. Levi questioned George and Benjamin. Both were clueless. The next day he sent Benji to bring Rosa home. Rosa not only didn't know Grace's whereabouts, she panicked, predicting fearful endings: Grace fell into a bog or Indians took her. She collapsed, becoming sick from worry and grief until the next day when George told her the truth. Uncle Levi went to Albion to ask about Grace's whereabouts. He learned that a drove of tan-skinned foreigners with bears in cages had gone through the county the previous week. Could Grace have been taken? He bought ten sheets of heavy paper and instructed Sarah to print placards which he posted in Albion, Mirriam and Wolf Lake:

GONE MISSING
GRACE BARKER, 23 YEAR
PLUMP, SCAR-FACED, CROSS-EYED
REWARD. LEAVE INFO AT ALBION POST OFFICE

The winter became unremittingly cold and snowy. Mr. Levi didn't mention again about Sarah hiring out. Once after visiting the post office he left to follow up a lead on Grace. Much to Sarah's relief, he came home empty handed. He became more dispirited each day. Since the ground was frozen they couldn't work on ditches, so he had too much time on his hands. As his depression deepened his attitude toward Sarah hardened. He was rude during every conversation. He stopped going to church, his one social activity. Elder Hyre visited occasionally, but nothing stirred him from his melancholy.

Spring was short lived that year with winter morphing into hot rainy summer. Everyone worked outside. They put in long days getting the crops in, planting clover and grain, digging ditches, and laying tile. Sarah and Rosa helped with plowing and planting. They put in a large garden. They were close to the swamp and mosquitoes were "big as birds and blood-sucking thirsty". Even though they wore nets under their hats the mosquitoes were an ever-present nuisance. The county agent warned them about chill blains, an illness thought to be caused by mosquitos.

One-night Sarah was awakened by Mr. Levi screaming in wild terror. She thought he was having a nightmare and hoped Benji would awaken him. In the morning, she took his breakfast to his room and was unable to wake him. Benji went after Dr. Mathys and by afternoon when he arrived Mr. Levi was complaining of body aches and was cold and shivering. Dr. Mathys diagnosed the chill blains which he also called malaria. He gave Sarah instructions for Mr. Levi's care, with the not-so-comforting platitude: "There's not much you can do except keep him comfortable, he will live or die regardless."

She was with him day and night during the two weeks he was most ill. His illness was so debilitating, his delusions so telling, and his death so imminent that Sarah's hardened core of resentment changed forever to understanding and yes, pity.

She needed Benji's help when the shivering was severe. No amount of covers warmed him. But the worst: neither Sarah nor Benji could bring him back from the war. Neither could tame his wild rantings.

At night, his body burned with fever. The bed clothes were drenched with the sweat pouring from him. This time he was regretful and despondent in his delirium: "sorry, Missus Hannah. Should'na brought you here. Too hard. Baby's gone...please, my sweet, don't cry." Sarah was discomfited by her intrusion in these private musings, long smothered.

The second week Mr. Levi's skin and eyes turned yellow. He itched constantly, leaving bloody, scabbing sores. He could no longer swallow the broth Sarah fed him.

Why was the terror always in the dead of night when Sarah was alone, when death came into the room, when breath became slow and raspy? "Don't die, Uncle Levi. Breathe," she begged. "Breathe," she shook him frantically. "You can't die!" Sarah whispered in the still, dark house. "Benji still needs you. This nice farm needs you. Whatever will happen to the farm if you die?" Then the vague musings from her mind found their place together in words: "And I need you, Uncle Levi. I want to know you now. I want you to get better. Do you hear me?" The words that tumbled out surprised Sarah, but they felt right. Quiet settled in the little room and she realized his breathing had cleared—he was sleeping. She no longer heard his struggle to breathe.

CHAPTER 10

The Joiner Farm

Sarah and Benji did the farm work that summer—Mr. Levi shuffling slowly as he supervised. He had changed toward Sarah. He was still taciturn and distant, but was willing to teach her how to work with the horses and handle the farm machinery. Sarah had known Benji was indispensable, but now she saw firsthand how hard he worked and how much he accomplished. For years he had soaked up knowledge about the farm and he took pride in teaching Sarah. She soon realized that she preferred farm work: caring for horses, turning the soil, planting a straight row, cutting the hay. She not only grew two inches that summer, she became agile and muscular—everyone but she noticed the change from girl to a striking young woman.

Her attitude toward Uncle Levi had changed as well. She was certain he was unaware of his words while delirious—he seemed to remember little from his weeks of illness. As his appetite improved Sarah suggested he eat with Benji, Rosa, and her in the dining room. He seemed pleased to do so, and while mealtimes were quieter with him present, they weren't uncomfortable. They even started going to church again.

One fall evening Uncle Levi came into the kitchen where Sarah was washing dishes. "I'm hiring a maiden lady to do the housework and care for the animals. Her name, rather unfortunately, is Nellie Smellis. She is Minnie Hyre's sister from Wisconsin. You've been a good help this summer and now have good experience to be a farm hand. I need to hire you out to pay Nellie's wage. She arrives next week. You'll be working for Elmer Joiner. I know little about his situation and will look for a better position by springtime. He'll come for you next week."

Sarah was not unhappy about hiring out. Life at Uncle Levi's was melancholy and dull. She was eager for new experiences. Though she couldn't verbalize it, she was eager for friendship.

The next week they were finishing their typical decorous supper when the back-porch door slammed and a booming voice called, "Yoo Hoo!" Like a tornado, she plowed into the kitchen and dining room, mumbling to herself and pulling an overstuffed grip. Their heads snapped as they all jumped to attention.

"Hallo, guess this be the place." Her curtsy seemed misplaced against her heft. "I'm Nellie," she smiled, buck teeth opening a plain face of indeterminate age. She was a force: tall and buxom with coiled blonde braids circling her head. She seemed to fill the room in her long, brown-sleeved dress, absent of decoration. "I have an assignment with Mr. Zumbrun," she said uncertainly, eying Uncle Levi and Benji, whose mouth was still standing open. Uncle Levi seemed shrunken as he stepped forward to take her bag and introduce her to the stunned family.

Benji jumped to attend to Nellie, pulling out a chair and stumbling her bag upstairs. Finally, someone with his stature. With her voice, she seemed larger: her speech was like a cannon shot in a closet and her laughter was like a volcano—it kept erupting. Sarah smiled, realizing Uncle Levi's machinations on Benji's behalf—he seemed smitten already. *Nellie will certainly shatter the dirge of placid mutterings in this house. I wonder how it will affect Uncle Levi's headaches,* she thought. As if on cue, Uncle Levi excused himself to his room, directing Sarah to settle Nellie in the room at the top of the stairs.

The next day, Elmer Joiner came in his wagon to take Sarah to her new home several miles away near Columbia City. Sarah thought about the last trip when she took Grace to the coach—they had been so afraid. Recently George had visited the farm, giving Grace's address to Sarah. He had visited her in her new placement with a family who had small children. This was perfect for Grace.

Mr. Joiner was scruffy and ill-mannered with yellow, broken teeth and more hairs in his nose and ears than wisped about on his head. His horses were hobbled and broken-down. Even so, Sarah was excited to get to her new home. At dusk, the horses turned into a short lane leading to a derelict log cabin with a barn out back. Sarah was disheartened, realizing she had taken for granted the comforts of a fine home. After feeding and brushing the horses, Mr. Joiner led Sarah to the cabin.

Two older sons, probably in their twenties and as unkempt as their father, openly gawked at Sarah. Another son was in his teens, a bit older than Sarah. The wife, a little bird of a woman with thin hair pulled in a knot, was putting supper on the table. No one acknowledged Sarah or suggested she wash up after the long trip. The wife gave each of them bread and pinto beans from a speckled tin pan. The white of her eye was bloodied with bruising around it. She was cowed, never making eye contact with anyone. While no one talked while eating it wasn't quiet as they broke explosive wind, expelled gaseous belches, and snorted, hawked, and spit into their sleeves and pant legs.

Sarah's enthusiasm waned as she looked around the small cabin with one bedroom and a loft. It reminded her of her childhood home, though that had been clean and tidy. This room was cluttered with tools, bags of feed, and manure brought in on boots. Where would she sleep? Certainly not with three men in the loft.

When the meal was over the men left the cabin. Sarah gathered dirty tins and followed Missus Joiner to the washbowl in the corner.

"Let me help clean up." When Sarah spoke, Missus Joiner startled with a squeaky little scream, dropping the tins she was carrying.

"I'm sorry," Sarah apologized, reaching out to her, causing her to jump again. This behavior boggled Sarah's mind. Living with Uncle Levi, she had grown up devoid of emotion, or even attention. But she hadn't been afraid. Missus Joiner acted like horses that had been mistreated. In Sarah's experience, children were punished when they misbehaved. It was a revelation to her that a woman would be abused. Now she was living here—what did this portend for her?

The men shuffled into the house bringing the cold November air. The youngest, Eddie, lit a lantern and grabbed her gunny sack of belongings. "Come," he said shyly, going out the door. Sarah followed him, appalled that she would be sleeping with animals in the barn. Eddie took her to an empty grain bin, hung the lantern on a nail and dropped her sack. "This be yer place," he smiled. "I'll bring some hay fer yer pallet."

"I'll need a blanket," Sarah said.

He looked dumbly, left the bin, then returned with a horse blanket. He went to the hay loft and brought several pitch forks of hay. Then Sarah was alone. As much as she wanted to cry and feel sorry for herself, she knew it would do no good. Uncle Levi wouldn't care that she slept in a grain bin.

She decided to take stock of the barn. She grasped the lantern and stepped out to the hay mow. Eerie shadows of cobwebs and bats flitted in her vision, reminding her of critters she *couldn't* see. She picked through a pile of trash, using her pocketknife to cut a length of twine for hanging the lantern. Pulling up two feed sacks she noticed a junk heap of broken gear and dilapidated farm equipment. She compared it with Uncle Levi's ship-shape, well-oiled machinery and tidy barn. Beside the hay mow, rickety wood stairs descended to the loafing shed where two cows, the two sorry horses and a mule, lifted their heads as Sarah approached. "This is my home too, so I'll be spending time with you." Sarah thought about all the unexpected twists her life had taken—she wouldn't have dreamed she would live in a barn. Again, she remembered Juda's words: *Don't let the hard times get you down. Pick yourself up and be strong.*

There was a water tank inside the door of the loafing shed. Sarah went into the stable where the cows were milked and found the lye soap used to wash the cows' udders. She went back upstairs to the grain bin to get her long johns. Returning to the water tank she washed the feed sacks she would use to cover her hay pallet, then removed her clothes, soaping and rinsing herself with the water from the tank. It was quiet and peaceful with the animals around her. She heard skitterings of mice and rats hunting for food. Then the skitterings began to sound stealthy, bigger than a rat. She felt a chill and the hair on her neck stood up as she realized she was being watched. She realized the mistake in removing her clothes. Her heart raced and her hands shook as she hurried to put on her drawers, her long johns, chemise and long dress. She was glad she had her pocketknife in the pocket of her dress.

While living at Uncle Levi's her interaction with men had been very limited. The occasional bedtime ritual with Benji sometimes seemed tedious and discomfiting, but because Benji was childlike and nonthreatening, it became customary.

Now she instinctively knew she had to protect herself from these men. Her body went into fight mode. Hurrying up the steps to the grain bin, she blew out the lantern. The bin had only a bottom-half door so she would need to stay alert. Sarah feared she wouldn't have strength to defend herself. Though the barn was pitch black, a bit of moonlight allowed her to see shadows outside the half door.

Every nerve was taut, her heart thrumming as she repositioned the pitchfork and opened her knife. She moved away from the pallet to stand beside the door. An attack from the rear may be unexpected to the person entering. Then she waited: fifteen minutes, thirty minutes. She was intent to the night sounds: close squeaks in the grain bin, a hoot owl, soft clucks of chickens rustling on the barn beams. Then she heard it: material brushing against itself as they moved with stealthy steps, two of them, whispering as they got near the door. She saw the shadow of a large man preparing to hoist himself over the half door. Sarah had never been so afraid; adrenalin pulsed through her bloodstream. She wanted to scream and attack him as he climbed over the door, but she waited until he was just inside, his back to her. She pounced with every ounce of frantic fear driving the pitchfork forward.

Contact! Howling, "You bitch!"

She almost gagged as the fork stuck. She lashed with the knife: slice, another soft slice. Yowling. Now there were two of them. "Bitch!" She tripped, losing the knife. She screamed. Could no one hear her? He was on top of her, stealing her breath, tearing at her clothes, pulling her hair. She felt her chest exposed to cold air. Her fingernails scratched. She kicked! She bit! Wild pummeling to her face. Then she felt her knife under her hip. Grabbing it with her right hand she stabbed and slashed as she was kicked with a boot.

"Butch, help me! The bastard stabbed me. I'm hurt!" he wailed, crawling off Sarah. The two brothers climbed back over the half door holding each other as they limped from the barn. Sarah was still enraged. Her body shook. She crawled to her pallet, covering herself with the horse blanket, fearful the brothers would return. She felt her body for damage: a large goose egg on her cheek bone would probably cause her eye to blacken, her chest was tender where it had been scratched, her right side was sore where she had been kicked. All in all, she was lucky; this time around she gave worse than she got. All night she sat, in a quandary about her situation. She was certain Uncle Levi would not break his contract with Mr. Joiner; neither did she think Mr. Joiner wanted to antagonize Uncle Levi by mistreating her. She was certain she was not safe here.

The next morning, she waited to go into the cabin until the family was eating. She walked in, standing at the table with a bravado she didn't feel. Chuck wasn't present. Mr. Joiner glanced sharply at her bruised face. She willed her voice not to shake.

"Last night I was attacked by Chuck and Butch who beat me, tore my clothes, and tried to take advantage of me. If I'm not safe here, I will return to Uncle Levi's. He'll void your agreement. Plus, he'll spread the word that you mistreat your help. I'm respectable; you won't take advantage of me. Do I leave now, or can I work here safely? Your choice." She sat down, pretending to eat her cold milk bread.

"Ya stupid good fer nothin' dicks," Mr. Joiner exploded. "Can' cha fools stay out a trouble fer one night? Don't tell me ya got kicked by the horse when ya went lookin' fer trouble. We're leavin' soon's chores 'ur done. Hitch up Liz and git yerself in the wagon. Eddie, if'n I hear any more sech goins on I'll vise-grip yer balls. Now git outa here, alla ya and git the chores done. Chuck," he yelled up to the loft, "Git yerself down here. I ain't feelin sorry fer ya."

Sarah was trembling from the confrontation. Mr. Joiner leaned forward with an insinuating smile, patting Sarah's hand. She jumped up, jerking away, the night's memory close.

"They din't mean nothin', Missy. They jest tryin' fer a bita free sugar. Won't happen agin. The older boys are goin' to work at another farm, leavin' this morn. Eddie's a limp dick—nota gonna bother ya."

"No one is going to touch me or spy on me, you included, Mr. Joiner. It will not happen again, or I'll involve Uncle Levi," her eyes bored into his.

"No, no, Missy. Don't git yer knickers in knots. Uh, 'preciate if ya didn't mention this ta Mr. Zumbrun if'n its all the same to ya," he bobbed his head as he backed from the cabin.

Sarah collapsed on the bench to settle her trembling body. The experiences of the past hours were a new revelation.

Missus Joiner shied over to the table, her eyes lowered, "Miss Sarah, Chuck's the mean one 'n he won't be here. Eddie's a good boy, he won't bother ya. The mister's a nasty drunk. Ya best fix a top to the door on the grain bin. I'll watch out fer ya," then she scuttled back to the dishpan.

"Do *I* need to watch out for *you*, Missus Joiner?" Sarah asked.

"Nah. I knows how ta handle him. He jest has ta git it outa his system," she said, rubbing her blackened eye.

"He shouldn't take it out on you, Missus," Sarah had the nerve to say.

That day Sarah disked a field for planting winter wheat. The job was mindless, so she reflected on the behavior of this strange family. Sarah realized she was hired because girls were paid much less than men. Mr. Joiner hired out Chuck and Butch and likely the family lived on their earnings.

It was unusual for her to forcefully confront men. She had no idea Mr. Joiner would back down so readily. Her new realization was, by acting powerfully, people saw her as powerful.

That evening before supper Sarah was looking in trash piles for things that would make the grain bin safe.

"Can I help ya?" Eddie asked shyly.

"I need to close off the top half of the door to the grain bin. I was hoping to find some scrap," she said as she poked around.

Eddie seemed delighted to help her, finding a scrap piece of roof tin. He nailed tabs on each side of the door to hold the metal in place. "Could Mama come here when Pop gits mean?" Eddie asked.

"Of course," said Sarah, "Does he drink a lot?"

"Perty much every day but he doesn't get drunk every day. If'n he's on a tear, jest git away from him—he'll hurt 'cha. But he ain't gitten this piece of metal down, I'll grant my hind leg."

Eddie helped Sarah find a wash bucket, an old broom, and soap. They filled in holes in the walls and she spread open the cleaned feed bags on her pallet of hay. That night Sarah curried the scruffy horses, just for the companionship.

The fall days got longer and frostbitten. Sarah and Eddie did the morning chores while Mr. Joiner slept. After breakfast Mr. Joiner helped with fieldwork, picking and shucking corn. By midafternoon he had disappeared or was staggering around, no help to anyone. Sarah observed how Eddie was always alert to his moods, coddling or covering for him when something set him off. As the day wore on he became more belligerent.

One freezing afternoon while Eddie and Sarah were picking corn they heard Mr. Joiner screaming from the barn. They both ran, finding he had fallen into the water tank. He was so drunk he couldn't tell up from down. He choked and sputtered, pummeling them as they tried to get him out. In desperation they tied ropes around his legs and chest until he finally flopped out, face down in manure. Sarah couldn't help herself, she doubled over in laughter, looking at the three of them, wet and bedraggled. She turned to see Eddie, his hands over his face, sobbing. Instantly she ran to him, grabbing his shoulders.

"I'm sorry, Eddie. I can't believe I'm so mean."

"Ya din't mean nothin' by it." Speaking through his sobs, "Ya hafta understand, he's my Pop."

"I know, Eddie." She tried to lessen his hurt, "He's a good worker."

"No, he ain't, Sarah. He's a drunk. This farm is a dump. I hate him! I hate him! I hate alla 'em!"

Sarah glanced at Mr. Joiner. He was oblivious, still hanging onto the tank. "I'm sorry I started all this. We need to get your dad in the house and into dry clothes."

"You din't start nothin'. This been goin' on long as I remember."

They walked Mr. Joiner to the house. Sarah heated some soup while Missus and Eddie cleaned him up. While sipping the soup, one thought permeated her mind: *God forbid that I ever drink alcohol. Look what it can do to families.*

Eddie came out of the bedroom. "Please don't tell Mom and Pop what I said," he dipped bread into soup, "but it's true."

* * * * *

Sarah was sleeping soundly. She awoke to pounding on the metal door. "Sarah, Sarah, let me in! Hurry! Hurry!" She jumped to open the door. Missus stumbled in, falling on the floor. Her hair was straggling around her face. Her lip was bleeding. She supported her arm which was twisted at an odd angle. Sarah quickly shut the door just as she heard Mr. Joiner enter the barn.

"Woman! Git cherself out here. Now!"

Sarah and Missus crouched in the corner of the bin. Thank goodness she and Eddie had fixed the door and filled the knot holes. They heard him staggering around the barn, edging closer to the grain bin.

"Ya pig-faced whore. Git out'n here. Ya ain't goin like it when I git cha." Now banging and stumbling against the door, just a few feet away, "Sari!

Ya in there? Open this door." Mumbling, he ambled away to a pile of trash, returning with a poker to bang on the piece of metal roofing that covered the top half of the door. Sarah stood inside, pushing the pitchfork handle against the metal, praying it wouldn't give way. Missus lay splayed on the floor, shivering and caved in on herself, her right arm twisted. It dawned on Sarah that this may be the first time she had disobeyed her husband. Maybe it was the first time she'd had refuge.

"Yu'll be a sorry bitch when I git my hands on ya." Loud, incessant banging reverberated in the small room. He slipped, landing with a thud on the barn floor.

"Dammit ta Hell," Sarah heard him navigating the steps down to the loafing shed. Her heart sank as the horses and cows bleated, apparently struck by the poker. The two women didn't move as he searched every corner of the barn.

"Where's Eddie?" Sarah whispered.

"Left this afternoon for the Grundy farm to see Chuck and Butch. He'll get back t'morra."

"I think your arm is broken. You need to get to a doctor."

"Probly not broken, jest dislocated. Happened before. Mebe you kin fix it. Can't wait till Eddie gits home."

Sarah whispered coarsely, "I don't know how. It looks broken to me."

They could hear Mr. Joiner stumbling around in the loafing shed, talking to himself, his ire diminishing.

"Sounds like he might sleep it off downstairs. Shur don' wanna wake him up by goin' down after the horse. No siree."

They waited till they heard snoring from below.

"We gotta git it fixed 'fore it gits swole. Cain't do it here where he'll hear us."

Sarah removed the piece of tin from the bin door, fearful of leaving the place she felt safest. They walked to the cabin; Missus's face was covered with perspiration. In the cabin Missus found a hidden bottle of whiskey, tipping back several good slugs.

"Don' worry, hit's jest like when a cow pulls out a leg."

Both women were whimpering now, Sarah so fearful of damaging her arm; Missus pulled into the chasm of unbearable pain.

"Grab me the dishrag. I cain't wake up the Mister. He'd kill us both." Missus lay on the floor, her injured arm extended at an odd angle. Sarah realized she'd been through this before.

"How often has this happened?" Sarah asked angrily.

"Who knows. Makes no difference." She directed Sarah to grip her hand, quickly pulling and rotating her arm.

"I can't do this," Sarah wailed.

Missus was becoming weary. She had never been so forceful. "You can and you will. You gotta pull hard. I'm ready," she mumbled, dishrag between her teeth.

Sarah held her shoulder with one hand and grasped her hand with the other, giving a hard pull. Missus growled a smothered scream from her throat and passed out in a dead swoon, her arm still extended at the odd angle. Sarah patted her cheeks. She had failed.

"Oh God...Oh God. Wake up...Wake up!" Finally, her eyes fluttered open. She saw her arm still extended.

"Haf ta do agin. Sometimes Eddie doesn't git it the first time."

Sarah took a slug of whiskey before passing it to her. "What will we do if I can't fix it?"

"You'll git it girl. Jest gimme a minute to catch my breath."

Sarah prayed frantically that she fix it this time. At least, having done it once she had a feel for what she should do; she would be more forceful this time. She felt the whiskey mellow her body as she patted Missus on her good shoulder. In some ways she was a weakling, but Sarah had never seen anyone so strong in tolerating pain.

"I'm ready," Missus nodded.

"I'm going to get it this time," Sarah said with confidence she didn't feel. She pulled hard. Missus fainted again but this time her arm fell back to her side. *Thank you, thank you.* Missus finally opened her eyes, a weary smile thanking Sarah. "I'm going to make a jar of squaw weed tea for pain."

"Git the sling in my top dresser drawer, also the Morton's Liniment. Maybe bring the whiskey so Mister won't find it." Missus rested her head on the table while Sarah made tea and gathered the few things they would take to the grain bin. She didn't relax until they were back in the bin and she had reattached the metal that covered the door opening.

Sarah rubbed the liniment on the bruising on Missus face and shoulder. She placed her arm in the sling and wrapped it against her body. Missus drank the hot tea.

"You can't live like this, with him beating you," Sarah whispered.

"What would ya do?" her voice thin and worn down with helplessness.

"Do you have family you could live with for a while?"

"They's in Mississippi. Don' know where. Ya see Sarah, he ain't a bad man. He has a black hole of hate inside hisself. I somehow stirs it up. It jest be the way it is fer some women. Sames fer my ma. It's okay. I'm gonna sleep now. Kin ya prop me some hay in the corner?"

Sarah piled up hay then covered it with the feed sacks making a soft reclining hassock. She couldn't control her helpless tears, much as she tried.

"Wish ya was my daughter, Sarah. Always wanted a girl." A tear slid down her cheek as her eyes closed, asleep.

In the corner of the bin, a tableau: A young fifteen-year-old with her arm encircling the elder. Yes, life had knocked her down, time and again, but as she lay there with Missus, certainty infused her being: this was wrong. Never should a woman not be safe in her home; never should a woman not have options; never should a woman settle for the black hole of hate. Who was the source of this certainty born in her: was it from the gene pool of Lucinda, her strong optimistic mother; from oft-remembered, feisty Juda; from independent, defiant Hannah; from stolid, though intrepid Grace? These were the women who birthed the seed articulating how she would be treated as she stepped from girlhood to womanhood.

CHAPTER 11

The Miller Home

"I now pronounce you husband and wife," Elder Hyre declared, smiling. The girth of the bride and groom made the guests appear as almost miniatures—and their elation overwhelmed even their size. Benji looked at Nellie with adoring eyes and, while a smile filled her face, on this special day she acted as coy and bashful as a teenager. Two weeks before Christmas Uncle Levi returned Sarah home from the Joiners. He was as expansive as Sarah had ever seen him, pleased with his success in finding a bride for Benji. He took Nellie to the general store in Albion to get material for a wedding dress. She was an experienced seamstress and would stitch the dress herself. She also was planning a fine wedding meal. There hadn't been this much activity and enthusiasm in the house since Missus Hannah was alive. Uncle Levi and Benji were finishing the couple's cabin built at the edge of the property.

Sarah served the meal to the wedding guests: the Hyres' family, the neighbors from farms on either side, and Rosa and her brothers. She thought how wise Missus Hannah had been in "freeing" Grace. Marriage that would have been a bondage to Grace was like a haven to Nellie. It was apparent to Sarah that in the few months since Nellie's arrival she had taken charge like a benevolent general. The property was tidy, the house spic and span, the food basic, but good, and the noise level in high decibels. Uncle Levi not only found a bride, he found a first-rate housekeeper.

One evening after supper Uncle Levi said, "You're halfway through the contract with the Joiners. When spring comes you won't stay long at one place but will move from farm to farm as the crops come due. How has it been, working for Elmer Joiner?"

Sarah was surprised he was discussing this with her. "He has a decent farm with sufficient acreage. Both Butch and Chuck are hired out. Eddie is around my age and he and I do most of the work. Mr. Joiner drinks, starting in the morning and is besotted by midday. He insists on running things but isn't able, so crop yield is low. He doesn't take care of his animals and he beats Missus Joiner. She hides in my room in the grain bin when he's on a rampage."

"I'm sorry to hear that. I rarely get to the north part of the county so didn't know the Joiners and hadn't seen his farm till I picked you up a few days ago."

"I'm learning a lot 'cause Eddie and I have to figure things out and I have more experience running the machinery. I do much of the field work."

In the time Sarah had lived at Uncle Levi's, he had been detached and unapproachable—she kept a distance from him. Now she was fifteen and made money for him. He was in such a good mood since the wedding, she decided to ask about her family.

"Now that I'm older, I'd like to try and get together with my family. I'm hoping you can put me in touch with Papa and Will and with Juda in Ft. Wayne. I'd like to write to them."

Just that quick his face went cold. Her question was an affront to him. "I don't appreciate the subject of this discourse. Why can't you be happy with the life I've given you?" he asked, his voice furious. "Why do you insist on opening this can of worms? Uriah is a deadbeat. Juda walked away from her last placement, so she's on her own. Good riddance. I've got no truck for this conversation," and abruptly he left the table. His instant anger and refusal to talk about her family left Sarah limp. He was insulted by her lack of appreciation. *He* was her family, there was no other. She believed he could help, but refused. Sarah cried in her bed that night, having nowhere to turn for help.

When Sarah prepared to return to the Joiners, Uncle Levi said, "You won't go back there; I've found a short-term job that will be more suitable." Sarah was relieved but knew this didn't bode well for the Joiners. Word would get around and Mr. Joiner likely would have trouble getting help. Eddie and Missus Joiner would bear the brunt of his anger. Sarah had cared for them. She was remorseful she had done nothing to improve their lives.

The next week Uncle Levi took Sarah to the Roy Miller family for a six-week placement. She would run the household while Mary Miller had their third child. "I think you'll find this assignment more suitable. They're a good family; you've seen them at church. You will go to church with then Sunday morning and spend the afternoon here on the farm." Sarah was overjoyed to get experience caring for a baby. Upon entering the lane, she observed the Miller farm was not as imposing as Uncle Levi's homestead, but was well tended and up to date.

From the beginning she enjoyed the Miller family. She shared a bedroom with eight-year-old Anna. That night before falling asleep, she thought of her room in the grain bin. She said a prayer for Missus Joiner and Eddie, wondering if they would ever escape their life.

A few days later Mary Miller knew her time was near. The midwife arrived and prepared for the delivery. "Okay, Sarah. I'll take Anna and Charles to the neighbors, then we'll be back for milking. Ya'all help Mrs. Amos bring this little'un into the world." Mr. Miller went over to the bed, tenderly kissing his wife and touching her face. Sarah stared brazenly. She had never seen a man kiss a woman or express affection in any way. His eyes were filled with love, his hands so gentle and soothing. Sarah's young heart melted; she saw the possibilities love could bring to a marriage.

Mrs. Amos, the midwife, explained everything as labor progressed. Sarah was torn between ecstasy and dread. She was excited to help with the birth, but her vague memories of her mother's labor and death haunted her. *Please God, keep Mrs. Miller and her baby safe. Don't let me mess up.* Sarah's job was to take the baby, wrap it in a blanket, clean its eyes, nose, and mouth, then bring the baby to Mrs. Miller to nurse. Until then, Sarah bathed Mrs. Miller's face with a cool cloth. After a few hours, the contractions were almost instantaneous—Mrs. Miller in her own world of grunting, grinding pain as she pulled on rags tied to each side of the bed.

"You're almost there. A few good ones and you'll be done."

Sarah was so caught in the drama she forgot to be afraid. She didn't realize she spoke aloud, "Oh, it's the head. It's coming. It's so tiny."

Whoosh! The whole baby was out. Mrs. Amos held the baby up. "You have a little boy, Mrs. Miller. A beautiful little boy."

"Wa-a-ah. Wa-a-ah." Sarah took the baby and cleaned his face. She couldn't help herself from checking his fingers and toes, tears running down her cheeks. "It's a real baby—you're perfect, little one. Let's go meet your Mama." She swaddled the baby and took him to Mrs. Miller.

Within several minutes the birth was complete and bedclothes changed. Mrs. Miller asked Sarah to get the family. She ran joyfully to the barn, giddily assuring Mr. Miller all was well.

Mrs. Amos and Sarah retired to the kitchen while the little family welcomed their new brother. Sarah heard Anna crying because she didn't get a sister.

"When I was eight my mother was in labor all day and most of the night. She and the baby both died," Sarah said.

"I'm so sorry. You did a good job today. Most births have no complications. If the doctor had attended your mother sooner, she probably would have been alright. It shouldn't have happened."

"You're right," Sarah agreed.

Sarah's days with the Millers were the happiest in her memory. She loved caring for baby Harry and tending to Charles and Anna who at six and eight years old wanted to help. They adored her, staying close whether she was gathering eggs, milking cows, or bathing the baby. Sarah idolized Mrs. Miller, a gentle yet independent lady who was the heart of the family. Fun-loving Mr. Miller was stable and hard working. Sarah basked in their attention, blossoming like a flower given water. On Sundays Sarah went with the Millers to the Dunkard Church. A few times they took her to the young peoples' meetings. Having little experience with friends, Sarah felt shy and out of place. She was befriended by Amy Gardner, a petite gal with a bubbly personality. Maybe because the girls were opposites, they became friends. Now Sarah looked forward to going to church and occasionally spending the afternoon at Amy's home.

Though she was with the Millers only a short time the experience greatly expanded her world. She saw a husband and wife who were in love, who were equal partners, and who were warm and tender with their children. She learned that young people her age had a social life, recognizing her own life as isolated and focused on work—a reflection of Uncle Levi's personality. While Sarah knew little about this world, she saw it as desirable.

Twice a year the Dunkard Church had communion and love feast. The Millers were going, and as a church member Sarah was encouraged to participate. Communion was a vital means of accountability in the life of the church. Each member prayerfully searched their mind for sins they had committed and went to the offended person to ask forgiveness. During the reflective somber communion service each member washed another's feet, as Jesus did his disciples before He was crucified, symbolizing the washing away of sin. Then, newly cleansed, everyone shared in a simple silent meal: bread soaked in beef and broth, unleavened bread, and grape juice, the symbolic body and blood of Christ.

Amy irreverently regaled Sarah with communion stories from years past. The young people looked forward to communion, though not always for the noble purpose their elders hoped. "First are the mechanics of modestly unfastening your long stockings from garters, knowing the young bucks across the aisle will be sneaking a peak. It's quiet and solemn so everything becomes funny. The young people giggle, causing the older ladies to furrow their brows and cluck-cluck their disapproval, inducing further chuckles."

The night of communion Sarah entered the church taking in the simplicity of the glowing candlelight, long tables covered with white linen and white crockery. Basins of water and white towels were on the floor at each end of the table. The men in their dark suits were on one side and women in plain dresses and white prayer bonnets on the other. Children, while not participating in foot washing, sat with their parents. The members were singing quietly while people assembled.

Sarah slid onto the bench along a table with Anna and Mrs. Miller on one side and Amy on the other. Mrs. Hyre was across the table, her slicked back hair parted in the middle, the doughy blobs beneath her eyes giving her a countenance of piety. *Oh dear, my first love feast and I'm across the table from the minister's wife*, thought Sarah.

Elder Hyre read scripture:

> Jesus knew that the time had come for Him to leave this world. He now showed them the full extent of His love. As the evening meal was being served, Jesus knew that the Father had put all things under His power, so He got up from the meal and wrapped a towel around His waist, washing His disciples' feet and drying them with the towel.
>
> "I have set an example for you. Now that I have washed your feet you should wash one another's feet. I tell you, no servant is greater than his master; nor is he who is sent greater than he who sent him."

"Let us proceed with the example Jesus showed us," Elder Hyre directed.

So, this is the tricky part Sarah thought, conscious of the men across the aisle. She lifted her skirt and petticoat and reached inside her drawers to unfasten her stockings and unroll them down her legs. Amy scooted the basin over and Sarah placed her feet in the warm water. Sarah appreciated the symbolism of this act, believing Amy would be special to her since she shared her first communion. As Amy squatted to wash Sarah's feet she lost her balance, almost falling backward. Her eyes were huge as she grabbed Sarah's skirt, splashing water but preventing the fall. The girls covered their mouths to prevent a giggle from escaping.

From across the room they saw six-year-old Charles Miller standing on the bench beside Mr. Miller. He called across the room to Anna. "Anna, stop looking up Mrs. Hyre's dress. It's not polite to peek at her ass."

A collective gasp! Mrs. Miller, eyes startled, covered her gaping mouth.

"What did Charles say?" Anna whispered loudly to her mother.

"Nothing, Nothing," Mrs. Miller whispered, trying to keep a straight face while Mrs. Hyre carefully pulled down her skirt, a rigid frown on her face.

"But I didn't hear him." Anna said, exasperated.

"Well everyone else did," Mrs. Hyre grinned, her frown cracking. As she looked helplessly at Mrs. Miller, the two women shook with uncontrollable giggles. Sarah and Amy joined them, the ladies covering their mouths and bending forward to prevent a full-throttled belly laugh.

Mr. Miller gathered Charles onto his lap, gently scolding into his ear.

"I wonder if they'll make Charles confess next Sunday," Amy snickered into Sarah's ear.

* * * * *

All too soon Sarah's contract with the Millers was over and Uncle Levi came to take her to the next farm. Sometimes she stayed at one place for a few months, sometimes just the duration of a harvest. One summer she spent a few weeks working for Mr. Gardner, Amy's father. At first Sarah felt awkward, uncertain how this would affect their friendship. Amy was true-blue, some days working in the field with Sarah. At night they shared her bed.

The months turned into years. Occasionally she worked close enough to Uncle Levi's that he picked her up for Sunday church and the afternoon at his house. He was living alone now, with Benji and Nellie's family just down the road. He continued to be cold, distant and very frugal with her, rarely giving her money. She was in demand, her reputation preceded her: she could run any farm machine, was excellent with horses, was a hard worker, didn't drink, and never complained. She cooked and did housework. Children loved her. Eventually the Millers had a long-term contract for her. Mary Miller told her that Uncle Levi hired her for the going price of a sixteen-year-old man.

Something was missing in her life. She saw herself for what she was: a work horse, plain and simple. She knew that other young girls had a better, easier life but she didn't know there were options for her. She was lonely. She never gave up hope she would someday find her family.

CHAPTER 12

Teen-Age Sarah

Sarah worked six days a week with little social life other than church. Typically, she went to church on Sunday morning with the Millers and spent the afternoon with Uncle Levi. He took her to the evening church service where she met the Millers, returning to their home. On rare occasions she spent Sunday afternoon with her friend Amy. On these days she went to youth gatherings before evening church.

Amy had planned a Saturday evening party for the youth group—a taffy pull. Sarah went to Amy's home for the party. She would spend the night and go to church with Amy's family the next morning. As they waited for guests to arrive Sarah gazed at her petite honey-blonde friend, "Amy, I feel jittery about this party, I hardly know these people. I'll probably spend the night in a corner."

Amy was one of the few people Sarah had told about the loss of her family. She felt protective of Sarah. "You feel that way because you haven't been out much. If you spent more time with these kids it would come naturally. You're quiet but that's better than being too noisy like me." She stood at the knock on the door, "Come in," she greeted everyone. "Leave galoshes on the porch, coats in the bedroom."

Well, I can at least smile, Sarah said to herself as she went to the door to greet the guests. Many of the young people had grown up together, while Sarah knew them by name only. She noticed some of the girls had waved their hair or used decorative clips. She wished she had arranged her hair with her Mother's pearl comb. Sarah felt dowdy in the frock Mrs. Miller had refashioned from one of her old dresses.

Sarah and Eloise took a turn stirring the candy. "What do you do at the Millers', Sarah?"

"Whatever needs doing, from tending the children, churning butter, milking, and whatever fieldwork is in season. Today I disked the field so we can start planting."

Isaac joined them. "You're an experienced farm hand. Even I have never run a disk. How did you learn all this?"

"I learned a lot when I lived with my uncle. The farmers where I work expect me to use all the equipment," she replied.

"Wow," Lydia said. "You must be strong. I didn't know a woman could manage the horses and get those big machines around the field."

"Oh, I'm strong all right," Sarah said with pride in her voice.

"Speaking of strength," Isaac said, "Jerry, I challenge you to an arm-wrestling contest."

"Yea-a! Okay," the group chorused. The guys paired off. When they were short by one, Sarah said, "I'll take a turn with Thomas."

"Go Sarah!" they yelled. By the time Sarah and Thomas sat at the table everyone was catcalling and cheering them on. In past years when Sarah worked with farm hands, they often arm wrestled in the evenings. She knew she was strong, but was surprised when she took Thomas down in sixteen seconds. The yelling quieted as everyone looked at her in disbelief.

Thomas looked embarrassed. "You know how to make a guy look bad, Sarah."

"Time to pull taffy," called Amy, as the men lost interest in arm wrestling.

Sarah went to the sink to wash the pans, observing the group as they pulled the taffy and cut it in pieces. She noticed that some of the guys and girls were couples. Art was especially attentive to Amy and when they pulled taffy their hands touched. What must it be like to have friends and be part of a group? While they were kind to her she felt like an outsider. Amy was her only friend and she rarely spent time with her. It dawned on Sarah that it had been a mistake to arm wrestle with the men; other women wouldn't have done that.

After the party, Amy and Sarah put on nightgowns and lounged on Amy's bed, rehashing the evening. "I noticed Isaac eyeing you tonight. I think he's interested in you," Amy observed.

"I didn't notice. I know nothing about men," Sarah said regretfully.

"So, what do you think about Art?"

"He's nice. It's obvious he likes you. Have you been seeing him?"

"He's taken me out three times for a buggy ride and last Sunday night I sat beside him at the evening service. Of course, that has everyone talking. I like him a lot. I've been wanting to tell you: Art and I are planning a big outing for our youth group and I want you to go. It's a German Baptist Youth Rally in Goshen this summer for all youth groups from northern Indiana. Young people prefer calling ourselves German Baptist rather than Dunkard, like the church here. I've helped with the planning. They're expecting seventy-five young people from Friday to Sunday. Art and Jess are each taking a wagon load from our Sunday

School class. The real reason you *must* go: I want to introduce you to my cousin, Judd Swihart, who lives in Goshen. You two will like each other and this is the only way I know to get you together. You should come—you need to do more than work."

"I'd love to, but I couldn't get three days off. Mr. Miller is always short of help. I have no money. I give my wage to Uncle Levi." Sarah eyed her dated dress hanging from a hook. "I have no party dresses or decent shoes. As much as I want to go, I just couldn't."

"Sarah, you're seventeen and almost grown. You make a good wage. What other woman do you know who does field work like you? Yet everyone takes advantage of you. Keep some of your own money. Please Sarah, you need to do this," Amy said emphatically. "Just put your foot down. Tell them you're taking Friday and Saturday off. I'm telling you; Judd is nice and good looking too."

"This trip would be a dream for me. I want to learn to talk to people. I'm too quiet and shy. I watched you tonight, Amy. You're so relaxed and friendly. And Art, he followed you around all doe-eyed. I hope someday a fella looks at me that way. Honestly, I've never been properly introduced to a man, so meeting Judd would be a first."

Amy turned down the wick in the lamp and they lay down to sleep, each with her own thoughts. "Uh, Sarah," Amy said sleepily, "Just a gentle reminder to give up arm wrestling. Your reputation will precede you and you'll never find a fellow," she giggled.

"I know. I thought about that too—not a smart thing to do," Sarah agreed.

"See, you're catching on already," Amy chuckled.

Sarah woke in the night with the moon shining in the window. She mulled over Amy's comments: *What other woman works like you* and *your people take advantage of you.* She understood it was the custom in their farming community for hired hands to give part of their wage to their parents. Uncle Levi believed women had little need for money. Her pay had always gone to him. Rarely he treated her to a bit of her own money. She thought over the previous years she had moved from one home to another, working as a farm hand. She had been careful not to become attached to these people. Being separated from her family as a child had caused her to build a protective wall against that hurt ever occurring again. When she contrasted her life with Amy's and others at the party, the truth hit like a hammer: she belonged nowhere and to no one. She was merely someone to do a job. She had one friend and few acquaintances. She was seventeen and had never had a young man as a friend, never mind being courted by one. Sarah felt an emptiness she had never allowed to surface as tears spilled onto her pillow. All the feelings of loneliness and abandonment she had suppressed over the years came home to her. Since living with Uncle Levi no one had looked out for her. This night she understood no one would, she needed to stand up for herself. That meant having a say in keeping her own money and getting more time off.

Then her mind heard Juda's voice from years before: *You must be strong, Sarah. Don't let hard times get you down. Mama would say 'pick yourself up, lift your chin and be strong'.* Sarah heard this as if Juda were in the room. The words were a salve to her heart, an impetus to be free of pity, to do something to find meaning for her life.

She got out of bed and gazed out the window. *Where are you Juda and Will and Papa? Will we ever be a family again? What should I do with my life? Can I be important to someone?* Sarah knew this night was a turning point. Things would be different from now on.

CHAPTER 13

Taking A Stand

Sarah knew she needed to talk with Mr. Miller when they were milking the cows, when he couldn't leave or ignore her. She enjoyed the early morning peacefulness with cows chewing grain in the soft glow of the lantern light. It was a cool morning, Sarah could see her breath as she entered the stable accompanied by Smokey the cat, a dependable presence at milking time. She first spread fresh straw bedding in the stable as two cows, Blacky and Spots, ambled into the milking area. They stood side by side placing their heads in the stanchions. She gave them their feed, washed the udders, and started milking, her head resting against the cow. Her heart was aflutter as she rehearsed her speech to Blacky.

Mr. Miller came in yawning, wearing his standard overalls, plaid flannel shirt and mouse-eaten straw hat. He carried his three-legged stool and sat down against Spots, his back next to Sarah's back. "Morning, Sarah. Gonna be a cool one."

For a while Sarah just heard the spray and saw the steam of the milk squirting into the tin bucket. Sarah had never asked for anything and she was almost sick with dread. She cleared her throat to steady her voice, "Mr. Miller, I need to make some changes in my wage arrangement."

"Sarah, I can't pay you anymore. Yer gettin' more than the goin' wage."

I bungled it already, she thought. "I'm not asking for more money. I want you to pay me directly. Then I'll give part of my money to Uncle Levi."

"Well, Sarah, you'd best talk to Levi 'bout this. I'll do with yer wage what he decides."

"I don't want to cause trouble or be disagreeable, but I need to work where I can keep part of my money. I'm seventeen and I need to have money of my own. I don't intend to waste it and I'll still give some to Uncle Levi, but I think it should be *my* money." Sarah's heart was pounding. Speaking up did not come easily for her. What if he told her to leave?

"Well, I'll be flummoxed." she felt his exasperation as he twisted on the stool to eye her back. "Seems to me yer gettin' a bit pushy and sassy here, Sarah. Where in the world are you findin' these ideas? We give ya a good home, yer room and board, and Sundays off." After a long pause he said, "I'll take this up with Levi at church next Sunday."

Sarah hated to upset him, but she couldn't give up. In her seventeen-year-old mind, her life depended on his agreement. Her voice was tremulous, "That doesn't seem fair to me. This needs to be between you, me, and Mrs. Miller. And since I've already upset you I might as well ask my other favor. I want to have two days off next month to go to a church youth group rally." Sarah heard the spray of the milk hitting the bucket at a furious pace and knew she had pushed him to his limit.

"What the heck has gotten into ya, Sarah," he yelled, prompting Smokey to jump off the feed bin and run from the stable. "You *know* that's haying season, and it takes everyone around here to get the hay in." Sarah scrunched almost under Blacky, trying to put distance from his impatience. "If ya weren't sech a nice girl and good worker I'd half a mind to tell you just forget it!" Under his breath, "Then I'd have Mary and the children to deal with." He removed his hat and wiped his face with his arm, gesturing with his hat. "What'm I to do here, Sarah? Ya got me over a barrel."

They were both spent from the tempo of their argument. Sarah knew Mr. Miller was a good person and a good boss, the best she could have. She decided to be honest and maybe he would understand. She had finished milking Blacky and she took her bucket of milk and squatted down beside him in the sanctuary between the two cows.

"Mr. Miller, I want someday to have a better life than being a farm hand. I've never had any say or choice in what I do. I'm not afraid of hard work, but I want more than work in my life. Most girls my age have a family to support them, so they have most basic things. I have no family so I must look out for myself. I need to be with other kids. I don't have nice dresses like other girls. I only got a few years of school; I'd like to take classes."

Mr. Miller had calmed down and was thoughtful as he continued milking. "How long ya been feelin' like this, Sarah?"

"I felt this way for a while, but didn't realize it until I was around kids at Amy's taffy pull party the other night."

"Well, I say, that must've been some party, to git all this started. I figured you were happy livin' here with us."

"I *am* happy here. You've been wonderful to me. This is the only place I've lived since childhood that feels like a home. I want to stay and work for you. I just need to have a say in my life."

Mr. Miller looked at Sarah steadily, "Mrs. Miller and I would hate to lose ya, Sarah. Yer a good worker, better'n most young men your age. I know Mrs. Miller don't want no other girl in the house. Put it this way, I'll talk to her. She's better at this stuff than I am, but I think I understand what yer sayin'," he nodded.

In the last months, Sarah had become close to Mary Miller. She was gentle and easy-going, but had equal say with her husband in decisions about the farm and family. She was soft-spoken in disciplining the children, but they knew she meant business. Though she was a farm wife who spent most days working outdoors, she was attractive and took pride in her appearance. On Sundays she took her hair out of the tight bun and styled it in waves and a loose chignon on her neck. Looking at her, you first noticed her deep blue eyes. Sarah thought those eyes could see into her soul. She had a fashion sense, and while the Dunkard women dressed plainly in dark colors and long sleeves, she always added decorative buttons, a bit of ribbon or a snippet of lace to give her a look of elegance.

The next day Sarah and Mrs. Miller were planting the garden together. Determined to protect from the sun they wore long dresses with long sleeves, gloves and wide brimmed sun bonnets. Sarah looked out over the small farm, especially lovely this time of year with well-tended white frame buildings surrounded by early blooming perennials. She took pride in the lush green fields she had helped plant. The three children, supervised by ten-year-old Anna, were given their own small plot and seeds for planting. Charles and Harry, the younger two, were content to dig holes and build mounds in the dirt.

Mrs. Miller hoed a ridge along the string line and Sarah followed with the seeds. "Mr. Miller says you want your wages paid to you from now on."

"Yes," replied Sarah, who was more comfortable having this conversation with Mrs. Miller.

"What do you expect Levi to think about this? He's our church friend, and we don't want to upset him. He *is* responsible for you."

"He won't like it, but I think I need the money more than he does. Mrs. Miller, please will you talk to Uncle Levi for me? I'm no good talking to him. I'll cry and I don't know the right words to say. He'll get mad and say, 'It's not done that way'."

"Why do you need the money, Sarah?"

"I just want to do things besides work, go to church on Sunday, and visit Uncle Levi. I want to be with other kids, have my own money, and go to young peoples' parties like I did Saturday. Next month there's a three-day rally for youth from the north part of the state. Mr. Weaver, the youth sponsor is taking twelve from our church. Amy Gardner invited me special to go with them." Her words, so long bottled up came tumbling out. "I just *have* to go, Mrs. Miller, but I don't have money or nice clothes. Before, I hardly went anywhere, so I didn't care that I looked shabby, but now I want to go out with young people, and I want to look nice like the other girls. But mostly, getting my own money and saving some of it is the only way I know to better myself, so I won't always be a farm hand. I want a better life. I want more schooling. Everyone says how smart I am, but I'm more ignorant than girls who have gone through eighth grade."

Mrs. Miller didn't say anything until two rows of beans had been planted. Sarah despaired, believing she hadn't been convincing, and knowing Mrs. Miller's agreement was essential. "Sarah, a farm family is always so busy," she said, looking down at her. "The work never ends, and there's always some calamity as you know. Seems all of a sudden you've grown up. I should've realized you're ready for some independence. You're right, you need to be having fun with young people. That bunch at church will be good for you." She stepped over to Sarah, putting her hands on her head, "You're such a hardworking gentle soul, we forget what *you* need."

She squatted next to Sarah. "I agree that I should talk to Levi first. I can let him know you're ready for this step, and we're in favor of it. But you need to talk to him too, and take care to temper your words. Your ideas will not go down easily with him. I think you'll do well explaining to him just as you did to me. You were very convincing."

Sarah jumped up, knocking off Mrs. Miller's sunbonnet when hugging her in a rare display of love and emotion, "Oh thank you, thank you. I'll make it up to you. I'll prove I can be thrifty."

Mrs. Miller grabbed Sarah's hand and swung the bonnet as they danced and pirouetted around the garden. "Watch out, everyone," she called as the children came running to join in the commotion. "Sarah is going to be the prettiest girl at the rally."

That night after they put the children to bed, Mrs. Miller called to Sarah as she opened her shuttle sewing machine. "If you want new clothes, Sarah, you're going to have to learn to sew. I'm not going to make them for you."

"Oh no, Mrs. Miller. I'll hand stitch them. I'm afraid I'll break your new sewing machine." Sarah knew the machine was Mrs. Miller's pride and joy. She wanted nothing to do with this new-fangled tool.

"Nonsense, Sarah. You need to learn to sew on the machine. It's a skill you'll always use. You said you wanted to better yourself; if you know how to sew, you could be a seamstress. It looks complicated, but once you learn, it's pretty simple. I'll show you tonight how to use the machine and when we get material and a pattern, I'll help with the first dress. After that you'll know how to do it."

Sarah saw in this simple act the profound message that Mrs. Miller intended without saying it in words: *I care enough for you to entrust this treasured machine for your use. You are smart and have ability. You can make something beautiful. You can BE beautiful.*

Sarah treasured her spoken and unspoken words. "How can I ever thank you? I'll be so careful with your machine. If I get good enough, maybe I can sew for you and the children." Sarah learned that night how to thread the machine, sew seams, pull a gathered skirt, and knot off seam ends. The next night Mrs. Miller set out patterns, got Sarah's measurements, and they both knelt on the floor laying out pattern pieces and pinning them to fabric. "You're a natural at this, Sarah. After you speak with Levi on Sunday, we'll be ready to shop for material. I can't wait to see what you choose."

"I'm so grateful to you for teaching me the machine. I never expected such kindness. I was afraid to ask you and Mr. Miller for my wages and for time off. I thought you might get rid of me and I didn't want to leave. I love living here, it feels like a home to me, not just a job." Sarah was tearful as Mrs. Miller gathered her in her arms.

"There, there, my dear," she soothed, patting Sarah's back and holding her close, her voice tender.

"I haven't had a real home where I felt wanted since I was a little girl. I thought I would never have it again. You make me feel like I'm somebody. I'll show you; I'll be the best I can be. Somehow I'll repay you."

"My dear child, you already have. You need do no more than what you do each day. You bring joy to us."

These tearful words and the tender embrace of this day, formed a lifelong devotion to this family. It revived Sarah's life. Finally, she felt loved. It made all the difference.

* * * * *

Sarah and Uncle Levi rode home from church in silence, the tension as thick as a cloud. She saw Mrs. Miller talking to Uncle Levi after church; now he knew Sarah intended to keep her wages. She almost felt sorry for him. He was now in his mid-fifties and while a successful farmer with a nice home, he was not a content person, if ever he had been. His actions, to Sarah, indicated he thought he controlled her, like Sox, one of his horses. As she had generally acquiesced, there were few problems, but neither was there a warm relationship. She thought neither of them capable of warmth.

This dispute would be a first and Sarah was terrified. Uncle Levi normally was cantankerous, but she had seen him show a fearful temper. He could force her to stop working for the Millers, insisting she return to his home and work without pay. She would refuse to do this.

Sarah and Uncle Levi sat down to their usual Sunday dinner of fried chicken, boiled potatoes, and garden lettuce.

> Our Heavenly Father, we ask Your blessing as we gather on this Sabbath. Thank You for this food and for Your constant provision to us. We remember those less fortunate and ask Your blessing over them. Bless those who preach to the heathen on the mission field. Guide us that we live in accordance to Your will for our lives. In Jesus name we pray. Amen

Most Sundays Sarah tried, usually unsuccessfully, to get Uncle Levi to discuss the Sunday sermon. Today she knew better. Uncle Levi was so agitated he could hardly sit in his chair. He shoved the serving dishes at her. She wanted to appear strong, but she was quaking.

"Uncle Levi, I want to talk…" she started.

He leaned forward, red-faced, his left eye twitching, "When did you get so almighty high-fallutin' you think you can make the decisions around here? What is this drivel about you keeping your pay?" he interrupted, his spit flying across the table with his explosive speech.

Sarah put down her fork so he wouldn't see it shaking. She looked at him directly, willing her voice to be steady. "I'm old enough to have my own money. I've given you all the money I earn, rarely am I given any."

"Young people give their earnings to pay back the ones who raised them. It's always been that way. I don't know why you think it should change," he said haughtily.

"I'll still give you some of my wages every month. It isn't fair to expect the Millers to buy my necessities. The only decent dress I have is one remade from Mrs. Miller's old dress. I'm going on a weekend trip with the youth group. I'll need money for that. I want to save some money. I won't be wasteful," Sarah responded.

"After all I've done for you all these years you would come back on me like a lily-livered coward. You run to the Millers begging for money." In a sarcastic imitation of Mary Miller, "'Our Sarah is going to need some independence'. You're getting entirely too cozy with the Millers. I've a notion to bring you back here where I can stifle your half-cocked ideas." He pounded his fist on the table, "Bah!"

Sarah stood, towering over Uncle Levi. Her voice cracked but she refused to cry or cower from him, "That will not happen. I'll go away and find my own job, but I won't live and work here again. I'm seventeen. I need to have a life. I need money of my own." Sarah walked around the table, sitting on a chair beside Uncle Levi. He refused to meet her eyes. She touched his arm, her voice gentle. "I don't know what happened nine years ago when you brought me to live with you. I'm guessing it wasn't your choice to have a child. In kindness you took me in and cared for me. I've been your responsibility all these years." Sarah leaned toward him, her voice tearful, "I'm grateful to you for being my parent. You did well by me. I'm saying I can start being responsible for myself."

Uncle Levi put his head in his hands, elbows resting on the table, a dispirited old man. "I was never meant to be a parent. What did I know about little girls? If God wanted me to be a father, he would have given children to Hannah."

"But you *were* a good father, you taught me responsibility. Now I'm a young woman; I'll be trustworthy," Sarah responded.

Sarah knew Uncle Levi thought she was out of line for a woman—she didn't care. She had succeeded in standing up for herself. This was the day Sarah became an adult. It was her first inkling that, for a woman to *have* power and independence, *she* needed to make it happen. She would observe women like Mary Miller and Lois Gardner, Amy's mother. These ladies were agreeable and mild-mannered, yet their role was influential and clearly pivotal in the family. She wanted to be like them. The first steps had been taken.

CHAPTER 14

The Rally

The household was in a state of excitement the morning Sarah left for the Goshen youth rally. The night before, ten-year-old Anna helped Sarah pack her clothes in a big bag. She held out her small rag doll, "I want you to keep Gerta, so you remember me while you're gone," she said, placing it in the bag.

Sarah knelt to give her a hug, "I could never forget you, Anna. I promise to take good care of Gerta. I'll hold her while I sleep, like you do."

That morning before going to the barn, Mr. Miller patted her shoulder, "Go off and have yerself a good time, Sarah." He couldn't resist a little dig, "Had ta hire two men ta take yer place," he mumbled as he went out in the dark morning to hitch up the horses. The children followed, insisting on carrying the bag.

Mrs. Miller stepped into the buggy with Sarah. "Do you have your lunch, do you have a hanky for each day, how about baking soda and toothbrush, extra hairpins in case you lose some, do you have your mother's comb and the new barrette?" Sarah nodded with each question, so Mrs. Miller clucked her tongue, urging the horses forward. Sarah stood and waved to the children and before the sun came up they were on their way to the church.

Art and Jess were in the church yard with their horses and wagons. Benches of wood along the sides provided seats for six people in each wagon. Confusion and excitement ruled as they packed bags of feed for the horses, water buckets and bags of luggage. Sarah noticed that Isaac was staying close as she followed Amy into Art's wagon and sure enough, he was on her left when she sat down. Amid all the commotion of whinnying horses and parents calling out last minute reminders, Sarah noticed the beautiful sunrise of pink and orange through the still-shadowed trees. Already the sun was warming the early morning air. Her heart was so full she chuckled, so much happiness just bubbled out. She reached down to clasp Mrs. Miller's hands with both of hers as the horses pulled away, then stood with the others calling their goodbyes. Sarah looked at the scene around her. Everything seemed right. Everything seemed possible. *I did it!* she said to herself.

With a big smile Amy turned and grasped her hand, "I'm so glad you're here, Sarah. You went through so much to make it happen and now, here you are."

As the long trip started everyone settled down, chatting among themselves in high humor. As it was early, a few fell asleep. Though Sarah hadn't slept much, she was too excited to sleep. She didn't want to appear rude by ignoring Isaac.

"Have you ever been to a youth rally, Isaac?"

"I went to one last summer at Manchester College. It was great. I met lots of nice people. They'll have activities planned. There's a big tent where the church ladies cook our meals. I'm glad you came, Sarah. You'll have a good time."

"I'm glad to be here. I didn't think I'd get to come. Mr. Miller is always short-handed in July, so I was afraid to ask for time off. Did you have a problem taking time off?"

"I work on my Dad's farm so it's easier for me. But I had to beg Mr. Baker at the grocery in Albion where I stock shelves. He was kinda upset with me. I work there Friday nights and Saturdays to earn money."

Their conversation was interrupted when Jerry started a game of keep away, throwing a ball around. Sarah concentrated, she didn't want to miss the ball or throw it over the side, requiring one of the fellows to jump out of the wagon to retrieve it.

Midday they stopped beside a stream and the men unhitched the horses so they could drink and graze. Sarah and Amy found a cool spot shaded by elm trees to eat lunch.

"Can we join you?" Art asked as he and Isaac strolled over. It was pleasant as they put out their lunches, each sharing and tasting. Mrs. Miller's sugar cookies were a big hit. Sarah was surprised how much she enjoyed talking to Isaac, as if she forgot her shyness.

After lunch Art said, "Isaac, let's cool off in the water." They took off shoes and socks, rolled up pant legs and walked into the shallow stream. "Woo Hoo!" soon everyone rushed to the water, the girls discreetly unfastening their long cotton stockings and putting them in their shoes. Sarah was a bit hesitant. *Is this allowed?* she thought to herself as she hurriedly removed her shoes and stockings, thrilling in the delicious coolness of the water. They had found a small pool with smooth river stones on the stream bed. The surrounding virgin forest shaded all but the wide shaft of light beaming into the pool and glancing off the sparkling water. A soft breeze pulled loose the girls' hair from restraining pins. The air was filled with teasing voices, laughter, and shrieks that faded into the woods. Even Mr. Weaver got in the water, running and splashing with the young people. Sarah was inexperienced with the playfulness and informality, surprised at the exposure of the girls' ankles and legs. Her hesitation was short lived as she hiked up her skirt to run away from Isaac.

Jerry's ball reappeared and a frenetic game of tag ensued. "No fair, I can't hold my skirt and catch the ball," Lydia yelled.

"Ah ha," called Jess, moving toward her with the ball. "Do you need help holding your skirt?"

"No," screeched Lydia, running to Sarah. Sarah grabbed the ball from Jess and threw it at Isaac who lurched to catch it, falling in the water. Everyone doubled over laughing as they helped him get his footing.

"Sarah, the back of your skirt is in the water," yelled Amy.

Eloise grabbed Sarah's skirt, "Okay. You guys can only do one-handed catches too," she called, throwing the ball at Thomas. They had a rowdy, wet game with everyone getting splashed. After a while Mr. Weaver yelled, "Time to get on the road. Last one out of the water has to hitch up the horses. Everyone, find a tree to hide behind. Men to the left of the river, ladies to the right. No peeking! Back at the wagons in five minutes."

When they gathered at the wagons the group gave Sarah and Isaac the prize for "biggest drips," not convinced they didn't get wet on purpose. Sarah, pleased with herself, thought: *that's the best prize I've ever had.*

Everyone climbed in the wagons tucking aside their shoes, socks, and stockings. The horses, rejuvenated, pulled with vigor. The worn-out youth began nodding off. Sarah was daydreaming and looking down in wonder at her friends' feet, exposed ankles, and clingy clothes: big feet, little feet; tan feet, pale feet; calloused feet, smooth feet; long toes, short toes; wiggly feet, still feet. She closed her eyes, resting her head against the side of the wagon. She smiled as she thought: *feet are beautiful things. What if Uncle Levi could see me now? Who would have dreamed...?*

Sarah jolted awake, immediately blushed and sat upright as she realized she had fallen asleep lying against Isaac whose arms rested along the side of the wagon. She looked quickly at Isaac and while his eyes were closed, she thought she detected a hint of a smile. Looking to see if anyone else had seen her, she blushed again when Eloise winked at her. She was having so much fun, she sure didn't want to ruin her reputation.

A few hours later they went north through the small village of Goshen arriving at a farm where the rally was already in progress. Art took the team up the slope of a large barn, the big sliding doors open to a gathering area filled with benches. Across the wooded yard was a two-story frame house and in between an open sided tent filled with tables and benches. Beside the house were three privies. Isaac was excited as he explained to

Sarah, "We'll have all our meetings in the barn, they'll open the big doors on each side, so it isn't so hot. We'll go to the tent now to register, pay, and get our sleeping assignment. The tent is where we'll have meals."

By supper time the tent was full. Sarah noticed from reading the agenda that everything would be led by young people, from prayers before meals, games, discussions, and church services. She ate supper with Amy, Lydia, and their friends from Nappanee, Isabel and Margie.

Isabel smiled, "Welcome to your first rally, Sarah. Once you go the first time you never miss. It's fun because you see friends from previous years."

"Sarah hasn't been able to be active in our local youth group, but she's taken care of that problem," said Amy.

Margie, who was sitting beside Sarah said, "I heard you singing the "Doxology" before we ate. You have a lovely voice. Each year at rally we have a choir that sings at the Sunday service. I was in it last year and really liked it. Why don't you join me?"

"I would love to, Margie. I've never been in a choir and I probably won't know the songs, but I love to sing."

"I may not know the songs either," said Margie.

Lydia leaned forward, lowering her voice, "Amy is going to introduce Sarah to her cousin, Judd Swihart, so wish Sarah luck with that."

Sarah blushed and put her hands to her face. She didn't know Amy had told Lydia. "Sorry, Sarah," Amy looked contrite. "Me and my big mouth. Actually, I haven't seen him yet."

Isabel nodded, "I'm not biased like Amy, but I've met him at past rallies and *I'd* sure be interested." She shoved against Amy, "Amy's never offered to introduce *me* to him. You must be special, Sarah," she smiled. "He's smart. I'm sure he'll be one of the leaders. I think he's a strong, dominant type. Can you handle that, Sarah?"

"Probably nothing will come of it anyway. We live too far apart. It took us six hours to get here today."

"I think Judd will need to stand in line," teased Amy. "Isaac stuck to Sarah like mud on a pig on the trip up here. I don't think he wants competition."

"Oh, competition is always a good thing for men," sagely remarked Lydia. Lowering her voice to a whisper, "Wait till the party games begin tonight. I can hardly wait. That's when l-u-v is in bloom."

This first evening was spent with everyone catching up with old friends and meeting new ones. Small groups of people spread blankets around the yard, the girls sitting primly in long skirts, fanning away the heat; the guys relaxed back on their arms, shirt sleeves rolled up. A young man playing the harmonica was occasionally interrupted by bawling cows in the near field. As the day slipped into night the setting appeared to be a cocoon in dreamy glow as young men hung kerosene lanterns from ropes strung around trees in the yard. A young man led the group in singing as everyone joined in a wistful love song:

Tell me why the stars do shine,
Tell me why the ivy twines,
Tell my why the sky's so blue,
And I will tell you just why I love you.

Sarah was sitting on a large blanket with several from her youth group, listening as the enchanting melody reached into the trees and beyond to the darkness. She saw Art reach for Amy's hand. All her senses were filled with the magic of the moment. Peace filled her being. She hadn't been religious but tonight she felt God. She closed her eyes and added her clear soprano voice with others:

Because God made the stars to shine,
Because God made the ivy twine,
Because God made the sky so blue,
Because God made you, that's why I love you.

Some songs were sung in "rounds" with groups beginning and ending at different times so one could hear swells of music from different locations. A fiddle joined in and the music became more upbeat and raucous. They began clapping, moving with the rhythm.

"Everyone, pick up your blanket. The party games will begin. Divide in groups of ten and spread out so you have plenty of room," called the leader.

"I've never done this before," Sarah said to Isaac. "I have two left feet; this may be bad."

Isaac took her arm and directed her into the circle they were forming. "I'm not good at it but I've done it several times and I remember some of the movements. I'll help you, but I'm sure you'll be fine. Anyone with a voice as lovely as yours will easily find the rhythm. We make the music by singing. Mostly you grab the hand of the person beside you and follow them. It's dark enough no one will notice if you mess up," he chuckled.

"Thanks, Isaac. I hope I don't embarrass myself and you," Sarah smiled.

They started singing and Sarah felt her friends pulling her along until she could easily follow:

If a body meet a body,
Comin' through the rye.
If a body kiss a body,
Need a body cry?
Every lassie has a laddie,
None, they say, have I,
Yet all the lads they smile at me
When comin' through the rye.

The group circled as they sang, the lead couple tented their hands as two-by-two everyone passed under, all joining again circling and going to the center of the circle. As she repeated the steps, Sarah relaxed, loving the music as skirts swayed with the skipping and swinging movements. Isaac leaned in to speak in her ear, "You're doing great. You're a quick learner,"

"You're a good teacher," Sarah said breathlessly.

They sang many songs and stepped to many formations, swinging, clapping, forward, backward, some music fast and boisterous, some teasing and slow. Sarah, unfettered and playful, loved the blur of movement, the touch of hands, the breathless energy, the rhythmic singing, and yes, the undercurrent of indelicacy. As the evening passed, she noticed she looked forward to returning to Isaac, her partner and "home base". His ready smile, happy to see her, warmed her heart. Finally, they all took a break, found their blankets and had popcorn and lemonade. Sarah was hot and weary but at the same time invigorated.

Local church people pulled up in wagons. The young girls from the Blue River and Ft. Wayne churches were assigned to sleep in the Bechtel's home near Goshen so bags were loaded and the eight rode into Goshen with Mr. Bechtel. By the time they arrived in Goshen the four Blue River girls were fast friends with the Ft. Wayne "city" girls, whose lives were vastly different. Because there was city transportation, these girls rarely drove a team of horses; they took the city hack, or their father or brother drove. That Sarah took a team pulling farm machinery around a field, was a foreign idea to them. They had commercial jobs: Elsie worked in a bakery; Polly was a seamstress in a small dress shop; Sally was a clerk in a five-and-dime store; and Rose worked in a library. While they lived with their families, they kept their own money. Elsie was engaged to be married and was planning her bridal trousseau.

They were so busy chatting they hardly noticed when they arrived at the Bechtel's large square farmhouse. The girls were given one bedroom. In addition, Mrs. Bechtel spread comforters on the parlor floor where the rest would sleep. The girls were eager to get out of their tight clothes and into a cool nightgown. They laughed as they looked around. The room looked like a ladies' shop with eight heaping piles: a full-length dress, ankle-high shoes, cotton stockings, stocking suspenders, petticoat, corset, chemise, and drawers. The girls all ended up on the parlor floor, whispering so as not to wake the Bechtels.

It was a short night as Mrs. Bechtel woke them for an early breakfast. They hopped back in the wagon to return to the rally. Several classes were offered for the youth: a Bible study, a class on Church of the Brethren history, and a group discussion: "Should Christians Be Involved in Political Affairs?".

Sarah and Margie joined choir practice. The young man directing the choir gave them their music. They would be singing "Alleluia! Sing to Jesus" and "Rejoice, the Lord Is King", songs Sarah didn't know. She hadn't learned to read music, so she sang quietly and tentatively until she knew the tunes. But she loved hearing the voices meld, she enjoyed the repetition to get it right, and she loved the more refined songs than those sung in the Blue River Church. At the end, they practiced familiar songs the whole group would be singing at the evening hymn sing.

As choir practice broke up, she looked across the yard to see Amy waving at her as she walked from the barn beside a fetching young man. *This has to be Judd, Sarah thought to herself. Oh my goodness. I'm glad I have on my new dress and thank goodness my hair looks decent. Too bad about the dark circles under my eyes from lack of sleep.* Judd appeared more "citified" than the boys from Blue River. She could see he was tall and well-built so she didn't need to worry that she would be taller. His dark hair was blowing with the breeze, falling onto his forehead. Heavy dark brows drew her eyes to his deep pools of brown, studying her intently. His strong jaw relaxed as he flashed a smile, warm and friendly. He exuded cool self-assurance, strolling confidently to her while extending his hand. It seemed somehow that the world around disappeared, like they were in a vacuum.

"Judd, I want you to meet my dear friend, Sarah Long," Amy said. "Sarah, my favorite cousin, Judd Swihart. We played together a lot as children until I moved. I miss him now."

Judd regarded Sarah carefully, holding her hand a bit longer than was customary. "I'm so pleased to meet you, Sarah. I was happy when Amy wrote that you would be able to come."

"I'm pleased to meet you, Judd."

"Are you having a good time? I know this is your first rally."

"I'm meeting great people and not getting much sleep, so yes, it's a good time. I enjoyed singing with the choir this morning."

Judd laughed, "No one gets any sleep at these rallies. Last year I think my horse found his own way home."

"Judd just finished leading the discussion on Christians and politics," Amy laughed and punched Judd. "When did you get interested in politics?"

"Oh, I just try to keep up with things locally, read the newspaper, attend a few meetings. I'm not really that involved."

"Judd, could you have lunch with Art, Sarah and me? I want you to meet Art, my new guy."

"That'd be great. I'd like that. I have to go to a meeting now to plan next year's rally. I'll see you in a bit. Nice to meet you, Sarah," he waved and walked off.

"Which session do you want to attend next?" Amy asked.

"I don't care. You choose." In her mind, Sarah knew she wouldn't be able to concentrate on any of them. Amy smiled knowingly, giving her a quick hug. "Your cheeks sure are red, Sarah."

At dinner time the two couples brought a blanket and their sack lunches to a shady spot. The heat had eased and there was a brisk wind, a perfect day for a picnic.

"You mentioned you practiced with the choir this morning. Are you a singer?" Judd asked.

"I enjoy singing just for myself. I think I got my singing voice from my mother. She was a good singer," Sarah replied.

"Was?" Judd questioned.

"Yes, she died when I was eight. One thing I remember is how she sang as she worked, and she sang to us at bedtime."

"I'm sorry about your mother," Judd touched her arm.

"Sarah has had some rough times," said Amy.

"Have you always lived in Goshen, Judd?" Sarah asked, wanting to change the subject.

"I was born a little south of here, but I only remember living around here. Our family has been to Albion a few times to visit Amy's family and Jess Swihart, my other cousin. That's pretty country down there."

"Do you help on your dad's farm?" Art asked.

"The last few years I've hired out," Judd answered. "My older brother is getting married and going out on his own, so I'll be moving back home to help my dad. Clarence my kid brother is still home too."

"I'm hired out too," Sarah said. Just then she saw Isaac walk past with his lunch bag and glance quickly at the four of them. *Oh, dear. I sure don't want to hurt Isaac's feelings. He has been so nice to me,* Sarah thought.

"Then we both understand how it is to work for someone. I'll be glad to move home and work for my dad. The man I work for is cranky and mean to his animals. I don't like that."

"Isn't your dad a minister?" Art asked.

"Yes, he is. That's another reason he needs me. As more people join the church, it takes more of his time. How do you get along with the family you work for, Sarah?"

"They're wonderful. I've had bad ones too. Since I've been separated from my brother and sister for so long, the Millers are my family now. I've been with them a year and a half. They've been so good to me. Because of them, I can be here today."

A bell sounded, calling the group to the barn for a meeting. A small Brethren college had recently been established in North Manchester, Indiana and the college president spoke to the young people to encourage them to attend the college. He answered questions about admission requirements, classes offered, and costs. Several young men asked questions but none of the ladies seemed interested. Sarah knew college was not possible for her as she had only a few years of primary school.

After supper everyone gathered in the barn for a hymn sing. They sang some of Sarah's favorites: "Just a Closer Walk with Thee", and "When I Survey the Wondrous Cross". The large barn with its rough-hewn timbers held soft hay in the mow so the music resonated as if in a cathedral.

A hay wagon was pulled to the end of the yard, the stage for the night's entertainment: a talent show. This was a favorite activity of the rally. Participants practiced for months, and competition was keen. Again, lamps were lit, and blankets were spread.

The Blue River group sat together. Just as the show was starting Judd came, sitting beside his cousin Jess, as fate would have it, placing Sarah between Judd and Isaac. Judd, oblivious, greeted her warmly. Isaac gave him a forced smile. Sarah thought she would die! Lydia eyed her sympathetically. *Good heavens, how did my simple life get so complicated all of a sudden?* she wondered.

It was a rowdy show with a variety of acts: juggling, a skit with two hobos, classic violin, a cowboy doing rope tricks with his horse, vocal soloists, magic tricks, a black-face minstrel, a flutist, and closing with a washboard band. Everyone had a great time as they cheered, clapped and whistled for each contestant. But Sarah was antsy, glad when the show was over, and she and the other girls could get in the wagon going to Bechtel's. That night as the gals huddled on the parlor floor the whispers bemoaned Sarah's dilemma. A great deal of stifled giggling occurred as the girls shared their calamitous encounters with men.

The Sunday morning church service started early as many had long rides home. After her "women talk" the night before, Sarah felt more equanimity about her problem with Isaac and Judd. It was still disconcerting to sing with the choir, looking into the audience to see both Judd and Isaac smiling brightly, their eyes focused on her.

After church was dismissed, Judd tapped her shoulder, "Sarah, would you take a walk with me before lunch?"

"Of course." They left the milling crowd to walk the short lane.

"I'd like to write to you if that's okay. Amy has always been a good judge of friends. I like being with you too. I know this summer will be busy and I'm not the best letter writer but maybe we can become better friends by writing letters."

"I'd like to keep in touch with you too, Judd. I know you'll be busy with your dad now that harvest season is near and you're busy with youth group activities. I'll give you my address at the Millers, and if you write me, I'll have your address." They turned onto the rutted path of the country road. Away from the crowd the air was still, the only sound was their steps in the tall grass and birds singing in the trees. After a short distance they sat down along the road.

"You have a gentleness that's very appealing, Sarah." Judd was thoughtful, looking at his hands clasped around his knees. "I guess I don't admire loud, bold girls so much. But I can look at you and understand you, your eyes tell me how you feel without your saying a word."

Sarah knew she was blushing. She glanced over at Judd, smiling, "Well, Judd, I think it's good if you can read my eyes 'cause I've not been around men much and I don't know the best words to say. I know I like being here with you, it will make me happy to get a letter from you, and I would like to see you again someday."

Judd nodded, acknowledging the obvious. "I'm sorry we live so far apart. I think we should start with writing and see how it goes. The good thing is I have two cousins near you. I could come for a visit and stay with Jess." He stood, reaching for her hand, "I think now we should have dinner with everyone. I know Jess is in a hurry to get started for home." Their return was silent, yet comfortable. They had both declared their feelings and were elated that feelings were mutual. They both realized the distance would make a continuing relationship difficult, but they would try.

The church ladies served a large Sunday dinner while the young people said goodbyes and exchanged addresses. Sarah bid farewell to her new friends with a promise to stay in touch. She felt unsettled and melancholy. Rarely in her life had she experienced sadness when saying goodbye. Since leaving her home so long ago, she had no one to miss.

Judd went with her to the barn to get her bag and stow it in Art's wagon. He touched her hand as she got into the wagon and whispered, "I'll write to you, Sarah." Judd looked quizzically at Isaac as he climbed into the wagon beside Sarah. The rally was over, they were on their way home.

CHAPTER 15

Isaac

Time was of the essence. The hay had to be in the barn before the sweet clover blooms dried, or it rained and toughened the hay. Everyone worked from sunup to dark. Sarah, Mrs. Miller, and Anna worked in the field cutting hay with a scythe. They used a large rake, making piles of hay which they lifted into a wagon. Mr. Miller and Elijah, another hired worker, used a grapple fork that clasped a large "bite" of hay, and with horses and pulleys carried it up through an opening near the roof of the barn, dropping it into the hay mow. The July sun beat down. Cutting and loading the hay was dirty and dusty, causing Sarah's eyes to water, her nose to run, and her skin to itch. The repetitious movements of the scythe caused every muscle to burn and complain.

She almost forgot these irritations as she told Mrs. Miller and Anna about the rally: cooling off in the stream, the party games, singing, sleeping on the floor, and the talent show. They whooped and laughed, interrupted, and asked a hundred questions.

Sarah confessed, "Unfortunately, I came home with a problem. One of the reasons I wanted to go to the rally was because Amy wished to introduce me to her cousin, Judd, who lives in Goshen. She thought we'd get along."

"Did you like him? Did you fall in love?" chortled Anna, pleased to be included in the women talk.

"Anna, you're being nosey," Mrs. Miller scolded. "How is that a problem, Sarah?"

"You probably didn't notice, but as we left the church, Isaac sat beside me in the wagon on the ride to Goshen. We talked and had fun together. He was my partner for the party games Friday night. He was easy to be with. I liked him."

"Oh, I see where this is going," Mrs. Miller nodded. "Sarah, get your rake and help me get this pile in the wagon."

"Omph," Sarah exhaled, heaving the hay. "Judd is so good looking. He's...more mature, smoother, and more self-confident. He was one of the main leaders at the rally. Everyone respects him—and he has a tongue like silver. We took a walk and he asked to write to me. Be sure to tell Mr. Miller not to miss a letter for me at the store."

In a sing-song voice Anna teased, "Sarah and Judd, sittin' under a tree. K-I-S-S-I-N-G."

"Anna, stop it, give her some peace." Mrs. Miller chided. "It's obvious you're smitten with Judd, Sarah. He's Amy's cousin, that's a good family."

"Oh, I am. But I like Isaac too. And Isaac lives here. I may never see Judd again," she lamented.

"It will be awfully hard to learn to know Judd, with him in Goshen. You'll both have to want it more than anything else. I believe God has a plan for each of us, and if it's His plan that you and Judd are together, it will be. I'd say you have a good problem. You have two men interested in you." She walked over, putting her arm around Sarah, "What happened to my little tomboy?" she chuckled. "Let's go get dinner for this hungry bunch."

* * * * *

In the last months, Sarah's life had taken on new energy and luster. While milking and working in the field her mind went a mile a minute. Would the mail bring a letter from Judd? What did Isaac mean when he said, "Hey Jerry, cool it with Sarah—she's taken"? Clouding her joy, her reverie always defaulted to a low hum of melancholy: where was Juda and Will? How could she convince Uncle Levi to help search for them?

The next week they were working in the field when Sarah looked to see a stranger dismount from his horse. Mrs. Miller met the stranger, then motioned for Sarah. As she drew close he called her name and she recognized her brother Will, now a grown man and a stranger. Sarah was overjoyed, she had dreamed of this day for nine years. Yet she felt shy with this husky man with a mop of fly-away black hair and shabby overalls. Will had no such reticence, pulling Sarah into his arms.

"I found my baby sister," he joyfully uttered, holding her close. "I told you I would find you." He held her away, his hands on her cheeks, "Sarah, if you aren't as cute as bees' knees," Will chuckled happily.

Sarah's laughter bellowed out. This was the funny, lighthearted brother she remembered. She was ecstatic, jumping into his arms as he swung her around.

"Let's all take a break and Sarah, you take the afternoon off," Mrs. Miller said. "Charles, you water Will's horse and Anna, you help me make some cold drinks." Eyeing Will, Harry sat on Sarah's lap as they settled on the porch swing. Will jumped up to help Anna when she tried to kick open the sticky screen door, nearly dropping the lemonade. "I wish Daddy would fix this dumb door," complained Anna, blushing shyly at Will.

They spent the afternoon chatting like two magpies, attempting to recapture the lost years. Sarah's reserve vanished with Will's concern and his kind inquiries. With each back and forth of the porch swing the years dropped away, the time apart filled in, the hurt eased.

Will turned to her, taking her hand, "Tell me what happened after you left home."

"Juda and I were separated even before I got to Uncle Levi's house. She went to a family near Ft. Wayne." Will winced, understanding the devastation to eight-year-old Sarah.

"I lived with Uncle Levi the first four years. At first I thought only of Mama, Papa, you and Juda," Sarah intoned. "When I was twelve, he hired me out for childcare and field work. I went from one farm to another, occasionally I lived in a barn."

The silence was long, deafening. "You don't show sadness." Will said quietly.

The frayed hurt lay bare in this fragile exposure of feelings. "Something broke in me, Will. I lost the softness a girl should have. It's like part of me is missing. Mrs. Miller once said I have tough where I should have tender. I don't think it can be mended."

"Don't say that, Sarah. I intend to help mend it; you see if I don't."

"Tell me about you and Papa. Where did you live?"

"It was easier for me because I wasn't totally separated from family. I wish it had been me instead of you." Will hesitated as if uncertain what to say. "I think when Mama died, Papa was taken from us too. He's not been himself since. Mostly we moved from farm to farm. At first Papa was able to work...but he lost his spirit. His hearing got so bad he couldn't work with anyone, now he hears nothing as far as I can tell. When I was about fourteen, I earned more money than he did. We had almost nothing, that's why I couldn't look for you. Papa is sad and bitter, not easy to be with. Sorry to say, he's 'bout as thick as manure and half as useful. He's my responsibility now. What do you know about Juda?"

"Almost nothing. Uncle Levi took me to meet her several months after I moved in with him, but I cried so much he never took me again," Sarah replied.

"I'm nineteen so Juda would be around twenty-three. She could be married with another name. Hopefully, Uncle Levi can help us find her."

"He's refused to talk to me about any of you. But Will, don't feel sorry, the bad is past. My life has been wonderful since I came to the Millers. They're the first family I've had since I was eight. I care very much for them; you will too. Mr. Miller may be able to help you find a job around here."

Sarah stood, "I should get started with the milking."

"Good idea, let's shake a leg," Will headed to the barn with her. They continued reminiscing while they did the evening chores, remembering Boss and Sol, their cows from years ago. Sarah listened to the music of milking, realizing that life had come full circle, she was again milking with Will.

Supper with the family was boisterous as the children competed for Will's attention.

"Charles, are you a fisherman?" Will asked. At eight-year-old Charles's eager nod, he asked, "How do you talk to a fish?" Charles furrowed his brows until Will answered, "you drop him a line."

"I've got one," Charles called, "what animal do you have to oil?" Will shook his head, "a mouse, 'cause it squeaks," Charles yelled.

"Will, help yourself to more potatoes," Mrs. Miller offered. "I love a young man who likes to eat."

"Thanks, I can resist everything 'cept temptation."

The adults dawdled at the table while the children went outside to catch fireflies. Mr. Miller gave Will names of farmers who might need a hired hand and suggested he put an ad in the Albion New Era Weekly Paper. The Millers promised to let the Dunkard community know that Will and his father hoped to move to the county.

Mrs. Miller insisted Will stay over, sleeping on the parlor floor, so he could visit Uncle Levi the next morning. He awakened early, going out in the dark morning with Mr. Miller and Sarah as they did morning chores. They enjoyed one of Mrs. Miller's farm breakfasts. As he saddled up his horse, the boys hung on his legs and Anna was dreamy-eyed from a distance.

Will hugged Sarah, "This is what I've been thinking about since you and Juda left. I'm so glad I found you, Sarah. We're going to be family again. Next, we'll find Juda," he said as he jumped on his horse, off to Uncle Levi's house.

* * * * *

After being at the rally with the youth group, Sarah's life changed drastically. For the first time she *had* a life. She became an integral part of the youth group and, though she was oblivious, her friendship was sought after by both men and women. She was tall and willowy, and she carried herself with an air of elegance, this being her natural reticence and lack of pretension. She was never the life of the party, but she was its soul; she had not a mean bone, but an innate kindness and generosity.

People were charmed by her and men especially wanted to protect her. While she was not wise in the ways of the world, she was staunchly independent and self-sufficient—after all she had pretty much raised herself. Sarah soaked up friendship like a sponge. Someone always made sure she had a ride to youth meetings. These friends were now the center of her life and she in turn gave them her big heart and joyful spirit.

In August Isaac was taking her home after a youth meeting. The moon was full and close, and the call of the tree frogs thrummed and swelled in the cacophony of night sounds. Isaac kept the horses at a slow pace as they rode through the nearly dark countryside, the soft light of the lanterns lighting the way. He was thoughtful, "I'm glad Will found you. I hope he gets a job around here so you can both look for Juda. Did you ever think this would happen?"

"You know, I couldn't bear the thought that I'd never be with my family again. I thought when I got older and had some money, I would try to find them. Uncle Levi gave Will an old address so maybe we can find Juda. So many good things have happened to me this summer, it almost scares me."

"Well, I'd say you've had enough years when things didn't go your way. It's high time you had some good." The buggy drew into Millers' lane, stopping beside the house. As the family was asleep, they had a lantern on the back porch for Sarah. "You suggested earlier tonight your father has changed—is old before his time. Are you eager to be with him again?" Isaac asked.

Sarah thought carefully before answering. "That's the big question: why did he have to separate us, especially since Juda was almost grown? I have thought of this often through the years, and again since seeing Will. I'm not sure I know how to answer." She paused, searching for words, "Papa was not a warm person, as I remember, especially compared to Mama. Will says he's given up, pulled into a shell. I don't know how it was for Papa when Mama died, but I'm sure it was terrible to have three children at home and lose your wife. I suspect I'll never be able to ask Papa why he separated us; I doubt he could tell me."

Sarah's voice broke and Isaac took her hand, "You're right, men don't usually talk about things like that."

"So, what good would it do me to be angry? I think I do better if I recognize there were things I'll never know about. If I believe he did the best he could in a bad situation, then maybe I can have my Papa again, maybe we can be friends, be a family again."

They sat in comfortable silence a long time, listening to the frogs and the buzz of the katydids. They could see only the idea of the other's face, it made words easy to send out, easy to hold tender. Their joined hands were enough. "Sarah, I want to talk about us now. Would that be okay?"

"Yes, Isaac."

"What you said, about your Papa," he said thoughtfully, "I so admire you. You seem wise and grown-up. I knew so little about your life until recently, but I know it's been hard and unfair. I've had things so easy. I think how furious I'd be if I were you, spilling out my anger." He leaned forward, his chin in his hands. "You just don't think that way. I don't know anyone like you."

"I don't know, Isaac. Maybe sometime I'll be angry."

"The times I was with you when we went to Goshen made the weekend special for me. I want to be with you, Sarah, but it's obvious you like being with Judd." He looked at her with a dejected smile, "I told Amy I didn't appreciate her intrusion with her cousin. Do you have an agreement with him, or do I get a chance in this?"

Sarah turned to him, touching his arm. "I hate that this has happened—it's so awkward. All of us: you, me, Amy, Jess and Judd, we have our loyalties as friends and family. I feel in the middle of a tangled, messy situation that's no one's fault. I don't want to upset anyone." She stood. "Let's walk. I think we can see down the lane." Sarah's pounding heart belied the stillness of the country night. "The best I can say is, I'll always be honest with you. I'm happy when I'm with you. I loved our time together at the rally, too. You're the easiest person to talk to; I don't feel shy with you. I hardly know Judd. We agreed we would write. I can only promise I won't be unfair to you."

They walked in the silent night, considering their dilemma. "If you don't want to mess with all this, I'll be sad, but I'll understand. Isn't it an irony, Isaac, that I had no friends for the longest time, now I'll probably hurt someone without wanting to?"

"As usual, you're the upstanding one in this," he chuckled. "I'm sure neither Judd nor I will compete as fairly as you." They walked in silence; he took her hand. His voice was bold, "I understand that I have permission to give Judd a run for his money, and by gum, I'm a man who likes a challenge." Isaac scooped Sarah up in his arms, running down the lane hollering, "Hang on Sarah for the fight of your life. The romantic Isaac will sweep you off your feet!"

Sarah grabbed around his neck, shrieking with laughter as they tumbled into the tall dewy grass along the lane. With Sarah still in his arms, Isaac touched her lips with a tender, feathery kiss and as Sarah softened, the kiss became passionate, a claim and a promise. Isaac smoothed her face, his fingers soft on her lips, "That will be with you till the next time I replace it. I'll try to keep it fresh." He took her hand, helped her up, and they walked back to the house.

* * * * *

Sarah put the cows in the barn for the evening milking. When Mr. Miller got back from the feed mill, he came to help finish evening chores.

"I went ta the store when I was in town taday and they gave me a letter for ya, Sarah. Put it on the dining room table. He seemed bewildered, "sure is somethin' how ya changed from girl ta woman, just like that. I say, don't get yourself in a blather over men, most of us aren't worth it. Keep 'em guessing is my advice, men like a little mystery in a woman."

* * * * *

August 17, 1893

Dear Sarah,

I thought I would get a letter to you much sooner. I've finally moved back to the home place. It feels good to be here. It's been very dry here, the crops need rain. We have the hay and most of the oats put up. We went to Nappanee last Saturday for my brothers wedding. He married Jennie Gardner. There were probly 30 people there, mostly relatives. They had a nice meal.

It was hard for my Mother. She didn't take the trip very good. She has not been feeling her usual good health. It's a good thing the horses pretty much take over the field work because my mind has been on you, not the work.

I know we didn't spend much time together at the rally, but I made the most of it, observing from a distence. I can tell that people like to be your friend (including me). I think it is because you really listen to people. You're quiet and don't try to get attention. You almost always had a little smile on your face. That is what I learned from watching you.

Sarah each night my last thought before I go to sleep is how nice you looked in your pretty blue dress and shiney black hair with the curls that don't stay put.

I am missing you more than I ever expected. I would like to come for a visit before the weather gets bad.

Your friend,
Judd

CHAPTER 16

Dilemma

No painting could be lovelier, no love story more poetic: sunset on an Indian summer day in a small Indiana village. Sweethearts out for a Saturday evening jaunt, their buggy lazily wandering the back roads to home. Going to Albion on Saturday was a regular practice. Sarah, Isaac, and the Millers joined neighbors and friends to do weekly shopping and absorb the life of the community. Isaac and Sarah left the Millers in town. It was Sarah's turn to milk.

After chores were done, they went to the kitchen and eagerly opened the box with pastries they had bought at the bakery—chocolate cake with thick butter cream frosting. Sarah boiled coffee to go with the cake.

"Where did you get your sweet tooth, Sarah?"

"I don't know, but I've always had it," she said, digging into her cake with gusto, her mouth smeared with frosting.

Isaac reached over, taking her chin in his hand, kissing her lips, then slowly licking the frosting from around her mouth. "You're my Sarah Cake, d'ya know that?" he said tenderly.

Sarah's head jerked from his hand, her eyes wide.

"What?" he questioned.

"That was my mother's pet name for me: Sarah Cake. No one has called me that until you just did."

"I'm sorry if I made you feel bad. Should I not call you Sarah Cake?"

She lifted her chin, her eyes seeing the distant past, "I'd like very much for you to call me Sarah Cake," she smiled.

* * * * *

Sarah paced, then sat, then looked out the window, then paced some more. Mr. Miller and the children were behind the barn where they could peek but still follow Mrs. Miller's instructions to "get lost when Judd arrives".

"I'm a nervous Nellie," Sarah muttered to Mrs. Miller. "I don't know how to handle men, let alone someone as fine as Judd." The cause of her distress was clear: she liked Isaac and she felt disloyal to him by being with Judd. She was glad Isaac had gone on a fishing trip. Lately she had felt his confusion and hurt—she was confused herself. She knew Judd was staying with his cousin Jess, who was also a friend of Isaac. This whole situation was a recipe for disaster. She believed she and Judd should have a chance to learn to know each other, but she also knew she would need to decide soon; this tetchy predicament was not good. "What in the world am I going to do with him for two days?"

"Stand still and let me look at you." Mrs. Miller adjusted her white collar and spit-polished a flyaway hair. "Talk about fine, you're one fine looking girl. Your new dress is perfect and that soft bow clutching your hair is exactly right. You have a nice weekend planned with the ball game today and Art and Amy tonight." She glanced out the window, "That's him, coming in the lane. Remember, he's probably more nervous than you are. Don't forget your sweater, it may cool down tonight."

Sarah went to meet him as he tied his horse. *As good as I remembered* she thought, noting his gray long sleeved shirt, black vest and black felt derby hat. "Welcome, Judd. It's good to see you again."

He jumped from the buggy, "You look lovely, Sarah. Even better than I remembered, if that's possible. I'm glad to finally be here." Sarah introduced him to Mrs. Miller then walked behind the barn to find the rest of the family.

"Who is you?" questioned four-year-old Harry, sending his older brother Charles into gales of laughter.

Judd knelt down to Harry, "I'm Sarah's friend. I've come to visit her."

Standing, Judd asked Charles, "Do you play baseball?"

"Yeah."

"We're going to a baseball game. Would you boys like to ride along?" Judd invited. Mr. Miller stepped forward, taking his sons by the hand. "Ya don't mean that, Judd. You'd have no peace. You'll have kids soon enough, I reckon." Then realizing his remark was inappropriate, he blushed and stammered, "I-yi-yi, sorry 'bout that," he apologized. "We'll be going ta town, might even see ya at the game."

Sarah and Judd left shortly, settling in easy conversation on the ride into town. "You have a nice horse," Sarah said, "She's a beauty."

"Star is a good horse. Yesterday was a long jaunt so I'm taking it easy on her today. My dad taught me to always buy first-rate horses and take good care of them. She's my baby, I'm very protective of her."

"I love horses too. There have been times when I thought my best friends in the world were horses. This is a long trip for you, and I know it's a hardship for your dad to have you gone. I really appreciate your coming," Sarah said.

"I wanted to come sooner, but I didn't think I should leave my folks," Judd stated.

"How is your mother? Your letter mentioned she wasn't feeling well."

"That worries me. She doesn't seem to be getting better. She has always worked hard on the farm and kept up with the garden and her chores. She seems to tire easily now. She's fifty-seven so I know she's getting old, but I've noticed a big change in her."

"I'm sorry to hear that. Is she seeing a doctor?"

"Yes, she sees old Doc Robinson. She takes his medicine, but I can't see that it helps. Enough about illness. Tell me about the Millers and their farm."

"They're a great family," Sarah enthused. "They have a large farm, nearly fifty acres. Mr. Miller is smart and well-liked by other farmers. He's been going to meetings of the county extension agent and is digging ditches and putting down tile to drain the land."

"I noticed yesterday there were quite a few low areas that aren't tillable," he nodded.

"The county agent says the crops will be better and it will be healthier because mosquitoes grow in the swamps. When I was a girl, Uncle Levi almost died from the chill blains. We're coming into town. You can see all the people waiting at the train station to go to Fort Wayne."

Looking down the dusty street they saw the two block long stretch of fine two-story buildings in front of the large red brick courthouse. Judd tied the horse and they mingled with bustling shoppers and those just passing the day.

"For such a little town, Albion has a lot," Sarah said, pointing out the three hotels, the ornate opera house and the general store. "Before we leave to go to the ball game, we must get some homemade ice cream from Halfertys."

A sign on the courthouse lawn read:

JOHN SINGLETON AUCTION
SATURDAY 2:00 PM

Judd took Sarah's arm as they were caught in the noisy chaos, moving around tables where people were putting out their wares, from baked goods and eggs, to furniture and goats. Judd glanced back, then returned to the table of an elderly woman without legs who was selling braided rag rugs. "I'd like to get Mrs. Miller something for inviting me to Sunday dinner. Could she use one of these by the porch door?"

"We don't have a rug there. That's a good idea, Judd. She would like that."

After paying they moved on to Judd's real interest, farm implements: an Oliver plow, a spike-tooth harrow, a Buck I hay mower and a McCormick twine binder. Sarah stood apart observing as Judd spoke knowledgeably to the salesman, then as other farmers joined the conversation they listened attentively to Judd's opinions, though he was young enough to be their son. After a time, glancing to see Sarah standing alone, Judd shook hands with the men and came to her with a sheepish expression, "I'm sorry for deserting you. When I get started with farm talk, I forget myself. Here you are standing in the sun. I apologize for my bad manners. Let me get you some water." They walked over to a big tub holding water, a chunk of ice and a dipper. They both took a long draft of the cool water. "You promised me ice cream. Let's cool off at the soda fountain."

"No apology needed. I was impressed watching you with the men. You certainly know what you're talking about," Sarah said as they entered the drug store and waited in line for their "two dips for two cents" ice cream. Judd got peach, Sarah strawberry, and after sampling each other's cone, each liked their own flavor best.

They returned to the buggy and drove east of town where many youth and young families had gathered. Sarah reveled in this proverbial small-town activity: Albion playing baseball with Wolf Lake, the small town to the south. This was the place to see and be seen on Saturday, a new mown hay field outside of town. A crowd of buggies lined the edge of the field. Men in derby hats and neck ties and women in bonnets and parasols strolled around to visit neighbors and friends. Children, their pent-up energy gone wild, had their own games: hitting balls and Andy-Andy-Over, or they clustered together giggling their secrets.

Judd had just returned to the buggy with lemonade. "I see all these ladies walking around and I think you're the prettiest one here. I'm the lucky guy to be with you," Judd stated.

Sarah chuckled, "They say absence makes the heart grow fonder. I may not be so pretty, but you may have eyes blinded by absence."

Judd nodded, "It's true, absence does make the heart fonder." He rested his arm across the back of the seat. "These last months at home I think of you all the time, and lovely romantic words fly around my head," he smiled. "Now here I am, finally with you and the beautiful words are gone from my mind."

The ball was hit into left field near them, but they were oblivious. Sarah looked deep into Judd's expressive dark eyes; she really wanted to know this man.

"It's not just pretty words that sway a woman. It was lovely to me when earlier you offered to bring Charles and Harry with us when I know that wasn't your choice. And when you bought the braid rug from the crippled lady—those actions mean a lot to me."

Judd grinned, "Those boys are cute little buggers. I wish we could spend time with them. It's just that my time with you is so short and precious. My competition has the advantage," he glanced aside for her reaction.

She nodded, "It's natural that Jess would talk to you about this. You're right. Since the rally I've been seeing Isaac. I would give anything for this not to have happened. I mean, what are the chances...?" her voice wondered off. "I never want to be unfair or hurt anyone." She turned to him, touching his arm, "I want you and me to have a chance. Can we just be you and me, no one else in our mind? What you said is true, this time we have is precious. Let's make the most of it. I'm just learning to know who you are. You need to know me. That's all, no one else can be with us for these two short days."

"I know, you're right." He ran his hands through the dark hair tumbling into his face. "It drives me crazy when I think of you and Isaac. I won't talk about it anymore. I want you to know that I'm serious and will do all I can to give us a chance. You're my kind of girl. Now, Mrs. Miller tells me you're becoming the family seamstress. You've made a dress for Anna. I've always thought I could pick the Dunkard ladies out of a crowd, but you're good, Sarah. Your dress is plain enough to satisfy the Dunkards and stylish enough to satisfy me. Of all the ladies here, you are the most elegant."

"I've been so lucky to learn from Mrs. M..."

"Yea, Woo Hoo!" The crowd cheered and whistled, throwing their hats in the air. The two in the buggy startled and looked around as a player ran the bases. The Albion shortstop had hit a homerun, winning the game.

* * * * *

The family returned from church and plowed through Mrs. Miller's farm dinner of beef and dumplings, mashed potatoes, fresh green beans, applesauce, and homemade peach pie. Mrs. Miller walked around the house with Judd's rug, then decided the porch was the best place for it. Everyone was sated and sluggish from dinner. Shortly the Millers went in the house to take a nap.

Sarah and Judd were sitting on the porch swing when Judd got up and walked to the screen door, lifting, tugging and checking the bottom corner where it stuck and didn't close. After a short inspection he said, "I can easily fix that. I brought my toolbox in case I had problems with buggy wheels on the way." He went to his buggy, returning with a well-stocked toolbox and a piece of wood.

"Judd, you don't need to fix our door, but it's such a nuisance I can tell you, Mrs. Miller will be in your pocket if you fix her screen door."

"It's not Mrs. Miller I'm trying to get in my pocket. I had a pretty little farm girl with blue eyes in mind," he pretended subtlety, with a sly glance. "It's a good thing I can fix the door with the same things I need to fix a buggy wheel. It's all in the physics. Will you please come and hold the claw of the hammer under this side of the door?" He knelt beside her, positioning her hands on the hammer, "or we could just spend all afternoon like this," he teased.

"No, we couldn't, my legs won't squat like this all afternoon," Sarah laughed. "How do you know about physics, anyway?"

"Let me bring you a stool so you'll be more comfortable. This will take a while," he said, bringing the stool; then measuring, trimming and sanding a triangular piece of wood to place on the upper corner of the door. "I only went through eighth grade. I liked school and it came easily for me, especially math. I've stayed in touch with my teacher and she loans books to me. I've been through the high school math books. Now I'm studying physics. I'm going to hammer on the top corner, so you'll have to hold it firm."

"How do you figure it out without a teacher?" Sarah asked. "I liked math too, but I'd have trouble teaching myself."

Judd hammered the wood to the door. "It's hard sometimes, especially geometry. You're good at it too or you wouldn't be able to figure out the sewing: making the pattern pieces, figuring the right amount of fabric and knowing how to lay it out. My mother didn't have much schooling and she's smart. I suppose since women don't have to figure for crop planting, construction and all, it's not as important for them." Judd paused in his hammering and looked at Sarah, "I've always hoped the woman I live with will be smart. I want her to keep up with me and I don't plan to always be a farmer."

Sarah's eyes looked past Judd and she thought, *Could I keep up*? Then with a lift of her chin, *Yes, I think I could.*

"Okay Sarah, release the claw and let's see if this door closes." The door settled into its frame without sticking, good as new. Judd squeezed her shoulder, "Thanks for your help. We make a good team." Then to himself, *Next time I come I'll bring something so it doesn't slam.*

CHAPTER 17

Juda

Mr. Miller hurried to the barn where Sarah was forking hay down the shoot into the cow manger. "Yippee!" he pulled a letter from his pocket and with fanfare sailed it to her. "Ya' must be livin' right girl—this is YOUR day." Sarah picked it up, grinning when she saw it was from Judd. He pulled off her hat, tossing it in the air. "I have even better news: I ran into Norman Beckman in town, a farmer near Columbia City. He just hired Will and your papa; they already moved in. He says Will is already an esteemed employee and your papa has come out of his cloud, showing interest in tapping their maple trees to sell syrup. Sarah, your family lives only ten miles from here."

Sarah squealed, pumping her arms. "This is the best day I've had in nine years."

"I'll kill a chicken. We'll celebrate tonight. I'll leave so you can read your love letter in private," he snickered.

My Dearest Sarah,

I had a good trip home from Albion. I just wish the distence wasn't so far. It took nigh to six hours from your house to mine with a rest stop for Star. Maybe you're lucky I'm not close or I'd be camping on your doorstep every weekend. That may discourage my winning your heart, which is my purpose.

Our family is having Christmas dinner at the church, one of the advantages of being the minaster. There are so many of us we will have a high-ho time. My mother goes all out on our favrites: ham, oyster stew, and mincemeat pie, plus all the food everyone brings. We'll stuff ourselves, eating and visiting the whole day. The only thing missing will be you.

My mother says I'm a sore trial the way I mope around since being with you. I don't want to be out of sorts for my parents, so I'd better chipper up.

My feelings for you were only made stronger by being with you. For years I've dreamed of my ideal woman. It seems I've found her in you. My heart will miss you until we're together again.

Affectionately,
Judd

* * * * *

Amy furtively pulled Sarah aside in the cloak room, "You *must* come home with me after church. We have to talk." Elder Hyre's sermon droned endlessly. Why would Amy be in such a tizzy? Had she heard from Judd? Sarah had received two letters from him. Surely, he wouldn't visit in the dead of winter. Sarah had been close to the Gardners ever since working on their farm a few years earlier. They often welcomed her for Sunday dinner with other cousins and sometimes Elder Hyre's family.

As the adults settled in to visit, Amy and Sarah bundled up for a walk in the woods. When they were away from the house, Amy grabbed Sarah's arms, jumping up and down, her curly hair flying, "He did it, he did it!"

"Who?" Sarah was excited but confused.

"Art. He asked me to marry him," she squealed. "And I said 'yes'!"

The two girls screeched their joy, hugging and dancing in the snow. "I'm so happy. Art is the perfect guy for you. When did he propose?"

"Just last night. I had to tell someone, or I would die. I knew you wouldn't tell. We haven't even told our folks yet."

"This is so-o romantic: you, married. I can't say I'm surprised. Art is so over-the-moon for you," Sarah said, rolling around a ball of snow for a snowman.

"This has been my dream, to find a man like Art. You never know if it will happen. I'm in a daze. Do you think Art is as giddy as me? I didn't sleep all night."

"Sure, Art is excited, but men are different that way. I'm betting he's not out with Jess or Isaac building a snowman nattering about getting married. When is the date?"

"We didn't even get to that. I'm sure we'll wait the decent one-year interval." Amy danced in the snow. Fanning her face with her hand, she let loose a bawdy guffaw for a Dunkard girl. "I sure wouldn't want to wait longer. Whew, Sarah, I'm finding I have some sizzle in my blood." The girls laughed uproariously, Sarah remembering her own kisses with Isaac. "Help me lift this ball on to the other one. This snow sure packs well."

"Enough of my news. I'm dying to hear about your weekend with Judd. Tell me I made a good match," Amy kidded as they rolled around a third snowball.

"Oh Amy, since you're betrothed, now you're the expert on love. I sure need advice about my love life. I guess love can make you happy, like you, or it can make you muddled, like me."

Amy threw her arms around Sarah, embracing her in a snowy hug, "I'm sorry. I guess it's partly my fault. Did you like Judd?"

"I did. But Amy, I think I'm in love with two men. How can that be?"

"Likely most girls never have that problem, but I can see how it could tear you up. Tell me what you're thinking. You know my lips are sealed."

"I know Isaac better, so of course he has the edge. You mentioned your blood sizzling, well I can tell you the sparks fly when I'm with Isaac. He knows how to play me like a symphony." Sarah rushed to Amy placing her mittened hands on her cheeks, her words heavy with urgency. "It's not that there's impropriety, don't get the wrong idea," she said, trusting her friend with her most secret feelings. "But he drives me out of my senses! Isaac is like me, countrified and earthy. I love that he's funny and not so serious, yet he cares about my feelings too. We talk about serious things. My brother Will has met Isaac and they hit it off."

"The timing was just bad. Had you and Isaac been an item I never would have introduced you to Judd, but I can see you two together. You seem happy when you're with Judd," Amy said.

"Judd," Sarah sighed with a dreamy expression, "he is swell. Such a gentleman. He'll do well 'cause he tries to better himself. He's smart and he's not satisfied to be average, so I think he would make me better too. Amy, you know I have no sophistication; I've never been off a farm. I think, because of the distance and the inconvenience of being together we both feel pressure to make it work. And Isaac's always there, even if he isn't really."

"Sarah, it sounds to me like you could love both these men, but I hear a softness in your voice when you talk about Isaac. I sense a natural rapport between you that hasn't had a chance to develop yet with Judd."

"Do you really notice that, Amy? I mostly feel in a muddle. I think Mrs. Miller would like me to pursue Judd. Of course, she doesn't *say* that. I know I can't have Judd making long trips here if I have strong feelings about Isaac. I need to decide. I wish I would get a sign telling me what to do."

"Well, he is happy," Amy said, putting an acorn smile on the top ball of snow. "You know all our secrets, Mr. Snowman. We trust you to keep them to yourself."

* * * * *

The budding green of the early spring landscape rushed past the train window. Sarah was entranced by the speed and the homely scenes of tidy Indiana farm life as she and Will took their first train ride to visit Juda in Ft. Wayne. She pressed her face against the train window when they arrived at the depot. "There she is! It's her," she grabbed Will. "She has Mama's comb in her hair," she said, reaching back to touch the comb tucked into her braided bun. "She looks so high-class and sophisticated," Sarah said, awestruck.

"And look at him, he sure favors city duds. Quite the dandy I say. And the little one with her white muff. They're most mighty a couple of high esteem—you can pin that in your hat. Let's quit yammering and go meet our long-lost sister."

Juda may have been citified but she ran to Sarah and Will with the alacrity of the fourteen-year-old who had lost her beloved siblings. The nine years dissolved to nothing; the tears of happiness replaced the tears of desperation from long ago at the schoolhouse, where Juda pleaded to stay with Sarah. The unbridled joy of this reunion could not have happened without the loss and grief of nine years of separation and heartache. That hard core of hurt was gone now—healing could begin. Juda was a tall, handsome woman with a rosy complexion and natural refinement. Her dark hair was styled, her long dress elegantly fitted. Even with this gentility she had a winsome pluckiness that hinted at the earlier Juda.

"Let me introduce you to my family," Juda's well-mannered grace asserted itself as she wiped her tears. "This is my husband, Josiah Hazen and Ella, who is four." The miniature of her mother with her dark curls and brown eyes, Ella was shy behind her mother's skirt.

"The three of you are a sight for sore eyes," Will remarked, shaking hands with Josiah who, while dapper and polished, had a generous smile and cheery disposition. He corralled them to the buggy for the ride to their lovely, though simple home where Juda had prepared a feast. As they told their stories it became obvious that Juda had been spared the privations that Will and Sarah had experienced. She had been cared for and well-treated by the families who took her in. At age seventeen she rented a room downtown and got a clerking job at Wolf and Dessauer, a new and prosperous department store. She soon was recognized for her decorative abilities in displaying merchandise and was promoted by Josiah, who was her manager. She loved her job and spoke enthusiastically about creating store displays: "that was the best time ever for me. When I got married and became confined with Ella I couldn't work anymore."

"Now she's a mother, the best job a woman can have," Josiah asserted. "See how nicely she has decorated our home?"

Little Ella was attracted to Will with his fun humor. She shook her head vigorously when Will teased, "Our little Ella is as cute as a bug's ear." He played finger games with Ella who was spellbound as he made fingers disappear and shaped fingers like birds and animals, slyly making deep-throat animal sounds. She was ecstatic when Will gave her a little bird he had whittled.

"I notice you're wearing Mama's comb," Sarah smiled. "It fits perfectly the way your hair is styled."

"I treasure it more than anything. It's the only thing I have from Mama. When you got off the train Sarah, you looked just like Mama with your black hair pulled back like hers."

"Thank you, that's a compliment. I thought she was beautiful. When I was at Uncle Levi's the thing I missed most was the three of us brushing our hair at bedtime. I thought I'd get in trouble when I took her comb, then I saw you had taken the other one. That comb has helped me through some tough patches over the years. I'm glad we both got one."

"No one ever noticed her combs were missing," Juda said thoughtfully. "My heart still pains when I think back to that time. Our lives changed overnight."

"Papa changed overnight too," Will added. They talked about Uriah who had seemed to give up when his wife died. He had refused to join them in visiting Juda. They chose not to fix on sad topics, instead reveling in their time together, nourished by memories and love of family. Too soon Josiah said they must go to the depot to catch the last train to Albion. "When summer comes, we will come to the country. Juda needs to see her father and spend more time with you. This is just the beginning," he promised.

"I believe I like fancy pants," Will whispered to Sarah, as they boarded the train.

CHAPTER 18

Again

Isaac wanted to go mushroom hunting, knowing the springtime woods would bolster their sultry spirits. They would make a fire when it got dark. *Yes, Sarah thought. We need to talk. My indecisiveness is making both of us uncommonly cranky.* It was a perfect evening, the forest greeted them with a mosaic of blooming pink dogwood and redbud trees vigorously announcing spring. The fresh dampness smelled crisp and earthy. They walked briskly, their breath catching, the effort restorative. As dusk settled, they collected wood and made a fire. The wet wood sputtered and sizzled, holding their eyes and their thoughts.

"What are we to do, Sarah? What is right for us?"

"If only someone would tell us," she muttered, clearly unsettled.

"When I have a big decision, I try to look at the pros and cons. I can tell you the pros, why I want to be with you. Maybe you can tell the cons," Isaac said.

"I think Elder Hyre would say our lives are preordained according to God's holy plan. If God wants us to be together it will happen. If something happens and we aren't together, then that's God's answer. I wish He would give us a clue. We don't *know* what is right for us," Sarah sounded frustrated. "Maybe I'm not right for you; I've had a lot in my life to make me unreliable. Tell me your pros."

"I love you. I think I have from the beginning. That's most important, if you feel the same. I've thought about this a lot, in fact I've been writing down my feelings, so I don't brashly spill them out to you, frightening you with my ardor," he laughed. "Mostly it comes down to we complement each other. You're the mature, thoughtful one while I see the more fun side in things. I'm optimistic where you see what's real. You're frugal because you haven't had a choice. I've saved money and will provide for you, but I also want to enjoy my money. I think you're more religious than me—I don't give a flip what Elder Hyre thinks about preordination. But like you, I have a deep faith and try to live according to scripture. I don't think religion will be our problem." He was thoughtful. "I believe both of us together are better than either of us separately."

Sarah laughed at his glib slang. "I'm probably not as religious as you think. Growing up, I didn't go to church as much as you did."

"What I'm trying to say is, I think we balance each other."

Sarah thought about Isaac's words. "I agree with you. We *are* good for each other," she stood and put wood on the fire. Returning to Isaac, she took his hand—the first they had touched. Her eyes sought his, "I told you before, I'm happy when I'm with you; you bring spice to my life. I like that you can be serious, but you are also fun. I love that you accept me as I am. You've never dictated what I should do—that's unusual in the few men I've known. With Roy and Mary Miller, he cares about her opinion and gives her equal say. I guess for me, that's what love is."

"I love you the way you are. I don't *want* to change you or push you to be different."

"I'm just afraid my insecurities will drag you down. The *cons* are my fear of being left, of never belonging to a family. I'm like a boat without an anchor. It *has* helped me to be with Will and Juda again."

"Those feelings seem to stay at the back of your mind—that those you love will leave you. It's like a cloud lurking at the edge of your thoughts. It's understandable. I make a commitment to you, Sarah. You can trust my word: I will never leave you."

"I'm not a quitter," Sarah said with resolve. She was quiet for some time, then took his hands. "When I do something, I give it my all. That's what I want to do for us. I want to give my best to help us be good together. I commit to that, Isaac."

They silently put out the fire and returned to the house without speaking. They had an understanding—no more words were needed. It felt weighty, too important for words.

* * * * *

As much as Sarah disliked raking and stowing hay in the barn, her spirits were light as she inhaled the savory freshness of the first cutting of spring hay. Her fickle mind soared of its own accord, off in a dreamy nether land where she and Isaac were cocooned in their own universe. She was a girl in love. After their talk, the puzzle pieces fit together. She no longer felt the turmoil of indecision.

"Sarah, come back from the clouds," called Mrs. Miller. "In case you haven't noticed, the wagon is full, you need to take it to the barn."

Sarah blushed, stuttering an apology. She must control herself and keep her mind on her work. This daydreaming wasn't like her. She determined to put a stop to it.

As she drove the horses to the barn, she noticed dust from a buggy that had turned into the lane. When she got to the barn, she saw it was Amy. Yea-a! She was excited by the unexpected mid-week visit, hoping she could stay for dinner.

Amy stepped from the buggy as Sarah ran up to her. "Oh Sarah," Amy's face crumbled as she bent into her sobs. "Oh Sarah" was all she could get out.

"What is it? What happened?" Sarah grabbed her desperately, black dread rolling like a freight train over her. Mrs. Miller ran to join them, kneeling before Amy on the porch swing. "What happened, Amy?" she asked firmly.

"Isaac is gone. He burned in their barn."

Without realizing what she was doing, Sarah ran from the porch—reasoning if she got away, the awful news wouldn't be there. With every frantic step her brain said...*no*...*no*...*no.* Running to the woods.... She must get away. She saw the scorched embers of their fire and she knelt to gather them, somehow, they were precious to her. *Please God. Not Isaac*...over and over she begged. She put her hands over her face to push away the reality. Amy, Mrs. Miller, and Anna joined her around the fire circle, all tearful except Sarah.

Amy's voice was choked, "It was in the night. The hay they put in the barn was green, it caught fire. Isaac must have awakened and smelled smoke. He was trying to get the animals out. He saved the horses. A burning rafter collapsed on him and evidently pinned him."

God, no. Hideous that he suffered in his death.

"Poor Ezra and Opal slept through it until a neighbor awakened them." Sarah got up and paced. She couldn't stand to hear this. She couldn't not hear it. "At first they assumed Isaac was in his room sleeping. His body wasn't found until this morning when the neighbors finished putting out the fire."

Sarah put her hands over her ears. "Give me some time, Amy;" she wandered away for several minutes. She returned to kneel again at the fire circle, oblivious that black soot smeared her hands and face and splotched her dress. "Okay," she whispered.

"His parents are heartsick. They feel responsible. Doc Mathys attended them this morning... they're both sedated and sleeping. To lose their only child—I wonder if they'll ever recover," Amy spoke thickly through her tears.

"They were so kind to me," Sarah whispered. "Isaac was fun and easy-going like Mr. Conner and kind and tender-hearted like Mrs. Conner. He was the best of both of them." *Like we would have been, she thought.*

Eventually they wandered back to the house where Mr. Miller, Charles, and Harry soon came for lunch. Sarah's heart came closest to exploding when Mr. Miller enveloped her in his big strong arms and stroked through her hair, tsk, tsking and awkward in his sympathy, "Ya couldn'a picked a finer friend, girlie. A fine chap he was. That laddie thought the world 'a ya. Wore it on his sleeve, plain ta see. Shouldn'a been like this. I'll never figure the Almighty on this one—a cryin' shame it is."

Mr. and Mrs. Miller soon left to go to the Conners to help clean from the fire. Everyone in the community would help, the priorities of their own farms subordinate to a neighbor in need. Likewise, Amy stayed with Sarah. Mostly they walked. Eventually the thoughts swimming in her head became words. She told Amy about their last talk and how things had felt so settled and "right". She spoke regretfully of things she had left unsaid. "I really love him, but I never said those words."

That night the youth group came to the Millers'. Sarah was so grateful for their friendship and tenderness, though she realized they came of necessity. There was sustenance in being together. Isaac was their dear friend. As sad as it was, grieving the loss together was easier.

The day of the funeral was heavenly, like springtime could not contain itself: a warming sun, insects humming and darting, trees flowering, a balmy breeze billowing sheets on the clothes line, dandelion puffs floating, warblers chirp-chirping—all airbrushed as on an artist's canvas. Elder Hyre, clucking the horses forward, basked in the beauty of the day, believing an angelic choir was ushering Isaac's soul to glory. Sarah, riding with the Millers to the white frame church, didn't notice. She did not want to feel or think or hear. Every ounce of her energy struggled to sustain this.

The youth group sat together in the front rows of the church, which was filled to capacity. Windows were open, a breeze bringing in the day. Sarah was between Amy and Eloise. The youth had been taught to be tough and hardworking, but they were innocents to death of one of their own. Their grief was brutal and consuming—hankies covering their eyes, shoulders shaking as sobs were stifled.

Rock of ages, cleft for me.
Let me hide myself in Thee;
Let the water and the blood,
From Thy riven side which flowed,
Be of sin the double cure;
Cleanse me from its guilt and power.

As the service progressed, Sarah was the only one with dry eyes. She took herself to other places and happier times, flitting between past and present: *Playing in the stream on the way to the Goshen youth rally: Sarah throwing the ball wildly at Isaac who slipped and got drenched. "Isaac and Sarah win the prize for biggest drips."*

She was pulled back by Elder Hyre's subdued, aching voice:

> I tell you the truth, whoever hears my voice and believes
> Him who sent Me has eternal life and is not condemned;
> he has crossed over from death to life.

Retreating to the youth rally: Clasping Isaac's hands as they sang and danced that glowing night: If a body meet a body, comin' through the rye. If a body kiss a body, need a body cry? Every lassie has a laddie. None, they say, have I. Yet all the lads they smile at me, when comin' through the rye.

Elder Hyre attempted to bring comfort for a meaningless tragedy. Sarah could hardly take in his words, let alone find comfort in them:

> The Lord is my shepherd, I shall not want.... Even though I walk through the valley of the shadow of death, I will fear no evil, for Thou art with me; Your rod and Your staff, they comfort me....

The starlit walk down Millers' lane when Sarah first spoke her feelings: "I'm happy when I'm with you. You're the easiest person to talk to. I don't feel shy with you," after which Isaac boldly picked her up, running with her as he called out, "By gum, I'm a man who likes a challenge—I will sweep you off your feet, Sarah Long!" Then as they tumbled into the long grass, he kissed her tenderly, his fingers softly touching her lips. "That will be with you till I replace it—I'll try to keep it fresh."

Sarah was jolted, her tender thoughts interrupted as Amy tugged her to stand as the congregation stood to sing:

> I'm but a stranger here, heav'n is my home;
> only a sojourner,
> Heav'n is my home: danger and sorrow stand,
> round me on every Hand;

> heav'n is my fatherland, heav'n is my home.

Sarah's thoughts returned to their last night together by the campfire. Her chest clenched so she could hardy breathe as she remembered Isaac's words:

"What are we to do about us, Sarah? I think I have loved you from the beginning.... We complement each other—you are the mature one and I'm the fun one. I believe both of us together are better than either of us separately.... I promise I will always take care of you. I won't leave you." Oh, to have that night back—so many things she would say.

Now they were walking to the little cemetery beside the church. Sarah was ramrod straight. She was only betrayed by silent tears oozing from her eyes.

> A time is coming when all who are in their graves will hear His voice and come out—those who have done good will rise to live, and those who have done evil will rise to be condemned.

"We commend Isaac's pure spirit to the ages, ashes to ashes, dust to dust," Elder Hyre intoned as the congregants sang a benediction for Isaac's short life:

> Yes, we'll gather by the river.
> The beautiful, the beautiful river.
> There with the saints at the river,
> that flows by the throne of God.

A solemn sadness pervaded her spirit. *It is over. My life with Isaac as it would have been is over. The finality was crushing. Lift your chin, Sarah. It is what it is.*

Few noticed when Sarah removed a small packet of sooty wood ashes from her grip and threw them into the gaping hole. *I love you Isaac. I will forever carry you in my heart.*

As the girls left the gravesite, Sarah felt a gentle touch on her shoulder. Mr. and Mrs. Conner, their faces pinched and strained in their grief—they had aged years in a few days—took her hands, too circumspect for a public embrace. Mr. Conner reached into his suit coat, withdrawing a black and white speckled secretary notebook, placing it in Sarah's hands. "This belongs to you, Sarah. We read his words, he started writing soon after the rally. We're grateful for the happiness you brought him this last year. We're so sad for you and for what might have been. He would want you to have this." They squeezed her hands then moved away, wounded and bent, leaning into an unseen wind and drought.

Sarah leafed through a few pages, recognizing Isaac's slanted, loopy handwriting: bold underlines, exclamation marks, and an occasional heart drawing. For the first time in days Sarah smiled in unrestrained and bounding joy, holding the notebook close. *Thank you, Isaac for leaving something I can hold. I can't have you, but I have your words.*

As on the two previous nights, Amy stayed over with Sarah. It was late, dark and quiet in Anna's room with only the katydids to compete with whispered voices and strangled sobs. Both girls were emptied, whip punched emotionally. Sleep would not come easily.

"Why do so many people I love die, Amy? What *is* it about me?" There! The horrific, all-consuming pariah voiced, thrown into the darkness.

Amy pondered, wanting to help, but youth, inexperience, and suddenly exposed mortality clouded a ready answer. "I can see why you feel that way—it never seems to quit for you. I wonder why you've had so much sadness while I've had everything good in life. It's so unfair. Just when you and Isaac were making plans to be together, Art and I are planning our wedding." The two girls faced each other, heads on soft pillows. Amy grasped Sarah's hands between them, her voice thickened and broke, "I can't be happy when you're so sad." A long pause.... "Elder Hyre would say the bad things make you stronger, that everything that happens is God's holy plan...but that doesn't seem right to me. Why you and not me?"

"This all weighs on my mind, Amy. I'm not satisfied with Elder Hyre's answers. Isaac wasn't either, we talked about it. I can't believe God didn't want Isaac and me to be together, causing him to die in the fire. Isaac doesn't even get a life now—that is cruel. God shouldn't be cruel. And if it's to make me stronger. Well, I'm already the strongest eighteen-year-old I know. Enough."

"Sarah, I've often thought about how you found Will and Juda this year: you had a family, then your mother died. You were separated for nine years, now you're a family again. The family circle was broken, but now it's repairing. There's almost a rhythm or balance to it. Maybe in years to come you'll find a circle in Isaac's death. Maybe it's something you can only see after a long time. I think for most people there is both good and bad times in their life. Girl, you should have smooth sailing here on out."

"I hope so, Amy. It's like my brain has exploded. I only see badness. Nothing makes sense. All these questions muddle my thoughts." Sarah paused, unsure of proceeding, "I've been talking to Isaac. Do you think he hears me?"

"Wow. I don't know."

"I know it's strange," Sarah admitted, "but when Isaac was alive, I'd think 'I must tell Isaac'. Now that he's gone, I still have things I want to tell him. I just wonder if he can hear me."

Amy was quiet so long Sarah thought she was asleep. When she spoke, her voice was sure: "you know how you can want something so much you set your mind to it and just make it happen? Some people have an illness that should kill them, but determination keeps them alive. Sarah, I think if you want it badly enough, you can talk so Isaac hears you."

"That's what I believe too, Amy."

CHAPTER 19

Friends Yet Again

Dear Sarah,

Amy and Jess have written me about the Conner's horrible barn fire and Isaac's death trying to save the animals. I never knew Isaac but everyone who knew him held him in high esteem and are grievously downcast. He was too young to pass to the other side with his life still ahead. Although I am not privy to your involvement with Isaac since I visited, I know you two had a special friendship. I express my simpathy for the loss of your friend.

It seems best if I give you time to heal. I will not visit or write to you, waiting for you to let me know if you're ready for us to commence. I care very much for you and hope you still want to give us a chance.

Your Friend,
Judd

Sarah called that summer the "humdrum of the doldrums." She felt fortunate to be living with the Millers who gently cared for her. Even the children, with their sweet antics and simple innocence raised her spirits and made her laugh. Mr. Miller was still laying drainage pipes to improve fertility, so this, in addition to the regular farm work, kept Sarah active and busy. Mrs. Miller always encouraged time with Sarah on the porch swing. Their conversations gradually nurtured her faith and restored her spirit.

It was the summer for sewing. It was therapeutic and occupied her evenings as she made patterns and sewed for the entire family. She became an excellent, creative seamstress; so much that Amy begged her to design and sew her wedding dress. Uncle Levi grudgingly allowed Sarah to take his measurements and make a tailored suit for him, giving her an excuse to spend time with him. He was crotchety when she brought the finished suit, but Sarah saw him secretly preening before the parlor mirror. He had a jaunty air and straightened his shoulders when he wore it to church each Sunday.

The best but worst time for Sarah was Sunday evenings when youth group met. For most of the previous year she had been with Isaac during these gatherings and it was painful to go without him. This was when she felt closest to Isaac, but also when her memories were most vivid and searing. For most of her life she had been friendless and alone, and not known loneliness. Now she was with beloved friends and felt lonely. But these were not the same kids who had gone to the rally the previous summer. They had all been tempered by fire: they were not so carefree. They plied Elder Hyre with questions and sometimes dismissed his answers. They had a closeness uncommon in adolescents.

Art and Amy had a fall wedding date. The strength of Amy and Sarah's friendship was evident as each girl gave succor and support to the other. Sarah determined she would not be a drag on Amy's happiness. She enthused over wedding plans, giggled and guffawed with girl talk.

Amy was at the Millers' one evening for a dress fitting. "It sure doesn't take much material for your dress," Sarah said, measuring Amy's waist. "You're no bigger than a minute."

"And what I wouldn't give for your tall hourglass figure," Amy countered. "Sarah, I have to ask you a serious question. You can think about it—you needn't answer tonight."

"What can be so serious, Amy?"

"You know Judd is my cousin and we've been close over the years. More recently Art and Jess have done things with Judd. We've thought about inviting him to the wedding. I don't know how things are between you two. Mostly I don't want to make you uncomfortable—how *you* feel is most important. We haven't invited him until we know your feelings about it."

The question hit Sarah like a punch in the chest. Her eyes clouded and searched Amy's face. "Oh, I hadn't thought about Judd being at the wedding."

"He doesn't need to be there Sarah, just say the word. We understand your feelings."

"I think your wedding is the most important day in your and Art's lives, you should invite who you want."

"Give it some thought. It's your choice. Whatever you decide will be fine."

"Judd has been the perfect gentleman through all of this. He's such a classy guy. You know, I always liked Judd.... Isaac was just...Judd said he would give me time...he wants me to get in touch with him when I'm ready. Did you say Judd was here and didn't try to see me?"

That night Sarah lay in bed, unable to sleep: *What is the right thing to do...? I don't want to hurt anyone.*

Across the fields, Amy lay in her bed: *What is the right thing to do...? I don't want to hurt anyone.*

* * * * *

Sarah couldn't help herself, she peeked down the stairs into the parlor and found Judd, seated, waiting for the wedding to commence. Her breath caught, her heart knotted in her chest: *my body betrays me, she thought as she secretly observed the willful lock of hair and boyish dimples, memorials to the child still camping out in this sophisticated handsome man.* She returned to Amy's bedroom.

"You're lovely Amy. The perfect bride. Art will swoon when he sees you."

"You must have seen him," Amy said knowingly. "You're blushing."

"Am I that obvious?" Sarah grumbled. "Only my bosom buddy could know me so well." The two girls encircled their arms and smiled into their mirrored reflection: one petite curly-headed honey-blonde and one statuesque and elegantly dark. Their dresses, which they designed and Sarah sewed, were classic and fashionable.

"Lois Gardner hustled into the room, "It's time." She appraised them, "How lovely—both of you. Sarah, you go first, after Art and Jess enter from the downstairs bedroom. Hold on to the stair railing so you don't trip." She opened the door and they slipped into the upstairs hall. Sarah hugged Amy, whispering, "Happy wedding day, Amy. Be happy, my forever friend."

Sarah mulled about with other guests after the wedding as Jess and Thomas rearranged the parlor and dining room for the wedding meal. As it was a warm autumn day the youth group sat around tables on the front porch. Sarah chatted with Lydia, Jerry, Eloise, and Jess, both couples betrothed and planning their own weddings. She felt Judd's presence before she saw him.

"May I join you?" he asked, seating himself beside Sarah. The small talk was about weddings, a common interest among this group, but awkward for Sarah and, she assumed, Judd. As everyone knew their history, Sarah was aware of quick glances and conversational lapses. She felt like they were on display, choice pieces in a museum. Art and Amy wandered by, giddy in their oneness. After swatting a fly, Judd unwittingly placed his hand over Sarah's, causing her quick intake of breath as she jerked to remove her hand from the table—an action noticed by all. *I wish Judd and I were not in a fishbowl this first time,* Sarah thought. As they ate, Sarah felt the rigidity in her body, struggling to appear relaxed. She collected dirty plates, returning them to the kitchen, just to do something away from the table.

As the wedding party broke up, Judd asked if he could return her to the Millers. Sarah nodded, "Yes please," she muttered. Alone in the buggy they began to relax, like kids let out of school. Though the big questions were unanswered, the foundation of their earlier budding relationship made it easier to be together.

Sarah interrupted their conversation, "Turn into this path on the left. It's a pretty spot where I sometimes bring the children to fish. We'll find a spot in the sun."

Judd let Star graze and the two settled on the horse blanket beside the stream. Judd, his relief obvious, lay on his back, his hands behind his head. "Thanks for bringing us here, it's just what I need. I'm glad we could be at the wedding, but it was a tetch awkward. I'm sorry you had to go through that."

Sarah was honest, "I never like being the center of attention and it certainly felt like everyone was watching us."

Judd sat up, turning to her, his brown eyes burning with intensity, "I just want to be with you and talk about ordinary things. I want to hear your voice, take away the forced smile on your face and the strain in your shoulders. I want to make you laugh. I want to touch your hand and you don't flinch." He restlessly pushed back his hair, "It doesn't seem like that should be too much to want."

"Oh-h…." Her eyes large circles, her hands went to her cheeks. It was like a lightning bolt went through her body: *Judd understands too…he feels just what I'm feeling.* There was indescribable comfort in hearing his words which perfectly mirrored her own feelings. The usually placid Sarah strangled a sob and burst into tears, her shoulders shaking with nearly a year's worth of pent-up emotion.

"I'm sorry I made you cry." He gathered Sarah into his arms, his hands coddling her head as her tears dampened his shoulder. "Oh, my dear, don't be sad," he begged plaintively, his own tears pooling. Sarah was totally overcome with wrenching, unladylike sobs. After a time, even being a man, Judd realized that this outburst was not solely due to his words. This had been waiting release. His voice and actions petted and soothed, letting Sarah cleanse and heal. She took his hanky, the gasping hiccoughs subsiding. She was totally spent.

"This is so unlike me," her voice still shook. She was embarrassed. "I *never* lose it. But Judd, what you just said, about wanting us to do ordinary things like a normal couple. I feel like you know my mind. That's what I want too. But then I get afraid. The bad that has happened always lurks in my thoughts. Sometimes I'm afraid to be happy, knowing it won't last." Sarah wanted to be open about Isaac but didn't know how. Showing feelings wasn't proper (buck up, lift your chin, Sarah) so it wasn't in her experience. Judd wanted to comfort her, to show he understood, but didn't think it was in his place to mention Isaac. There was a solitary wistfulness between them. Isaac's death was a mountain too big for them to ever climb. Sarah wiped her nose and sidled beside Judd. He took her hand, his voice decisive. "It seems we're in agreement in wanting to be together again so that is where we start. When we met at the rally a year-and-a-half ago I knew the distance would be a problem, but I had no idea it would be *this* hard. If we can make it after this, we'll know we can get through anything. So, I'll come to your house tonight. We'll play checkers or something with Anna and Charles."

"That would be perfect. I would like to be together as friends, I don't much care what we do. I often play games with them and they'll love your attention. They're not good losers though, so play at your own risk."

"Do you feel comfortable if we go to church together? I think since people saw us at the wedding, church should be a piece of cake."

Sarah was hesitant, "I must say Judd, bringing you to church will be hard." She thought about it. "I guess we should just get it over with."

Again, Judd realized he wasn't privy to Sarah's life; he needed patience in inserting himself into it. "Jess and I will plan an outing for you and Eloise after church. If the weather is still good we can have a fall picnic. This is a nice little stream, maybe we'll come back here. They stood, folding the blanket. Sarah returned his soppy handkerchief. "Thanks for your patience. I know this hasn't been easy for you. Most men would have given up on me a long time ago. I *was* happy to see you at the wedding. It feels good to be with you again."

No one feeds on drama and gossip more than small church congregations whose members' lives are an open book. Judd and Sarah ignored the nudges and side-long glances of the adults and open-faced staring of the children. They breathed a sigh of relief with the benediction.

Jess's mother had prepared a picnic feast: fried chicken, potato salad, and chocolate cake. Jess had filched a bottle of blackberry wine "so we can toast the wedding couple, wherever they are," he said, grinning slyly. It had its desired effect as they spread the blankets beside the stream, the sunbeams and golden leaves gently raining down. They were relaxed and lazy, greasy from gnawing chicken. They watched a squirrel dig into their leftovers, they skipped stones, and practiced birdcalls. They removed shoes and stockings and rolled up pant legs to wade in the shallow stream.

Sarah's color was high as she reached to Judd for support, "I seem to be a bit unbalanced; that wine is swimming in my head and tangling up my feet," she giggled. The two couples drifted apart when Judd and Sarah left the stream and walked barefoot through the woods. They sat on a downed tree. Judd turned toward her as if inhaling her... searching... memorizing. Sarah held his eyes with a coy smile, "I'm not being a good girl," she demurred, as close as she ever came to coquetry.

"I like you like this, my sweet. I'm going to bring blackberry wine every time I visit," he laughed. "This is what I want for us. I want us to court like other couples. I was thinking last night, I've known you a year-and-a-half and we've only been together four times. From now on, I'm going to visit more often. I can stay with Jess. With winter coming, I may get snowed in down here." He took her chin in his hand, "Now that might be fun," he said with a wily grin.

"You've planned a perfect day for us, Judd. I haven't had so much fun...in a long time. I want you to visit as much as you can. When I don't see you...it's like you're not in my world."

"I'm going to come for Christmas. My parents have enough family around, they don't need me. Someone can help my dad if the weather gets bad."

"That's not many weeks away," Sarah grabbed Judd's hands, "It will be good. We'll plan lots of parties." Judd gathered her into his arms, their kiss needy and jubilant, their courtship renewed with fervor.

* * * * *

"Do you think we should go in the parlor door since Mr. Levi invited us for a social visit?" Mrs. Miller questioned Sarah as they turned the buggy into his driveway.

"No, I always go through the back porch. He would think it odd if I went to the parlor. I can't figure out Uncle Levi. He never has company other than Benji's family."

Upon entering the back-porch Sarah saw a long line of ladies' bonnets on a pantry shelf. Her hands flew to her face as she turned to the Millers. "What's going on?" she asked skeptically.

Mr. Miller touched her arm, "Sorry, m' girl, we were pledged to secrecy. Not our idea."

"Judd wanted to have a surprise party to announce your betrothal," Mrs. Miller took Sarah's hands. "He's so happy, none of us had the nerve to dissuade him. Paste a smile on your face, my dear, and act surprised. We best go in now."

"Surprise!" The wooden doors between the dining room and parlor were open, both rooms full of people. Uncle Levi greeted her with a big smile, pleased to host the big event. Nellie and Benji, smiling broadly, had decorated the house with fall flowers and Sarah saw several trays displaying Nellie's culinary expertise. Indeed, this would be a fine party. Benji lifted her, swinging her around, "Sarah, are you surprised?" As much as she disliked the limelight, she was soon drawn into the celebratory spirit.

Judd, his eyes sparkling, touched her arm, "I wanted us to celebrate our good news." Sarah was in a jumbled rush of close warm bodies, friendly greetings, and convivial back slapping. Faces flashed before her: Will, her brother gave her a cheeky smile with his hug, Elder Hyre and Sister Minnie, all the youth group, Amy's parents, Rosa and her brother George. Judd brought his parents to meet her, "Papa, Mama, I would like you to meet Sarah Long. Sarah, please meet my father and mother, George and Elizabeth Swihart." *So, these are my in-laws. I hope they approve of me.* Sarah was eager to meet Judd's parents, as she assumed she and Judd would likely live with them until they could afford their own home. His mother allayed Sarah's anxieties with her gentle manner and kind words, "Don't you worry, Sarah. You and I will get along just fine. Judd has made a good choice."

His father added, "The way Judd talks, I thought you'd have a halo. Welcome to our family."

Uncle Levi called for quiet. Sarah looked up at him, her hands folded, a reserved smile on her face. "We welcome you here today to share the happy news that Sarah Long and Judson Swihart are betrothed. Judd asked for Sarah's hand in marriage and I give them my blessing for a long, happy life together."

This feels like a dream. I can't believe this man will be my husband.

Unlike Sarah, Judd was at ease in the limelight. Assured of his stature, the words came easily, "I think I'm the luckiest man alive to have found Sarah," though he was unaware of his blunder.

But I hardly know you.

"Each of you have been important in our lives and we want you to celebrate this happy occasion and the wedding we plan for the fall."

I will have to leave the family I just found... Amy and Art... the Millers... my friends.

"I want to introduce my parents, George and Elizabeth Swihart."

He wants someone smart who can keep up with him—he'll go far.

"I especially thank Mr. Zumbrun and Nellie and Benji for preparing the food and the pretty decorations. I encourage you to stroll in the yard and enjoy Nellie's beautiful flowers."

I'll show you, Judson Swihart. This girl will work her fingers to the bone to get you where you want. You just got yourself another good workhorse.

CHAPTER 20

Married

"I have no idea what I'm expected to do, Amy. I've seen what cows and horses do but that's no help. You're the only person I can ask." Sarah was embarrassed and acting contrary to her nature in discussing the unmentionable subject. Art, Amy, and Sarah were in a wagon on their way to Goshen for a Swihart reunion (Amy and Judd's mothers being sisters). For the first time Sarah would meet Judd's brothers, sisters, and extended family. Art was almost asleep in the front seat, driving the team on this steamy August day, while the girls were in the back, their heads together, their tongues wagging. Amy, the tried and tested bride of almost a year was unusually forthcoming with Sarah, who would marry Judd in a few months.

"Actually, I think it *is* easier for farm girls who have grown up around animals and seen their instinctive nature. You don't need to do anything. Men know what to do and they do it. Don't look so aghast; amorous congress isn't as bad as you might think, and it gets easier the longer you're married. I've learned to enjoy the closeness you have with someone you love. Once you're intimate it's easier to share in other matters. My mother told me men's desires are different than women's. Our duty is to keep our husband happy and do it with a smile. We listen and support their opinion—even if it's wrong and they fail. We never chide or pretend to be superior. As Elder Hyre preaches, it's better if we're submissive. Our job is to make a nice home and take care of manly needs."

"I don't know. That sounds hard for a stubborn girl like me. It seems the husband takes, and the wife does all the giving."

"But in a good marriage the husband wants his wife to be happy, so it balances. Obviously, the husband has the hardest job in earning a living. Our responsibility in bearing and raising children is important, noble even, but certainly easier."

"Marriage has been good for you, Amy. You and Art seem happy together."

"We've not been married long, but for me it keeps getting easier and better. I don't know how I'll stand it if I live till I'm seventy," she laughed. "It will be good for you and Judd too. I always thought you two were a match—and you proved me right."

* * * * *

"As a married man of almost a year I'll give you the advice my friend, Don gave me before I married Elma: keep your eyes wide open before the wedding and half closed afterward." Will joked with Judd as they drove the buggy to Albion to get the marriage license.

"I plan to keep them wide open for a good while," Judd chuckled at Will's saucy humor. "I can't wait to be with Sarah."

"I'm partial, but I guarantee, you struck gold with that girl. Whatever she does she gives her all; she is not like any other woman. It's said, 'In the beginning God created the earth and rested. Then he created man and rested. Then God created women, and since then neither God nor man has rested!' That's Sarah. You'll be hard put to keep up with her. Here's the courthouse, let's tie up and get this license. She gave me this one job to do and you and I are going to get it done."

* * * * *

This is the right thing...this is the right thing....

The speech in Sarah's dizzied mind repeated as she walked the small aisle between guests in Uncle Levi's dining room. She joined Judd before the blazing fireplace in the parlor. Judd looked somber, befitting the occasion, then broke into a dazzling smile when she reached his side. Sarah reassured him with her own gentle smile. Had Judd been able to read her thoughts he would have heard: *You made a good choice, Judd. I've handled everything life has thrown at me and landed on my feet. That's what I'll continue to do.*

Elder Hyre intoned:

> Dearly beloved, we are gathered here together as Ezra Judson Swihart takes the hand of Sarah Catherine Long in holy matrimony.
>
> *This is the biggest day of my life and it's all a blur. Why can't I settle down? I know it's right—I'll make it right.*

> I, Judson Swihart take thee Sarah Long to be my lawful, wedded wife to have and to hold from this day forward in the holy estate of matrimony. I pledge to love, honour and keep thee for better or worse, in sickness and in health, for richer or poorer and forsaking all others keep only unto thee so long as we both shall live.
>
> I, Sarah Long, take thee Judson Swihart to be my lawful, wedded husband, to have and to hold from this day forward in the holy estate of matrimony. I pledge to obey and serve thee, to love, honour and keep thee for better or worse, in sickness and health, for richer or poorer and forsaking all others keep only unto thee so long as we both shall live.
>
> With vows pledged, Elder Hyre presented Mr. and Mrs. Judson Swihart: I now pronounce you husband and wife. Whom God hath joined together let no man put asunder.

Sarah and Judd had a quick moment before they received their guests. "You're the prettiest bride I've seen, Sarah." He touched her ivory voile skirt, "The dress you made is lovely. I'm glad you're my wife. I meant what I said in there," he motioned to the parlor, "but the words didn't sound like me. More than anything I want to take care of you and make you happy."

"You *do* make me happy. We're going to make a good life together."

Their private moment was interrupted by Uncle Levi welcoming the wedding guests: "We welcome all of you, especially Judd's family who have come a distance. Nellie and Benjamin have outdone themselves to prepare Judd and Sarah's wedding." He placed his hand on Sarah's shoulder, his eyes gleaming, "After our supper we know you will all want to join Judd and Sarah at the Blue River German Baptist Church's communion and foot washing. We ask God for His rich blessing on this new marriage. Let us join in prayer."

Though her face remained impassive, Sarah grasped Judd's hand during the prayer, hoping to convey her chagrin that they were now committed to attending communion on their wedding night—a time they would most choose to be secluded. Was Uncle Levi just oblivious to a young couple's desires or was he being purposely mean? Sarah would not reward him by expressing her distress. As the prayer ended, her eyes sought Judd's, "I'm so sorry," she whispered.

That night at communion, Amy stayed close in sympathetic commiseration. Always uncomfortable being the center of attention, the strain enveloped Sarah—her head ached, her hands shook, she held tears in abeyance. Her head cleared on the buggy ride back to Uncle Levi's with Benji and Nellie. The November night was cold and dark, and it was nice to cuddle in a heavy blanket with Judd.

Nellie and Benji led Sarah and Judd into Missus Hannah's room. "We got it all nice for you, Sarah: the pot, a basin with warm water, and a towel and washcloth." He went to the bed touching the colorful, expertly-stitched quilt, "Nellie made you a quilt. It's our wedding gift. Do you like it?"

"It's beautiful Nellie," Sarah's hands stroked the decorative material.

"It looks warm. Thank you." Judd smiled.

Nellie took Benji's hand as they left the room, giggling like ten-year-olds. "We go now Benjamin so they can roll in hay. Call us if you need something," she said, closing the door.

Sarah sat on the bed, her face in her hands. Judd went to her, "Is something wrong, Sarah?"

"I don't think I can stay in this room tonight. I'm sure Benji and Nellie meant well. The quilt is a treasure. I haven't been in this room since I cleaned it after Missus Hannah died—Benji and Nellie wouldn't know. It was a horrible death; I still have nightmares of blood everywhere. She was so white—in my dreams she is a ghost. I can show you stains I could never get out. Really Judd, I don't think I can sleep here. Let's check if the girls' room is empty." They tip-toed up the stairs, hearing snores from Levi's room. They peeked into the empty girls' room. "Yes, a room for the newlyweds," she smiled.

"I believe I'm going to like married life," Judd teased much later. "Are you doing okay, my sweet?"

"I'm taking to married life just fine. Mrs. Judd Swihart fits me to a tee."

CHAPTER 21

Newly Weds

Awakened from a deep sleep, Sarah could smell the cold late-winter air on Judd as he knelt beside the mattress, his chilled hand bringing goose bumps on her arm.

"Wake up, my sweet. We need to have breakfast and get into the field. I've done the morning chores. I'm surprised the roosters didn't wake you."

"What time is it?" she asked sluggishly.

"A little after six o'clock."

"For crying out loud; what is wrong? It isn't like me to diddle around in bed. I think I'll skip breakfast. My stomach is upset from the venison we had last night. I'll get the horses harnessed. By then it'll be light, and I can start plowing. Do you think your mother has a Willard Antacid Tablet?"

"With all her stomach problems I'm sure she has something."

Sarah was surprised when she vomited on the way to the barn. *Not like me to be sick. That venison didn't sit right.*

Judd soon joined her in the barn. "Hey, how's the little mother?" he folded her in his arms.

"What?" Sarah looked puzzled.

"Mama thinks you have a bun in the oven. She says you have all the signs."

"I do?" Sarah seemed surprised.

"I'm glad," Judd said. "Now people can't say we don't know our way around the barn like they gossip when it takes too long."

"At least I know why I've been feeling so puny and under the weather. Honestly, I was hoping we'd have more time with just the two of us, but we'll take what comes."

"Now I'm glad I talked to Lamar Hoke a few days ago. I want to get a better paying job. We need to get our own things: a wagon, another horse, tools, and some basic home goods so we can get our own place. Lamar has a little log cabin on his truck farm where we can live. He would like us to get there in time to plant spring vegetables."

"I'll miss being with your parents, especially since your mother is failing so much. We can still go to your dad's church, can't we? I'm just learning to know a few people, but then I forget, in a few months my stomach will be too big for me to go out. I wonder if Mr. Hoke will let me work in the field?"

"Maybe for a few months. I expect any free labor would be a bonus to him."

A few weeks later Judd's father drove them to their new home with all their worldly goods: Star, Judd's bed and straw tick mattress and bedding, a dishpan and kitchen utensils, a few tools, and their clothes. Sarah was in high spirits until the jostling wagon prompted several "throw-up" stops. So far, the tiny intruder hiding in her lap was giving her little respite.

The Hoke farm was a perfect place for the newlyweds. They worked together in the fields, in the summer planting and tending vegetables, in the fall, picking apples. They lived in the cabin away from prying eyes, snuggled in their oasis of love. Sarah was in her element, nesting and growing their baby while tending the vegetables. She felt succulent and vigorous, basking in Judd's gentle tenderness.

They were having their nightly walk. "I talked to Papa at church today. John Ricci has a good horse and wagon for sale. Papa thinks we can pay for it with what we've saved. With another horse we can rent land and put in our own crops. We don't have anything now, but I want to make a nice life for you and our baby. It'll take a while, but we can do it."

"You make me happy, Judd." Usually undemonstrative, Sarah threw her arms around him. "Can you believe next month will be our first anniversary? This has been the best year ever."

* * * * *

Some babies choose the worst time to announce their discord from the protective shelter of the womb. A January blizzard froze all movement excepting Judd's sleigh bringing Mrs. Shank, the midwife, to the cabin. Sarah's relief was evident, her tears mingling with drenching perspiration when they blew in on a cold gust of wind. She was afraid; her mind wanted to return to a similar cabin twelve years earlier when her mother died. Sarah also was laboring long, her energy and resilience spent. Mrs. Shank brought castor oil and a take-charge demeanor. Several hours later baby Edith shouldered herself into the world, bellowing her clamorous displeasure.

"You did good, little mother. Birthing shan't come easy for you. Now drink this raspberry tea to get a clamp on that womb." Sarah was whipped, her body felt pulled inside out. She had hardly enough energy to wash her face.

"I've worked till I thought I'd drop during haying and threshing season, but nothing compares to birthing a baby." Sarah reached her arms to gather little Edith to her breast. A glimpse of Heaven opened in her eyes when she saw her newborn—all the beauty in the world molded into this tiny baby. Every good thing in Sarah's life brought her to this moment, a soul-grabbing love not known before. Baby Edith warmed to this swelling emotion, her brown eyes wide and searching.

Life in the little cabin was idyllic as Judd, Sarah, and Edith learned to be a family. Because of the blizzard they were alone, Judd tending to Sarah and helping with the baby. After a few days Judd was able to go to his parents' farm, bringing back Mama Elizabeth who would help during the two weeks Sarah was bedridden. Sarah adored her mother-in-law and treasured their time together but was concerned that the housework and long hours would take a toll on Elizabeth's health.

"You're a good mother, Sarah. It comes naturally to you."

"I learned from Mary Miller when she had Harry. She was the best mother I've known. She believed you won't spoil babies by holding them."

"I'm going to hold this baby every chance I get—because I won't be able much longer."

Sarah's breath caught. Having seen steady deterioration she was afraid what Elizabeth would say. "What do you mean?"

"When I was having so much pain after Christmas, George took me to the doctor. He said I probably won't see another Christmas. I have a tumor that has invaded my innards. There's no more they can do for me. My belly is getting as big as yours was. It's been hard for me not to pity myself, but this is God's will and I trust His ways. Selfishly, I want to be part of my children's families."

Sarah was devastated. It seemed her life was wave after wave of loss—she couldn't get up from one before the next knocked her flat again. Her new-mother body was ill-prepared to grieve with equanimity. She sobbed, clutching Elizabeth who was seated on her bed. "I'm so sorry they can't make you better. I felt like I finally got a mother. Now I'm losing you too. I'm sorry for my children—they'll never have a grandma."

"These last days have been hard. My faith has been sorely tested. But Sarah, I recently heard a new hymn. The words have brought me peace. Elizabeth sang through her tears:

God hath not promised skies always blue,
Flower-strewn pathways all our lives through;
God hath not promised sun without rain,
Joy without sorrow, peace without pain.

But God hath promised strength for the day,
Rest for the labor, light for the way,
Grace for the trials, help from above,
Unfailing kindness, undying love.

The two women enclosed a sleeping baby, their voices thick with tears: "But God hath promised strength for the day, Grace for the trials, help from above."

* * * * *

Judd got his new draft horse. Nell was strong, though easily excited. She would be an excellent work horse with the right guidance and Judd was diligent in his instruction. He enjoyed the training and Nell flourished under his tutelage. He decided to buy and train horses for an extra source of income.

Like Nell, baby Edith was fretful. After nursing her, Sarah gave her a sugar tit, a rag tied around a dollop of sugar. Sarah no sooner started chopping wood when she would hear Edith crying mightily from the cabin. Neither were the nights restful. Every feeding brought pacing and the quest to find relief for an infant with the gripe.

When spring came Sarah swaddled Edith inside her apron top and helped Judd plant vegetables for the Hokes. Her constant movement and the brisk air settled Edith and she slept, finally becoming a sweet natured baby. Sarah also recovered from her difficult confinement. With the spring work she came out of her sleep-deprived fog.

After watching the ads in the Goshen Daily Times, Judd took a leap, agreeing to rent twenty acres near the Michigan state line close to the small village of Bristol. It was cheap because it was remote, ninety-minutes from Goshen. But for Judd it was progress; instead of being a farm hand for the Hokes earning eight dollars weekly he would oversee his own land, keeping half the crop that went to market. In a good year he could make twice as much. They would be on their own without close neighbors. Judd had only visited the property once, confessing to Sarah their new life would be meager. But hardship didn't seem daunting. They were optimistic and robust, on their way to blue skies and flowery paths.

Dusk was settling when Sarah saw the rough-hewn log cabin and small barn in a stand of poplars. There was no lane, and the tall grass came over the sides of the wagon.

"Welcome home, Mrs. Swihart," Judd spread his arms expansively.

"It's a beautiful spot. I didn't know it would be this hilly. I can't wait to fix the cabin." They walked over to appraise the logs which desperately needed repair.

"It will take work." Judd murmured. "You'll need to shingle the roof first then chink the logs. I hope winter holds off a few weeks. See the cleared acres to the south? I'll plant that right away in winter wheat. All the stumps to the east need to come out. I can use Clyde's plow and planter to get the wheat in the ground. We're lucky to have Star and Nell; we'll trade using Clyde's implements and I'll pull his stumps this winter. It will take a few years, but I'll get this land all cleared. We'll get the cabin fixed up and make furniture."

"Caring for Edith will slow me down. I'll have to figure some way to watch her while working outside. At least she still takes long naps," Sarah said.

"Clyde suggested he may sell us some land in a few years," Judd said, already dreaming of being a landowner.

The first task for Sarah was reroofing the cabin. She ran up and down, in and out, trying to satisfy Edith. Too often she hammered to the scathing accusation of her crying baby, the early morning wails giving way to fussy mutterings. After several days, the roof was finished, and Sarah started replacing the mortar on the logs and chimney. This was tedious and time-consuming. Edith was content when Sarah swaddled her to her chest while she worked on the lower logs, though the winter was frigid and icy in this north country.

Judd was making good progress on stump removal; the next summer they would have twice the amount of tillable acreage. They both worked in the forbidding grayness of the freezing weather, the beauty of snow on the evergreens a dulled pleasure. Despite the struggles of that first snowy Indiana winter, the spark of ambition rarely sputtered.

By February Sarah didn't need her mother-in-law to tell her she was with child: the morning waves of nausea left her bilious and green. The sensitivity and little slights she nursed, and the all-day-every-day listlessness that drowned her body and mind left no question. Her hyperactive nerves strained her patience with Edith's need for attention.

Oh, the joy that springtime brought their spirits. The sun, like a soft syrup, melted into their hunched-forward, knotted muscles. Skin-cracked and calloused fingers healed in the fresh warm air. Edith luxuriated in her freedom, toddling away on her chubby baby legs. New birds arrived, industrious in their homemaking, splashing their morning song and shrill gossip across the sky.

Sarah put in an early vegetable garden, her hands competent, the dirt therapeutic. Judd impatiently waited until Clyde finished plowing and planting before he could use the implements to get corn and oats in the ground. Then a rainy spell further delayed planting. He became concerned that he was late for the spring growing season.

For the first time they did something besides work, spending Saturday afternoons in Bristol, enjoying a band concert or browsing at the farm implements. They swam in the nearby creek and had late evening picnics.

The high tenor of summer was crushed when they received a letter summoning them to Elizabeth's deathbed. All work came to a standstill as they prepared for the long trip to Goshen, intent on arriving before she passed to the other side. Sarah was several months into her confinement, a concern the bumpy ride could push her into early labor. The heat was punishing, but especially so for Sarah. She sat on pillows and Judd held Edith so she wouldn't jump on Sarah with her knobby elbows and kicking feet.

Before she died, Elizabeth squeezed Judd's hand, acknowledging his presence. Family and friends mourned this much beloved lady who had suffered so long. Judd couldn't dismiss the feeling that wounded his heart: he shouldn't have moved so far away when his mother was ill. Regrets filled his mind and despair prevented solace. If anything, it was hotter on the trip home. It was an introspective, withered couple that shouldered back to Bristol, cocooned in the relentless heat and dust from the horses. They folded into their misery, buried in a dark place in their minds. After reaching home they put Edith to bed and Sarah walked with Judd through the parched fields, their spirits desolate.

"If we don't get rain soon there'll be no corn crop. We've had no rain for a month."

"Is the drought affecting everyone?"

"I had to wait to borrow implements, then it rained for a week. My crops are about a month behind most. If they do come up now, they'll be scorched. It's a waste of seed money."

"This isn't your fault Judd."

"If we had been closer to Goshen, I could have shared implements with my dad. I couldn't find a place to rent there. I regret not spending time with my mother this year. Sarah, I feel I've been selfish. I was too ambitious."

"I know your regrets concerning your mother. You're too hard on yourself. She encouraged us to move here, Judd. Look what we've accomplished. You've cleared three acres. We have a cabin that's in good repair."

"Thanks to you, Sarah."

"Yes, and I have regrets about neglecting Edith. We're doing the best we can. The drought isn't our fault. We've carried water to the garden, so we'll have food to put in the new root cellar. We have our chickens. I think we still have enough money for seed corn and oats for next spring."

"I know you're trying to be encouraging, but it doesn't look good to me. You've worked so hard and you never complain. If we don't get one good cutting of alfalfa and some corn and oats to feed Star and Nell, I'll have to borrow from my dad. I'd hate that."

"We have to get a heifer calf. With the baby coming this fall, Edith will soon quit nursing."

The drought took on a life, like a dust storm that beat down everything living. The ten acres of corn were burned and shriveled when they poked through the ground. There were only two cuttings of hay, the fall crop puny. The heat made Sarah miserable, her oversized body felt like a furnace. She carried water to keep the garden vegetables alive; she knew they would eat a lot of potatoes this winter. In the heat of the day she and Edith napped under the shade trees, waiting for the rare breeze to ruffle the long grass.

Edith was still asleep one September afternoon when Judd came home from Clyde's farm. He tied the horses and slogged to the blanket as if weights pulled his legs. He lay flat, his hands over his eyes.

"What's wrong?"

"Just when I thought it couldn't get worse, it got worse." He hesitated, dreading to unload his words. "We have to move."

"Oh no, not that." She felt an unknown force grabbing and crushing her future. Their dreams, their future was here in these woods. This dark earth melded with her skin, found home in her hands, was part of her sweat. She felt Judd had just yanked part of her away from her body.

"But the baby is coming in a few weeks," she screeched.

Judd turned away from her on the blanket. "We don't have to move until spring, if that's any consolation," he said bitterly. "I told him there's no possibility you could leave now, and it will be winter after your confinement. I was so mad at Clyde. I don't know if he's being honest with me or if he's taken advantage of me, but I'm sure the fool. He says his well is going dry, so he has to move here. How can he stay there all winter on a bad well?"

Sarah banged her fist on the ground. Her fury startled Edith awake, her wails echoed around the trees. "I chinked those logs and mortared the chimney when it was blustery and freezing—when I should have been inside caring for my baby. You were out until dark all last winter pulling stumps and clearing *his* land." Sarah stomped after Edith who was still fussing.

Judd stood, gathering his arms around the two of them. "Be careful, Sarah, don't hurt yourself. I don't think Clyde expected us to fix it up this nice. He had suggested he would be open to sell to me, but we didn't shake hands on it."

"So, were we supposed to live in a cabin with snow coming in and a cracked chimney with broken mortar? With a *baby*!" Sarah couldn't contain her anger or the certainty they'd been wronged.

"I think I wanted it to work so much I wasn't as cautious as I should've been. If he does have a well problem, he might have put us out anyway. We certainly wouldn't have had it paid off. Today I tried to drive a bargain and I think we'll be all right if we can find a place to live. Come spring he'll give us a fresh heifer, a sow, and four bags each of seed oats and corn. We'll feed Star and Nell from the alfalfa in the shed. I think Clyde tried to be fair with me—he acted very sorry. The drought messed up a lot of people, Sarah."

She settled, somewhat mollified. "You did get a good trade for us, Judd. This caught me by surprise. I think I had planted my feet here; this felt like my home. I'm sad we don't get to stay."

"Me too. I pushed myself to make this a good farm—even though it wasn't mine. I'll always regret that we missed the last year-and-a-half of Mother's life because we were so far north. Now I need to get busy finding something else. I hope we can be nearer to Goshen."

CHAPTER 22

Ligonier

For the rest of her life, when Sarah remembered the three years in Ligonier, she had to strain to summon memories. She only ever knew those years through a mist; her mind never really "latched on" as new baby Esther did in finding her mother's breast. Her head never got above water, she constantly felt she was being pulled under. The broken dreams from Bristol left a bitter taste of defeat. She didn't even think about chinking the logs on the decrepit two-story cabin. In truth, her one searing memory was of brutal, never-ending cold.

This home was even more remote. She felt swallowed in the forest with her babies and the animals. She now had the twice-daily chores of caring for the livestock: she milked Boss, fed the baby calf, slopped the pig, fed chickens, and gathered eggs. Since they had a cow she churned butter and made cottage cheese. She hoped they would never again have to eat potatoes every meal.

Judd awoke in the dark mornings to run his raccoon trap lines, earning ten cents for each pelt. He spent most of each winter day cutting logs, hauling them to mill and pulling out stumps. This was stressful, exacting work. Men or horses were injured or worse when the huge poplar logs accidently moved. Star and Nell were so well trained they sometimes worked without direction. In season Judd planted, tended, and harvested corn, oats, and wheat.

Edith was three, baby Esther had her first birthday, and by fall Sarah was with child again, trapped in the weary and mind-numbing depletion associated with a gravid body.

"You're being a tease, Edith. Give Esther her sock doll. Come, try on your dress. Mama let out the seams; I hope it will get you through the winter. I heard Papa come home. He needs to look at your leg before you go to bed."

"It hurts, Mama."

"I know it does. You're my big girl, Edith. Show Papa how brave you are. He'll make it all better. Bring your torn stockings so I can mend them."

Judd brought in the nippy fall air and hung his jacket and hat on a hook inside the door. "My three favorite ladies waiting up for me. I'm a lucky man," he smiled.

"Papa, I cut my leg bad. Make it better."

"Come here, Edith." Judd unwound the clean rag bandage. "Ouch. That's a nasty slice."

"Will she need to go to the doctor?" asked Sarah.

"I've no money; you can't get blood out of a stone. I'll put a bacon poultice on it overnight. If it looks okay in the morning, I'll stitch it myself. Edith, bring your shoes to me. Mr. Webb in the general store had a little piece of scrap leather that will be big enough to make you a new pair of shoes. If you're a brave girl, tomorrow Papa will make you new shoes."

"New shoes for me! I'll be brave."

* * * * *

For many women subsequent births would get easier, but this was not Sarah's lot. The long pounding labors left lacerations, infected tissue, and scars that ripped again with every delivery. Each new fetus stormed into Sarah's body bringing a tribulation of gut-wrenching vomiting, uneasy foreboding, and mind-numbing weariness; all the while she still nurtured a suckling newborn. Nothing of her body or time belonged solely to her, nothing about her was really thought about, not by her or anyone. It was the ordinary life of a frontier woman. She was the pivotal workhorse, shackled to the grindstone, circling the unending path that smoothed the way for grain to become meal—for the family to be nurtured.

In September Mrs. Kline, the midwife was brought to the cabin. Even she sounded disappointed when announcing the birth of a little girl. After checking baby Ruth, Judd brought cold water to Sarah, then returned to the fall corn husking. A successful farmer must have sons to help with the farm work. Sarah felt the disappointment keenly. She loved her precious little girls; she just wished she had more time to mother them. Did other mothers feel so overwhelmed and perpetually guilty: for leaving them to cry in the pen, for falling asleep the rare moment she held them, for never having enough clean diapers?

The cold winter put down roots. The couple collapsed on their bed in the freezing attic, exhausted from running daybreak till dark. Judd reached for Sarah. "Please not that, Judd. I haven't the energy."

"What's wrong, Sarah?"

Sarah was hesitant to admit her shortcomings. "I always wanted to be a mother, but now that I am, I feel like I'm not doing right by the girls.

Ruth is so sickly. I'm always tired—sometimes I want to sleep rather than care for them. My mind is always in a fog. I get impatient when they do the normal childish things. Sometimes I feel so blue, not like myself. The thought of having another baby so soon—I'm not sure I could handle it."

"I just figured you were content with things, but it *is* hard for you. It's near impossible for you to get away. You're always so sick during your confinement. You don't seem to have your normal spirit since Ruth was born. Remember the picnics we used to take when Edith was a baby? Maybe I should take you and the girls when I go to the feed mill and the store. Would you enjoy the ride?"

"I would love to get out but it's so cold. I don't think it would be good for them, especially Ruth. I don't know what the answer is, but I'm sure it's not another child."

The winter of 1900 was a black time—funeral in its desolation. Whirls of snow blew in through cracks in the cabin and settled for the winter. The girls had chest colds that hung on. Baby Ruth was especially sick, sometimes too weak to nurse. Each day Sarah replaced the onion poultice on their chests, and rubbed camphor oil under their nose. Judd slept in the bed with Edith and Esther using his body to warm them. Sarah slept in the overstuffed chair, holding Ruth upright against her chest, her gurgling breaths punctuating the still night.

Rock bottom came when Sarah recognized the dreaded signs: vomiting, melancholy, and fatigue. Every morning she slogged through chores, unable to be rid of the roiling that clutched her physically and depleted her mentally. Day after day she was shrouded in a constant refrain to God: *Give me the right spirit to accept your will. I trust in Your wisdom. I need Your help in carrying this load.* She was chopping wood when she noticed dark spots in the snow below her. She touched it, recognizing it was blood.

She was alone. Judd wouldn't return until night. She went to the cabin to get rags. She knew the right thing to do: rest and get off her feet to save the seed in her womb. Without knowingly deciding, her body enticed her in another direction. She saddled Nell, galloping her across the frozen land, back and forth at high speed, her body jarring with complaint. Her mind was a void, empty and cold as that field. She knew she should think about what she was doing, but later, not now. When the muscle spasms in her abdomen intensified to contractions, she turned toward home. She returned Nell to the stable, fed and watered her, milked Boss, and finished the evening chores before returning to the cabin and her crying babies. She changed and fed them, cuddled and played their baby games. She went to the bed and delivered a small mass of tissue which she wrapped in a clean towel. She found a sturdy box and held it to her heart as she knelt beside the bed. "God, be close to me your child and hear my prayer. I know I've often done wrong. Today was a great wrong. Understand that I love You and want to do the right thing. I love Judd and Edith and Esther and Ruth; I can't handle more just now. I ask you to receive this...being into the place you have prepared, and keep its spirit in your care. Amen."

* * * * *

For Sarah, one day blurred into the next: no day or week distinct from another. One morning she was surprised to see the apple trees in bloom. She had coasted through winter, almost missing spring. It was time to move outdoors and start the planting season.

"I just heard Baby Carl wake from his nap. Edith, you change his diaper and put him in the wicker carriage and go for a walk. Take Ruth with you."

"I'm playing in the grass. I always have to take care of babies," Edith whined.

"Esther is planting corn. Would you rather do that?"

"No, I don't want to work."

"You're the best baby tender I have, Edith. Get him before he starts to cry. Ruth, you stay right beside Edith on the road. Stay out of the ditch."

"I *like* work," Esther said as she diligently planted seeds in the furrow.

"You're my helper today, Esther, because you can count five kernels of corn for each hole. I never thought you would teach yourself to count at four years old. You're smart, like Papa. Edith is good at making Carl smile. So you each have something you do best. Oops, I'm going to lose my breakfast," Sarah said bending over, gagging wretchedly.

Esther ran to her, hugging her knees, "Mama, you got bug in your tummy?"

"I guess I do—and that isn't all," she said softly. "I'm going to sit a minute while you count the corns in this row." She leaned against a tree, silent tears dropping to her apron.

"Your sick tummy makes your eyes hurt?"

"Yes, my eyes hurt too. I'll catch my breath, then I'm going to teach you to gather eggs. Since Carl is the only boy and he's a tiny baby, I'll teach you the outside chores. You're the only one responsible enough. You won't leave eggs behind or drop an egg."

" I 'fraid of chickens."

"I'll show you how to sneak the egg from the chicken. You'll help me till you're ready to do it alone. You're a big girl, I know you'll do a good job. Maybe you'd better go check Edith and see how she's getting along with Ruth and Carl. Come right back."

"Mama, Mama! Come."

Sarah startled awake, hearing the fear in Esther's voice.

"Carriage in the ditch!"

Sarah's legs couldn't move fast enough. Her chest seemed to contract; she couldn't breathe. Way down the rutted road she saw Edith and Ruth playing in the grass.

Oh, dear God, why did I let them go alone? Please God...don't let anything happen to Judd's boy.

Esther was screaming behind her, sensing the catastrophe. Now Edith and Ruth were frightened and running to meet her. She streaked past Nell and Boss, grazing and now curious, lumbering toward the fence. She could see the buggy upside down at the bottom of the ditch where there was a thin stream of water from recent rain.

Sarah tumbled down the ditch, slinging the buggy and grabbing Carl who was partially submerged. He was immobile, his face gray-blue.

"Oh, my baby...no...no." In a panic she held him upside down and shook him. Water drained off him, running down his face. "Please God...help...make him live." Without thinking she carried him up to the road, put him on his stomach and pressed on his back and sides. A thin stream of water dribbled from his nose and mouth. After long seconds he gagged weakly. Encouraged, she pressed again on his back. Now a weak cough, his gray face breathing life. He turned his head, his eyes vacant. She was crying, bouncing her baby as he gagged and sputtered, then bawled—a heavenly sound.

Sarah sat beside the road, her four babies, Nell and Boss, a watery soup of still-nagging panic, hysteria, mud, and giggling silly relief. She nestled Carl in her arms, her face heavenward, singing in a weepy timorous voice: "Praise God from whom all blessings flow...."

CHAPTER 23

Move to Southwest

Judd burst into the cabin bringing the cold winter. His face was red, his eyes sparkling. "I've a surprise. We're moving back to Goshen. I didn't want to get your hopes up till I was certain." He pulled Sarah from her knees where she was mopping the floor, baby Carl and toddler Ruth crawling and grabbing her skirt.

"Well good riddance to Ligonier. I'll not miss this forlorn place."

"Chester at Lacy's Livery in Goshen is buying both horses I trained this winter. With the money we've saved, it's enough to buy a parcel of land a few miles from Goshen in a village called Southwest. Levi Hoke said we could move back to his cabin; I know it'll be tight with the children. We'll work in his truck patch through the summer while I build our house. We can move to Southwest before you have the baby in the fall."

Sarah reached to stroke Judd's face. "I have such good memories of our time at the Hokes. We were so young and in love. It's hard to believe it's been six years and going on five babies since then. I was so untried, so new at being a wife. Now I'm a broken-down old woman," she held out her roughened hands with dirty, torn fingernails and looked down at her expanding belly.

Judd took Sarah's hands, "I know it'll be hard for you. In two years, you'll have had two babies and moved three times," he mused, shaking his head. "Our life hasn't been what I hoped for you; it's been one struggle after another. I need to find something better than farming and hauling logs."

"You did the best you could. You leave the house at four o'clock in the morning and don't come home till after dark. It's hard times, Judd. Everyone struggles now."

Months later they moved into an unfinished frame house in Southwest. Her labor started when she was working in the field with eight-year-old Esther, already a dependable farmhand. "You'll have to finish sowing wheat, Esther. You know how to do it; be sure to spread it evenly like we did this morning. Show Papa you're a good worker. In the spring we'll see the tall green wheat, and you'll be proud because you did it yourself. I need to lie down. I'm not feeling well. Papa will soon leave to bring Granny Smith."

Judd was on the roof pounding shingles while Sarah labored to the steady crack of the hammer. "I understand why your deliveries have been hard," Granny opined, busy preparing for the birth. Granny was a tiny bird of a woman: her dark eyes darted, her voice was chirpy, and she was even spritely colored with red hair and rosy cheeks. She was a spinster lady who moved from home to home managing deliveries and caring for new babies. "Your body wasn't built to birth babies and all four have left their mark on you. Here, take this Mother Wort. Let's get this baby moving along."

"It won't make the seizing hurt worse, will it? The midwife in Ligonier gave me something that made the pains much worse, and I still labored several hours."

"Hit's preordained, Sarah. Pain in childbirth is the curse of Eve. The Bible says women will bring forth children in sorrow. This is a privilege given us by God. Laboring is soon enough over and forgotten with a new baby in the family."

"This is the problem, Granny; we have too many children. I get so tired and discouraged, I feel like I'm drowning. My body doesn't heal from one baby till another is on the way. I hardly get to know them as a baby before they're second place," Sarah moaned as another contraction pulled her into its grip.

"We're not to question God, Sarah. He'll not give more than you can bear. And don't worry, the self-same hen that scratches for one can scratch for ten."

"But we can't provide for ten children," Sarah hissed in her desperation. "Can't you give me a potion to strike my seed?"

"Hit's not in my place. Now this be no kind of talk when we're about to bring one of God's young'uns into the world. Such talk will beckon the evil eye and bring all sorts of calamnity."

By eventide Esther had sowed the field with wheat, Judd had shingled the roof, and Sarah was sleeping after birthing her fourth girl, baby Clara. Granny Smith had cleaned away all evidence of the birth, and after bathing Clara, handed Edith her new charge. Though Sarah may have been discouraged, eldest daughter Edith, at age nine, was all agog with this living breathing baby doll. She took to mothering without a backward glance. The day was hardly an interruption in the ebb and flow of the family. Defying the two-week bedrest recommendation, within three days Sarah was in the field helping Judd and Esther husk corn.

* * * * *

At four o'clock in the morning Sarah slowly roused from a drugged sleep. *What day is it? Monday. Wash day. The clothes will freeze on the line so I won't have to sprinkle them. But no mind, all days are the same: dull, dull, dull, boomeranged in her head. The bone-chilling cold and darkness infused her body like death. The days presented themselves vaguely, it was like slugging through life with smudged glasses—her brain foggy and gray. Where was the color, the clarity, the sparkle that grabbed hold of you and lifted your spirit?* she wondered.

She shuffled up the steps to the attic. "Esther, Edith." She shook the little girls, their braids and spindly arms entangled. "Time to get up and start milking. Edith, hurry and bring in a bucket of corncobs so I can start the fire."

Already buckling down in earnest, Esther was inching into the freezing clothes she had folded at the foot of the bed. "I noticed the wood bin is almost empty. I'll chop wood before I milk Boss and feed the calves."

"Quit fiddling around. NOW, Edith. Carry in the wood Esther chops and fill the bin. After I feed Clara, I'll come and help with milking and feeding the animals. Hurry. You can't be late for school."

Nursing her babies in the dark morning, before the chaos of the day, was the oasis in Sarah's life. Their sweetness and innocent baby love were the only things that could pierce the dull day-in, day-out litany of gray monotony. The soft baby hand brushing her cheek brought succor and a warm smile.

Sarah's mind was pulled from frying mush by crying babies and loud arguing. "If you were careful, Edith, you wouldn't always make a mess," Esther complained. "Now Carl's hands are all sticky and it's in his hair. You're so careless."

"Well la-de-da. I wouldn't want to be prissy like you. You think you're the cat's meow. I can't believe you saved your piece of chicken from Sunday to take to Mr. Thompson. Teacher's pet—that's you," Edith snipped with derision, grabbing Esther's carefully organized homework and tossing it in the air.

"Stop it Edith. You'll get it all sticky. Mama, make Edith give me my homework."

"Give it to me Edith. Now girls, come hither." She put the dish cloth down, kneeling with an arm around each girl. "It makes me sad to hear you girls argue and spat with each other. You're lucky to have a sister. When I was your age, my sister Juda was sent away. I didn't see her for many years. I missed her terribly. Treat your sister kindly, like you would a friend." She looked Esther, then Edith, full in the eye, "Don't forget what I said about sisters—it's important. Now get your tail in the wind. The miles will go faster if you hustle along."

By the time the girls came home from school the clothes were washed, hung on the clothesline and rolled up damp, filling two bushel baskets. Tomorrow Sarah would bake twelve loaves of bread and while the stove was hot, heat the irons and press the clothes. She was particular about her families' appearance. They were poor, yes, but it didn't cost anything for clothes to be clean and neatly patched. As she was often with child, she seldom left home, so *her* clothes didn't matter but she wanted the girls' school dress and apron to be neat and their stockings patched. Now they were part of a community; no one would accuse *her* family of slovenly appearance.

Before chore time Sarah needed to muck out the stable. As the day had warmed, the girls were grazing the cows on the road. Her heart warmed as she heard the medley of their voices cheerfully singing:

> She'll be comin' around the mountain when she comes,
> She'll be comin' around the mountain when she comes,
> She'll be comin' around the mountain,
> She'll be comin'around the mountain,
> She'll be comin' around the mountain when she comes.

Her heart warmed as she remembered her talk that morning to Edith and Esther. Maybe they had taken her lesson to heart. Her two oldest had different temperaments and too often they provoked each other.

> Eeny, meeny, miny, moe.
> Catch a monkey by his toe.
> If he hollars let him go.
> Eeny, meeny, miny, moe.

As she looked out the window to watch her girls hand-clapping the little ditty, she saw Judd's wagon pull in the drive and stop midway. "Whoa!" he yelled as he jumped off the wagon. Looking out the window she saw him, red-faced and mad-as-a-hatter, stomping toward the unsuspecting girls. His wrath was frightening. "I just made that gate," he yelled. "It's not a toy to have the three of you hanging all over it and pushing it around. You're not to play on it," he bellowed, grabbing Esther who screeched like a kicked cat, her eyes wild with fear. He spied a discarded picket fence stake and spanked her with all his strength, dropped her and grabbed Edith, who defiantly was ramrod straight and had no tears. The sweet sounds of singing had given way to sobs and wailing. His anger not spent, he lifted little Ruth who was beyond terrified and spanked her equally as hard. "I will teach you a lesson you won't forget: gates are not to play on." He left the crying girls clutching each other as he led the horses to the shed.

Sarah resumed shoveling manure. As much as she wanted, it wouldn't do for her to attend to the girls. She felt responsible for their anguish. *Should I have known they shouldn't be on the gate? Could three little girls damage a gate?*

It was a silent, somber household that night as everyone gave Judd wide birth, afraid of another lashing. While he was in the barn, Sarah put Jimson Leaf Salve on their bruises, swells, and scrapes, her heart broken by the grievous battering. She took each of the girls in her lap in the rocker while she sang to them:

I've got love like an ocean
I've got love like an ocean
I've got love like an ocean in my heart.

She put them to bed with a tender kiss, patting them until they were asleep.

CHAPTER 24

Good Neighbors

Sarah saw light at the end of the tunnel for the first time in years. It was brilliantly hued with purpose, optimism, and independence. After moving to Southwest, Sarah had her Saturday morning route into Goshen, selling fresh eggs, butter, milk, and dressed chickens. She added extra-heavy cream to her cottage cheese, and always sold out. This gave her money for groceries, time to visit with customers, and linger at shop windows. Daylight for Sarah was also friendship with near neighbors, Amos and Elsie Martin who lived on the next farm, pie suppers, and other activities at the Yellow Creek Church of the Brethren. Sarah had been welcomed into the Sister's Aid Society—church women who met monthly to sew for missions and share a potluck dinner.

Judd was also establishing himself. He subscribed to the Goshen Weekly Times and on occasion went to downtown Goshen on Saturday nights to hobnob with farmers and businessmen. He was invited to join men who went to South Bend to hear William Jennings Bryan speak before the fall election.

"Sarah, I've never seen such a crowd of people. There was a band and hijinks of all kinds. Bryan has such a silver tongue. You won't believe this, but I could almost be convinced to vote with the Democrats."

At threshing time, he joined neighbors to hire a farmer with a threshing machine. They ate meals together and became friends. Judd was respected for his willingness to assist neighbors with projects. It was common knowledge that no one knew horses as well as Judd Swihart. He could spend thirty minutes with a horse and know if it had a sound body, had been injured or abused, was lazy or excitable, or would work well in a team. What might have been a vocation for him was information freely given.

The community recognized the Swiharts struggled to provide for their large family, but saw their resourcefulness in making the most of their meager goods. Sarah's cooking was plain, mostly what they grew. They ate potatoes cooked with peelings and fried in lard, mush, and white beans. She used spices, butter, and cream to advantage, and her dishes at potluck dinners always came home empty.

"My stomach is upset. I'm afraid I'm going to puke," Esther coughed and held her stomach as she trudged to the breakfast table. "I feel too bad to go to school today." The fact that she was sick on butchering day, the most fun day of the year, was not lost on Sarah. "You were fine this morning when you were milking. If you're so sick you can't go to school, you need to stay in the attic," she said, thinking to dissuade her. "We don't want you to make the neighbors sick."

Esther, quite pleased with herself, thought this a fair trade. She sidled to the attic window watching the activity below: Amos and Elsie Martin arriving with their squealing pig, the two pigs bled out, then the carcasses suspended on tripods while Judd and Amos skinned them and removed the entrails. A fire was made under a barrel of boiling water where the hide simmered, loosening the hair. Sarah and Elsie scraped off the hair and carefully cleaned the intestines. It was a cold winter day and Esther, wrapped in a quilt, saw the warm vapor breaths puffing in the cold air as the two couples visited and laughed while they worked. Smoke from the fire and steam from boiling water mingled and dissipated into the morning air as the men cut away layers of fat from the hide, cooking it down to lard in a big black kettle.

Around noontime Esther's mouth drooled when the pungent smell of frying pork and potatoes wafted up to her perch in the attic. *I hope Mama doesn't forget I'm here,* she thought. When a child had dyspepsia Mama always gave them bread soup, but Esther was really hoping for fresh pork and potatoes.

Mama came to the stairs, calling to the attic, "How is your bilious stomach, Esther? Do you feel like eating dinner? Should I make you some bread soup?"

"Yes, Mama. I feel much better. I think I could eat some fresh pork and potatoes if there's some left."

"What a speedy recovery you've had," she remarked with a smile. Shortly Mama returned to the attic handing Esther her lunch. "Papa says it's bread soup for you today."

"Thank you, Mama. Bread soup will be fine." Esther's eyes lit up when she saw Mama had added several cracklins, pieces of crispy fat, that she could chew on all afternoon.

After dinner, Judd ground the meat scraps and added spices to make sausage. The ladies stuffed the intestine casings and coiled the sausage into crocks, covering it with lard. Stored in the potato cellar it would be preserved until summer.

They made a cure of brown sugar, salt, and spices, which was rubbed on the hams and shoulder meat then put into a potato sack to protect from the flies. These they hung in a smokehouse over a slow fire. Every part of the hog was used: the head, backbone and feet were used for gelatin and minerals. Lard, stored in five-gallon tins, would be the shortening used to fry and bake. Sarah used the birthday present Judd had given her—a case of Ball Mason Jars. This new method of food preservation involved putting the pork in glass jars and boiling them in a water bath until they were vacuum sealed.

Butchering day brought satisfaction and fulfillment to Judd and Sarah. As difficult and meager was their life, they knew if they had meat preserved and grew a summer garden they could feed their growing family.

* * * * *

Carl was not yet two years old the winter the children got measles. Edith and Esther, exposed at school, had some itching and fever but were better after a few days. Clara the baby was next, and Sarah had been up several nights with her. This was her third night with Carl and her reserves of energy were depleted. She had just fallen asleep in the rocking chair when his simpering, pitiful cry startled her awake. "Carl, hush!" She lifted him off her shoulder and held him aloft, shaking him. "Just hush for once," her voice was raspy with wrath. His fevered body could only answer with a mewling whimper.

"What is wrong with me?" Her voice shook as she guiltily jumped up from the rocker to pace the floor, jiggling the baby. How could she get angry with a helpless, sick baby? The gray melancholy overwhelmed her in that dark early morning, sucking her into a black hole which held her captive. A sudden rush of nausea erupted from her gut as she charged forward to reach the bucket behind the stove. The retching brought tears as she understood her condition. It explained why her energy was depleted and her spirit so sore. Another baby. So soon. How would she manage? Her spirits sank as she realized that by summer she could no longer go out—too hot for a concealing coat. She would have to give up her Saturday deliveries to Goshen and the earnings from that. Her small slice of freedom was so fragile.

Weeks later Sarah was awakened during the night by pounding at the door. "Judd, Judd. Wake up. Someone is at the door."

Judd opened the door to find Elsie, their neighbor, collapsed on the doorstep. Her torn clothes were splotched and sticky with blood from a cut on her eyebrow. Her eye was bruised and swollen, her nose was bleeding—it appeared to be broken. Her long hair, usually styled in a neat bun, was straggly and blood soaked.

Sarah rushed forward helping Elsie to a chair. "My Goodness. What happened to you?" she knelt, holding her neighbor in her arms.

Now in a safe place, Elsie's pent-up anxieties burst in low agonized moans as she rocked forward, holding her hands to her face.

Judd handed her a wet cloth, "How did you get hurt, Elsie?"

Her hands fluttered about as she realized the indecency of her ripped dress and dabbed at dripping blood. Normally reticent, she was clearly embarrassed. "I'm sorry," she whispered as not to wake the children. "I'm sorry to get you involved. Everything is such a mess," she shuddered. "What will I do? It's Amos. He's so upset with me. I'm afraid of him. He's lost his senses." Sarah and Judd startled, searching the other's eyes to understand.

"It's hard to believe this of him, Elsie. He's a good church member. He's my friend," Judd said, shaking his head in disbelief.

"He seems so...reasonable, so in control—even gentle," Sarah voiced disbelief as she wrapped Elsie in a blanket and cleansed her wounds.

"He *is* reasonable until he loses his temper. Then he becomes a different person. This is why I've never told anyone." Fresh sobs convulsed her body, "No one will ever believe me."

"I *do* believe you," Sarah interrupted. "These injuries didn't just happen. I'm glad you came to us."

"I believe you as well," Judd nodded. "But the man who did this isn't the Amos I know. It's hard for me to imagine. In a minute we'll get you cleaned up and I'll stitch your eye. Start at the beginning, Elsie. Tell us what brought this on. Maybe we can help you."

"It started six years ago when my mother died. In her will she left our fifty-acre family farm in my name only. Amos wants the farm. It drives him wild that he works every day on land that isn't his. I've wondered if he married me to get the farm. According to him, women have no business owning property. He sees no point—I'm never going to work the land. For years he has tried every way to get me to retitle it to him."

Judd nodded, his face serious, "I see the problem."

"But Judd," Elsie winced as she rose from her chair. "It's *my* family farm. It's where I grew up. Why can't it belong to me?" she questioned, naked pleading in her brown eyes.

"It can, Elsie. Amos must not know about recent changes in property laws. It used to be when a woman married, any property she had was forfeited to her husband. A few years ago the Indiana law was changed allowing women to own property. It seems your mother understood that when she wrote her will."

"He just can't get past it. He's getting more perverse and hateful. Tonight, he accused me of infidelity." Fresh tears flowed. Elsie was a diminutive, pretty lady with a timid and gentle soul. To bare this private misery went deeply against her nature. "Why would he say that? I'm afraid of what he might do to me to get the farm. He beat me bad tonight with the fireplace poker. He pulled me around the house by my hair then threw me out the door in the snow. I didn't know what to do but come here."

"What he did to you was wrong. The Bible teaches that a father shouldn't spare the rod in teaching his children, but a man is supposed to love his wife as God loved the church," Judd remarked thoughtfully. He gathered needle and thread, using vinegar to cleanse the wound. I'll do my best here, but I reckon you'll have a scar. I'll take you to the courthouse tomorrow morning so you can check the title and get advice about the law."

Sarah held the lantern as Judd made small, perfect stitches. Sweat droplets made paths down Elsie's face as she absorbed the pain without making a sound. "There must be some answer to this that satisfies both of you. Leastways you can't continue getting this ill treatment," Judd observed, applying a potash and vinegar plaster over her wound.

Elsie slumped, discouraged and hopeless. "I just want to be sure the farm stays in my family and goes to my sons," she said softly. "My grandfather made a trade with the Potawatomi Indians to get this land. My father built our home and buildings from our own lumber. I guess I'm being selfish," she said bleakly. "I know I'll have to go home and make things right."

* * * * *

"Mamma, take your coat off. It's spring, you'll get hot." Esther was in hearty spirits, thrilled to accompany Sarah on her Saturday delivery route. Judd insisted that, in her condition, Sarah shouldn't harness and drive the mules. Esther was more adept in handling them.

"If I get hot I'll take my coat off. I'm glad you're helping me today, Esther. Yonder comes the interurban. Maybe you should pull over. You don't want the mules to shy. Oh, look at that pretty dress in the Chicago Fair Shop."

"Oh, it's beautiful," Esther's eyes widened. "I love the bright pink. Mama, you would look good with those lacy ruffles."

Sarah's spirited laughter tinkled like musical chimes as she imagined herself in such finery. "I don't think your father would agree with you," she smiled, her jocular mood undeterred by her own shabby attire. "We have one more delivery before we go to Bradford's Grocery." Suddenly Sarah leaned forward gripped by a sharp pain in her abdomen. "I changed my mind; we need to turn around and get home right now." She reached to take the lines, "Hurry Esther. Go like greased lightening."

"But Mama, we didn't get groceries." Esther was exasperated that her outing was cut short.

"I'm sick, Esther. My stomach hurts. Smack the mules." Sarah's lips pursed in a thin line as she clutched her abdomen. Blood gushed from between her legs soaking into her shoes and across the wagon floor.

"Mama, it's blood. You're bleeding." Esther's panicky voice screeched as she beat on the mules, rushing them home. Her eyes darted swiftly between guiding the mules and the blood pooling on the wood floor and staining Sarah's dress. "What is happening? Are you going to die?" Her eyes were wild as the wagon flew, weaving, bouncing, and nearly tipping.

Sarah's calm demeanor belied the emergency. "No Esther, I'm not going to die. Something in my stomach needs to come out. It's like when you have the runs and can't control it. That's what I have, only its blood. When we get home, I'll clean up and everything will be fine. I hope we don't have to get Granny Smith. You're doing a good job, Esther. Thank goodness you were with me today. I see the house ahead. We're almost home."

CHAPTER 25

Clayton Farm

This time Sarah cried. Her crooning sobs were confined to a rare solitary moment while milking in the stable. To leave the Southwest home that Judd built for them only two years earlier seemed catastrophic. Words played in her mind: *It's a sin and a shame. Is there no end to the misfortune that plagues us? Why is God testing us with such cruelty? There must be a way through this. Give me faith in Your leading, God.* She felt too downtrodden to bolster Judd and the children who were foul-tempered and rancorous in their disappointment. They would lose everything. Again. Their acreage was insufficient to make enough money farming, and Judd didn't make enough hauling logs to keep up the bank payments. The girls would have to leave school, and the family would leave behind friends in the church and community. Sarah could no longer have her weekly delivery route as they were moving far from Goshen—to the two-hundred-acre Clayton farm south of New Paris. She would be cloistered again, her life confined to children, the farm, and her garden. Once more she would be caught in an eddy of demands, lonesome in a vortex of chaos. Judd had been hired by Egbert Sanders to haul logs, but as the lumber yard was several miles from their new home, she and the children would rarely see him. Leastways his income would be steady at $1.25 a day. They were moving in the middle of a smallpox epidemic. At Southwest, their family had escaped the frightful pox, but Sarah was fearful of sending the girls to a new school. They would leave early in the morning. It was bitter cold. The roads were snow-clogged and icy so the move would take all day.

"Mama, Esther won't give me her crate to pack in the wagon. You told me to pack everything," Edith screamed, chasing Esther who refused to relinquish her precious "things".

"You're not getting my crate. You're not careful with things. Your stuff will get lost or broken, you just see," Esther sniveled haughtily, rushing from Edith.

"Quit yammering. You girls are a sore trial," Sarah chided, her patience worn thin. "With everything I have to deal with, why can't you two get along?"

"I'm sorry, Mama, but Papa said I could ride on the hay wagon tomorrow. I'm going to take my valuables with me."

"Like a book from your first-grade teacher or the beat-up stocking doll you had when you were a baby. Some treasures," Edith taunted.

"You two are filled with devilment today. Each of you finish your jobs and don't say a word to each other. Edith, leave Esther's crate alone." Sarah lamented the discontent between Edith and Esther, now ten and nine years old. Edith was poorly motivated but wily with a mincing tongue. Because Judd gave Esther so much responsibility, she was old beyond her years, steadfast, and a pleaser. She was nimble-witted but too seasoned with piety for a child. It saddened Sarah that her oldest daughters were so often at odds.

The Clayton farmhouse was big, cold, and drafty. The only warmth was around the wood stove, prompting Sarah to awaken early to start a fire so the children would have a warm place to dress before braving their chores in the winter cold. The upstairs was freezing in the winter with hoarfrost on the windows and water frozen on the sills where snow dusted in.

The Clayton farm had an endless supply of lumber. When Sarah and the children finished chores there was always wood to chop. Even little Ruth and Clara stacked wood. Judd sold it at the lumber yard for six dollars a cord.

The girls got started in the Kime School. As before, Edith was a lackadaisical student while Esther strove for perfection. She liked the regimen and orderliness of learning. In the evenings she pretend-played being a teacher to Edith and Ruth though neither was interested in her tutelage. She was good at spelling and usually won the school spelling bee.

One evening she came home excited. "Mama, Mr. Markle says the winner of our school spelling bee will go to Goshen to be in the county contest. I want to win. Will you help me practice?"

"Of course. Edith, why don't you practice with us?"

"I'm no good at spelling. I don't like to get in front of everybody. Let Esther be the smarty pants."

Mr. Markle gave Esther spelling books, and every night they sat by the kerosene lamp, Sarah repeating words. A few weeks later, Esther came home happy as a possum: she would represent Kime School in the county contest. The next day Mr. Markle came to their house to talk with Sarah. In two weeks, he would take Esther on the interurban to Goshen High

School where she would compete. He brought a silver ribbon sash with Kime School written on it for Esther to drape over her shoulder. She could hardly contain her excitement as she practiced words while wearing her sash. Sarah bought a pretty feed sack and stitched her a new dress—her first dress that wasn't a hand-me-down.

On Thursday before the spelling bee Judd came home just before bedtime. Esther was wearing her new dress with the sash pinned to the shoulder.

"What's all the foolishment here?" he asked, eyeing Esther.

"I'm going to Goshen on the interurban with Mr. Markle to be in the county spelling bee," Esther pirouetted to show off her new dress.

"Is Edith going too?" Judd asked.

"No, she doesn't like spelling bees," Esther twirled, no inkling of impending trouble.

"And I suppose you're going to pay for this excursion, are you?"

"It's only eleven cents." Esther's eyes clouded as she sensed Papa's disapproval.

"Listen to you, only eleven cents. That's eleven cents more than I have for you to hightail it to Goshen on an outing the other children can't enjoy."

"Judd, Mr. Markle is depending on her. No one will be there from Kime School if Esther doesn't go," Sarah beseeched. "She has studied two weeks to get ready."

Judd's brow darkened and his jaw clenched as he looked dispassionately at Sarah, "You of all people know we don't have money to waste."

"Please Papa, I have to go. I have a sash and a new dress," she howled, naked pleading in her teary eyes. "Pl-e-a s-e Papa," she begged.

"Esther don't be a sorehead. You're not going, so get over it. I've no truck for this ado over nothing. Now where's my supper?"

Sarah's voice was thick with tears; Judd's decision clawed at her heart. "This isn't ado over nothing. This is important to Esther. Your supper is on the stove. Esther, come upstairs and get ready for bed."

Sarah sat on the girls' bed, cradling Esther's head in her lap. Even Edith and Ruth were tearful and sad. "Stop your tears, Esther. They do you no good." She ran her fingers through Esther's hair. "I know this is hard for you. I'm very proud of you; you learned lots of new words. You deserved to go—I'm sorry you can't. You girls are growing up. You'll have many sore disappointments, even worse than this. When I was little and bad things happened, my mama said, 'Pick yourself up. Lift your chin and be strong'. That is the lesson to learn from this."

"I wanted to go so bad, Mama. Why won't Papa let me go?" Esther's voice was plaintive, still wretched in her disappointment.

"He doesn't understand little girls, I guess." Sarah tendered. "Show him your mettle now. Show him what you're made of."

"That's what I wanted to do," Esther said softly.

* * * * *

After two years the family moved again, though not far away. The Leer farm was also south of Goshen, in what Edith called "the boondocks".

Mrs. Price, the midwife in the area, was the first visitor when she came to deliver Floyd, their sixth child and second son. She stayed for a few days until Sarah was on her feet. Six-year-old Clara was enamored of their guest and followed the midwife as she packed her belongings to return home.

"Floyd sure is a nice baby. I'd like to take him home with me," she teased Clara. Judd arrived to carry Mrs. Price's grip, assisting her to the wagon.

"Wait, wait!" yelled Clara, running out of the house with baby Floyd wrapped in her coat. "You can have our baby, Mrs. Price," she called, handing Floyd up to her. "You want a baby and we have too many—we don't need this one. You can keep him warm in my coat."

Judd and Mrs. Price guffawed, "You can't give away our baby, Clara. Let's take him back in the house," Judd chuckled. "Come with me."

"I think Mama is sad, Papa. Maybe she doesn't want a baby."

"Sure, Mama wants our baby. She gets tired sometimes. You'll have to help Mama," Judd said, placing the baby in the cradle. "Here now, you rock the cradle while I take Mrs. Price home."

To bring in extra money Judd agreed to drive the school hack. It was a large wagon with benches along the sides. A metal frame was covered with black oilcloth except for a door and window near the front. A small wood-burning stove put out heat. As Judd hauled logs, it often fell to Sarah to run the twice daily school route. For hauling he needed the best horses, leaving Sarah with the mule and a young horse, an untried team. On a bitter January evening, Sarah was standing at the front of the hack trying to protect her face from the wind and snow when Sam, the young horse became spooked, rearing wildly into a gallop. The mule stumbled, then both ran out of control.

"Mama," Esther staggered forward, grabbing the reins of the mule while Sarah pulled on Sam.

"S-T-O-P! H-E-L-P! O-U-C-H!" Wild screams from the children filled the quiet country air as they were thrown like matchsticks, banging around the wagon. The door of the stove broke open, spilling out the fire, coals chasing the flopping children. The noises of the neighing and snorting horses caught up with the grinding and screeching hack as it flip-flopped back and forth, tipping to one side, then the other. Neither Sarah nor Esther was strong enough to stop the runaway horses.

"I have to get to the horses," Sarah screamed. "Keep pulling both reins as hard as you can."

"No Mama, you'll fall. They'll trample you." Sarah stumbled to the door, grasping the wagon, then staggered out onto the doubletree that connected the wagon to the horses. One misstep and both she and the children would be dragged and tossed. She grabbed both reins, running and staggering between the two flying horses. "Whoa! Whoa! Sam. Whoa!" trying to bring calm to the panicked horses. When she thought she could no longer hold on, she sensed the horses slowing, settling, and then stopping. Thank God!

Esther held the horses while Sarah collected the hysterical children as they rushed off the hack, needing to be away from the terrifying mayhem. She wiped their tears, only with effort controlling her own. She soothed and rocked them. With her usual answer to every crisis she started to sing. Soon the sweet lilt of a childish chorus echoed across the snow:

Whisper a prayer in the morning.
Whisper a prayer at noon.
Whisper a prayer in the evening.
To keep your heart in tune.

God answers prayer in the morning.
God answers prayer at noon.
God answers prayer in the evening.
To keep your heart in tune.

CHAPTER 26

Leer Farm-1909

In a rare moment of togetherness, Sarah and Judd leaned on the fence looking over the farmland they were working. "I 'spect Esther won't finish that field till God comes home," complained Judd. "I vow, she's slower than molasses."

"But look at the perfect swath she plows. You never need to redo her work. You forget she's only thirteen," reminded Sarah.

"I reckon she's as good as any boy would be. It's been a good spring—in a few days the crops should be in. Will you look at that orchard? We'll have a bumper apple crop. The thought of your apple butter makes my mouth water. It won't be long we'll be eating from your garden. Sarah, you have a prettier garden than anyone I know."

"I plant and God nurtures. I must say, that garden looks like the pictures in the seed catalogue," Sarah couldn't help a bit of smugness. "We'll need more canning jars the next time you go to the Waterford Feed Mill."

"This morning I looked behind the barn at the blackberries. By next week you can have the little ones pick berries before the birds get them. I need to get the fixin's for wine, too. This is a shabby old house, but we sure have used the basement potato cellar. The ice I harvested from the creek last winter is still frozen solid. When the garden comes in we'll have plenty of storage space."

"It's nice to have you home more, Judd. My spirits revive when the sun is shining and I know you are close by in the field. Those long winter days when you were gone logging seemed to last forever."

Judd clasped her shoulder, "I like being home too, but I don't think I'm meant to be a farmer. I hate the uncertainty of it: we're always getting tossed off a farm 'cause of either drought or too much rain; the bank takes over the farm; or the owner wants to move back on the farm; it's always something. I need to find a job with more stability."

"You will, Judd. Something will work out for us."

"I'm capable of better than this. I'm fed up working so hard with nothing to show for it." He pulled the time piece out of his overalls, "It's time Esther started milking. I best relieve her."

A few days later, the family rushed through a late supper, as talk wasn't permitted during a meal. They were eager to hear Papa and Carl talk about their trip to Goshen. Such a trip was the greatest treat ever, only happening once or twice a year. Of course, nine-year-old Carl, being the boy, was chosen to go with Judd. He had carried in a parcel, and the girls were on tenterhooks, unaccustomed to such excitement. Judd brought out his cobbler tools and a large piece of leather to repair Esther's shoes, while Sarah opened her sewing box.

"We saw a horseless carriage," squealed Carl. "It went fast and was all dusty. The driver wore goggles and a cloth over his face," Carl was cocky, being first to see this wonder.

"What are goggles?" asked Clara.

"They looked like eyeglasses that fitted over his eyes—to keep dust out of his eyes."

"Can you believe, in the few years we've been in the country, there are over one hundred cars in Goshen? Lots of people consider them a menace. They scare the horses. Sometimes they go off like a gun," Judd exclaimed. "I bought us a newspaper, Sarah."

Everyone was jostling and talking at once. "I want to read the paper too," Esther begged. "Let's open the package," Edith said enthusiastically. "I want to open it," Clara ran to get scissors. Carl plopped down the package, teetering restlessly from one foot to another in his anticipation. "I carried it in, but I don't know what it is either," Carl admitted.

Judd opened the package revealing a Sears Roebuck catalogue. "It's just a book," Clara said disappointedly.

"Look at all the hats." Esther thumbed the pages.

"Girls, this isn't a book to read. There's a big store that sells everything in this catalogue. We can't buy anything; we don't have money to pay for it. See here, you have to pay $1.50 to buy that hat. But we can keep the book and look at the pictures when our work is done."

The children grabbed the book and lay on the floor around it. "Careful, we don't want to tear it. Let's take turns turning the pages," Edith said.

"I only spent ten cents, truly Sarah. John at the mill told me I could go to the post office and get a catalogue. I knew my girls would love it."

Esther jumped from the circle and in a rare display of affection, hugged Judd. "Thank you, Papa. We love the book you got us," then she quickly scrambled to her place on the floor.

Sarah placed her hand over Judd's, "I'm glad you got it—such a treat for the children. It will occupy them for months. I wonder when I'll get a chance to see it," she laughed.

"I promise, someday we'll be able to order things for them. That will be a happy day for me. I want to move back to Goshen, Sarah. So much has changed there. Many homes have electric lights. They're putting bricks on Main Street. There's a new place for families to visit called Blosser's Park. It's by the dam. We could go for picnics. Look at this advertisement in the paper: they're bringing a famous preacher, Billy Sunday, to speak at the Jefferson Theater. They call him an evangelist. Wouldn't we love to go to something like that? I can just see you all gussied up pretty," his eyes fondly teasing her. "Goshen is up and coming. I want us to be part of the progress. This life is too countrified for both of us."

"It will happen, don't doubt it. I can feel it in my bones," she smiled.

* * * * *

For the past months, Sarah had known the stony feel of a freezing desultory day in a flock of days that never flew away. The gloom nested in her spirit. As usual it was accompanied by lethargy, a sick stomach, and an expanding belly. It was different this time—something wrong from the beginning.

Sarah lay in her bed in the middle of the day—unheard of for her. Certainly, with seven previous confinements, she was complicit with the pain of childbirth, but this pain was beyond the pale. She should have summoned Mrs. Price, but Judd had been gone all day. The children were all in school except for Floyd who toddled around the bed, off-put and shying from her restless moaning. She gritted her teeth, shielding her abdomen, moaning and caving in to the agony. She knew this baby was too early. Not fearful by nature, she was surprised she felt afraid and alone. She had been cramping and oozing blood all day. The pain in her back was unremitting; her mind was overwrought, blurring her concentration, lacking lucidity. *Dear God, don't let me die like this. I can't leave my children: Edith...Esther...Ruth...Carl...Clara...baby Floyd...my two buried babies with no name. Help me, God...take away this pain....You know my heart, God...sometimes they feel like more than I can handle...let me live, God. I will be better.*

The baby was coming. In her misery Sarah felt the tiny head. *Help me, God.* She had to push—three pushes. The baby slid onto the towel.

"Oh, my sweet boy. Papa will be happy...but you're too little...Oh baby. Oh my baby... breathe... breathe... please God." Tears fell onto the blue motionless infant. In seconds Sarah knew the baby was too small to live. She swaddled him, holding him close to her heart, crooning: "my baby, my baby."

Her pain was still intense, her groin determined to push, and push again. "What is happening?" Her muddled mind realized another baby was coming.... "We have two baby boys." The second baby opened his eyes, seeming to study her intently.... His tiny chest throbbed.... He did not breathe. Sarah grasped the baby, holding him by his feet, tapping his back. "Breathe.... Breathe, baby.... God, make him breathe."

Nothing.... She slumped forward, laying the babies between her legs in the bloody detritus of birth. Sarah's busy fingers frantically examined each baby again, then again: sweet little button noses that would never smell fresh clover; little heart-shaped mouths that couldn't cry or ever give her a smeary kiss; wispy tufts of dark hair her fingers would never tousle; translucent skin that would never see the sun; twenty little fingers that would never milk a cow. These two precious lives extinguished before their first breath—before feeling a mother's touch.

Her bloody hands covered her tear-filled eyes. Her wretched sobs joined her frightened toddler's screams as she rocked her lifeless babies. "Why, God? Are you punishing me because I don't love my children enough? Am I so lacking that you had to destroy their whole future? So bad that they will never be Judd's twins, but only a dream and a memory for us?"

An ocean wave of sadness swallowed her as she kissed and wrapped her infants. Some part of her died, oozed through her fingers to settle with the babies. She felt like a candle flame, so insubstantial and empty was her essence. She wiped her eyes, straightened her shoulders, lifted her chin.

"Come to Mama, Floyd. Oh my sweet love. Now, now, it's alright. Don't cry, love. Would you like some jelly bread? Mama will feed you and put you down. I wonder if a nap will erase your bad memories."

By evening when the children came home, Sarah was resting in the rocker with Floyd. It was a day as any day. After supper, Esther was inquisitive as Sarah hurried the children to bed. "Are you okay, Mama? You seem quiet today."

"It's been a long day. I'm ready to rest. Clara's hair is all snarly. Will you brush it before bedtime?"

"Her hair is snarly because it has too many curls. I'll give you a big hug; that will make you feel better. Be sure to tell Papa I said good night. Gadzooks Mama, you're hugging me too hard. Night, night. Sleep tight, Mama."

Sarah served warmed potatoes and sauerkraut. "Supper is light tonight," she said, joining Judd at the table. "Did you sell any wood today?"

"Three racks. At this rate, I'll be able to make a trip to the feed mill next week. As long as this cold weather holds out."

"I need to talk to you, Judd." With a quick glance he noticed her tears. He jumped up, reaching for her. "What's wrong? You never cry."

She impatiently brushed at her tears, "I'm sorry. With all my heart, I'm sorry." She took his hand and led him into their bedroom. She had bathed the babies and dressed them in the homemade kimonos handed down from the children. They lay on a blanket on the bed—two tiny babies.

Judd ran forward, reaching out before stopping. He looked at Sarah with puzzlement, her arms holding herself as if cold, her tears falling softly. He sat on the bed, pulling Sarah into his lap. He held her head to his shoulder, his fingers stroking her hair, loosened for bed—this loving gesture more eloquent than words. After several minutes, he asked with a quiet husky voice, "Are you alright, Sarah?"

"They are perfect little boys, Judd. Just too little. They never took a breath."

Judd picked up one of the babies, handing him to Sarah, then held the other baby, touching and learning his little body. "So tiny. Yet so perfect." He brought little fingers to his lips. "Wouldn't we have enjoyed twins, Sarah?"

"Aren't they beautiful boys? They look like your mother. I'm so sorry."

"But Sarah, this is God's plan. We weren't meant to keep them. I'm sorry you had to go through this alone. I can't imagine how hard that was. You're a brave lady." He reached to stroke her cheek. "I'm just glad God saw fit to spare you. I would have loved to keep our twins, but Sarah, I couldn't live without you. Let's come to bed, now. We can have them for one night."

CHAPTER 27

Goshen Home, New Job

Esther left home early for the three-mile walk to the new West Goshen Elementary School. On this first day she wanted to arrive before her four rowdy and uncouth siblings. She knew their family would be viewed as unschooled country bumpkins and she wanted to present herself as a more scholarly, serious student.

"Why are you in such a hurry?" Carl called, catching up with her. "Settle down, Esther."

"Aren't *you* nervous about starting in the new school? Everything in Goshen is strange and noisy and fast. I feel dumb. Aren't you afraid kids will make fun of you?"

"I don't give a whoop for school, so I'm not bothered. I'm glad we moved back here close to town, though. I can tell Mom and Pop like it better. Mom likes having her delivery business again."

Esther needn't have worried. At thirteen the characteristics that would serve her in womanhood were already budding. As second oldest child and the workhorse of the family, she had been given significant responsibility, so she was dependable and disciplined. Just as rigorous was her moral compass: "I just want to do what is right". These scruples she adhered to because she wanted to please her mother. One might expect her peers would be off-put by such lofty maturity. She was saved by being a social butterfly, and at this young age had realized that her coy modest smile and a slight flutter of her skirt enticed beaus as bees to honey, much to sister Edith's chagrin. She was favored with the dark complexion and thick black hair from her mother's Indian ancestry.

The whole family flourished in their new home. They lived in a large brick house down a one-mile lane. The snowy winter of 1912 brought a worst-ever blizzard to northern Indiana challenging Judd to keep the lane open to the county road.

One evening when he was clearing snow from the lane, the man plowing the county road stopped his team, waved and walked toward Judd. "Hullo. Name's Howard Burger. Every time I plow this road, I notice how good your lane is plowed. The county is having trouble keeping up with all the snow this winter. If you have the time, I think they could use you and your team on a temporary basis. Think ya might be interested?"

"I haul logs for the lumber yard during the day, but I suppose I could leave early and help in the evenings," Judd replied.

"You'd be doin' us a favor. Ya need to talk to Sam Jones. Office is in the courthouse. I notice a few of your neighbors' drives are always cleaned out. Someone else around here have a plow, maybe lookin' for work?"

"Nah," Judd answered. "We have some elderly neighbors and a widow who can't keep their drives open, so I try to keep up with it."

"Mighty good a' ya. Sure they 'preciate it. I'll tell Sam you'll be in to talk to him. I think you'll be satisfied with the pay."

"I'll go tomorrow," Judd stomped his feet from the cold. "Thanks for stopping."

So began Judd's work with the Elkhart County Highway Department. He plowed roads evenings and weekends. Because the pay was good, with earnings from both jobs, they were able to put aside a little nest egg. In the spring, Sam called Judd into his office.

"How would you like to work for the county full-time, Judd?"

"I'd like that. The road work is easier on my team than felling trees and hauling logs. The pay is better, and I like the men I work with. Yes sir, it would be my privilege to work for you." Judd was ecstatic. He knew this was the break he had hoped for—steady work that paid well.

"Of course, full-time pay is better. You'll get $1.60 a day, $40 dollars a month. Good, it's settled then." Sam stood, reaching to shake Judd's hand. "I've checked you out this winter, and I must say you impress me, Judd. You're one of the few temporary workers who didn't pad your hours. You have a capable team, and you handle them well. I haven't had to replace broken fences you knocked down. The men like to work with you. When Howard told me you plow the driveways of the neighborhood widow ladies, I knew you were my man."

"Much obliged, Sam. I'll always be honest with you and I'll put in a good days' work. I appreciate the opportunity you're giving me. You won't regret it."

Judd wanted to dance a jig as he left the courthouse; his smile filled his face. "I know just what I'll do," he said, walking to Hawks Hardware Store.

He arrived home early that night carrying a big box. The children came running, their curiosity aroused. "We did it, Mama!" He touched her shoulder, his eyes glowing. "I got a full-time job at the highway today. Sam was very encouraging—he likes my work. We're going to be okay now, Mama."

"What is it?" Carl yelled as they lifted out a wooden bucket and a crank attachment with a metal container.

"We'll celebrate this weekend after Mama goes to the grocery. It's a hand-cranked ice cream maker."

"Well gadzooks. We can make ice cream at home?" Clara asked, watching the crank handle spin the tin churn.

"We still have river ice stored in the potato cellar. We'll have a party, Mama; invite the neighbors."

The children all spoke over each other, taking turns with the crank and removing the lid from the shiny churn. As excited as they were, their voices were hushed staccato: they had never seen such shiny luxury in their home.

Not comfortable showing affection around the children, Sarah surprised Judd by grabbing him in a big hug. He spun her around, yelling, "Yahoo, my Sarah cake!"

Sarah was ebullient. "You did it, Judd. I always knew you would. All your hard work paid off."

A few days after the ice cream party, Carl didn't want to get out of bed. "I'm sick, Mom. I can't go to school today."

"Oh Carl, you're too ornery to get sick. Get a move on. The calves have to be fed."

When he shuffled in from the barn complaining of a sore throat and unable to eat, Sarah leaned her cheek against his forehead. "Well I'll be hornswoggled. You're burning up. What's wrong with you, son?" The next day the fever was working him furiously, and Sarah saw a prickly rash on his stomach. Usually plucky and boisterous, he was achy and lethargic. Frightened, Sarah sent Judd to get Dr. Ash.

She was on edge watching Dr. Ash look at his throat, tongue, and feel the glands in his neck. By now the rash covered his body. "We made ice cream on Saturday. Could that have made him sick? We all ate it, and he is the only one who is sick."

Dr. Ash shook his head, "No, no, Mrs. Swihart. The ice cream isn't the cause. He has scarlet fever. He probably got it from someone at school—we have a batch of cases. It's easily spread and while it isn't usually deadly, it can be. You need to watch Carl very carefully in case it progresses to rheumatic fever, pneumonia, or kidney disease. The high fever can also do damage, so when he feels hot you must use cool baths or cloths on his body until the fever breaks. Try to get lots of liquids in him, which will be hard because his throat is sore. He must be quarantined inside this room for two weeks. None of the family must have any contact with him except you. When you go in his room, wear a bandana over your nose and mouth, so the germs don't spread to you.

Any time you touch something he has touched, you must wash your hands with soap. All his utensils must be boiled for ten minutes. Because you'll be with him, you must stay away from the family as much as possible. By law, I must put a yellow tape around the front of the house and a quarantine sign on the front door. I'll come back in two days, but if he gets worse, send Judd for me."

Sarah's voice quavered, "Dr. Ash, if you're trying to put the fear of God in me, you've done so."

"That's my intent. Keep your children home. Preventing the spread is paramount. An epidemic of scarlet fever is catastrophic, many will die. So far, Goshen has a limited number of cases. Even so, they're closing the schools and churches."

Always a paragon of cleanliness, Sarah went on a mission, determined that none of the family would get sick. It was a war to kill Carl's germs and everyone joined the effort. Everything in the house was washed down with bleach water. During the first week when Carl was so sick, Sarah stayed in the bedroom. He slept much of the time. She sponged, forced liquids, read stories, and sang to him.

Fortunately, it was springtime, and the weather was fair, so the rest of the family stayed outside. It was time to plant crops and put in the garden. The rest of the family worked all day and collapsed in their beds at night. Each new day Sarah was thankful no one else was sick.

At the end of the first week Sarah sensed they had turned a corner. Carl's temps spiked less often and were not as high. He was awake most of the time, complaining about his sore mouth, his itchy skin, and his headache. Sarah set food and water inside the bedroom. She got activities from the teacher to keep him busy, but ten-year-old Carl wasn't a complacent patient.

Esther had been planting corn in the field along the lane. She ran into the kitchen. "Where's Carl?" she asked Sarah.

"He's in his room. Probably taking a nap—he hasn't pestered me for a while."

"I think I saw him walking up the lane," Esther said, sticking her head in the bedroom.

Sarah rushed after her, seeing the empty bed and open window. "That scoundrel! I'll be bound, I'm going to throttle that boy." She rushed out the door, meeting Carl in the lane, shaking him till his teeth rattled. "You ornery varmint. What possessed you to go off half-cocked?" Sarah grabbed his ear, dragging him up the lane.

"Mama, I wadn't going to hurt anybody. I'm tired of being penned up like a coot head."

The children were bunched together at the edge of the garden, keeping their distance from Carl. They were aghast, their eyes wide. Never had they seen their mother so angry, her face beet-red, her spit flying. She dragged Carl into the house, his feet unable to match her speed. "Quit talking rot. You risk Pop losing his new job 'cause you're tired of staying in the bedroom? You know what happens when you break quarantine? If someone turned you in to the police, they would have taken you to the pest house," she hurled him toward the bed where he cowered, fearful of this out-of-control, maniacal woman. "I give my oath Carl Lester Swihart, you pull this stunt again and *I* will take you to the pest house myself. This family does not break laws or cause trouble—you'd best learn that now. Quit sniveling. I'll hear no more about this. If you're lucky your sisters won't tell Pop about this calamity."

And they didn't. Judd, happy when the quarantine was lifted and impressed with Carl's acquiescence while ill, decided to take him to an end-of-season coat sale at the Chicago Fair Store on Main Street. Being the first boy, Carl was lucky to always get new clothes. He was a bit of a dandy, showing interest in duds that showed him to advantage.

"We'll get it big so you can wear it a couple years before Floyd wears it. What do you think of this brown one?" Judd asked.

"That looks cheaper than a skinny chicken," Carl sniggered. "I don't like the hood."

"It's not cheap. It costs two dollars. Don't trifle with me, Carl."

"Look at this blue plaid one, Pop. I like the big buttons. It really looks warm," he commented, trying it on. "I like it Pop. It's only three dollars—not that much more."

"Try this one, Carl. It's nice and heavy and is two dollars."

"I don't like the things on the sleeves. I want the blue plaid one, Pop. It's my favorite."

"I don't want to pay three dollars when these two-dollar coats are perfectly good. These five coats are two dollars, and you'll have time to grow into them. Which is your choice?"

"I want the blue plaid, Pop. The others are too plain."

"Well, I guess we're done shopping then." Judd proceeded to return the coats to the rack and leave the store. "Too bad, you'll have to wear your old coat another year. The sleeves are halfway to your elbows; I can imagine what it'll look like by next spring."

As he took the coat off the hanger, panic edged Carl's voice. "Okay," he said grudgingly, "I'll choose the one with the thing on the sleeves."

"Too late, son. You well and truly bungled it. No new duds for you. Remember this lesson when you forget your humble station and think you haf'ta have the best of things. Our family doesn't have money to waste on frippery. You drive the horses, Carl. Shopping wears me out. You can go home and pick bugs off the potatoes."

* * * * *

Esther walked into the stable, greeting Ollie, his mule ears twitching, and Sam, the feisty young draft horse. This was her favorite time of day—her last job before going to the chaos of the house for breakfast. She disliked the shoving, spilling, and slobbery eating of her noisy siblings, much preferring outdoor work. She even liked the muscular rigor of chopping wood and working opposite Papa cutting trees with the crosscut saw. These moments alone with the horses were a time to clear her mind, say a prayer, and order her day. Why did Mr. Shank want her to come to school early? Never one to misbehave, she was the best student in the school. Maybe he wanted to talk to her about the solo she was singing for her eighth-grade graduation ceremony. She loved school and was sad to be graduating.

"You're probably wondering why I called you in. You'll be graduating in a few weeks. As a teacher, I don't often have a student with your aptitude. You have a gift, Esther. It would be a shame if you don't develop it. You would be a wonderful teacher."

Esther blushed with pleasure and squirmed in her chair from unaccustomed praise. She brought her hanky to her mouth. "Oh, thank you, Mr. Shank. I'm surprised by your kind words." She dropped her chin, lowering her eyes. "I don't know what to say."

"I would like to see you go on to high school. You have the intelligence, but you also have an air of culture and a sense of curiosity unusual in a young girl. You amaze me with your high grade of elocutionary ability. Have you thought about high school?"

"I've never thought it would be possible. You know I'm second to Edith. She helps in the house with the children and I do the farm work. I've always wanted to be a teacher, but my parents need me on the farm." Esther looked down, shaking her head. Her downcast expression revealed the reality of her future.

"I want you to talk to your parents. They are good people. Leastways tell them my thoughts on this. If there's any way I can help you, I will. You are capable of so much more than eighth grade."

"I've thought about teaching children's Sunday School. Do you think I could do that?"

"Yes Esther. I'm sure you could teach Sunday School...but what a waste," he mumbled into his hand.

"I didn't get that?" Esther said, leaning forward.

"I said you will be a very good Sunday School teacher."

Esther enjoyed attending the Inbody Church, a small country congregation a two-mile walk from her home. It didn't occur to her she was different from her family in her devotion to church—it just seemed the right thing to do. She attended Wednesday night prayer meeting and twice on Sunday. She volunteered to teach children's Sunday School, a challenge as there was one class for all ages. She organized the children to dramatize Bible stories, sometimes presenting a skit to the adults. The Sunday School children were more teachable and obedient than her siblings; she felt like a real teacher.

Fall revival meetings were guaranteed to draw a crowd. Brother Lutes, the guest minister, was locally recognized as a good exhorter. It was a cold rainy night, Esther arrived chilled to the bone but soon warmed with the fervor of the sermon. The Women's Christian Temperance Union was picketing around the country. Elkhart had recently voted to be a "wet" county, allowing alcohol, so ministers and their congregants were up-in-arms against the devil rum.

A fire roared in the wood stove in the little church. The country folk, bundled in their winter coats, leaned forward on the wooden benches, nodding and swaying, receptive to the exhortations of plump, pulpy Brother Lutes. His pate was shiny with only a fringe of gray hair, his face buried in a profuse beard. His voice ranted, his body struggled and pummeled, a pugilist battling the devil himself.

"Christians, you are asleep on your feet. The devil is triumphing over the church. Whoever enters the door of a saloon, whoever loses sobriety, whoever votes for the saloon—it'll be hell and eternal damnation for you! Christians today are so self-satisfied; you sit in the pews until you mold. You must be like a policeman, rushing to a crime scene in your labor to save those enslaved to whisky. You must bring these sinners to Jesus Christ. What have you done for Christ today? What are you willing to do to save the lost? Give your life to Christ. Sisters and brothers, pour out your heart to Jesus. Confess your sins. Don't just warm the pew but together we must do the work of Jesus. Come forward during our last hymn. Wash away your sins in the blood of Jesus."

Softly and tenderly, Jesus is calling,
Calling for you and for me.
See by the portals He's watching and waiting,
Waiting for you and for me.
Come home, Come home,
Ye who are weary, come home.
Earnestly, tenderly Jesus is calling,
Calling, Oh Sinner, come home.

Brother Lutes is speaking to me. I don't want to be the kind of Christian who just sits in the pew. I want to lead sinners to Christ. I want to live the Jesus way. Esther walked forward, responding to the altar call. She confessed she was a sinner. She gave her life to Christ and was baptized in the river on a wintery day.

* * * * *

Life changed in the Swihart home after Judd got the job with the highway department. His confidence restored, he became more outgoing and hearty. Sam, his boss, soon recognized his intelligence and leadership potential. He was chosen to represent workers in the field at monthly meetings with administration. Still he was surprised that summer when he was assigned the plum job of the year: preparing and scraping the one-half-mile oval track for the horse races at the Elkhart County Fair.

"Can you believe I get paid to spend a whole week at the fairground keeping the horse track primed? I'll be around all those horse people. Think how much I'll learn from them."

"This job is good for you, Judd. You get so many opportunities. Like going to that meeting at the Grange with the mayor. He knows your name now."

"Let's take the whole family to the fair for a day." Judd said excitedly. "Wouldn't they get a bang out of that? I'll bet they'd allow Carl to ride on the scraper with me. He'll think he's a big shot," Judd chuckled.

"You know I can't go in my condition," Sarah reminded him. "But it's a great idea for the girls. I'll keep Floyd home, so nobody has to watch him."

"But I want you to get an outing; you never have any fun. Don't you think if I laced your corset real tight you could pass? Some heavy women have a stomach as big as yours."

"I don't want to embarrass you, Judd. But you're right, sometimes I feel as confined as a pig-in-a-poke. I could visit the women's pavilion early before a lot of people arrive, then stay seated in the bleachers during the horse races. That's what I want to see most. It's a wonderful idea. Thanks so much."

"Let's surprise them. We'll take a picnic lunch. Maybe you can make deviled eggs. I can just hear 'em hoop 'n holler."

"Just so you don't tie my corset so tight I pop the baby at the fair," Sarah chuckled.

* * * * *

"You have a healthy boy, Mrs. Swihart. Do you have a name for him?" old Dr. Ash asked, handing the baby to Sarah.

"Judd wants Noble. For the middle name we'll give him Judd's name. I vow I don't see a baby holding the name Noble; I bet he'll get a nickname before he's out of diapers. Dr. Ash, this isn't a proper question for a lady, but I need to ask you what I can do to prevent more babies. I have seven living children and four that died. I'm thirty-eight years old. It's hard for us to make do for seven children."

Old Dr. Ash blushed and sharply turned away. "I've always thought God in His wisdom knows the plan for families. I saw a woman in my office the other day who wanted my knowledge for making her seed fertile. Some things doctors don't have answers for. Your female parts are tore down so it would be better if you had no more babies. I can advise you on three things: if your husband can withdraw his organ before spilling his seed, a baby may not commence; you're most fertile during your monthly illness so refrain from coupling at that time; and third, I'll write a prescription for a douche kit. Collins Drug Store stocks them. Follow directions on the package, but basically after relations you rinse away the male seed with warm water. It's not difficult to do and it causes no pain. Some women find they're not comfortable touching their tender parts, but you'll not hurt anything. Most ladies have difficulty discussing these things with their husband, but Judd seems like a good man. You tell him I recommend these actions."

"Well, a douche wouldn't be worse than what I go through during confinement and delivery. Thank you for the information, doctor. I didn't know anyone else who could help me."

"There's no guarantee, Mrs. Swihart. This is just my best professional knowledge."

* * * * *

It was one of those hot August days when the sun squeezed the breath from you—and it was only nine o'clock in the morning. The girls were well into their Saturday task: canning three bushels of peaches. They were working in the summer kitchen just behind the house.

Edith was blanching the peaches in big kettles of boiling water, keeping her eye on Clara who was taking care of baby Noble. Esther was sitting on a crock peeling the peaches, removing the pit, and filling the jars. Ruth added syrup, closed the jars, and placed them in a water bath to seal. This was their never-ending summer task when they weren't working at the Chase Bag Factory. A family of nine ate lots of food during the long Indiana winters.

"I'm going in the house a minute, Clara. Watch Noble, don't let him near the stove," Edith warned.

"Mama said we can call him Tobe," Clara said, "So that's what I'm calling him. Whoever heard a baby called Noble?"

Sarah brought the mule and wagon to the house and began loading the food for her delivery route.

Esther jumped up. "Do you need help, Mama?"

"Yes, thanks. The chunks of ice are heavy." She glanced askance at Edith, coming out of the house in pants.

"Haw-w! What are you wearing?" laughed Clara.

"I can't work by this hot stove in a long skirt and apron. Carl's pants are much cooler."

"That may work till Papa comes home; then you best get your tail in the wind or he'll take the strap to you," Esther warned.

"Edith, will you start the bread so I can bake it before we go downtown tonight? We have a gang of twenty coming tomorrow and I need to dress chickens and make pie after I get home. Giddy up, Ollie," she called, starting down the lane.

"What's that mark on your hand, Edith?" asked Esther.

Edith jerked her hand back. "Only you would notice." She lifted her chin insolently. "For your information, I went to the Romany Camp after work yesterday. A gypsy lady told my fortune. She put the mark on my hand. I'm not supposed to wash it off."

The girls' heads snapped to attention, their eyes unbelieving. Ruth recovered first, "But Edith, they're the devil."

Esther leaned forward, her dress unbuttoned and laid open at the neck, her skirt hiked to her knees. She used her hanky to wipe sweat from her face, replacing it in her sleeve. "Did you go by yourself, Edith? Did they try to capture you?"

"Don't get a bee in your bonnet, Esther. I'm not dumb enough to go there by myself. Olive from work went with me. It was quite fun. The fortune teller was in a tent with red satin curtains. She was dressed in satin and wore a turban that had dangling jewels covering her face. A ball on the table in front of her had an eerie glow!" Edith was captivated by the drop-jawed reaction of her sisters, proud of her brazen disobedience.

"Edith, you're scaring me," screeched ten-year-old Clara, always easily spooked. She ran out of the summer kitchen, staying well within hearing distance.

"Girls, she really had supernatural powers. She knew I lived in Goshen and came from a large family. She knew I sew for my job; there's no way she could have known that."

"Do you think maybe she noticed the needle pricks when she put the mark on your hand?" Esther asked sagely.

"She foretold my future: I'm going to marry a man who is quiet and intelligent. We will move away. We'll have children but not as many as in my family. Isn't it amazing she can predict that by looking at my hand?"

"Did she steal your handbag?"

"No Ruth. It was all above board. Clara, you need to change Tobe's diaper. Give him some water and get him out of the sun. His face is all red."

"How much did you pay her?" Esther asked.

"Only fifty cents. It was worth it to know my future."

"Edith. That's half a week's salary. Mama is going to ask when you give her only half your pay. We'll have to each give some of ours so Mama won't be suspicious. You'd better get a story together, Edith. Clara and Ruth, we can't tell Papa. Edith, you know well and truly, if he finds out he will put you out of the house."

Ruth complained, "Esther, this is unfair. My pay is already short this week."

"And why might that be?" Esther asked, jaded by the peccadillos of her sisters.

"I gave Hershel Bales ten cents to give me a ride in his roadster. We went clear to Nigger Town in Elkhart. I got to wear goggles and a dust veil. He went thirty miles-an-hour," she said, stretching deliciously, pleased to have her own story.

Ruth had certainly piqued Esther's interest. "Hershel is too old for you, Ruth. Where did you run into him? I never see him around."

"At Abe Roth's gas station. Lots of chaps hang around there," she said, fanning herself with her sunbonnet.

"It's not prudent for you to go where men congregate, Ruth. It's not seemly, or even safe. Mama wouldn't like it and Papa would punish you within an inch of your life. The Bales aren't a family Papa would approve of."

"Esther, it was just a few times—it's not like I'm keeping company with him. Don't get so worked up. I go with Cousin Leah. Abe is usually there working on cars. Once he gave us a co-cola. For crying out loud, you're being an old fogy, Esther," she complained saucily.

"Look at my cartwheel, Edith. I can do three in a row."

"Watch out for Tobe, Clara. Don't get so close to him. There's a buggy coming up the lane. I wonder who it is; I can't be seen in Carl's pants."

"I think it's the medicine wagon. I hear bells jingling. He's the purveyor of the bag balm Mama uses. Bossy cut her teat on something. I'll get money from Mama's jar," she said, going into the kitchen. "Clara, take this change and buy bag balm. If I go he'll take an hour trying to sell me his cure-alls. Edith, do you want to shop when we go downtown tonight? I want to talk with Mrs. Plaut."

"Aren't *you* hoity toity? Like Mrs. Plaut is your best friend." Her voice reflected exaggerated snobbery.

"She's nice, you'd like her. She knows the latest styles and can tell what looks good. I'm going to get material for a white blouse. To her I'm not just a farm hand. Don't make fun Edith, but she told me I have "class" somehow in the way I carry myself. She wants to help me look my best. Even if I don't have much money she never makes me feel poor or like I'm wasting her time."

"I know I torment you, Esther. Mrs. Plaut is right. I don't know the words but there *is* something about you that people notice. I think you're like Mama. You're fetching and mannerly—it comes naturally to you both. That's why I don't often go places with you; no one notices me when you're around."

The two sisters were sitting alone in the summer kitchen, heat from perdition, flies and gnats sluggish on every surface. Their clothes were damp and sticky, hair loosened in straggles, they were barefoot and smelly. Somehow this day they could be loving and truthful about who they were at the core.

Esther touched Edith's arm, "I had no idea. I don't mean for you to feel that way."

"I know. I guess it's why I go to the gypsy lady and you go to Mrs. Plaut. I'm going to Blosser's Pavilion this evening and dance the night away." Then the girl who never sang opened up, full throttle:

> Goshen gals won't you come out tonight
> Come out tonight
> Come out tonight.
> Goshen gals won't you come out tonight
> And dance by the light of the moon.

CHAPTER 28

A Family Homestead

"Open your eyes, Esther. I have a surprise for you." Awakened that morning with the rooster, Esther had dug up a wagon load of potatoes to take to the market. She helped Papa shovel them into the bin at the grocery store, then collapsed from overheated weariness on the ride home.

"Whoa." Judd pulled the horses into a drive on Berkey Avenue, closer to town than their home down the long lane.

Still sluggish from her nap, Esther looked at him quizzically, "Why did you stop at this house?"

Judd's voice cracked; his eyes danced in his excitement: "we're buying this house, Esther." He shook her shoulder in his intensity. "I already put 25 percent down. We have five years to pay it off. I'll sign the papers next week. Do you think Mama will like it?" he chuckled tremulously, his voice thick with pride.

Esther took in the well-kept large white frame house and barn. Pleased that Papa shared the surprise with her, she broke into a smile. "Mama will love it. We'll all love it." *Can we afford it? Not a good question to tamp Papa's run-away enthusiasm.*

"It's perfect for us. We have seventeen acres, enough to grow sufficient crops for the animals and have Mama's big garden. You can't quit farming yet, Esther," he teased.

"This is the nicest house we've ever had. Mama's going to love the porch across the front shaded by the oak trees."

"The first thing I'm going to get is a porch swing. You know Esther, your mama and I courted on a porch swing at the Miller's house where I met her." His eyes fixed on distant memories. "I sure didn't think it'd take me this long to get her another porch swing. Been married goin' on twenty years," he shook his head, unbelieving. "Maybe once we move into this house she'll invite Juda's family—none of our homes were fit before. You remember your cousins from the reunions, don't you?"

As if hung in a new frame, Esther visualized Judd and Sarah like the hard times had delivered them: Judd with webbings of fine wrinkles furrowing his face, hands calloused and rough, hair receding and tinting gray; Sarah, the toll taken by unremitting hard work and childbirth—congealed weariness stamped into every tissue, her shabby sacrifices blooming brightly on her body. On the threshold of adulthood, Esther could see through the gauze of Judd's words and memories: *they are aging, worn, and won't be around forever, but forever good people and decent.*

She touched his hand. "Thank you, Papa. This is the best surprise you could give us."

* * * * *

The family thrived at the home place on Berkey Avenue, the last of eleven moves and their final home. The sturdy house was ample for the large family: in the downstairs a parlor, sitting room, large kitchen with a table for fifteen, and Judd and Sarah's bedroom. Upstairs there were six bedrooms with a central hall. The basement, which included the potato cellar, could be entered from either inside or outside. There was a summer kitchen behind the house and a barn with a nice stable.

Who would expect a home to define and flourish a family? It was perfect timing when the Swiharts moved near downtown activities, likely because cultural mores were allowing women more independence. Their home restored their innate dignity. Judd's jocularity and Sarah's gentle sweetness and generously laden table attracted family, friends, and neighbors. Because of frequent moves and Sarah often unable to appear in public, their church attendance had been dormant. Now they found sustenance and fellowship at the nearby West Goshen Church of the Brethren.

Esther's best friend was Mary Huber, her cousin. They answered the alter call together during revivals at West Goshen, Esther baptized for the second time. The girls were active in the West Goshen youth group and with young people from Brethren Churches in the area. Because both girls had nice singing voices they often sang special music during church services.

Esther had grown into a lovely young woman. She waved her thick dark hair, spooling it on the crown of her head. She was Sarah's daughter in every way and strove to emulate her mother. She had a gentle propriety but conveyed a flavor of happiness. She easily learned subtle ploys to please young men. She would sidle modestly up to them with a flick of her skirt, eyes wide, leaning in to listen intently. Soon her tinkling laughter would fill the air. She would blush as she lifted her hands to her face, "Oh, such wit!" The young men swarmed about her; she was not innocent of her power over them.

Esther made regular visits to Mrs. Plaut's dress shop. Nellie Plaut had "adopted" the young farm girl who dreamed dreams no one else noticed. They looked through Vogue magazine for fashion ideas. As purses were a new trend, Esther decided to stitch a purse using scraps of cloth from the Bag Factory. She blushed modestly when Mrs. Plaut said she could sell fifty of them—but she did make a purse for each of her sisters. As Mrs. Plaut advised, the girls were now catching rainwater to wash their hair, pleased by its soft manageability.

As would be expected, with Sarah recovering from Ruby's birth, four nearly grown women and three rambunctious boys ripping around the house, a breeze didn't blow that a cross-current didn't whip up a storm.

While Papa didn't allow talking at meals, often he was working and Sarah easily lost control as she hovered between stove and table, dishing out food and refilling plates. B-E-L-C-H. Carl rolled out a profuse soggy belch, laughing delightedly. "Bet you can't best that one," he dared.

"Boys, enough of this foolishment," Sarah chimed absently, worn down by the constant fracas.

Floyd, whose life was devoted to keeping up with Carl, proved equal to the challenge with his own watery propulsive fart. Both boys laughed uproariously.

Esther shuddered. "I *hate* crudeness. If we can't have a pleasant meal without all this indecency then you boys take your leave so the rest of us can enjoy our breakfast."

"Go do your chores, Carl," Sarah said, sipping her coffee and humming a hymn.

"I wonder if Roger's Band is going to be at the Pavilion Saturday night?" Edith wondered aloud. "They're old, but I still love their sound."

"I think I'll go with Papa to the Grey's baseball game," Ruth said. "Do you know if he's going, Mama?"

"No, I..."

"Get away from me," Carl yelled, running into the house with a full bucket of water, splashing through the kitchen, into the sitting room and out the front door. Close behind was Floyd with another bucket, running up over the sofa in his bare feet.

Quick as a minute, Sarah grabbed her broom, chasing the wild boys, giving their backsides a wallop as they ran. "Get out of here, you hoodlums," she yelled. "If you get my sofa dirty I'll have your hide." She brushed off the sofa. "How is a woman to keep a clean house with those two around?" She and Edith mopped the spills. "It's no sin to be poor but it's a sin to have a dirty house," she muttered her oft-repeated creed.

"I need to talk to you," Esther whispered to Edith, grateful that Ruth and Clara had already left for work. In the privacy of their bedroom, Esther admitted, "Something's wrong, Edith. When I went to the privy this morning there was brownish stuff all over my drawers. I'm not sick and I know I didn't dirty myself. I really want to go to work today. This is the day we get smallpox vaccinations. Do you think I can go?"

"I know what it is, Esther: you started your monthlies. It happened to me a while ago. You're not sick, but every month you'll have several days when you bleed down there and feel poorly."

"Well, I never heard such," Esther grimaced with disgust. "If Mama told you about monthlies why didn't you warn me? I thought I was rotting from the inside."

"Because Mama didn't tell *me* nothin'. Olive explained it—she calls it 'being on the rag'. You need to keep your nose clean around guys during this time—though you being Miss Perfect, we don't have to worry about that." Edith couldn't resist a dig about Esther's principled behavior.

"No, I suppose not," Esther agreed.

Edith opened her bureau drawer and pulled out sundry items from under a pile of bloomers. "This is a sanitary apron. You'll have to cut up a bunch of rags—old diapers work best—and pin a rag to the apron, tying the strings around your waist. I'll have Olive get you a sanitary apron from Mayberry's Drug Store. She won't mind; things like that don't bother her like it does us."

"This is humiliating," Esther said, stepping into the contraption. "I can't believe this. How come I didn't know about monthlies?"

"Because your nose is always in the air," Edith teased. "Surely you've hung Mama's rags on the clothesline with her bloomers, there between the sheets. Then again, I think maybe she doesn't have monthlies very often since she's often expecting or has a baby hanging from her tit."

"You forget I never work in the house or wash clothes. I'm always outside. I don't know about house chores and women's things. Are there more surprises I should know about?"

"Not that I can tell you. We've got to hurry, or we'll be late signing in. As Olive told me: 'Now you're a woman, Esther'."

* * * * *

Sarah was exhausted and almost asleep when finally putting Ruby into the cradle. Judd pulled her to him. "I'm feeling frisky, my girl."

Exasperated and dog-tired, Sarah pushed away his grasping hands, "It's too soon after Ruby. You're going to have to do something else about frisky. With my luck I'll get knocked up again."

Judd caught his breath, surprised at the vehemence of Sarah's smutty talk. "Your lips are loose for a refined lady. Heaven forbid you start sounding like those women who marched in South Bend: 'Women Unite. Your Body Is Your Own'," he chanted in falsetto. "Their problems would be solved if they'd stay home and get married. I don't even know what they mean—your body is your own," he said, grumpy to be turned aside. "Does it mean you don't need to wake up and feed Ruby tonight 'cause you're tired?"

Sarah realized this was a delicate subject—it wouldn't do to set him off. "I don't agree with the rallies and the ladies' brazen behavior. But I agree that ladies should have some say as to how often they are with their husbands and, as much as possible, how many children they have." She reached for his hand, seeing his dear face in her mind's eye, but right now afraid of his closed attitude. "I shouldn't be having more children," she pleaded. "Two doctors have told me that. Dr. Ash told me three things we can do to prevent the seed from taking hold. I want us to try what he said." Sarah was glad the lights were out and the children all asleep. She had worried weeks about this conversation, fearful and embarrassed to bring it up. At least they were talking.

"Don't tell me you brought this up with Dr. Ash. Sarah, he'll think you're a slut. He probably thinks I force myself on you, that you hate your own husband."

Sarah's voice trembled with feeling. "He doesn't think that. He's a doctor. He sees it from the health point of view, and so do I. That and the money. Children cost money we don't have."

Judd dropped her hand, his voice steely cold. "I thought I was taking damn good care of all of you."

Sarah was hurt and frustrated at her inability to convince Judd. Tears ran down her face, wetting her nightgown. She sniffed.

"Stop crying. You know I can't stand it when you cry."

"I just want you to understand how I feel. I'm sorry I can't say it so you understand." There was a long silence. It felt like a chasm separated them.

Judd's voice was surly. "Well, I'm wondering what you expect me to do? I'm a man. God made us with desire. If a man isn't with a woman, his manhood will fail. You want me to be with a whore? You want me to touch myself in sin rather than be with you?" She felt him sit up on the side of the bed, his voice disgusted. "I can't believe I'm talking like this to a woman, leastways my wife."

Her voice held a hint of starch, "It occurs to me if God made man with desire, then either God or man should start carrying some of these babies. Frankly, I think I've done more than my share." Sarah slipped over to sit beside him on the side of the bed. "I don't mean to say we can never be together again. It just seems we're overly prone to have babies. For my health, can't we use some moderation? Dr. Ash has some suggestions I think we should try—though he gives no guarantee." Judd shook her hand off his arm.

Sarah sat there deflated, grateful for the darkness, knowing that to speak as they were could not happen with a shred of light. After all her years with Judd, there were many ways they couldn't be in the light of day. She wondered about that. How well does a woman really know her husband? What will happen tomorrow morning when we wake up and see each other in the light, she wondered?

CHAPTER 29

Esther, Age 14 – 18

The home on Berkey Avenue was a maelstrom of hyperventilating anticipation and pent-up rowdiness. The kids worked like dogs all week. They wanted to shed the grit with lavender soap and Old Spice and catch the seven o'clock streetcar. It was the night to change underwear, haul the galvanized tub behind bushes in the back yard, bathe, and wash hair. If their ramblings brought a bit of wanton mischief or piss and vinegar—well, young lives need some spit and shine.

"Stop girl! Where do you think you're going?" Judd bellowed as Edith tried to skulk out the kitchen door, her cloche hat at a perky angle. "Look at me. What's that red paint on your face?" he harangued.

"Just a little lip rouge, Papa," Edith said, regretful she hadn't made it to the door. "Everyone's wearing it."

"I don't give a whoop who's wearing it. You'll go right over to that sink and wash it off. Use lots of soap. No girl of mine is going out of my house looking like an Indian. And what's that bag you're carrying? It's too bright—everyone will notice it."

"It's the purse Esther made for me with scraps from the bag factory."

"Esther made that?" he looked again, determined to hide any approval.

"I made it in colors I knew she'd like," Esther said, getting up from the table and taking her dish to the sink. "I'm off to the party games at West Goshen Church. The Rock Run Youth Group is joining us tonight. Papa, isn't Fred Wilson on one of your road crews? I think he'll be there." Esther engaged Papa, giving Edith opportunity to get out the back door. "Carl, are you going to Roth's Gas Station? You sure are good at talking your way into a cruise around town."

"I say, it's nice to have friends with cars," Carl agreed.

"I'm going with Carl. He's sweet on my friend, Esther, so maybe I'll get a ride too. What say, Carl?" Ruth punched his shoulder.

Esther felt a deep draft of well-being as she carried her lantern to walk the few blocks to church. It was a perfect summer evening for games with unusually low humidity and a good breeze. She loved being with her friends and couldn't wait to meet the fellas from Rock Run. Actually, she was relieved her siblings rarely chose to go to youth group activities. She wanted to "put on a good face", and it was just easier not having to deal with her unpredictable family. Indeed, Esther thought Edith was unfair in accusing her of stealing away her suitors.

Esther was pleased with the new white blouse she had made on Sarah's new sewing machine. She had soaked it in Argo starch and ironed it carefully. Again, using scraps from work, she had pieced together a colorful neck cloth which she knotted at the V-neck. She had on new black and white button-up shoes with a tassel in front. She rarely got new clothes, so tonight she felt special; she hoped the young men would notice.

While Esther took delight in the young men, the girls were her true friends. Mary, Carolyn, and Maude tittered their falsetto feminine sweet talk as she joined them.

"How pretty you look," Carolyn raved, primping the collar of her new blouse. Esther ducked her chin, "Thank you. Mrs. Plaut showed me the design and Mama helped me sew it. It's the first time I used a Butterick pattern. I hope you don't see all the mistakes I made," she averred modestly.

"I love your patchwork neck cloth. The shades of yellow are perfect with your black hair," Mary cooed.

"At work they throw these scraps away, so I've been making things. It's like quilting."

"Hey gals, we need some partners," Chas, Fred, and Ray came to the girls. "Esther, will you be my partner for the first go-around?"

The pink-coral evening slipped behind the trees into darkness as the youths stepped spritely and swayed to their music, a breathy chorus: "By the light of the silvery moon…." Swinging, skirts swirling, open-air innocence, tripping, and laughing. "Say, Esther. I like your new dancing shoes. You're steppin' high tonight," Howard said…."Are you ready for a breather? How about I get us some punch and cookies," Chas said…. "You West Goshen gals are quite the saucy ladies. I hope we get together often," Fred said.

"Some of us are taking the streetcar to the Olympia Candy Kitchen. Would you like to join me? I'll see you to your home." John took Esther home by eleven o'clock. The house was quiet and sleeping as she said a proper goodbye. Esther hummed as she undressed, replaying her evening. She felt cosseted and charmed, her social life placid and altogether satisfying. She listened for Edith to enter the unlocked back door and slip silently up the stairs.

"What happened to you?" she hissed quietly, seeing Edith's dirty bloodied face. "Are you hurt?"

"No, I'm not hurt, though I might be when Pop sees me. Can you help me clean up?"

"I have the wet cloth I used to wash up. If we go downstairs, we may wake Papa. Oh Edith, what have you done?"

"Now that I can't say for sure," Edith cackled, hinting at tipsiness.

"Shush! If you wake Papa, you'll be in big trouble."

"Olive and I went to the women's suffrage rally in Elkhart. It was a peaceful march; the ladies were all well-behaved. Then an old man about Pop's age, grabbed Olive's sign and in the scuffle I got hit. It didn't seem like much, but I didn't have anything to clean with."

"Yes, I think you're lucky. Most of this is washing off. I'll get you some Jimson Leaf Salve. I bet Papa won't notice. Mama will, but she won't say anything."

"After the march we sat in the park, just talking. We've been taught that because women bear children, their role is to nurture the family, rearing well-behaved children who will yield a moral, God-fearing society. And of course, women are always subordinate because men earn money that supports the family. They make the decisions." Edith's voice became intense, whispering passionately as she paced around Esther, gesticulating, and grabbing her hand. "Think about it, Esther: you've always done the work on the farms where we've lived. But if something happened to Papa, Carl would own the farm, having no idea how to operate it. Women do some of the same work as men at the Bag Factory, but we're paid a fraction, and they lowered only *our* pay 'cause of the Great War. As long as women don't have the vote, none of this will change. Please don't jaw on me, Esther. This is important."

"No, I won't tell. I had no idea you were interested in the suffragette cause," Esther said, looking confounded. "I thought these women were unbefitting. Don't you think women should stay out of politics, that it isn't seemly?"

"I wish you would talk to these women, Esther. Actually, they're more like you: they're smart, they know the right words to say, and they champion what they believe. These women will change our lives." She snickered, "They see the day when we can drink wine openly, not steal it from Pop's potato cellar."

"I wish I were brave like you, Edith. You're not afraid to say and do what you believe. I get bogged down with people disapproving and judging me. You have the nerve to stand up for rights. I don't stand for anything; it's not how I want to be. I wish I had your backbone."

"I think if *women* don't stand up for women, who *will* stand up for us? I look at Mama's life—it's been all hard: work and having babies. I can't see much happiness for her. She's the invisible backbone of the family, but she has no say in anything. Pop controls everything."

"Like you wearing lip rouge?"

"Yes, there's that. When we were marching, I thought about Mama and almost cried. Tonight, everyone in the family went out to do fun things: Pop, me, you, Ruth, Carl, and Clara. None of us thought about what Mama wanted to do. She was home alone running after Floyd, Tobe, and Ruby, her belly about to spit out another baby. It makes me sad for her."

"You think Mama's not happy?" This thought had never occurred to Esther—it was just the way it was.

Edith paused, then shook her head, "I can't believe you have to ask that question," she said softly. "So, you wondered why I went to the rally—well, it was for Mama. We've got to step up. We girls are going to take turns staying home on Saturday nights so she can go out, or if her belly is too big to be in public, she can have an evening to rest."

"Yes, of course. I'm ashamed I never thought about these things."

"I almost forgot to tell you: I met a nice guy, a successful reporter for the Elkhart Truth newspaper. Name is Wilbur and he's all for women's rights."

* * * * *

It was another balmy Saturday night when the children would scatter, each finding their own tempting folly. Ruth would stay with Mama and the little ones. Esther was trying to rein in Edith, to keep her away from imprudent pursuits.

"Papa's getting suspicious, Edith. You never know what he'll do to keep track of you. Go with me tonight. Then maybe he'll relax with you."

"Go to church party games?" she squawked, as if that was the worst imaginable punishment.

"I'm just saying, Edith. You know how Papa can be. You might have fun. Several chaps are quite fetching. Two you have to leave for me: if Earl's there from Rock Run Church, he's all mine." She danced around, her long hair flying. "He makes me swoon when I see his mop of curly hair blown by the wind," she giggled. "I'm also sweet on John from West Goshen. He's good at party games and he comes every Saturday night. I think he takes a shine to me. You can have any of the others."

"Listen to you," Edith laughed. "Haven't you got *your* knickers in a roar? I'm not looking for a man; I already have one. But I'll humor you and check these fellas out."

The girls were in good spirits as they took off together in the wagon. Edith still thought Esther's festivities a bit stodgy, but she was surprised she was having fun. The kids were friendly and welcoming and a few of the guys were quite attentive.

Midway through the evening Esther joined Edith. "It doesn't look like Earl's coming. Shucks, I was hoping you'd see him—he is *fine*. A bunch of us are going to the Candy Kitchen. Do you want to come along?"

"I'm pretty tired; I think I'll cash in early tonight."

"You take the wagon then. John will bring me home."

"Sure. I hope Pop doesn't catch you. I'll probably be asleep when you get home."

"Thanks for coming with me tonight, Edith. It was fun having you. I'll see you later."

After leaving the Candy Kitchen, John took his buggy the long way to Esther's home. He and Esther had been heating and stirring the tender coals of friendship, coaxing them to flame. Esther's intuition was right: John hoped to stake a claim on Esther. A chaste kiss was on his mind as he turned into the driveway.

"Just stop here, John. I'll walk the rest of the way. I don't want to disturb my parents."

"Of course." The horse stepped to the ditch to nibble grass. The top of the buggy was folded back, the sky carpeted with a million stars, a night burgeoning with promise.

"It's so quiet here. It feels like we're the only two in the world," John relaxed his arm behind Esther, looking at the stars.

A tall figure jumped from behind a bush, hurling toward the buggy. "Stop right there," an angry voice yelled. The horse startled, jerking the buggy into the ditch.

John jumped up, his face congealed in terror. "Who's there?" he yelled. Esther felt herself being grabbed and pulled out of the buggy. She screamed with every ounce of strength. The dark nightmare tumbled around her. "He has me, John," she screamed, feeling John grab her arm, then release her so suddenly she fell over the side of the buggy into the ditch.

She scrambled to get away from her attacker to see John staring straight into the face of... "Papa?" She collapsed on the ground. "What are you doing?" The pieces of the nightmare didn't fit, nothing made sense.

Judd yelled at John, "Get the heck out of here. NOW, you scoundrel. I'll take care of Esther.... You better believe I will. GO!" he shouted angrily. Esther glanced back to see John standing transfixed with a puzzled expression, then with a small wave in her direction, he left.

Rage flashed before her eyes. Nothing would placate her anger and humiliation. Her feet caught in her skirt; she stumbled, and he manhandled her upright.

"So you thought you'd pull a fast one, sneaking home with a man," he yelled, yanking her arm and dragging her up the drive. "You're no better than common. Dammit, I'll teach *you* to trifle with *me*." He pulled her up on the porch, turned her over his knee, and paddled her: Bang...Bang... Bang.... "You...will...not...disobey...me! You're confined to your room," he jerked her upright. "You're going nowhere, not even to work. Do you understand?" He drug her into the front room where Sarah sat huddled forward in her nightgown, her face gutted, unable to do anything to help Esther. Judd kicked her toward the stairway. "Get out of my sight. I don't want to see you." he yelled.

Esther put on her nightgown and got into bed beside Edith. She felt around her body, checking for damage. She realized she was less physically hurt from his pounding than she was mentally distraught. All her layers of undergarments had been protective.

"Are you okay?" Edith whispered, puncturing the dark silence.

"No...I'm not sure I ever will be." Esther lay still and unmoving, every cell in her body hyper vigilant. "I won't live in this house anymore," she said with resolve.

"Oh Esther. We heard him beating you clear up here. What are we going to do?"

"I have a lot of thinking to do," she said somberly. I guess I have all night and tomorrow to make some decisions." Her voice was sad, "I wish I didn't have to hurt Mama."

"Well, if anyone can wield clout over Papa, it's you. If you leave, he'll have to work the farm," she laughed angrily. "I sure don't think he has time or inclination for that." Edith was silently musing, realizing the seismic eruption embroiling their family. She scoffed, "Good for you, Esther."

Esther lay awake for hours, her thoughts whirling and anxious, underneath a black melancholy. Her senses grasped to find anchorage, a toehold to her life before. Strangely she felt alive with waves or vibrations coming to her from around the house—like everyone was awake, their angst conveyed to her. Scores of sounds reached her: every bedspring was complaining; soft footfalls were pacing—Sarah, downstairs; then bouncy Clara—such the little worrier; a throat-clearing bulbous hawk—that would be Carl; a sleepy outcry from a dream—restless babies. Esther was comforted by the messages coming through the walls to her. Maybe her family couldn't vocalize their distress, but she heard their cautious night sounds, and it gave her succor.

Esther was looking out the window of her room the next morning when Sarah brought a plate of fried eggs, bacon, and toast—a special treat. She sat quietly while Esther ate, her dejected demeanor reflecting her wounded heart.

"Mama, I have to leave. I can't live here anymore. I won't be able to give you my salary."

She reached for Esther, heart of her heart. Her hurt was transparent in her red-wrecked eyes and sallow cast. "It was wrong what Papa did last night. But please don't leave. I'll talk to him."

"Mama, I did nothing that Papa should chastise me. I'm eighteen years old. I have a right to be with friends. Now everyone will know what happened, not just how he treated me, but how rude he was to John." Her ire percolated to fuming rage. "Of all us kids in the family, I'm most obedient. I've never given Papa reason not to trust me—and this is how he treats me? By spanking me like a child?"

"Everything you say is true, but Esther, would you tear our family apart? If you leave, the girls will leave too."

"I don't want to leave you Mama, but I've been thinking all night. I *am* going to work tomorrow. I'll go out with friends without asking his permission. He can never hit me again—why does he think he has that right?" Esther spun around, crying, "I've worked like a dog for Pop and I've never caused trouble. It's unfair. I'm not going to be treated this way anymore."

"I'll talk to him. We have to straighten this out. I can't change the way he is, Esther. If I could, I would. All I've ever wanted is for my daughters to have a life easier than mine. I've only wanted to protect you." Her shoulders slumped... "I've failed. Go to sleep now, my dear. None of us got any sleep last night."

The next morning Esther went to work as usual. For several days Judd left early and came home late.

"It's okay, Esther. You don't need to leave. Pop won't interfere with your activities or your time with friends. He understands you're an adult and can't be treated as a child. He'll never hurt you or touch you. Papa learned his lesson; this won't happen again to any of you girls. From his point of view these admissions are near impossible, yet he has agreed. He won't go back on his word. He wants to do the right thing." As she did throughout life, Sarah mediated between Judd and the children. While he was the hot pepper in the soup, she was the starch in the pudding. She intervened with his punitive harshness to meld and reconcile, always the soothing power undergirding family unity.

* * * * *

Esther was besotted; the recipient of her affection was Earl Phillips, a young man from the Rock Run Brethren Church. Even *she* believed herself daft in the head: she wrote poems, she daydreamed, she dropped her hanky to prompt an excuse to talk, she left the gate of the horse stall open, and she pulled daisies apart (he loves, he loves me not). Every conversation was Earl, Earl, Earl. Her friend Mary was shocked by her out of character behavior.

Esther's voice shivered with ardor, "I can't help it, Mary. Every time I see his shy dimple and that mop of springy curls I have to grab my hands to keep them out of his hair. It's obvious he tries to manage it and it's just not to be," she was so tickled and smug, tossing her head and smoothing her own wayward curls.

"Oh Esther, you've got the bug; you're caught—hook, line, and sinker."

"Do you think he likes me? He's so shy. Sometimes I just want to shake him and say, 'notice me, Earl'."

Mary laughed, "You're not used to his offhand manner. You've always had any guy you wanted lining up after you. Earl's driving you bonkers. I think he's the smart one after all," she teased.

"Well, I don't think so," Esther's impatience was palpable.

That night in bed, Esther started her "Earl" refrain: "He was there again tonight. I think he's interested in me. He never used to come to all the meetings."

"I tried to talk to Mama..." Edith started.

"One time when I turned to look at him he was staring straight at me," Esther interrupted.

"Esther, listen to me. I need to talk to you," Edith raised her voice and reached to touch Esther's arm.

"Oh sorry. What do you need?"

"If you weren't so smitten you'd notice others have lives too. I tried to talk to Mama, and she walked away, so I guess I need you to help me. Please don't have a conniption-fit."

"What?" She had Esther's full attention now.

"There's no good way to say this: I got knocked up." Edith couldn't look into Esther's eyes, her chin quivered. It had been hard when Mama didn't help her, and she knew Esther was a neophyte in these matters. But so was she.

It seemed the bedroom filled with firecrackers and sirens, the noise in Esther's head felt like explosions. Seeing Edith hunched and shriveled in the bed, yet trying to affect an attitude, her only thought was: *Be kind.*

"Oh, my goodness," burst from her mouth. She touched Edith's arm, her thoughts in a muddle. "You actually...did the...deed? How do you know you're...? Are you sure?"

"I haven't had my monthlies for a long time. I couldn't understand why I was throwing up. Then it dawned on me that Mama throws up before her belly swells. Truth be told, Esther, I think Mama and I both have a bun in the oven. I ran out to the privy one morning and Mama was in there, heaving *her* breakfast while *I* heaved outside. Good lands, our family is as queer as a nine-bob-note. Mama's fertility knows no bounds." Edith leaned forward, her hands attempting to smother hysterical laughter, which subsided into sniffling sobs. "What will I do? Look Esther, I'm getting a little pooch in my belly already." She stretched her nightgown, exposing a surprisingly large bulge.

Esther couldn't stifle a sharp wheeze of breath. *How had she not noticed that?*

"You're the only one who knows, Esther. I haven't told anyone."

"Do you know who the father is? Is it someone you keep company with?" Esther was trying to say the right things, getting the information she needed so they could make a plan. Already though, she felt her mind suffuse with crushing shame—shame dropped like a weight on their family. Now they'd be at the core of gossiping whispers. How could Edith do this to Mama? She'd never hold her head up again. What would Esther's friends assume about *her*, now from a tainted family? Oh, her cheeks burned to remember her silly chat with Mary: *"I just want to shake him so he notices me."* Maybe no respectable boy would want to be with her anymore.

"Contrary to what you think, I don't spread my legs for every man that whistles down the pike," Edith said, fiddling her finger nervously over the nub end of her braid. "Actually, this may all work out. I've been seeing Wilbur since the suffrage rally." She grabbed Esther's shoulder, suddenly effusive. "Remember the gypsy fortune teller told me I was going to marry someone intelligent? Maybe this was predestined." She was seeing what she wanted to see—a good outcome. "Wilbur is intelligent, he's a reporter with a good job. I've even thought this may work out for him; married men can't be conscripted into the army for the great war in Europe. I think that'd be worth *something*."

"Tell me about Wilbur," Esther asked.

"You'd like him. He's medium size with brown wavy hair and blue eyes—quite handsome, if I do say. He's serious, quiet, and very attentive to me. He's really caught up in this war. He seems like a decent person."

Then how come you're in this condition? Esther wondered. "Do you think you can pledge yourself to him?" Esther asked, her chest seizing with the momentous decision Edith faced.

"Let's just say Pop would like him better than most fellas I take a shine to."

"Pop will disown you. But this will be the end-all for Mama. She's so…untouched by smut, so innocent of wrong. She doesn't fathom us girls…impure in any way. What this will do to her…" Esther didn't care that she offended Edith—to do this to Mama, she deserved every lick and stripe.

"You think I haven't thought this one-thousand times?" Edith's withered voice sagged in futility.

Esther deliberated, then spoke, "You need to talk to Wilbur soon. If he's a decent sort he'll marry you. Then I'll tell Papa and we'll have a little wedding here at the house. I can take care of that. If he doesn't want to marry you, he'll be hanged, drawn, and quartered by Papa. I'm sorry. I wish you didn't have this facing you. I know this isn't what you wanted."

"It may turn out better than we think. He's quite a decent chap. I think I have good faith in that gypsy lady."

CHAPTER 30

The Great War

Buy bonds and avoid bombs! By 1916, war fever had struck a match across the country. Because of the war, many men had been laid off work—those between the ages of twenty-one and thirty had been conscripted. Food lines formed and sugar, flour, and gasoline, had been rationed. People who had never gone hungry now worried how they would feed their children. People were anxious and agitated—a tinder box waiting for a spark.

The Swiharts were more fortunate than most. Judd was now supervisor of all the road crews. Skilled seamstresses at the Bag Factory were at a premium, though the girls' wages had been cut. After working all day, Ruth and Clara cut and packed bandages at the Red Cross, or went door to door selling savings bonds. Esther and Sarah planted, tended, and harvested grain for the animals. They planted potatoes by the ton to sell and feed the family. The seventeen acres were a bonanza during the war years.

Judd wasn't surprised when Sam called him into his office and closed the door. "The men have taken this last layoff hard; they're just looking for something to set them off. I didn't have a choice. I have to say Judd, I was surprised to see you walking the picket line yesterday with the road crews. I need to know where you stand on this."

"I'll tell you where I stand, Sam. These men—their children are hungry. They see a cold winter coming. Some are afraid they're going to be sent to fight in Europe. Sometimes frightened people do things without thinking. I believe if I picket along with them, things are less likely to get out of control. Last week at the Goshen Milling Company, men rioted and started a fire. Sir, I don't want that to happen at the highway. I figure if I'm there, I might be able to keep a lid on it."

Sam mused, "I think you're right. I know your men trust you. I agree, your place is in that line with them."

"Yesterday I got to thinking, you know that woods behind the shop? Could some of the men, instead of walking the picket, cut down those trees and chop them for firewood to take home? This would give them work to do and they'd appreciate the county giving them wood. They may be less likely to tangle with us."

"I know where you mean. I'll bet the mayor would be happy to get those trees out. A terrific idea. I'll get back with you on that. Thanks Judd, I appreciate your work. I feel like you've got my back."

"That's my plan—to have your back."

That night Edith, Wilbur, and baby Emory, were coming from Elkhart to meet Sarah and Judd's months-old baby, Merle. Even though there was a trolley to Elkhart, Edith had been scarce since her awkward "shotgun type" marriage. This occasion was meant to "bury the hatchet" in a numb sort of way. Sarah was dressing two chickens, unheard of on a Tuesday—the chicken supper a bland acknowledgement of recompense to Edith.

It was voting day: the 1916 presidential election between Republican Charles Evans Hughes and Democrat Woodrow Wilson. The men left for the courthouse when supper was over. Wilbur, reporting for the Elkhart Truth, needed to be at the county courthouse as election returns came in. He hoped to demonstrate to his new father-in-law his reporter's tenacity and his high status among important politicians. For his part, Judd, who was anticipating a run for Elkhart County Trustee, wanted to see and be seen. He could schmooze with the best of them and he liked rubbing shoulders with the dapper Elkhart reporter who he knew would show well—mayhap a symbiosis that could work for both.

Back at Berkey Avenue, the women were sitting around the kitchen table, each with a cup of sassafras tea, the picture of domestic harmony. They were overjoyed to be together again but realized the dynamics of the family had changed: a bit like a summer shower that couldn't decide if it wanted to thunder and flash or drizzle a rainbow. With Edith married and with a baby, the atmosphere was incredibly changed, nuanced with coded words, hooded eyes and weighty pauses. The unspoken crux was the stilted dance between the daughter with an unsavory premature baby and her mother with an unseemly ripened birth.

"Guess what Edith," Clara gloated, "Papa's going to get a Model T Ford. We'll be able to visit you every week."

"Edith and Wilbur don't want to see this tribe every week," Sarah stated.

"These peaches are good, Mama," Ruth said, "Do we have some to can?"

"I have a bushel, but they won't be that good because I can't get sugar."

"You can, Mama. Wilbur wrote an article for the paper this week. Families with lots of children can get a permit for extra sugar rations."

Sarah stood to jostle Merle who was fussy and refusing the breast. "I should think I'd qualify at the top of the list," Sarah said.

"Mama, you should get one of those sucking tubes for Merle. It's like a rubber nipple. Emory liked it better than a sugar tit. It put him to sleep every time."

Sarah looked skeptically at Edith, "So now you're giving me advice about babies?"

Edith, abashed, turned to Esther, "Are you and Earl secretly betrothed yet?"

Esther blushed sheepishly. "No, but I haven't been seeing anyone else."

"Esther and Ruth compete for dibs on the parlor," Clara said, "But I can tell you, Ruth and Vail are a lot more lovey-dovey. It's a good thing for them that Papa has meetings downtown most nights."

"I see no point in being in a big rush," Esther said primly, then gasped, glancing at Edith, realizing her words could be hurtful.

"I don't know what you're talking about, Clara," Ruth blushed.

"Well, I overheard Papa tell Carl, 'Ruth is shaking hands with trouble with that Vail fella', just saying what I heard," Clara shrugged.

"Wilbur's mother introduced me to a new friend. Her name is Jeanette Osborn. She's a spiritual leader from Chicago who's recruiting people from Elkhart to the Lemurian Fellowship. Mrs. Cripe has been her follower, and is taking training to join the order."

"Be careful, Edith. Is it Christ-based with the Bible as the inerrant word of God?" Sarah asked skeptically.

"I've only gone to a few meetings, but Sister Osborn is developing quite a following. The Lemurian Order believes all religions have value and, yes, the Christian Gospels are part of their Bible. Members are to constantly try to improve themselves so when they die they'll be reincarnated in a new body at a level nearer to perfection. The part I like is that all members have to help each other improve; you can't do it alone, but in society with other members. They learn to improve themselves by channeling or speaking with members in other levels of incarnation. I'm not explaining it well; I have lots to learn. I've noticed a change in Wilbur's mother since she's taken the classes—she seems happier."

The family stared impassively, wondering at Edith's words. It sounded foreign; they didn't know how to answer such ideas. They didn't want to hurt her feelings.

"I'm glad you're going to church," Esther finally said. "Does Wilbur go with you?" she asked, knowing how important the church was to her and Earl.

"Not yet. He's interested when I talk about it." She grinned, "At this point we'd both rather go dancing."

Finally, both babies settled. The ladies reached into their knitting baskets; hands were never idle as everyone knit socks for soldiers. In the early morning, Judd and Wilbur returned with the news that Elkhart County went for Woodrow Wilson.

* * * * *

Judd and Sarah were sitting on the porch swing on a spring evening watching the coral, pink, and blue, slip through the patchy puffs of cloud as evening changed to night.

"Where is everyone?" Judd asked.

"Most of them are at the Grey's baseball game. Esther is upstairs sewing a middy blouse to wear tomorrow when Earl takes her for an outing. She's all het up. I think she's expecting a proposal, so you should be prepared for him to ask for her hand."

Judd offered the bowl of popcorn to Sarah. "Well Earl should fish or cut bait," he said, his feet tapping to pump the swing. "He's not such a bad egg I suppose—just poached, maybe," he grinned at Sarah.

"I don't know what you're complaining about. Frank and Alice Phillips are an upstanding Brethren family. It's different with Vail Hazen—we know precious little about his family over in Ohio."

Judd sat up abruptly, his ire provoked. "That Vail isn't worth a plugged nickel. He's too bigheaded—struts like a peacock. He's a sluggard, doesn't do honest work far as I can see. Ruth is enamored with his movie star looks."

"Unfortunately, I think you're flogging a dead horse. Ruth is smitten by him." Sarah reached for popcorn. "I always say, no one is so bad you can't find some good in them."

"There you have it, you always see the good in everyone. A year ago, I wanted to hornswoggle Wilbur, but I think Edith is happy. He's a good provider."

"Has it occurred to you that maybe no man is good enough for your girls, huh Judd?" Sarah teased, poking his arm.

The next day Esther, the proverbial romantic, was checking her appearance in the mirror. The lip rouge she had snitched from Ruth was an emboldened touch. She was pleased by the stylish middy blouse with the knotted blue tie. She pinned her straw hat at various angles, absentmindedly humming, "The Sunshine of Your Smile".

"Where would you like to go, Esther?"

"Why don't we go to the dam and sit by the water? We can even take a walk if we want," Esther suggested.

"Sure, good idea," Earl turned the buggy south, driving to the dam on the Elkhart River. They parked in the shade of tall oaks, watching fishermen and pleasure boaters.

"This is perfect," Esther smiled at Earl like he had created the setting himself. It was one of those days when nature was bursting with promise: springtime growth and sunlight collided in multi-hued tones, giving the appearance of a pointillist painting.

"I should have rented a rowboat," Earl suggested. "I'm not very adventurous."

"I think it's good you didn't. As clumsy as I am, I would probably tip it over and drench both of us," she laughed.

"I'm not one to take chances or try new things. I'll probably always be a farmer."

"We'll always need farmers—it's a good vocation. Since your father has a good size farm, he'll need help."

"You know my brother George is at Manchester College. But Esther, I just never wanted to go to college. He's going to be a minister. Can you imagine, getting in front of a church full of people and giving a sermon?" Earl waved his arms and shook his finger like a performing evangelist. "Why, I'd die of fright," he shivered at the reprehensible thought.

Esther was quiet, then she shifted and reached her hand to Earl's cheek, turning his head to face her. "It seems like you're apologizing for being the way you are," her voice was gentle. "You don't need to. You're a good, hardworking, Christian person. You don't need to be like George or anyone else. My father was a farmer. I farmed all my life because we didn't have older boys, and I'm proud of it. You should be too."

"Well, what you see is what you get," Earl said offhandedly. "My dad is impressed by your father's work at the highway department. He says Judd has turned that place around. It's good he's running for trustee. I'm sure he'll be elected."

"Papa has always worked hard. He's good with people, though too strict with his daughters," she glanced at him, figuring he had heard rumors. "I can tell you there were many lean years for our family before the highway department."

"Let's take a ride out to the country. Then we can get an ice cream." Earl untied Jock from the tree, and they meandered south toward New Paris. Esther was bemused by this conversation—certainly different than she had anticipated. Earl became more relaxed, like a weight had been lifted from his shoulders. He even dallied with Esther.

"Why Esther, the first time I went to the West Goshen Church party games I saw this pretty little black-haired filly and I said 'Earl, git over and nab that gal'. I rushed in a bad hurry and I was still fourth in line. You were the queen bee. I followed you all evening like a hang-dog puppy and you didn't even know I was there."

Esther turned to him, her head bobbing. "Oh yes I did. I asked Mary who was the fella with the brown curls." She shrugged her shoulders, "I couldn't be so forward that I set tongues wagging."

Earl led Jock along the river at the Mill Race, a wooded place frequented by church baptisms and young lovers. "It doesn't take much to get gossip started. You probably don't remember the time we danced the Quadrille and you girls jumped so much your hairpins fell out. Esther, I watched you thread your fingers through your silky hair and your hands were like magic: you twisted and coiled and tucked, then stuck in the pins and combs and you looked so fresh and beautiful. That was when I fell in love with you. The gossip mill would have gone wild had anyone been watching me. I'll bet I was drooling," he chuckled sheepishly.

Esther's eyes widened in naïve innocence, "Why Earl...."

He took her hands, "I hope you know I love you. I want you to be my wife. I think we can be very happy together," his shaky voice was earnest.

Esther couldn't breathe. These were the words she had dreamed, but hearing them in real life boggled her mind and stilled her tongue.

"Oh Earl...."

"I was kinda hoping for a better response than that," Earl looked at their entwined hands.

She was so excited that her high passion overcame her modest propriety. Esther jumped from her seat and planted a not-so-chaste kiss on his lips.

"I want to touch your curls," she gasped. She pressed his head against her chest in naughty clutching wickedness, burying her face in his curls, twining her fingers through his hair, kissing his hair...eyes...lips....

"Does this mean yes?" Earl was red-cheeked and breathless.

"Yes...Yes...Yes...Yes..." she chortled.

"Whoopee!" Earl shouted, his relief plain to see.

Esther sat down sedately, repositioned her hat, smoothed back her unruly hair and folded her hands primly. Her breath was racing, her cheeks were rosy, her smile was a mile wide.

"Phew! I've wanted to do that for a long time," she giggled with a lingering sigh of pleasure.

CHAPTER 31

Earl & Esther Wed

It was a gusty November day, the wind thrashed through the trees. *Too bad my wedding day is in the middle of the potato harvest,* Esther thought as she shoveled up a pile of potatoes, the loose dirt blowing back on her. She tapped Nell on the flanks, signaling him to move the wagon forward. She was on schedule with wedding preparations: the three-tier wedding cakes had been baked and decorated, green beans snipped, potatoes peeled, and ham basted. The house was spotless with Sarah's fall flower arrangements in the parlor. Her dress needed the hem ironed. Mrs. Plaut had helped with her wedding dress, ordering special china silk fabric in a light gray color. The Inbody sisters tailored the dress that had lace at the collar and cuffs and a wide sash with tassels. No society matron in Goshen would have a more fashionable, classic, wedding dress. Esther would quit work early this afternoon, leaving time to pamper herself with a rainwater shampoo and a scented bath.

She was ignorant of premarital qualms. Though she had no close married friends, didn't confide in Edith, and her mother was averse to discuss such topics, she had read that "love is friendship set to music". Her love for Earl passed all bounds and she sentimentally visualized their marriage arm-in-arm together, gliding through the seasons of life, confident their faith would soften the snags and storms.

In the afternoon she helped Sarah in the kitchen, then carried the galvanized tub and buckets of hot water upstairs to her room. She pulled down the window shade and luxuriated in the tub, brushing dirt from rough hands and feet, trimming her nails and shampooing her hair.

Edith entered her room as she was dressing, "You look pretty, Esther. You look like a bride in a catalogue. The silk is so soft, it sways when you move."

"I'm so excited Edith. I've waited forever for this day."

"You'll love being married. I know I messed up and the folks might never get over it, but I love having baby Emory and being married to Wilbur. My life is much easier. I have one baby to watch instead of four, and Wilbur is much easier to live with than Pop. You'll be a good wife—you're easy-going, you're a pleaser, and a hard worker. You'll be a good partner for Earl, at least once you learn to cook."

"That's the first thing I've got to learn. I'm hoping Mrs. Phillips will be patient with me."

Sarah entered the room. "Uncle Clarence is here to start the wedding. Edith, you'd better get to your seat."

"Don't forget you and Wilbur need to sign the marriage certificate. Be sure Earl's brother George, and his wife Gertrude, sign it too," Esther reminded Edith as she left the room.

Sarah placed her hands on Esther's shoulders, her eyes filling, "This is your special day. I know you'll be a good wife to Earl."

Esther's own eyes teared, "I'm so happy Mama, but I'll miss you every day."

They stepped into the hall where Earl was pacing, his harvest of curls domesticated with lemon oil, his pink cheeks wreathed in a shy, affable smile. He reached for Esther's hands, "You look beautiful. This is the best day of my life." The old family pump organ burst forth with the Wedding March as Earl and Esther slowly descended the stairs to the parlor.

The next day Judd and Sarah took them to the train station where family and friends gathered to see them off on their honeymoon. Conscious of their newlywed status and hoping for anonymity, their secret was broadcast when they were pelted with rice as they entered the train. They would spend a week in Ohio with Sarah's brother Will, and his wife Elma, while their church had revival meetings. Will was still the fun-loving jokester he had been when Sarah and he were reacquainted when she was a teen-ager living at the Millers. While Esther didn't know him well, she had met him at occasional family reunions. Always the life of the party, he was known for funny stories and his spicy, irreverent language. Sarah always had a soft spot for her brother, so was pleased when he invited Earl and Esther to honeymoon at his home.

Traveling by train was a new experience for the couple. The trip took a long day, time for the self-conscious pair to bond. While they behaved with prudent modesty, they had eyes only for each other and their tender ministrations and sentimental touches expressed a youthful poignancy. They nibbled from a basket of food Esther had packed, and spent time in the observation car.

It was late when the train arrived in Pioneer, Ohio. The couple were instantly endeared by Elma, a jolly sprite with her sunny eyes and genial air, settling them in the kitchen for hot chocolate and her famous chocolate pie. Will, with his jaunty, amiable good will and bantering chatter, helped the reticent pair to relax. In his mid-forties he had a thick head of brown unruly hair, dark complexion, and smile-furrowed eyes. He dug into his pie with gusto.

"Earl, have you heard the one about the wife who looked in the mirror and told her husband, 'I look old, fat, and ugly. I really need you to give me a nice compliment'. 'Sure,' said her husband, 'your eyesight is perfect.'" Will guffawed, slapping his knee as Elma smiled benignly, rolling her eyes at Esther.

"Seriously, Esther, I'm glad we can spend this time together. I'm guessing Sarah hasn't told you a lot about her childhood. I think you should know about it," Will added.

"You're right, she rarely mentions it. I know it wasn't easy."

"Earl and Esther are tired, Will. Don't start that tonight," Elma said.

"Right. Let me take you to your bedroom." Will picked up their suitcase and grabbed the broom."

"Why are you taking the broom? The room is clean," Elma asked.

"It's for Esther." He showed them to the room, pulled down the shades, pointed to the pot under the bed and the pitcher and bowl for washing. "Now Esther, I don't want you to be immodest and shock Earl's eyes. Be sure you stand behind the broom when you undress!"

Esther couldn't hide her smile as she tittered and blushed, lifting her hand to her mouth to cover her embarrassment.

"Alright!" Earl crowed. "Be sure to leave the broom, Will."

When they were snuggling in bed, Earl said, "Today was a good day. The train ride was interesting. Do you realize it's the longest we've ever been together—and we're still getting along? I believe I'm getting into this marriage thing," he teased. "I'm glad we came to Will and Elma's."

"He's like I remembered. They're going to be a lot of fun." Esther giggled, "Undress behind a broom, where do you suppose he got that idea?"

Her hands threaded through his rebellious curls. It felt so right—to be permitted. He caressed her cheeks, his lips sought her body in the dark, exploring and discovering, sensing the other's response and fondling a reply. Ah-h yes, marriage was good. Spent, they lay fulfilled, shy now and uncertain.

"Are you okay, Esther?"

"I'm better than okay."

"You seem quiet."

She shifted toward him. "I worry we could have an early baby and people will think we had to marry," Esther confessed.

"But that couldn't be. We're just now married," Earl said questioningly.

"Babies can come early. Then people would talk. Oh Earl, I never want there to be a question that I'm an honorable person. My sisters and Carl, I think they're what people call loose. To live as a Christian doesn't seem important to them. You know Edith and Wilbur had to get married. Ruth and Vail's behavior isn't prudent, same for Carl and his girlfriend. I want to be able to hold my head up. I need people to know that at least one of the Swiharts is moral, like Mama and Papa."

"I know how you feel, Esther. I'm always compared to George. I don't want to have an early baby either." They lay in silence.

"I think I can fix this," Earl said. "I'll ask Will if he'll take me to the drug store. I'll buy some prophylactics. It'll be embarrassing, but no one knows me in Pioneer, Ohio."

Esther sat straight up. "You mean there's a way to prevent having babies?"

"My cousin told me about it. He's pretty easy with the women and that's *his* solution."

"Someone should tell Mama about this," Esther said quietly. "I love you, I love you, I love you," she found Earl's lips in the darkness. "I'm so glad I married you. You're good at solving problems."

Earl smiled in the darkness; his chest puffed a bit. *She needed him. He was used to being in the background. People hadn't much noticed him, let alone NEED him. In that moment he vowed he would forever do all in his power to make her happy.*

"You do want children sometime, don't you?" he asked.

"Oh yes, I just don't want anyone to question my honor," she answered.

In the morning, Earl washed his face, then sat on the side of the bed as he buttoned his union suit. "I'm going to leave so you can clean up. Why don't you relax in bed for a while? After all, you're on your honeymoon."

Esther luxuriated in bed a few minutes, hesitantly touching her body. She felt alive and succulent, ripened like a fruit to pluck. She stretched languorously—life was delicious. A satisfied chuckle escaped her lips as she hopped out of bed and went to their suitcase to choose a clean blouse. Accidently she pulled out a black silk stocking from under Earl's pile of shirts. She dropped it like a hot coal. Why would Earl have silk stockings? Her heart raced, the well-being of the morning was quashed as she folded the stocking and slipped it back under his shirts. Her mind grasped for an explanation. While she didn't understand, she sensed that a man who wore silk stockings wasn't "normal". She had heard Carl refer to a fellow at the gas station as a "nance" in a deprecating tone. What was a nance? While washing and dressing, her mind was abuzz. Was this a test? Was there a reason it took him so long to pledge to her? Was her love for Earl sufficient if he was "different"? There had to be an explanation. She would go on as usual, certainly not mentioning it to Earl. But the glow was burnished; now unwanted questions flitted about in her mind.

The week flew by. Will and Elma's daughter and her new husband entertained them. The four of them attended a band concert, permitting Earl to slip away to the drug store. Esther received succor from revivals every night, inspired by the minister's words: "trust in the Lord".

On Saturday, Esther helped prepare food for Sunday when the extended family would visit. In the afternoon Elma began heating water, as all of them would take a Saturday bath. "You and Earl get started now so Will and I can get our baths before supper," she suggested.

Earl called Esther into their bedroom. He seemed skittish and had a sheepish expression on his face. "You've got to help me," he said, going to the suitcase and pulling out the black stocking. Esther gasped, now the truth would out. "Don't laugh or make fun of me," he begged. "After I wash my hair, I have to put a stocking on my head to mash down my hair till it dries. Otherwise, it's totally frizzy and wild—even more than usual. But I can't stay in the bedroom for an hour hogging the tub so no one else can bathe. I can't leave the room with a stocking on my head; leastways Will could have a heyday with that. I know it looks silly, but a stocking is the only thing I've found that works. My mama uses it sometimes. I've got wild hair just like her."

Esther wanted to shout "hallelujah"; she was so relieved. No longer did she need to wonder if he wore garters and silk stockings under his pants. She chuckled, ruffling his hair with her fingers, "You know how I love your curls, Earl. If it takes a stocking to tame them, we'll find a way." She sat beside him on the bed, thinking. "Do you think it would be too indecent if we were in here together while we bathe? We *are* married, after all. You can go first then let your hair dry while I bathe. I wouldn't do it with our parents, but I think Elma and Will are more open-minded. That's what we'll do, Earl," she said decisively. "Go out to the stove; the water is hot." She leaned into him and whispered, "This could be fun."

Since no one knew when Earl and Esther would return to the train station from their honeymoon, the two decided to carry their suitcase and walk to Esther's folks on Berkey Avenue. The family stayed up late to hear about the train ride and their visit with Will and Elma. Esther noticed that Ruth was preoccupied and jumpy. Before going to bed she went to Ruth's room.

"What's wrong, Ruth? You seem upset."

"Thank goodness, you're finally home. You've got to talk to the folks. Pop is going to kill me. Vail and I got married. He's sending money for a train ticket to take me to Ohio."

Esther tried not to show her horror. "How can you be married? There wasn't a wedding. Vail isn't even here." She was exasperated by Ruth's impertinence.

"Vail was here over the weekend. While you were going to revivals we went to the courthouse and got married. We eloped."

Esther was beyond flummoxed, "I've never heard tell of such. I doubt it's legal. Maybe since Papa is county trustee he can find a way to cancel it." She sat beside Ruth on the bed, taking her hand. "Ruth, you don't want to leave your family and go far away. We'll lose you." Esther's voice broke, tears streamed from her eyes, "Surely this isn't what you want. Is Vail forcing you? Are you...like Edith was?" Esther despaired. In their world, it was unheard of for a woman to marry in the courthouse, then leave, unchaperoned, on a train to another state.

"What's done is done. I know Pop thinks Vail is a stuffed shirt and a scoundrel, but I'm his wife now. I'm going to Ohio."

"You know what this disgrace will do to Mama; word will spread with the speed of plague," Esther couldn't conceal her true feelings.

Ruth was looking out the window into the night. "I might as well warn you: you've got lots of company."

Esther ran to the window. Soon the deafening noise of car horns, noise makers, and people screaming for Earl and Esther, flooded into the upstairs room.

"It's your shivaree. I knew they were going to bell you tonight. I got some of your underwear and hung it on the mirror in the parlor. They got Earl's long johns—you can see them flying from the mailbox. Oh, look at Earl; they put a ball and chain around his ankle. Mama knew they were coming and made cookies. Let's go join the party."

"I'll be bound, what a strange night. I'll talk to Daddy tomorrow, Ruth." She pasted a bright smile on her face and went downstairs to join the noisy post-wedding celebration.

The next morning, Esther rose early and followed Judd to the basement where he removed ashes and shoveled coal into the furnace. "I hate to return home and be the bearer of bad news, but Ruth asked me to talk to you. Last weekend she and Vail went to the courthouse and got married. Vail is sending money for her to take the train to Ohio. She insists she will leave next week."

His face flared with hot and choking indignation. He picked up coal chunks and threw them against the stone wall. "By damn!" his expletive came out windy and urgent. "That no-account son-of-a bitch sold my girl down the river."

Esther stepped back from his vicious anger and coarse language, "She calls it eloping. She seems certain it's legal."

"That high fallutin' good-for-nothin' blue blood. I knew he was trouble. What can we do, Esther? What's our obligation here? To make it right, do we need to have a real wedding with a minister?"

"I don't know, Papa. I've never heard of anyone who eloped. I guess you'd better check at the courthouse where they give marriage licenses. If it's legal, there's not much you can do."

"You know this will break your mama's heart—more talk and gossip," he said with righteous wrath. "She won't understand," his head rested in his hands, dispirited. "I can't explain it to her; she's so pure-like...she's always been that way. I saw it the first time I met her at the rally. It's like you can see the angel in her." He sat on the coal bucket, his hands shielded his eyes, "You'll have to tell her, Esther."

"Oh Papa, don't make *me* tell her."

"You'll have to. I told her about Edith. I can't do it again."

"We're going to have to live with Vail for many years. Ruth likely is leaving next week—who knows when we'll see her again. To send her with anger does no one any good. We've got to make the best of it."

"She made her bed, now she'll have to lie in it," he said miserably.

Esther met with Sarah that evening in her bedroom. "Mama, I need to give you some news about Ruth and Vail." She spilled out the few details she knew. Sarah collapsed on the bed, her body seemed to wither. She lowered her head, silent for a time.

"What a failure I've been as a mother—that two of my flesh and blood would dishonor me so. The most important task in my life, I've failed. I grew up with morals and values. I was young once, I understand. Believe me, I loved with my heart, body, and soul...but we were honorable. The war has changed women: the way they dress, carouse with men, smoke. It sickens me that the values I hold dear, I've not instilled in my children."

"You *have* taught us, Mama. It's not you who've failed. This is why Ruth isn't here talking to you—she honors and respects you so much. She feels her behavior soils you and she's ashamed. Right now, she loves you too much to be close to you. She's grown now. She'll leave us, but your example will always be with her—as it will be for all of us."

* * * * *

The next months were an extended honeymoon for Esther and Earl. They lived with Earl's parents, Frank and Alice Phillips, on their substantial farm east of Goshen. Esther's life changed drastically; for the first time she did household tasks instead of farm work. Gentle Alice took Esther under her wing, teaching her wifely chores: how to cook, wash and iron clothes, shop, twist the neck off chickens, and prepare meals for a crowd. For once she had spare time to learn to crochet and cross stitch. She was surprised to enjoy this domesticity and was flattered when Alice complimented her artistry in rolling a nice pie dough, decorating cakes, and cross-stitching pillowcases. The couple went with Frank and Alice to the Rock Run Church of the Brethren, Earl's church throughout childhood. They had Sunday School picnics and get-togethers with other young-married couples.

Esther had grown up with young siblings, but she had never been married with youngsters in the home. Eight-year-old Paul was the proverbial smart-aleck kid brother. He knew Esther resented his ubiquitous presence: if the couple took a trip to town, took a walk in the woods, or sought privacy in their room—like a buzzing fly, there was Paul, cozying to Earl and excluding Esther. Paul being a favored child, Alice and Frank thought his shenanigans charming, especially as neither Earl nor Esther seemed capable of dealing with him.

A more troubling dilemma was the country's call to arms for the 1917 war in Europe. Many townspeople went to the train station every time another delegation shipped off, waving handkerchiefs, and shedding tears. Earl's brother, George, was required to garrison and train for deployment to Europe. The military believed farmers were needed at home for growing crops to feed soldiers and the populace. A minister, however, was expendable for the war effort. Gertrude, George's wife, was bitterly angry and jealous of Esther because Earl safely stayed home while George was put in harm's way. Gertrude could never overlook the injustice in the brothers' assignments and found every way to blame and begrudge Esther, who carried the cross of Gertrude's ire. Esther could never confront her with the obvious: she had no input in either brother's military posting.

In the spring, Alice gave Earl good news that he promptly relayed to Esther: they were going to have a baby. She had noticed Esther's morning sickness and changing body. The couple was pleased, their honor intact, since it had been several months since their wedding. Used to being the Swihart "tomboy", Esther was touched by Earl's tender ministrations. It wasn't like them to be effusive about "being in the family way". Her changing body was not something readily discussed—that was the way of the times. But Esther felt Earl's concern and solicitous attention. Though it wasn't a common practice, he encouraged her to see a doctor to learn recent advances for ladies of delicate condition. They followed his advice to the letter: Esther stopped wearing a corset; Earl poured her a glass of creamy milk twice a day; and they took walks so she got lots of fresh air. Alice made her a housedress that hung from the shoulders so the hot summer would be less stifling. When she could no longer be out in public, Earl was content to stay home with her.

Earl wanted them to have their own home. Frank bought a farm a few miles from the family farm, planning that the couple would eventually buy it. Frank and Earl would work both farms. Earl was eager to raise white-faced Hereford cattle. They were excited about the attractive and roomy white frame house where they would raise their family. They moved in the spring, bringing hand-me-down furniture from both parents.

One sunny September day Esther went to Alice's home to make diapers. She had yards of outing flannel which they cut, stacked in layers of three, then stitched on her sewing machine. She adored Alice and was more comfortable asking her questions about her condition than she was her own mother.

Returning home in the afternoon, she heard a roadster approaching from behind at great speed. Before she could pull the horse over, the wagon was struck. She felt herself flying, then all went black. When she came to, she was lying on the road where the horse had been. Her confused mind surveyed the damage: the wagon was practically destroyed, with both wheels broken and the back of the wagon in splinters. Immediately her mind went to her baby; *move baby, please God, send someone to help. Protect our baby,* she repeated over and over. She checked her injuries: she could move her arms and legs; a large swelling around her eye obstructed her vision; her nose felt tender and misshapen; and blood still dripped on her stained dress. This was a country road; it could be a long time before someone came. She called the horse to no avail. She leaned against the broken wagon, slipping in and out of consciousness. It hurt to breathe. The severe pain made her dizzy and nauseous.

Though time seemed to creep, after long minutes she heard a car approach. A man rushed to her, "Did you get hit?"

"Yes," Esther answered weakly. "He didn't stop. It was a big black roadster. My horse is gone too. I hope he's not injured."

The man noticed, but didn't mention her enlarged abdomen, "We need to get you to a doctor. Do you think you can walk to my car?"

"I think so. Sir, thank you so much for helping me. I'm sorry to trouble you."

"What is our world coming to when a man would leave an injured lady in your condition along the road?" he said angrily. "Let me help you to the car. You need to get to Dr. Starkweather."

Esther was in and out of consciousness on the drive into Goshen. "You are so kind, sir. Thank you so much," she murmured each time she roused.

Dr. Starkweather, known as a women's doctor, was the quintessential small-town physician with his fringe of gray hair, kindly eyes behind glasses, and hands that poked and prodded, searching for injury. His office was in his home on Main Street. He hurried to help the good Samaritan bring Esther into his office.

"We must take care in moving her. She probably has internal injuries." He listened to her heart, then placed a Pinard horn at points around her abdomen to detect a fetal heartbeat. "I hear a heartbeat, Mrs. Phillips. Your baby is alive."

More fully conscious, the gravity of the accident, the pain, and the sympathy of the doctor brought tears spilling down her bloody, dirt-encrusted face. "Oh, thank God," she murmured, trying to find a comfortable position. "My mother has a telephone now, doctor. Could you please call her so she can come? Her number is 736."

"Mr. Stump, the man who rescued you, is using my phone to contact the authorities. I'll have him call your mother. You'll need to be in bed until your baby comes; I'm guessing, in about two months. I'm giving you a mild pain medicine; we need to be cautious due to your head injury. I'll see other patients then come back to tape your broken ribs. I want to watch you closely for internal bleeding. I'll need a urine sample to take to the hospital to check for blood."

After taking the pain pill Esther dozed. She awakened to see Judd and Sarah huddled in the corner, his arms around her shuddering shoulders, his fingers wiping her tears, then his own. Esther had rarely seen Sarah cry, and certainly not Judd.

"Don't cry, Mama. The doctor says I'll be okay. He heard the baby's heartbeat, and I've felt movement."

Instantly Judd and Sarah brightened their faces as they rushed to her bed. "You're going to be okay, Esther. We talked to Dr. Starkweather. You'll have to be on bed rest till the baby comes. You'll stay at our house; Clara will be only too happy to care for you. We sent Floyd to get Earl. Thank goodness we have the car to take you home."

"Papa, Earl has to find the horse. It's probably injured. I doubt the wagon can be salvaged."

"Do you remember what happened?" Judd asked.

"I heard a loud car coming behind me. I looked back. It was a big black roadster, going too fast. I didn't have time to pull the horse over. When I came to, I was on the road. That's all I remember."

Dr. Starkweather re-examined Esther. "Good news: your heart rate is nearly normal, and the baby's heart rate has slowed. This would suggest there isn't internal bleeding. If we're lucky, your worst injury is several broken ribs. He proceeded to tape her chest and abdomen. "This will be tight and uncomfortable but it's necessary. You'll be better off at home than if I put you in the hospital ward with sick and infectious patients. The next few days you are most at risk to lose the baby. It's too early—the baby won't live if it comes now. I'll explain all this to your mother. With the bump on your head, you probably won't remember. I wish you well, Mrs. Phillips." His voice hardened, "I know they're looking for the man who hit you. I hope they find him and bring him to justice."

The next two months Esther stayed with her parents on Berkey Avenue. A hospital bed was moved into the parlor. Dr. Starkweather visited regularly, and Earl came every few days. The accident and its aftermath profoundly changed the couple. So young in their lives and so early in their marriage they learned that life can be taken in an instant. The accident brought the wisdom that every day together is a treasure; irritations are incidental to the bedrock of a greater love. They both leaned inward, mutually making decisions and solving problems. This remained the pattern throughout their marriage.

Soon after the accident, Earl brought the news that the man driving the roadster had run his car into the ditch a few miles after hitting Esther. He was found to be drunk. The policeman informed Earl the driver agreed to give them three hundred dollars if they would not press charges.

"You shouldn't settle so soon. Your horse could go lame and you don't know the total of Esther's medical bills. If he offered you three hundred dollars, he assumes you'll counter higher," Judd suggested.

"Judd, this isn't your decision to make," Sarah said.

"Yes, you're right. I'll stay out of it. I was just trying to help."

Later when alone with Esther, Earl asked, "What do you think about the money, Esther? I believe they need an answer. We wouldn't press charges anyway; our church doesn't believe in taking legal action to settle disputes."

"Do you think it will cost us more than three hundred dollars till we pay the doctor, fix the wagon and get another horse if need be? It *was* his fault—he was driving drunk. We shouldn't get stuck with any expenses."

"Yes, you're right. You should ask Dr. Starkweather if he can estimate his bill."

"Sure, I'll ask him. Do you think we should try to get more in case there are other expenses, like Papa suggested?"

"It wouldn't be right to take advantage or *make* money on this."

"Well, let me talk to the doctor. I would think three hundred dollars would cover it."

Judd and Sarah grew to appreciate Earl during these months when he was a frequent visitor.

Sarah noticed Esther freshened up before his visits, combing her hair and fixing her face. If she was weary before his visit, she was romantic and feminine in his presence. Earl was "steady is as steady goes", eager to please and never querulous. While preferring to be in the background, he was always friendly and helpful. Nearly every visit he brought something that put a smile on Esther's face: flowers in a canning jar, a roast for supper, or a Ladies Home Journal magazine.

As time for the birth approached, Dr. Starkweather determined that a new obstetrical technique should be used. Esther would have a caesarian section surgery to deliver the baby. They would use a mask with ether to put her to sleep. She would go to the twenty-seven bed Goshen Hospital, recently converted from a residence. A special doctor from Elkhart would come for the surgery, never before done in Goshen. This was noteworthy, the story of the young mother injured by a drunk driver was featured in the Goshen Daily Democrat. Even beyond friends and relatives in the extensive family circle, the whole community offered concern and prayers.

The delivery was scheduled for November 23, 1918. There was a hive of activity outside the surgery suite, so no one noticed Sarah and Earl standing outside the open door of the nursery room.

"Oh Earl, the baby is blue," Sarah gasped as a doctor rushed past with the baby. A nurse and doctor encircled the infant. The doctor lifted the limp, dusky baby by its feet, gently spanking its bottom and snapping its feet.

"Come on baby. You have to breathe," Sarah didn't realize she'd spoken aloud.

"I'm going out with Judd; I can't take this. Come tell me if something happens," Earl said as he hurried away.

It seemed they worked forever before the infant took a breath. Without realizing, Sarah felt her chest heaving; her attempt to breathe for the baby. *Please God, after all we've been through, don't let the baby die.*

She heard sounds of relief and quiet cheers, "Okay, she's trying to breathe. Come girl, let's have a lusty cry," the doctor said. Then Sarah heard it, a mewling, whimpering sound—a sigh more than a cry.

Sarah swallowed a sob as she ran down the corridor to the waiting room. "You have a daughter, Earl, and she's crying!" Earl jumped up, hugging her with months of pent-up emotion.

"We have a baby," he shook Judd's hand. "She'll be named Helen after Dr. Starkweather's wife. I think my girl will be a fighter, she's been through so much already. Sarah, Dr. Starkweather was just here. They're finishing the surgery. Esther will be asleep most of the day. Everything went as planned. They'll let us see her for a few minutes this evening. How soon do you think we'll get to see the baby?"

"I don't know anything about hospital deliveries, Earl, but she seemed pretty puny. It may be awhile. I think she'll take after the Zumbruns. I saw a thatch of black hair."

"I hope it's not curly like mine," Earl said.

The next day when Earl went to the hospital, Esther was lethargic and nauseous from the anesthesia and pain medicine. When she moved, she threw up, which was painful after major abdominal surgery.

Earl went to the baby's room. "Would you like to hold your baby?" the nurse asked.

"Yes, very much." Earl sat in the rocking chair with Helen in his arms. His heart was captured by this little one who was having a hard go of it. He was glad she favored Esther's family with her round face, black hair and dark skin tone. Her eyes were dark and searching.

"Can I unwrap the blanket?" he asked the nurse.

She seemed to question his request, then relented, "Sure."

Earl unwrapped the blanket and checked Helen's little fingers and tiny feet. Immediately he noticed something wrong. He glanced at the nurse who had busied herself at the desk across the room. Both his hands hurried to Helen's tiny arm, exploring. It felt flaccid and her fingers seemed unnaturally splayed. He noticed the left arm was reaching and punching the air; the right arm didn't move. *Oh my dear, what has happened to you?* He lifted her kimono and saw the twisted and misshapen right foot lying motionless, and the left leg waving its baby dance. He lifted the tiny lumpy foot to his lips, the silky baby skin so soft on his cheek. Tears filled his eyes—not of disappointment or sadness, but of overwhelming love for this babe God had tucked into his arms and his heart. He knew in that instant he would do anything for this child.

Within a few days, Esther's body was rid of the effects of the medications, her mind clear of the fuzziness that had stuffed her head. Helen also picked up, her dark eyes bright and probing. She latched on to the breast with aplomb. Feeding times, when the nurse brought her swaddled baby, were the highlight of Esther's days.

"I've never known a baby who fusses less than this little girl; she only cries when she's hungry," the nurse commented.

After several days, Esther went back to her hospital bed in Sarah's parlor. This was the first time she diapered and checked her baby. She was awed by the miracle of this little one who so quickly captured her heart and gave her life purpose.

"Mama, come here," there was panic in her voice. Helen lay placidly in her diaper, her dark eyes reaching for her mother. *See me, Mama, her eyes seemed to be saying. Aren't I SOMETHING!*

"Mama, something's wrong with her," Esther was coddling her rigid fingers, lifting and dead-dropping her right arm and leg. "She can't move them," she said frantically. She was caught up in acquainting herself with her baby. "Her whole right side seems paralyzed. She doesn't cry when I move her so it must not hurt." Sarah sat on the bed, her arm around Esther's shoulders. Esther's eyes rushed to Sarah's, "Did you know something was wrong?"

"I did. Earl told me a few days after she was born. I didn't see until yesterday when you came home."

"Earl knows?" she asked.

"Yes, and I can tell you there is no man alive who will love and care for this child more than he will."

"Mama, I'm so lucky to have him. And now this precious baby," tears swelled in her eyes.

"All of us in the family will help you give Helen every possible benefit. Life will be hard for her."

"Did Earl talk to the doctors? We should never have settled for three hundred dollars."

"Dr. Starkweather didn't have much to say when Earl asked about the damage to Helen's right side. They feel certain it's a result of the accident. He emphasized there is no sign of brain damage. Though she had a tough start, she's very alert. They say only time will tell the extent of her handicap. Exercises may strengthen her muscles."

Esther lifted her new baby, kissing her eyes, her fingers, her toes. "You're my perfect little angel, Lovey. We best start working on you. You're going to need to walk someday."

CHAPTER 32

Sisters Edith and Clara

Esther was determined to be home before Christmas. As grateful as she was for Sarah's assistance, she had been away from home three months. Judd packed all the baby paraphernalia in the Model T and took them home.

"It's time for us to be a family again," she told Earl. "Mama wanted to send Clara to help, but I just want to be with you and Helen."

"I almost forget what it was like to be married. I'll help—I know you're weak and far from healed. I'm just happy to have you and Helen to myself," Earl replied.

The next week they went to see Dr. Starkweather. "This little babe looks in fine fettle. She's regaining some muscle tone. I want you to get Relevo Liniment and massage her muscles at least twice a day for twenty minutes. Bend and knead her hand and foot, even if she cries. Do everything you can to get her to use the damaged limbs. As she gets older, make her reach for things with her right arm and stand on her right leg. Get her a walker she sits in. I wish I could assure you these exercises will help her muscles develop normally, but I don't know that. There's a doctor in Elkhart who works with people with damaged muscles. Maybe he can help your Helen." As if on cue Helen gave him a bright smile. "You have a special child here," he said, shaking their hands. "She could have died twice, and here she is smiling at me. She's a fighter, that's for sure."

"I guarantee, we'll do as you say." Earl promised.

* * * * *

Armistice! Armistice! 1918—the end of the war to end all wars. Earl didn't even tie the horses before running into the house after his return from Hawk's Hardware. Small town fervor was high. Everyone's lives had been put on hold as people scrimped to buy war saving stamps and liberty bonds. Every housewife was eager to stop rationing sugar, flour, and coffee. Over three thousand Goshen men would return from the war.

Women could quit working.

"The war is over. They've called an armistice. You wouldn't believe the celebration downtown. All the stores have flags; there are signs welcoming home the soldiers. Store clerks are wearing Uncle Sam hats. Tomorrow night they're having a big party; too bad it's so cold or I would suggest we go," Earl said.

"Thank God, that's wonderful news." She ran to Earl, caught in his embrace. "Now maybe George will come home and Gertrude won't be so nasty to us. I would love to go to town for the festivity. It feels like I've been penned up for ages."

"Do you think your folks would come here in the car and take us to town? That way you and Helen wouldn't be out in the cold."

"I'm sure they would if they haven't promised a ride to someone else," Esther said.

That's all Earl needed to plan the outing. The next night they were with Judd and Sarah driving downtown. "Land sakes, I believe everyone in the county is in Goshen tonight," Sarah exclaimed. "It's good we came early."

"Confound it, look at all the cars." The goosey sound of Judd's horn punctured the air. "This is Goshen's first traffic jam."

"I declare, now *that* is a bonfire." Earl looked up, "I hope they don't burn down the courthouse."

"Look Earl, there's the new motor-driven fire truck; we'll have to check it out. I'm going to park here in front of the Chicago Fair Store so you ladies can see the action."

"You fellas better watch out; I see some cheek-to-cheek dancing out there. I thought that was outlawed in Goshen," Sarah chuckled.

"Tonight, anything goes—God Bless America," Esther cheered in celebratory spirit.

Sarah and Esther were secluded in the Model T; the pulsing light of the bonfire illuminating, then casting shadows, on their surroundings. They observed the gaiety, cheers, speeches, and drunken hijinks around them. Along came a rowdy chain of young folks, singing as they weaved in and amongst the crowd: "Oh, Johnny! Oh, Johnny! How you can love! Oh, Johnny! Oh, Johnny! Heavens above!"

This was a treasured moment for the two women. With the passage of time they were more than mother and daughter: they were each other's best friend, confidant, trusted advisor, and partner in faith. "It feels so good to be out, even staying in the car bundled in comforters and warm bricks is exhilarating. Thanks for coming to the farm to get us."

"You'd better get used to it, Esther. I rarely get out of the house. It was kind of Clara to stay home with the four young'uns. She'll have her hands full. With you out at the farm we rarely see you. I was spoiled having you home so long; I miss our talks. I've been so concerned about Edith. She's changing, Esther. I could understand if her faith in the church was lax, but the direction she's going is so misguided. I would even say it's evil."

"Is she still involved with that Osborn lady in Elkhart?" Esther asked, opening her bodice so Helen could nurse.

"She's totally wrapped up in it. You know how Edith has always done her own thing? I hoped Wilbur would drive some sense into her head, but now he's in it as much as she is."

"I'm sorry to hear it. You say it's evil. What do you mean?"

"Oh Esther, it breaks my heart. They discourage members from associating with anyone outside the Lemurian Community—even their own family. It seems Edith is getting more distant, and when we see her all she wants to talk about is "the brotherhood"."

"But what *is* the brotherhood, Mama?"

"It's all gibberish to me. Tommy rot, Pop says. They think a Lemurian civilization existed thousands of years ago on a continent called Mu. It was very progressive and powerful. They taught Christian principles, but the people were wayward, so the continent was submerged under the ocean and destroyed—like the flood in the Bible. I don't make sense of it; they compare it with Christianity today." Sarah's voice was interrupted by a troop of drunken young people, cheering and holding aloft flags and sparklers. "Isn't that fella staggering around Al Baker's boy? He better not get pinched by the police for drunk and disorderly. His mama leads all those rallies for the Woman's Christian Temperance Union."

"Look, he fell down.... His friends are helping him. Mama, does Edith's group have a church she attends?"

"I think this Jeanette Osborn rents a theater where she preaches. She's got a large following. It scares me what this world is coming to. They believe they can communicate with the dead. I think their faith is in the fortune teller, not in God. Edith and Wilbur take Emory to these séances where people do all sorts of indecent activities. They keep it dark, so people don't have to account for themselves. Now I didn't hear *that* from Edith, but I can tell you it's not on the up-and-up, and no place for a toddler. Supposedly they channel a dead person, and their body gets taken over by the spirit of the dead. I know people scream and cry, speak in tongues, and pass out when they connect. That's what I say is evil."

"It certainly seems so. Nothing a God-fearing Christian would get involved in."

"I'm afraid for Edith's family, Esther. I can't see anything good coming of this."

"Edith is an adult with her own family. There's nothing we can do to make her see sense. Like Papa said about Ruth, 'she made her bed; she'll have to lie in it'," Esther said, burping Helen over her shoulder.

Sarah mused, as if an afterthought: "what is happening to our family? I need to be more urgent in my prayers. It won't surprise you that Carl's in trouble at church again. The West Goshen minister came last week to talk to Judd about Carl playing baseball on Sunday."

"But doesn't Papa watch him play?"

Sarah smiled. "There's the problem. Carl isn't going to listen to the minister when he knows his dad doesn't agree with the church's teaching about acceptable Sabbath activities." Sarah turned in her seat, "Hand Helen to me. It's been too long since I held our little dumpling," she said reaching for the baby. "Honestly Esther, sometimes I think Reverend Fike just goes looking for ways to discipline us. Why, they want us to report a church member going into a saloon. Wait till they find out Carl goes to the bowling alley where all the lewd women hang out. Even your father can't corral that boy—though I don't think he tries very hard. He doesn't treat *them* like he did you girls. The boys are all spoiled is what they are, and they run me ragged. I vow, they'll be the death of me."

"One thing is certain: even Clara who naïvely sees the best in everyone, would *never* say Papa spoiled us or neglected to discipline us girls. I wonder why he's easier on the boys. Why the difference?"

"Because boys are favored, Esther. Talking about Rev. Fike, do you remember Minnie Huber, the little lady at church who sits near the front. She has just one big tooth in the front of her mouth. She was taking a walk when Rev. Fike visited her. He reprimanded her for wearing a sun bonnet over her prayer covering—said he'd bring the issue up at council meeting. At our last council he asked her to come forward, saying she had sinned by hiding her covering under a sun bonnet. Everyone felt sorry for that little humpbacked lady as she slowly shuffled to the front. She straightened her shoulders, her eyes looked at the men's side of the church in a straight and level manner, then turned to Reverend Fike, 'I notice that Brethren men can wear no hat, or any style that they want. It seems fair to me the sisters should have the same privilege, especially around their home. I plan to continue wearing a sunbonnet when I'm outside', then she returned to her seat. I tell you Reverend Fike got red and blotchy to the top of his head, like his self-righteous piety went right to seed. I heard someone snigger. There wasn't a lady there who didn't want to stand and cheer. At Ladies Aid meeting all the women fawned over Sister Minnie; she did what no one else had the nerve to do. We thought she was this meek little pansy. As it turns out, she's a sunflower, tall and strong in her way—her face holding to the sun."

"I do remember Sister Minnie," Esther said. "She's probably the last person I would've expected to speak up to Reverend Fike. I think the suffragettes are influencing women to believe our opinions count and we should have a voice. I don't go to rallies like Edith, but I hope women *do* get the vote."

"Goodness knows, Edith has always said her piece. I see Helen is moving her right arm. She reaches for the rattle now. Your exercises are working."

"I spend every spare minute working with her. I see progress but it sure is slow. She says words like bye-bye, ma-ma, and da-da so her brain is developing normally. I figure if she has a good brain, I can bring the muscles along. She tries so hard and she never fusses. She wants to roll over, but the right side holds her back. She manages to scoot a bit, if you put out a toy she works till she reaches it. She's going to have a tough go, but determination is just stamped in to her body. Look Mama, here come the fellas in Uncle Sam hats."

Judd got into the car, sputtering and fuming, "Mama, I'm glad you didn't come with us. It would have ruined your evening. We saw Edith dancing the Charleston in a short swingy skirt. Wilbur is off reporting, and she acts like Jezebel. It was obscene. She needs a good licking."

"I'm sure everyone in Goshen saw her. I wonder how many ladies will have the pleasure of telling me." Sarah muttered.

* * * * *

"Stand up, big girl. If you want to walk you're going to have to stand."

Step, Step One
Step, Step Two
Step, Step, Step, Step
Run, Run, Run, Run, Run.

Esther sang the childish song while helping Helen put weight on her feet. Helen slobbered and sang along in her baby gibberish.

The back porch door flung open and Clara stumbled in, bringing the damp springtime. "I'm glad I finally got here." She removed her coat and rubbers, then sat on the floor, grabbing Helen in a hug. "How's my girl? I miss you, Sweet Pea."

"Don't tell me you walked here from Goshen. Papa's men haven't grated the road since winter; it's a sea of mud and potholes. Why aren't you at work, Clara? Is everything okay?" Esther was alarmed, knowing something was wrong if sixteen-year-old Clara missed work and walked seven miles from Goshen.

"Mama doesn't know I'm here, but I had to talk to you, Esther."

"What's in your bag?"

"A camera. Floyd said I could bring it to take pictures of Helen. You know Floyd—trouble follows him around. Last week he was showing off when he jumped off the school bus and ran in front of a car. His leg got broke, the bone was sticking out and everything. Mama called Dr. Bowser and Papa came home from work. They pulled the bone back in place and now he's in a cast. The doctor put the smelly cloth over his nose, but Floyd screeched like a kicked cat. The man who hit him felt bad, and the next day he came back with this camera. I'd say a pretty good deal for Floyd. Now Tobe and I have to do his chores."

"Poor Floyd. I bet he'll look next time before running across the road," Esther said.

Clara, holding a rattle for Helen to grasp, watched as she struggled to lift her arm a few inches. "Such a sweet baby," she said, nuzzling her cheek. "It's too bad she's so handicapped. She's adorable, even if she'll never walk."

Esther looked at Clara quizzically, her brows furrowed, "What do you mean, her handicap? I don't understand."

Clara's chin lifted to see Esther's face, her eyes probing to judge Esther's sincerity. She stammered, "Well, she…she can't move very well. Her hand and foot are…not right, they're… useless. She can't…."

"Oh Clara," Esther said with assurance, "trust my word, she's *not* handicapped. She won't always be like this. Now she has a developmental problem, but she'll catch up with other kids. Why, it's only been a few months since she was born, and she moves her arm and leg. You'll be surprised what *this* girl will accomplish."

"You're right," Clara said softly. "I'm not looking at Helen right: I see her limitations, what will hold her back. You see the possibilities when her body mends. You're right, she's moving better than when you stayed at our house after she was born."

"I agree with you, for some babies, her problems could be a handicap, but not for our Helen. Now Clara, tell me why you walked seven miles to talk to me. It looks like you brought dirty clothes in your bag."

Clara's eyes clouded, the veins beat in her temples. Her hurt was transparent as she hunched into herself. "I'm so ashamed. I don't know if I can say the words," her voice was shaky, her well-being extinguished.

Esther reached for Clara, treasuring her gentle spirit. "I know you, Clara. You're a good person. It can't be so bad we can't make it better."

Clara dissolved in tears, her hands covered her face. "I'm not a good person anymore. I'm a sinner."

"Tell me, my dear."

"Last night my friend Mary set me up with a fella. His name is Jack. He goes to Goshen City Church of the Brethren. She said he was 'hunky-dory'. Mary was with her boyfriend and the four of us went to the McDowell farm. We were supposed to meet some of their friends, but we didn't see anyone when we got there." Esther's heart broke as Clara curled into a fetal position, shrouding herself with Helen's blanket, as if protecting herself from hurtful memories and hideous shame. Her voice became a whispered monotone, dry and achy. "Suddenly the lights went out. They drug me into another room. Mary, I don't know where.... I heard her calling me. She was crying too. My drawers and stockings are torn and bloody. All the buttons popped off my dress. But I found them and I have them. I saved the buttons, Esther," she said with pride. "It hurt; it felt like something tearing. It seemed like forever. I don't know how many there were. Suddenly the lights came on. The hired hand who lives upstairs heard Mary and me and got suspicious. The guys all ran out the parlor door, got in their buggies and took off. That's when I looked for the buttons, till I found everyone. I'm glad I saved something. I'm defiled, Esther. The preacher said so. I'm not clean anymore. I wanted to be a lady like you, but now I'm a sinner. The hired man put Mary and me in his buggy and took us home. I can't tell Mama, and definitely not Papa. I could only come here."

Clara's words exposing her rape were like a foreign language to Esther. In her perfect world she couldn't conceive of a hate that would cause a man to violate a woman. How could such a thing happen to her sweet little sister with the sunniest, most trusting heart? For the first time, she felt a crack in her unconditional belief in church teachings and in her trust in a loving, caring God. Esther's tears were of anger and futility. Could Clara ever feel whole again? She felt a suffocating inadequacy to know how to help or say a healing word. She looked at her dear innocent baby, sound asleep. She despaired that mothers can't always keep their children safe in this world with lecherous men from their own church, bootleg liquor, the shimmy dance, and fast cars. She curled next to Clara, encircling her petite, fragile body.

"Cry, my dear. Your tears will help you heal. There, there." She smoothed her hair tendrils with her fingers as she talked. "This wasn't your fault. You did nothing wrong. You must keep repeating this until you believe it in your heart. The sin isn't yours, Clara. Remember the day you accepted Christ into your life? When you did that, He washed you clean. You can never be dirty again. You are God's child, as pure as driven snow. Today can be a fresh start, like you've been whitewashed. You must put last night out of your mind."

Esther softly sang the words of a favorite hymn:

Lord Jesus, I long to be perfectly whole;
I want Thee forever to live in my soul;
Break down every idol, cast out every foe—
Now wash me and I shall be whiter than snow.

Whiter than snow, yes, whiter than snow.
Now wash me and I shall be whiter than snow.

Even with Esther's classic sense of decorum and virtue she was sufficiently tolerant to set aside the teachings and platitudes about fallen women endorsed by the church. She would salve a broken heart, console, and open a niche where wholeness could one day thrive.

CHAPTER 33

Helen Meets A Tramp

"Toodle-oo Mama," Esther called out as she and Helen entered the kitchen door at Berkey Avenue.

"You're bright and early," Sarah smiled, lumbering to catch Helen against her swollen belly. "How's my little girlie?"

"I'm a *big* girl, Grandma. I'm three." Helen held up three little-girl fingers. Sarah reached for a chair to pull herself up.

"Look at that plucky little tyke. I vow Esther, I would never have believed the progress she's made."

"All those stretching exercises and massages are paying off. I 'llow, we'll have to keep a close eye on her today. She'll get out the screen door and into the road as fast as greased lightening. What happened to your door? It's cracked and the window is broken."

"Oh, that door. Pop is going to fix it as soon as the glass comes in at Hawk's Hardware. The boys are so full of foolishment, and Pop is as bad as they are. Pop bet Carl, Tobe, and Floyd they couldn't wrestle him under the kitchen table. In all the wrassling around all four of them went through the door. I get so flustrated with the lot of them."

"You do look a little peaked, Mama. It's going to be warm today. I brought two bushels of corn for canning—it's in the summer kitchen. I don't know how many bushels you have, but I don't want you to be on your feet all day in this heat. The girls can help me finish when they come home from work."

"I'll get along, Esther. I always have. I'll sit to cut the corn off the cob. Let's go start the pots boiling to blanch the corn. I'll wager, it's harder on me than it used to be. A lady my age isn't meant to be worrying about childbirth," she said scornfully. "It's a mortification to have four grandchildren older than my own baby."

Esther contemplated, "Mama, does Papa...uh, does Papa...."

"Pop thinks it's a woman's lot; it's God's will, blah, blah, blah. I'll get Floyd and Tobe to shuck the corn. Ruby can watch Helen. I'm glad you brought your copper tub. We'll get two water baths going."

"Clara told me in church yesterday that something is going on with Edith—said she saw you crying. She was so worked up; she thinks the world is coming to an end when she sees you cry."

"I'm sorry Clara saw me. I reckon that's how it feels to me—the world ending. Pop and I are just sick," Sarah's voice was shaky and cracking.

"It's the Osborn lady, isn't it?" Esther asked. "I told Earl yesterday, that woman is just trouble."

Not wanting to upset the children, Sarah's voice dropped to a whispered alarm, her tears dotting the bib of her apron. "I can't bear it Esther. I'll be chastened for having hate in my heart, but I detest Jeanette Osborn. Edith and Wilbur are following her to California, taking those two little boys. They may as well be dead to us; we'll probably never see them again. She has stolen them out of our family."

"Mama, try to settle down. It's bad for the baby when you're so overwrought."

"I would rather she had gone in with the Papists or Jews; leastways she would have stayed in Elkhart," Sarah leaned forward, covering her face with her apron, her body shaking. Esther feared for her mother's health.

"I must cleanse my spirit. The Bible says, 'The Lord giveth and the Lord taketh away', so I guess this will pass, but God gives a sore trial."

"Mama, Mama," Helen came clumsy-limping into the summer kitchen as fast as her legs could go, grabbing Esther's skirt, "I skered," her voice panicked.

"She's afraid the train whistle will get her," Ruby said.

Esther lifted Helen, coddling her with a soothing voice. "You're not used to the train whistle, are you, Sweetie? It can't catch you Helen. You're a big girl. You run too fast."

"This is a good time to stop for dinner," Sarah said. "Ruby, tell Floyd to bring in the bag of cottage cheese from the clothesline. We'll have it with maple syrup and some of this sweet corn. Helen, do you want a molasses cookie after dinner?"

"I want a cookie," Helen said, her cheeks moist with tears—though the train was forgotten.

After lunch Sarah whispered to Esther, "I'm going to call Dr. Bowser to make sure he can come this evening. Looks like the baby will come today."

"Oh Mama, is it too early? I knew you got too riled this morning. Go in and lay down. I'll finish the corn. I'll stay tonight and watch the children. You should call Pop's work to be sure he gets home in time."

"Yes, it's time. This baby is well-nigh big enough," Sarah grimaced.

That night Sarah delivered a hefty baby boy. Esther washed the infant, bathed Sarah and changed the bedclothes. "What's this little fella's name?" Esther asked.

"Satisfaction," Sarah said, mincing no words and looking pointedly at Judd. "I hope everyone's satisfied," she said in a world-weary voice.

"His name will be Donald Edward," Judd pronounced. "God is good. We have five fine sons," he said.

After a weighty pause, Esther added, "and five fine daughters."

"And four in the ground," Sarah muttered. At forty-five years of age, she desperately wanted to be done with childbearing. Her body didn't easily rebound after Don's birth. 1918 was the first year she couldn't plant and tend the family garden. In the fall she took to bed with a high fever and cough, succumbing to the flu that swept through Goshen and the rest of the country.

* * * * *

"Come and see your baby sister, Helen. Careful big girl. You can't jump on Mama. Stand on the stool by the bed," Sarah said, leading Helen into the bedroom. "Don, you can come too."

Esther leaned toward Helen, "Here's Erdene, your new sister. You can pat her head if you want."

"She's noisy, she chugs like the engine that could. Does she have an engine in her mouth?"

Esther glanced sharply at Sarah, "Our baby has a hole in her heart, so it's hard for her to breathe. That's why she makes that noise," Esther told her.

"Can she play?" Helen's soft voice was awestruck.

"You're too big to play with her—you're five years old. Helen, let Don up on the stool. Since he had measles he can't see very well."

"Children, go wash up for dinner." Sarah sat on the bed, "Hold to your faith, Esther. The doctor said to love this child for as long as we have her and that's what we'll do. He also said it's possible the hole will heal."

Tears sat in Esther's eyes, "But Mama, Erdene can't breathe while she nurses. How am I going to feed her? She gets blue and chokes. It scares me to death she'll die in my arms." Esther cried, her sniffles a duet with the baby's rhythmic wheezing. "Don't tell Earl I'm a crybaby," she said, her face blotchy with emotion.

"With every birth I've had, and I've had enough to know, the days following birth have been full-up with discouragement. I was overwrought with the thought of caring for another baby. But we find the strength to carry on—mothers just do. Esther, I confess, when Helen was born, I thought she'd live in a wheelchair. Look at her now," her laughter tinkled. "She's learned to do what we thought impossible. She's a miracle; you've made her that way. You'll learn to care for Erdene as well. You're a wonderful mother, you'll figure things out."

Esther took her hand, "If I learned anything, Mother, it was at the hands of a master. Don't tell Earl. He doesn't need to know when things get me down."

Esther arrived at the one-room Prairie Flower School in Millersburg at the end of the school day. She drove the horse out of sight, hoping to observe Helen, who had recently entered first grade. She didn't know the teacher and hoped he would enlighten her as to Helen's adjustment to school, maybe even suggest activities to strengthen her right hand and foot. As soon as Helen left on the school hack, Esther went into the school room. The teacher sat her across from his desk in one of the student's seats. He busied himself cleaning the classroom while Esther waited, surreptitiously observing him: Mr. Garman was stolid and big boned. His thick brown hair was slicked back, his thin lips pursed in a line. His dress was a bit shabby like a man who lived simply and frugally. He finally sat, measuring her as if in reproach: "Yes?"

Esther felt intimidated, a supplicant before God, "I want to talk to you about my Helen, to see how she's doing."

"She's doing fine. We're off to a good start this year."

"Are the other children...mean to her, uh, because she's different? I saw one of the children trip her so she fell just now, when she walked to the school hack."

"Mrs. Phillips, you and I both know kids will be kids. They pick on the one with the softest underbelly. You're right, Helen is different, so she arouses hectoring. They don't hurt her; they just make fun." Mr. Garman unconsciously smoothed his mustache while he talked. "Some of the children exaggerate her limp and call her "claw hand"." Esther's head jerked upright as though she'd been struck, her eyes swam with tears. "Yes, she's probably been tripped."

"Might, I mean...might it be good to explain...to teach about kindness. She's just a little girl; she can't help she's different. Maybe ask how they would feel," Esther realized she was stammering; she wasn't helping Helen. She felt desperate. She wanted to scream and beg. Yet she felt helpless to say words that would make a difference.

"Mrs. Phillips, I don't believe in showing favoritism."

"Oh no. I don't mean favoritism."

"I daresay she'll face repetitions of such childish behavior. She needs to learn early on how to live with it and ignore it—tempered by fire, so to speak. Actually, I'm quite impressed; she's a plucky sort with lots of spirit and determination. It almost seems she blocks out what she doesn't want to see and hear."

"Yes, yes. But I don't want her spirit to be broken."

"Is there anything else, Mrs. Phillips?"

"Why, why, yes, there is. The muscles in her right hand are spastic and contracted. She can't use it. When you begin teaching penmanship she'll use her left hand. She's quite adept, she eats with her left hand."

"As I said earlier: I don't make allowances or give any student an easier regimen. They'll all write with their right hand."

"I...I don't think so. Thank you for your time." Esther rose from her chair with one goal in mind: *Please God. Don't let me cry in front of him* her mind repeated until finally on the road her tears gushed as from a spigot, a keening sound as from a cornered animal. She felt hapless shame that she couldn't stand up for her daughter. What kind of mother would cave in and stutter—a mealy-mouthed paragon of empty effort. If *she* couldn't stand up for Helen, who would?

* * * * *

"Mama, there's a man walking up our driveway. He's dirty," Helen ran into the house letting the screen door bang. As usual Esther was feeding Erdene, a scrawny six-month-old who was hardly bigger than a newborn. Everything she ate she threw up. Esther looked out the window. "It's a tramp. He's one of God's children down on his luck. Go lock the screen door. Tell him to rest on the porch and I'll bring him a plate of food. You stay inside where I can see you from the kitchen."

Helen stood at the screen door in her mud-spattered pinafore, her child's curiosity aroused. The man was young, having a tasteful countenance despite his shabbiness. He had a stringy leanness and walked with a pronounced limp.

"Mama would come and visit with ya' but she has to feed my sister. She throws up her milk *all* the time. Her stomach looks like she swallowed a ball. She has to wear an asafetida bag with stinky weeds around her neck. Pee-uuu! It's supposed to make her better, but it doesn't work."

The tramp sat against the porch post, his legs in front of him as he observed Helen through the screen door. Water was still dripping off him from washing in the rain barrel. He began eating the leftover ham and beans and potatoes in a leisurely and proper manner.

"I think ya' forgot to say grace," Helen reminded him.

"You're right little girl, I did. My mama would be ashamed of me," he said, bowing his head and whispering a prayer.

"I'm sorry your sister is sick," the man said, removing his sweat-stained hat and running his hand through thick brown hair.

"Ya' see that cow there? She's Grandma's cow, Boss. Grandma and Grandpa brought her here last night cause her milk settles Erdene."

"Boss sounds like a good cow," he nodded, his speech spare.

"Yup. She's a good one all right. It's my job to feed her and watch she stays off the road. We have to go to grandma's house tonight for Aunt Clara's wedding. She's my favorite aunt; on Sunday she plays croquet with the little kids. Ya' might have to leave then."

"Oh, I'll leave here pretty directly—unless your mama has work needs done."

"Daddy says it's a shotgun wedding so I 'spect it'll be noisy. I don't like loud noises."

"I'm with you, girlie. I don't like loud noises either. Too many loud noises lately."

"Mama said there's more ham and beans if you want more."

"No, I've had plenty. It was very tasty." The tramp pulled up his pant leg and rubbed his ankle.

"You have a bad leg like me? How'd you hurt your leg?"

"It got blown up in the war."

"Does it hurt?"

"Yes."

"My arm and leg got messed up in an accident before I was borned. Mine doesn't hurt anymore. Do people make fun of the way you walk?"

"Sometimes they shove me. They think I'm a lazy good-for-nothing."

"Yup. They trip me too. I hate wearing high-top shoes, 'specially when jumping rope. Mama says they're ignerent. She says people like us are special—we have our own way of walking an' all. I figure everybody's got something: Erdene's got a hole in her heart and throws up, Grandma's boy, Don, got measles in his eyes and can't see good. They put eggs in his eyes every day, but it doesn't help, he still can't see. You have a hitch in your leg. That's just the way of it. I'm good at school but I'm not good at running or jumping rope."

"Good for you. It's better to be good at school than good at running."

"I 'spect so."

"I'm going to be on my way now," the tramp got up and limped to the rain barrel, dipping his hat. "Tell your mother I really appreciated dinner. She's a good cook."

"I'll tell her. Nice ta' meecha."

"Yes, I enjoyed our visit, little girl."

"My name's Helen."

"My name's Bill."

"Bye, Bill."
"Bye, Helen."

CHAPTER 34

Helen's Injury

"I've been thinking of Helen's birthday coming up. I can hardly believe she'll be ten. I thought we'd have the grandparents in for homemade ice cream. That'll be the best treat. We'll have to buy ice, but we can splurge this time," Esther said as she and Earl relaxed after supper with a cup of coffee.

"The years sure go fast. Then again, she seems older than most ten-year olds. She's so much better than I would have believed; you've done so much with her, Esther."

"It's all her, Earl. You see how determined she is; nothing stops her. And her mind is so sharp. It's good she's natured that way 'cause she has plenty of hurdles to overcome. I'm amazed at her mind," Esther chuckled. "Last night she asked me who I'm going to vote for—said I should practice my voting rights. Where do you think she heard about women getting the vote? She reminded me I want to talk to you about the election. I wish my first-time voting was more exciting. Neither Harding nor Cox appeals to me. I don't think I'd have voted for Woodrow Wilson had he been nominated again, but at least I knew something about him."

"I don't know much about them either. I don't think anyone does. I'm going to vote for Warren Harding only because I usually vote with the Republicans. I want someone who won't take us to war. I'm tired of war."

"What do you think of McCray for governor?" she asked.

"I'm going to vote for him because he has a farming background. Maybe he'll be good for farmers."

"I've already decided I'll vote for Bill Charnley for mayor. Cleota Roth says he's a good man. Remember she and I have that meeting at ten in the morning and I won't be back till after noon. I'm taking Erdene with me, but Helen will be here. I'll set dinner out for you and Harold."

"It's the last cutting so it shouldn't take too long. When you get home, we'll go to Goshen and vote."

The next day Esther went out to the barn hill where Earl and Harold were bringing a load of hay into the barn. "Helen, stay away from the horse and the machines. Practice your somersaults over here in the grass." She waved her arm to get Earl's attention. "I'm leaving," she called.

Harold worked in the hayloft pulling the sling-load of hay into the mow and dumping it. Earl was in the loaded wagon, forking the hay together to be grabbed by the hay sling. The large pincer-like sling attached to a rope and pulley was tethered to the horses, so when they pulled the rope the loaded sling was lifted to the top of the barn within Harold's reach. It was hot, itchy and mindless work. The morning drug on. Something drew Earl's eyes away from the repetitious forks full of hay: red...red...red! Helen was astraddle the rope with both her hands and dress pulled inexorably into the pulley, helplessly caught, her hands pinched and mauled.

"WHOA!" Earl ran to the horses, backed them up, hoping to free Helen's hands. She was screaming, her face streaked by sprayed blood. "Oh no...no...." He saw blood swimming over glistening bone, muscle, and tendons, dislodged fingernails, and skin ground to a pulp. Harold came running, "I'll get my car." Earl carried Helen to the house to wrap her hands in towels, then ran to the car as Harold drove up.

"It hurts, Daddy. It hurts, Daddy," she moaned weakly.

"I'm sorry, I'm sorry," Earl cradled her in his arms. "I never heard her cry, Harold. I just happened to look up and saw blood. If I hadn't looked, she could have been pulled in up to..." he shook his head in disbelief. "Go as fast as you can, Harold. I sure hope Doc Bowser isn't on a house call."

When Dr. Bowser unwrapped the towels he stood transfixed, a look of horror on his face, "Oh my goodness, we have a problem." He held an ether-soaked pad over Helen's face, then reset bones, stitched tendons, and cut away damaged tissue, reshaping fingers and hands. Earl sat beside her, thankful that ether allowed her to sleep through the surgery.

When the doctor finished bandaging the two little hands he sat down with Earl. "I'm just a country doctor, Mr. Phillips. This injury is beyond my expertise. I want Helen to be able to use her left hand—it was the most severely injured. She wasn't using her right hand much anyway. This little girl needs one good hand. I want you to take her to the orthopedic specialists at the medical center in Indianapolis. It's a long drive, but it's what we need to do."

"We'll do it. We've not been to the state capitol, but we'll figure it out."

Two days later Judd drove Sarah, Esther, and Helen in his new Willys Overland to the Indiana University Medical Center, a huge journey. They left before first light and didn't return home until early the next day. They stopped several times for Judd to patch flat tires. The busy city and large hospital complex were intimidating. They waited a few hours in the Riley Pediatric Clinic, observing children with fearsome medical conditions.

The specialists were impressed with the small-town doctor's surgical repair. They recommended daily soaks in a hot medicated solution. Each day was torture when Dr. Bowser removed the dressings. After a month, Dr. Bowser was satisfied that Sarah could dress the wounds. As Esther was with child, she was never permitted to see Helen's injury; it was believed this would imprint on her unborn child. The only benefit from the accident was Helen often got to stay at her grandma's house. She played with Ruby, Merle, and Don, who all vied to feed her since she was unable to feed herself. After the skin healed, the tendon and muscle stretching exercises were agony. The miracle after many months of rehabilitation was that she had a functioning left hand.

* * * * *

"Mrs. Phillips, keep your legs together. We can't have this baby before the doctor gets here," Mrs. Robinson's voice was shrill, with an edge of panic. Her hair, pulled inside a brown knit hair net swayed in time with her long skirt as she paced between Esther's bedroom and the kitchen window, watching for the doctor. She'd been hired to care for Esther after the birth; she had no experience with deliveries.

Esther expelled a guttural groan, "I need to push. The baby's coming."

Mrs. Robinson held her legs together, "Don't push, don't push." The back-porch door banged as Earl ran through the house, "I see him! He's just down the road. He'll be here in three minutes."

The minutes seemed forever before Dr. Bowser rushed into the bedroom, "Let's have a baby," and immediately the baby was born.

"You have a little girl, Mrs. Phillips. Do you have a name for her?" Dr. Bowser asked.

"She'll be named after my two best friends, Rose and Mary. We'll call her Rosemary." Esther said wearily.

"Doctor, come check the baby," Mrs. Robinson beckoned. The doctor stepped over to the bassinet to observe the infant. "She's having a spasm, or seizure as some call it. It will stop shortly. Turn her on her side so she doesn't choke. It happens sometimes after a difficult birth," he said.

The doctor returned to Esther, "The baby was having a little spasm, Mrs. Phillips. If you see this happen again, you needn't worry unless it lasts longer than a minute and the baby turns blue. Let the spasm run its course—there's nothing you can do to stop it. You'll see saliva foaming from her mouth. Just lay her on her side so she doesn't choke. I'm guessing she'll have several more, then will outgrow them. You don't need to be afraid of the spasms."

Esther's eyes clouded with worry; doctors always left so much unsaid.

"It's one more thing to deal with. I'm sure we'll manage."

In the afternoon, Mrs. Robinson ushered Earl, Helen, and Erdene into the bedroom to meet Rosemary. Helen's hands were scarred but healed, her left hand pulled off the blanket to check the baby. Erdene toddled behind with her breathy shuffle. She was beginning to gain weight and lose the blue orb shading her mouth. The hole in her heart was healing; she no longer "chugged" when she ran through the house. Esther and Earl smiled, taking in their idyllic family, all the more precious because of the struggles and hardships they'd endured.

"I'm the luckiest man," Earl smiled, "I have four women to take care of me."

* * * * *

In the fall, Esther's thirteen-year-old sister Ruby came to stay for several days so Esther could help Earl husk corn. Esther had always loved working outdoors, so this was like a holiday. The brisk fall breeze spilling golden leaves invigorated her as she and Earl moved together down the sodden rows, scratched by the dry corn stalks. "Helen said Mr. Garman moved her to the eighth-grade reading group—and she's just in fifth grade. She's ahead in arithmetic too. Academics certainly are her strong suit. I'm thinking we need to help her in this, Earl."

"I already see how it will be when she grows up: people won't see past her lame leg and crippled hand. She'll likely be a spinster lady," Earl twisted off an ear, husked it, and threw it into the wagon.

"That's what I've been thinking too. We'll need to set her up so she can take care of herself. Rosemary and Erdene won't need it because they'll marry. It's hard enough making ends meet, but I think we need to save for Helen's education."

"Git up," Earl called, moving the horses forward. "I'm going to start a bank account for her. Even if we save a few dollars a month, by the time she's ready for college we'll have something to help her get started."

"Hopefully, our medical bills will soon be paid off. I just realized the other day that Rosemary hasn't had a spasm for a few months. Erdene is stronger and gaining weight. If we can stay clear of the measles that are spreading around Goshen we should be okay. Mama said she'll buy material for a dress for each of the girls if I sew a dress for her. She wants a dress with a lace collar she can wear to the Rock Run Brethren Church, then remove when she goes to the Dunkard Church, where lace isn't permitted. I can't fathom what's gotten into my brother, Carl—he's so religious all of a sudden."

"Carl? That's a surprise. I always thought he had a wild streak." Earl said.

"He did. Maybe marriage has changed him. Mama and Pop have been perfectly happy at Rock Run Brethren. Now Carl wants them to change to the Dunkard Church."

"I have trouble seeing Judd a Dunkard; they have beards and all."

"Doesn't it beat all, Earl? You know the Dunkard men wear the stand-up collar, like papist priests? Well, Papa said if he had to wear a stand-up collar to be saved, he'd not join the Dunkards. So they appeased him; said they'd make an exception for him. I vow, I think Mama should wager for her lace collar too."

"It sounds silly when you put it like that: churches getting upset over people's dress—collars, for goodness sake. Just so they don't pressure *us* to turn Dunkard."

"Mama tried. She said since our Rock Run Church burned this would be a good time for us to switch to the Dunkard Church."

"Oh dear, Esther," Earl grimaced, stopping his work to look at her. "Are you serious?"

"I told her the truth; I said I prayed about it and we're happy at Rock Run Brethren."

Earl exhaled, his pause ominous. "I reckon it's just another reason I won't measure up in your family."

"It's funny you say that Earl, because I feel the same about your family. George is such a well-known minister and Gertrude never lets me forget it. Paul can't get his nose out of the air since he's going to Manchester College."

"I guess we'll be the dark horses of the families," Earl said, his voice cast down. "The wagon's full. Let's unload it in the corn bin."

Esther yelled, "Earl, what's that noise?" She looked all around, then dropped to her knees, not finding the noise that shook the ground. Earl could hardly control the horses, shying and prancing around.

"Look up Esther," he yelled. "It's an aeroplane. Whoa, Whoa Jock. I wish the girls could see it. I read about it in the paper. It carries the mail. It's landing in a field close to the Mill Race. Gadzooks Esther, it was so close I could see the pilot waving. You can get up Esther, it's gone."

* * * * *

"I don't think I've ever mashed so many potatoes. It's a good thing they're from our garden." Esther's arm was sore from pounding down the potatoes in a large bowl.

"Can you believe how prices are going over the moon?" Dora and Esther lived on adjoining farms. As the families did many projects together, she and Esther were dear friends. "So many men are losing their jobs, or are on strike. We're lucky our husbands are farmers with secure jobs. This is a scary time. I'm not too proud to say we're feeling the pinch. That's how I got the idea to invite you over to make donuts. Our families are due a treat after all the skimping we've been doing."

"I'm glad you called. I definitely needed a day for women talk. It's nice for the children to play together too. What a treat to have mashed potato donuts. I think they're Earl's favorite, after angel food cake."

"I know what you mean about women talk. Sometimes talking only to children and Fred for days on end, I think I'll go stark raving mad. A woman needs nitty-gritty talk with a woman," Dora exclaimed.

"Since you're my best friend, and I know I can trust you not to gossip; I don't know what to do about having another baby," Esther's voice lowered confidentially. "Rosemary is four years old. If we're going to have another baby, we should be getting to it," Esther blushed. She was so uncomfortable her heart raced, making her voice shake. She hadn't talked about such a sensitive topic with anyone—not her mother, her sisters, or her husband. She walked over to where Dora was frying donuts, "Earl doesn't say, but I know he wants a little boy. One more child is the most we can afford; even that will stretch our finances. We seem to just have girls, so I don't know if I want to risk trying for a boy."

"Oh my," Dora's eyes widened. Her voice dropped, "What should I do?" she said under her breath.

"What do you mean?" Esther asked.

"I know how to determine if you have a boy or a girl. Someone very reliable told me, but I pledged to secrecy; it's not to become common knowledge. But I know it works, Esther. It's been proven with all three of my children." She was silent, the ticking clock seemed to fill the room. "It's not fair that I know this and don't help you Esther, but you have to promise to tell no one."

"Oh, I promise, Dora. I won't ever tell." Esther's eyes filled, she took Dora's hand to convey her worthiness to hold the promise.

Dora whispered, "When you have relations, if you want a boy, you immediately turn from your back to your right side. If you want a girl, you turn to your left side. That is the secret."

"I'll remember that, Dora. Thank you for telling me. I'm amazed it's so simple. You can trust me with the secret."

"Well, I hope it works for you." She giggled, "We wanted women talk, I guess we got it. I think we need to dip some of these donuts in cinnamon sugar and have a coffee break."

* * * * *

Esther was redding up the dishes after supper. "Let's take the girls for a buggy ride, it's such a nice evening. I feel like I've been stuck in the house forever."

"Come girls," he called. "Who wants to go for a ride?" Soon the family was plodding down the country road.

"I'd like to get an auto, Esther. We'll soon have four children, and it would be nice to drive to church and to town on Saturday nights. The gas won't cost so much. My brother George is getting rid of his eight-year-old Model T. He's going to seminary and thinks he needs a new Model A. He said he'd give me a good price on it."

"What's a good price, Earl?"

"One hundred fifty dollars."

"It's not that I mind driving around in Gertrude's eight-year-old car; I'm not that prideful," Esther ruffled her shoulder wings. "But Earl, I hate to be indebted to Gertrude. Her pious eyes and self-righteous nose in the air will hold that debt over me every chance she gets."

"I think we could pay it off soon. The crops are good this year. The thing is, we can't afford a newer auto, and I know George takes care of his auto like a baby."

"Whatever you decide, Earl. It sure would be nice to move with the express crowd. The baby will come in the fall, and I always hated taking tiny babies out in winter weather."

Esther called to the girls riding behind, "Girls, look at the new baby horse at Ulreys. Isn't that a beauty?"

"We've seventy dollars for a down payment."

"How times are changing. I have to go to Goshen Hospital to have the baby. Dr. Bowser doesn't do home deliveries anymore. I don't want a repeat of Mrs. Robinson holding my legs together till the doctor got there. I still believe that's why Rosemary had those spells."

* * * * *

The ether made Esther's mind hazy. She felt like she was in a tunnel where noises reverberated and voices echoed. "The baby is dead. Give her a shot of phenobarbital. We need to put her to sleep."

She woke that night in the maternity ward. *I'm going to throw up, she thought. Oh, the whirling dizziness when she moved her head. Then she remembered the doctor's words. Oh God. Don't let it be true.* Tears slid down her cheeks. She wanted this baby so much. Everything had seemed normal. What could have gone wrong? There was no one to ask and soon her troubled mind took respite in sleep.

The next morning Esther woke when the nurse brought her breakfast tray. The white noise of kindness exploded in the silence of the ward, settling like lead in her heart. The other two mothers worked intently to appear occupied. The nurse pulled the curtain around Esther's bed. She heard the simpering baby sounds and the mothers trying to stifle them. It was a relief when Earl shrugged through the curtain and entered her cubicle. His pain was evident in his weary, bowed carriage and his blotchy tear-swollen eyes.

"Oh Earl," she reached for him, her eyes probing. His jaw clenched and unclenched; his face quivered in a futile struggle for composure. They clutched each other as in a death grip—as indeed it felt. They wailed in a silent turmoil of watery pain. Esther wiped away his tears, "Tell me," a strangled whisper.

Earl used her sheet to dry his face. His words were quiet, raspy, "We had a beautiful little boy, he was perfect. The umbilical cord was wrapped around his neck. He died just before he was born. Dr. Bowser said he couldn't prevent it."

"A little boy," it was like a shard in her heart.

"I named him James Randall as we decided. He's at Culp's Funeral Home. We'll have a graveside service tomorrow, probably just the minister and our folks. What do you think about the girls going to the cemetery? They know we had a baby, but they don't understand."

"They'll know something is wrong. We lost our baby. Probably they should go to the cemetery with you," Esther said.

"Oh, my dear, I wish you could have seen our baby. He was so filled out and pudgy. He had quite a lot of dark hair, about a half-inch long." A fresh barrage of tears silenced him.

"I want to see him, Earl. Talk to the doctor or someone."

"They don't think it would be good for you to see the baby when you're so delicate. They said there's a rule against bringing dead bodies to the hospital. If you'd had a home delivery you could have seen him."

"Please Earl, see what you can do."

The next morning Esther was still asleep when Earl slipped into the ward and drew the curtain around Esther's bed, holding his index finger to his lips. Floyd Culp, the mortician brought in the little casket, opened it, and rested it on Esther's lap. He grasped her hand with both of his, then went out in the hall so the parents could be with their baby.

"Floyd said if someone comes in they'll make him take the baby away, so we won't have long." Earl whispered.

"Oh-h, my little one," Esther touched his little fingers, brushed his baby cheeks. Earl, just look at him; he's perfect. He looks so nice in the little dress and sweater. Thank you with all my heart. I so-o wanted to see my baby."

"It was Floyd. He sneaked us in the back door. I hope he doesn't get in trouble."

"Don't you think he looks like the Swiharts? But he has your long fingers."

"Cleota is going to come and be with you this morning while we're at the cemetery. I didn't want you to be alone."

"She's the friend I would have chosen. You've taken care of everything, Earl. I could never go through this without you. It feels like we've had more than our share of trouble, but losing James is by far the hardest. We'll get through it, Earl. They say when life is hardest, that's when God is closest."

"I don't know, Esther. All night I felt so desperate and angry...I thought I couldn't tell you."

"I feel the same. Don't you think God understands why we have these feelings? We hoped so long for this baby boy. He would have been perfect with our girls. But I know our little family will be okay. You and I will be okay. Our love is bigger than the hurt of this." Esther took Earl's hand and brought it to her lips. She placed his other hand around James's tiny one, then she completed the circle, holding the other small fingers. This circle, meant to last decades, instead would last minutes. "Good-bye my sweet baby boy. I carried you in my womb. Now I'll carry you forever in my heart." She kissed the little cheek. "You can take him now, Earl, before we get in trouble."

Losing their baby was like a seismic crack imploding their world. A relentless winnowing and depletion culled away the vitality needed to endure the day-to-day. Esther the more so because she chastened herself for attempting to "play God", believing her punishment was the death of her perfectly formed son. Of course, she never could confess this to anyone as she parried peoples' awkward condolences.

For Earl it was a loss of what could have been: pride in a son to carry his name, to work on the farm, and carry on the family heritage. With a more morbid mindset, it was easier for him to succumb to the black hole and darkness of gray. Nothing felt like their life before: daytime, nighttime, eating, driving the horses, or sweeping the floor. Only the vague hope that if they kept doing the same things, sometime life would right itself.

The catastrophic October 1929 stock market crash came just a few weeks after their personal misfortune. No one knew how the country would be affected but uncertainty was a smothering fog over every decision for years to come. For Earl and Esther an immediate effect was a glut of farm produce on U.S. commodities and foreign trade markets.

Earl's bounteous corn and wheat crop could hardly be sold. Paying off George's car was out of the question.

One spring evening Earl's parents came to visit. Earl and his father often farmed together, and visits were common, but their demeanor unsettled Esther. Their unease indeed was a portent of bad news: "we have to sell this farm, Earl. If we don't, we'll lose both farms," Frank said apologetically. His hands clasped the back of his head as his tall, lean body paced around the kitchen.

Alice removed her wire-rimmed eye glasses to wipe her eyes, "Our plan was to pay it off and let you buy it from us, deducting the amount we've given the other children for their education."

Esther rose from her chair to hug this tiny woman she loved like a mother. "You've been more than fair with us. This depression is affecting everyone."

"If we wait, the bank will take it over, it's as simple as that. I hate to do this after everything you've been through," Frank shook his head, his eyes troubled.

"Everything else has gone wrong. Might as well lose our farm too," Earl shrugged with sullen defeatism.

Frank clasped his shoulder, understanding his discouragement. "I've been asking around about farms to rent. Frank Yoder is looking for someone. That's on Berkey Avenue close to your parents, Esther."

"That would be nice if it works out. Don't worry about us," Esther said, striving for optimism. "We'll manage. These are bad times for a lot of people, and it doesn't look like it will soon get better."

The back door banged as all three girls ran into the kitchen. "We didn't know Grandma and Grandpa Phillips were here," Erdene said. "Did Grandma bring cookies?" She ran to Alice who scooped her on her lap. Older and more intuitive, Helen stopped inside the door, noticing the long faces of the adults. She sidled to her mother, asking quietly, "Are you sad, Mommy?"

Esther smiled, embracing her, "How could I be sad when I have three special big girls?"

CHAPTER 35

The Depression

By 1930 the depression had marched across the country with a knock-out punch, battering rich and poor alike. The country's mood fluctuated dizzily between patriotic fervor and an ominous fear that life would never be as before. Instead, a clawing hand-to-mouth struggle ensued for most families.

This was true for Earl and Esther who had been rousted from the substantial farm they had planned to buy from Earl's parents. Now they were renting the Yoder farm a few miles west of Goshen on Berkey Avenue, about a twenty-minute walk from Judd and Sarah's home. The five of them rambled around in the six-bedroom farmhouse down a long lane from the road. Chopping wood for the kitchen cook stove and a wood stove in the living room was a daunting task, so they congregated in the kitchen, and the rest of the house stayed dark and cold. Nighttime felt spooky to Helen, Erdene, and Rosemary; the privy was a long walk from the house through wet grass and hooting owls. Its roof leaked, causing the Sears catalogue to be stuck together, brown-stained and soggy. Eerie shadows from the lantern danced along the outside path and inside through the drafty, shadowy rooms, up the staircase to their bedroom where they slept together for warmth.

Earl, in particular, had been cast down by the welling sorrows of the death of baby James and the loss of "their" farm. He had wallowed in shame and fear since yesterday when the Goshen Implement Company repossessed and hauled off his beloved Farmall Tractor. They had agreed to operate the thirty-acre Yoder farm. How could it be done with only horses? Esther would have to become a full-time field hand. His shame ate like a worm in his belly.

Esther woke at four o'clock to start the milking. The dark morning had a stealthy damp chill, as penetrating as a smothering fog. It felt like something that could swallow her whole. Several minutes later, Earl, stooped and woebegone, shuffled into the barn. A grimace was frozen on his face. He was preoccupied and distant as he started milking. Esther dumped her milk in the strainer and walked to Earl, holding his head against her thigh, knowing he wanted privacy for his emotions.

"We can't let these trials get the best of us, Earl. We have each other and we have our faith. We'll take one day at a time and plow through it, just like when turning over a new field. Someday we'll look back at the dark furrows of this time and be grateful we came out of it tolerable. Our life will get back on track, but we've got to dig in today. We have three little girls who trust in us. You're a wonderful father, do it for your girls."

Earl's shoulders shuddered while milk streamed into the bucket. He spoke brokenly. "It's just so much at once. About the time I get through one thing, I get slammed down again. I just don't see how we'll make it this time."

"None of it is your fault; that's what you have to tell yourself. This depression has hit everyone and someday it'll be over. We'll work together every day, and one day we'll be okay again."

The udder was emptied, flaccid. Esther picked up the filled bucket and poured milk into the strainer. Together they finished milking, washed the milking equipment, and carried the heavy milk can to the horse trough to cool.

Everyone in the family awakened in the dark to do their jobs. Helen, at twelve years, did the farm work, shake straw in the loafing shed, feed the livestock, and grind corn to meal. Because they didn't have sufficient land for grazing, each day Esther and Helen walked a mile to a rented field to herd the cows and tie them to a fence while Esther milked them. The job Helen hated was going into the woods at night to bring the cows back to the loafing shed. She worked in the field at corn husking and thrashing time and helped plant and tend the garden. Rather than being coddled, she adapted to her disabilities—proving Esther's long-ago prediction that she didn't have a handicap. Six-year-old Rosemary loved the animals and the out-of-doors, happily toddling after Helen until eventually taking over her tasks. They raised rabbits for food and Earl hunted squirrel. That left young Erdene doing the inside housework, freeing Esther for the field. She trimmed the wicks, washed the lamps, and filled them with oil. Even as a child, Erdene could put her hand inside the oven of the cook stove and know when the temperature was right to bake bread—soft inside with a crunchy crust. They ate a lot of gravy with pork rind or boiled eggs, slathered over bread or cornbread. While their food may not have been enjoyable, they usually had something on the table.

"What's for supper, Mama?" Helen's tummy gurgled and complained while she did chores. The potato she had for lunch was long forgotten.

"We're having popcorn tonight."

"But Mama, we had popcorn last night," complained Rosemary.

"Ah-h, but there's a treat tonight. You get maple syrup on top." Esther sat a large pan of warm popcorn on the table. Daddy said grace before Mama dipped each of them a bowl, adding a drizzle of syrup.

"Yum-m. Maple syrup on popcorn is good. Can we have it like this every time?" Rosemary asked.

"No, just for special."

"I'm pretending it's Grandma Swihart's wieners and potato soup. That's *my* favorite meal," Erdene said.

"We're thankful to have popcorn. When Helen went to the chicken house this morning, there were four chickens missing—stolen during the night. We aren't as hungry as some town people who have no animals or garden. They're so desperate they steal to feed their family. I feel sorry for them. We're some of the lucky ones; we've never had to go to the county to get food. We mustn't forget to put the cows and pigs inside at night. We'd be bad off if *they* were taken," Esther remarked.

They walked or took the buggy everywhere. They were still making payments to George on the Model T that sat in the barn, hardly used. They had no money for gas, and rubber to patch flat tires was expensive and hard to get. People stayed home more, less likely to go downtown Saturday nights because they had no money to spend. Most shopping was trading a chicken for flour or such when the huckster truck came. Rock Run Church was front and center in their life. During fall revivals, Helen went forward during the altar call, committing her life to Christ. She wanted to be like her mother and live the Jesus way.

Entertainment was likely a church pie supper, or a pound supper with neighbors, where everyone brought a pound of something, like biscuits, bologna, or apples. If someone had a birthday, homemade ice cream was churned and cakes were baked. It seemed the poorer people were, the more generous their spirit. Because everyone was needy, they all looked out for each other, sharing what they had.

Helen, Erdene, and Rosemary knew unending work, never being warm, and unappetizing food, but they thought their life charmed. They lived in a neighborhood of cousins. Many summer days they walked to Grandma Swihart's house where Aunt Ruby and Uncles Don and Merle and a passel of cousins would harness the pony to the wagon and away they'd go on another adventure. Some of the Swihart children and grandchildren dropped in at Judd and Sarah's almost nightly, gathering around the old piano to sing. They were good singers and never tired of the old hymns. They often went to Grandma's for Sunday dinner: delicious fried chicken with all the fixings and chocolate pie. There was lots of raucous jousting and hilarity among the adults, cousins to play train on the front porch swing, croquet, and Grandpa's peppermint candy. In the fall when neighbors threshed at each of the farms, nothing was more exciting that sliding down the giant straw stacks with all the neighbor children.

In the spring they received a formal invitation to attend Earl's brother, George's, graduation from seminary. The ladies of the Elkhart Church of the Brethren where he pastored, were serving a sit-down dinner. Esther had never seen an engraved invitation with fancy script. "What do you suppose RSVP means?" she asked Earl.

"I have no idea, it's too high falutin' for me. Do we have to go?"

"We not only have to go, we get to contribute to a monetary gift. Gertrude added a note, saying George has a meeting in Goshen on Friday morning. He wants to pick up Erdene so she can stay overnight with Dorothy. I almost forget Dorothy is Erdene's age, she acts so much older. Oh Earl, we don't even have decent clothes to wear to church. We'll look like paupers at this fancy affair."

"I'll be planting corn then. It'll waste a whole day going to Elkhart for this confounded party," Earl griped.

Esther shrugged, knowing the two of them would worry this to death. She thought belittling remarks directed at her and Earl were all too frequent from both their families. Snide comments among her siblings were commonplace. The others laughed and gave back as good as they got, but she and Earl were too meek to be sassy—then they stewed about it.

In the middle of the night, Esther had a brainstorm: she would cut up her wedding dress. There was enough material for a dress for each of the girls. If she worked every night she could get them done. She would go through Mama's remnants to find trim, so they didn't look alike. She hated to destroy her wedding dress, but it seemed the only solution. There was nothing to do about shoes; they'd have to buff up the old ones.

In three weeks, the dresses were finished. Esther was modestly pleased. They were all different, a soft flowing gray with different trim. She also spruced up her own church dress, letting out the seams, using Mama's left-over lace, and borrowing one of her nice brooches. This would be one of her last public outings as she was beginning to show. With the freshness of spring and turning of new earth, the couple's spirits found an eager optimism, imbued with the tender hope that a baby brings.

"Come Erdene, let's get your clothes packed. Uncle George will be here soon. Hang the new dress as soon as you get there so it doesn't wrinkle. Wait to put it on until just before the ceremony; you daresen't mess it up."

Earl had put gas in the T, patched the tires, and washed it till it shone. Esther was proud of her family, praying they wouldn't get a flat tire on the way.

"This sure is a nice big church. George must have some rich parishioners," Earl said as they entered from the parking lot. Gertrude was coming up the basement steps with Dorothy and Erdene as they entered the imposing front doors. She looked like a mannequin in Stephenson's, the posh Elkhart department store. Her blonde beauty-salon curls were styled as if waxed. Her lime green hat, dress, jewelry, purse, and pumps, were all accented and shaded perfectly. Her lips bloomed a subtle rose. Her hand grazed down the whalebone ridges supporting her figure before she extended it to Earl.

"Welcome, we're glad you could come," she said with practiced cordiality. "I saw you drive up in the old Model T. How is it working for you?"

"Hello Gertrude," Earl shook her hand. "It works just fine. This is a proud day for you and George."

"Yes, it is. He has worked hard. Dorothy, shake hands with Mr. Earl and Mrs. Esther."

Dorothy tossed her auburn curls molded from rags, curtsied, and shook their hands. Esther stared at this real, Kewpie doll girl attired in a rose voile dress with matching patent leather shoes. Her eyes slipped to Erdene's anxious expression, stunned to see she was wearing a bright yellow taffeta dress, her feet swimming in yellow slippers. She knelt to greet her.

"Hi Dearie, what happened to your dress?"

Gertrude straightened the ribbon in Erdene's hair, "She'll be sitting with Dorothy all day and the dress you sent wasn't appropriate. Doesn't she look nice?"

Esther straightened, unwittingly clutching her abdomen—she felt she'd been stabbed in the gut. Her face was impassive as she patted Erdene's shoulder, "Yes, you look really nice. If you're sitting up front, be sure not to squirm."

"Since the girls are with you, we assigned you to one of the back luncheon tables with the other families. I hope we'll find time to visit after lunch. We enjoyed having Erdene. I wish the girls could play more often—they're like two little peas in a pod." She guided the girls ahead, "We must go, I don't want George to wonder."

"The pompous old peacock," Earl muttered as they found a seat. "She just stirs up bad blood." The two struggled through the party, lacquered smiles in place, another slight gouged in the belt of their memory bank.

Life only got worse. One snow-blown February day in 1931 Judd plowed up the long lane in a county truck, clearing the snow. Esther stood to fetch him soup beans they were having for dinner.

"No time. Come Earl, we've got to go." He grabbed Earl by his shirt while wiping his frosty scrunched face on his coat sleeve. His agitated behavior attested to his alarm. "I just heard a rumor that State Bank of Goshen has failed. We need to try to get our money out before they close the doors." Earl's face crumbled as he found the bank book and grabbed his coat, following Judd to the truck.

With all they'd been through, Esther's faith gave her confidence that God would not give more than they could handle. The troubles could mow her down, but she always clawed back, stronger than before. They had so little, yet they'd sacrificed to save money to send Helen to college; she would be a teacher. Esther went to the dresser to check their budget ledger: $138 in a savings at State Bank. To lose that money would be the final defeat.

She prayed all afternoon while mucking out the loafing shed. When the girls trudged home from school, she peevishly complained they played in the snow while walking up the lane, delaying chore time. She could hardly breathe—her heart so heavy with dread. It was the girl's bedtime when she saw Judd drop Earl at the far end of the already drifted lane. She knew the outcome by the lantern's glow on the stooped, disheartened stance of her dear mate, arduously plodding up the lane. The money was gone.

Even though Judd and Sarah had flourished and were considered people of means, their struggle during the depression was difficult because they had so many children still at home: Floyd, age twenty-four; Tobe, age twenty; Ruby, age nineteen; Merle, age seventeen; Don, age thirteen; and Merle Kendall, a friend of Tobe, who was a boarder. The county government didn't have money to pay their workers. They kept cutting back Judd's days, then only "paying" with IOU's. Judd and the boys were back to cutting down trees and hauling timber to the telephone company to be used for telephone poles. Judd was fifty-eight, his body sinewy, his face furrowed and engraved by weather. Sarah continued to care for the animals, tend her large garden, preserve food, and put food on the table for eight children and other family who often visited. While she still had her delivery route she got only eight cents for a dozen eggs and ten cents for a gallon of milk. Most people had no money. She was more successful with sewing. She worked up feed sacks that she bought at the elevator for five cents, sewed them together with felled seams and sold sheets, bedding, and towels. At fifty-six she had no gray in her hair, but her body was haggard and tired. She kept to herself the nagging pain lingering in her abdomen.

Sarah and Judd had joined the small Dunkard Church where some of their children were members. While they attended regularly they ignored some of the rules required of other members. He didn't wear the "cut" coat with stand-up collar, nor did Sarah wear a prayer bonnet. He smoked cigars, causing Sarah to complain that she went to church with her clothes smelling like a "stogie". They had a forbidden radio and listened to their favorites: "Ma Perkins", "Amos and Andy", and "Fibber McGee and Molly". When Sarah finally went to a doctor and was told she needed surgery she went to the West Goshen Church of the Brethren minister for an anointing and healing service.

"We got another letter from Edith today," Sarah told Judd at supper. "From the sound of it, California is heaven on earth. The weather is sunny and in the seventies. They walk out their back door and pick an orange for breakfast. They go to the beach and play in the surf every weekend. Wilbur has been hired by a studio to write movies. I wonder if it's really as good as she says. We have no way of knowing except what she writes."

Judd snorted, his eyes flared, "There's a sucker born every minute."

Ruby was enticed by the gay glitter of exotic places. "I don't know. I might go off to live in seventy-degree weather and free oranges," she smirked, sending a coy glance at Merle, Tobe's friend who was living with them. "Maybe Wilbur can get me an acting job. That sure would be better than waitressing six ten-hour days a week for five dollars."

"She doesn't say anything about Jeanette Osborn or any of that faction. I wish they'd give it up and find a good church."

"It won't happen, Mama," Floyd stood up, taking his plate to the sink. "Edith never did like going to church."

Since recuperating from surgery, Sarah was forbidden to do farm work. Her mind wandered as she busied herself washing feed sacks, cutting them to size, and sewing them into sheets. Her children and grandchildren were continuously in and out of their home, sometimes staying five minutes, sometimes weeks. She knew they were all struggling. *We should do something special. Maybe have a supper for everyone after Christmas. I could make oyster soup. That would be a treat for them. We'll make it a tradition.*

It was a given, though unspoken, that Sarah was the pillar of the family—the safe haven in a storm. Hers was the attentive ear to hear their dreams and secrets. She succored them and each felt most loved and favored. She listened with tenderness and gentle acceptance, never censure. A lot of her day was given to prayer. While she was soft-spoken and reticent she didn't miss anything. Her mother's intuition knew how her charges were faring in life.

Now she was thinking about Ruby's behavior with Merle, Tobe's friend who was living with them. This situation may have worked with Esther, but Ruby had a wild streak. Could it be the Zumbrun Indian and Jewish blood? With her dark skin and black hair, it made you wonder. She had seen the two coming in the back door late one night. If Ruby and Merle were enamored, Merle would have to leave. She could not abide another tainted daughter.

And why did Ruth, living in Cleveland, want to come with her young boys to her mother's home for her delivery and lying-in? She wrote saying she hoped to stay several months. Ruth's letters weren't forthcoming, but something didn't sit right with Sarah. Judd always said Vail was a scoundrel. It would be good to have Ruth and her children home. A baby in the house would be nice.

A car turned into the drive, dust flying. *My lands, who would be driving so fast?* The car screeched to a stop and Clara came rushing to the house, car door left open. Sarah hurried to the door.

"Clara...what?"

"Mama, Mama!" Clara grabbed Sarah, bursting into tears.

"My dear...."

"Harry told me I couldn't come...I could get you and Papa in trouble. But I couldn't leave without seeing you. We're leaving in the middle of the night." She went to look out the front window. "I hope no one followed me here. Harry says they're dangerous...from South Bend." Clara collapsed on the couch, bending and rocking her body, her hands covering her face.

"What are you saying, Clara? You're leaving? Where are you going?"

"I only know it's somewhere in Virginia. Oh Mama," she reached to take Sarah's hand. "It's so far away. I don't want to leave you," she sobbed.

"But why...?"

Clara jumped up, pacing, her voice blubbering in her distress. "Harry got himself in trouble; I don't know much about it. He borrowed a lot of money to buy an airplane. Some deal fell through. They're bad men—not the type you and pop associate with. They're after him."

"Why would Harry be buying an airplane, Clara? This sounds shady to me."

"I have no idea. Nothing makes a stitch of sense," her voice was aggravated. I didn't know any of it until this morning. We can't take anything with us. Harry's going to get someone to bring our stuff later." Clara's face was agonized with pain. "I have to go, Mama. The children are in the car. They know something is wrong. They get scared when they see me cry."

"How can this be?" Sarah muttered. "You'll get in touch with us?"

"Harry says we have to lay low for a while. Don't say anything to Papa yet, in case someone looks him up and asks questions." Clara squeezed Sarah's hands, holding them to her lips, "I can't live so far from you, Mama. I don't think I can do this," her tears started afresh.

"Of course, you can, Clara. You're a strong woman. Maybe Harry will be able to satisfy these men and you'll soon move home. You'll be all right. Each day you pick yourself up, lift your chin, and go on."

"I'll miss you, Mama," Clara's voice keened in her despair, their bodies clasped in a final embrace.

"My prayers will be with you every day. As soon as I hear from you, I'll write. We'll stay in touch with letters. Now wash your face and get yourself together. I'll take some of Grandpa's candy out to the children. Be safe, my dear. Be strong."

* * * * *

Sarah was determined to get through the Sunday afternoon family gathering without exposing her anguish. It wasn't like her to show anger, even when her children's behavior crushed her spirit. Esther had just taken her aside in the kitchen to whisper that there would be another hurry-up wedding in their family. Evidently she hadn't sent Merle packing soon enough; Ruby was going to have a baby. She felt her body soak up the guilt again—honor seemed so elusive. As a mother was she so lacking in demonstrating to her children the Christian virtues of decency and high morals? Her brood seemed determined to bow her head in shame. If they wanted to hurt her, they knew where she was most vulnerable. Sundays were hard for her at best since Clara moved. They all missed her, the child who relished life and could charm a fence post. Her naïve innocence was a buffer—they all wanted to please her. Clara's family had been in Virginia a couple of years, and while she would always be homesick when away from Goshen, they seemed safe and settled. Clara never again mentioned the debt for the airplane. Sarah guessed she knew no more than she did two years ago.

Sarah's thoughts were brought back to the dining room by a sudden timbre of hilarity, the boys cheering and jocular. Judd was giving them tickets for the Chicago World's Fair.

"Where's my ticket? Gimme my ticket" Don lurched to reach the magic papers.

"You're too young to go," Judd said. "You and I will stay home and work to pay for the tickets. Even though the highway department got discounted tickets, I still had to pay. They weren't cheap."

"No fair," grumbled Don.

The brothers were making plans for this first-ever outing from Goshen. "I read about the exhibitions. General Motors has an assembly line where they put a car together," Carl said.

"I want to see the house of the future that cools in the summer, and has a box in the kitchen that washes dishes," Floyd added.

"It'll be a long drive. You should leave here by four o'clock in the morning. You have to plan on two or three flat tires," Judd started to organize the trip.

"Why don't you all sleep here so you get an early start," Sarah suggested.

Friday night Carl, Floyd, Tobe, and Merle were in a sporting mood as they prepared for the trip. Carl was busy greasing the car. "Floyd, get a couple bottles of Pop's blackberry wine. I need to wet my whistle."

"Do you think Pop will notice if I get a couple bottles for the picnic hamper? I don't think Mama will put it in. We should take the extra tire tube and plenty of rubber patches." Floyd said.

"I'm going to fill a lard can with water for the radiator. Do we have a funnel?" Tobe asked.

"Stick some rags in," Merle suggested.

"Is Mama going to pack our food tonight?" asked Merle, always thinking of his stomach. "Don't forget a thermos for coffee."

"Don't worry about food. It'll be ready by the time you leave," Mama called from the kitchen.

"I'm making another trip to the cellar," Floyd said. "The night is young. We should get a card game going."

"I hear the hit of the midway is Sally Rand's strip tease show in the Paris exhibit. That will be our first stop," Tobe smirked and lowered his voice as not to be heard from the kitchen.

"Whoopee!" Merle pumped his arm. "Carl, you can't go 'cause you just started a Dunkard Church. Can't have an upstanding minister checking out Sally."

Carl sniggered, "What happens at the world's fair stays at the world's fair."

The boys were jolly as they laid out starched white shirts, vests, tweed trousers, and fedoras—dapper to a T. No one would accuse *them* of being country bumpkins. The anticipation was delicious, as good as the real trip.

The next morning Judd and Sarah awakened at four o'clock, expecting the boys to be dressed, with the car loaded. They found them in the living room passed out on the couch and splayed across the floor, empty bottles a reeking testament to their night of decadence. Not wanting to be around when Judd lost his temper, Sarah scurried to the barn wondering how the boys would sweet-talk their way out of this calamity. One never knew with Judd, but she had a bad feeling.

Judd's eyes blazed with deadly and righteous wrath as he picked up steam, kicking legs and bashing heads. "You no-account pissants!" he yelled. "All my trouble and expense to get your tickets and put gas in the car, and I find you in your cups!" His voice was contemptuous and disbelieving.

The boys jerked awake, eyes wide with terror, baffled and clumsy in their effort to get away from Judd's fury, his voice a boomerang in their heads.

"We're all ready to go, Pop," Carl grabbed his shirt, awkwardly starting to dress. "We'll clean up here and get the car loaded."

"And where do you think you're going?" Judd's booming voice was smothering in contempt.

Carl's bleary eyes avoided Judd's gaze, "Chicago," he said with a curdled dread of premonition.

"Hogwash. You're cutting logs today. All four of you," his voice was hard as stone.

Tobe, chastened, walked over to Judd. "I know we messed up, Pop, but we can drink some coffee and be ready to go in twenty minutes. This trip is a chance-in-a-lifetime. We can't waste the tickets. Please don't make us miss it."

Floyd sat with his head in his hands, wretched and disbelieving. "We've had so little to look forward to. Last night was such fun—getting ready. We got carried away," he said with regret.

"Next time you decide to loot my wine cellar, you might consider the consequences. Get your work clothes on—we've got logs to haul," his voice surly as he left the room.

That was the last anyone mentioned the world's fair.

CHAPTER 36

Louise Born

"Please Esther, I can't ask Mama to do it. She's been so down-in-the-mouth lately. She's not been herself since surgery." Esther and her sister, Ruby, were on their knees, overheated and ungainly with bulging stomachs as they knee-shuffled along, planting Esther's garden. Esther grabbed her sunbonnet to fan her face, "You want me to make you a light summer dress to wear out and about?"

"I can't take the heat. I know you'll wear your coat until you quit going out, but I don't see the point of stopping my social life because I have a protruding stomach."

"I'm slowing down and staying home already," Esther acknowledged. "After what happened to baby James, I'm scared about this one. I don't think Earl or I could take losing another. I'll make your dress, but on one condition: you don't wear it to family gatherings where Mama will see you. You're right, she's not herself, and it would upset her. Pop would raise cane too. Let's cool off a bit. I need to check on Helen," she said, walking toward the house. "The principal just told us her grades are good enough she doesn't have to write her exams. Now she's glad she got the measles. She gets bored though, lying in a dark room all day. She'd love it if she could have a book but of course her eyes need to be covered. She still has a fever."

It was weeks later that Esther told Earl to call Dr. Young; the baby was coming. They held each other, filled with dread. What would go wrong this time?

Earl made the call. "He's going to see the patients in his waiting room, then he'll come. He said, 'tell Esther I'll see this through with her. She needn't worry about a thing'."

"I'm glad he's our doctor, I feel good about him. I'll send the girls to Grandma's."

Two hours later, Dr. Young, the quintessential small-town doctor, knocked on the front door. "How are things coming, Esther?" His booming voice and tall, husky body filled the house. He went to the bedroom, opened his bag, straightened his glasses, and examined her. "I'm glad I didn't rush over. We've got some time yet," he said, pulling up a chair by Esther's bed. "I've got a job for you, Earl: I want you to log when the pain starts and how long it lasts. Also, the time between pains. That'll give us an idea what's going on. Now Esther, you got any of your molasses cookies around? Maybe a cup of coffee? I missed my dinner. You know, my mother made molasses cookies and I thought her cookies beat all, but I declare, yours take the prize. Have you got your corn planted yet, Earl?" The afternoon was spent with his stories interspersed with Esther's labor pains. He had Earl laughing till he cried; they forgot to be afraid.

"Okay Esther, I want you to drink this, then you and I are going for a ride."

"But I have my nightgown on."

"Where do you think I'm taking you? To a dance?" he chortled. You need some fresh air. My idea is to end up at the hospital. I'll call you, Earl, when we get there."

He took Esther to the country roads bungled with potholes. "My sakes, this is a bumpy road," Esther said, jostling and bouncing to beat the band.

"It sure is." Dr. Young gripped the steering wheel jerking in his hands. "You need to tell your dad to get his men out here and grade this road."

"Maybe if you didn't go so fast it wouldn't be so bumpy," Esther suggested.

"Hang on Esther. I know this railroad track up ahead is a humdinger. Here we go!"

"Land sakes alive," she gasped. "I think we were flying there."

"Did you like that? Let's turn around and do it again."

"Oh, I don't think...."

"Here we go. Hang on."

"Dr. Young, I think maybe we should turn around and head toward the hospital."

His eyebrow shot up and he smiled ear to ear. "You're the boss, lady. Let's go have this baby."

"Yes, I think it's coming," Esther groaned. When they got to the hospital, as he was helping her to a wheel chair, Esther said sheepishly, "If I didn't know you, Dr. Young, I'd say you took that bumpy ride on purpose."

His eyes sparkled, "Now Esther, would I do that to the lady who makes Elkhart County's best molasses cookies?"

Everyone said Louise was the sweetest, prettiest baby ever. She had a full head of dark curly hair, a little rosebud mouth, and large wide-set hazel eyes. She was the first of Esther's babies born without health problems. It took a few months for both parents to enjoy their active chubby baby, and not make problems where there were none. She was so placid, Esther hardly knew she was in the house. The girls fussed over who would take care of her: thirteen-year-old Helen was the perfect age to love on a baby, and even seven-year-old Rosemary was good at amusing her. She ate heartily, slept well, and was precocious in development.

From the beginning she had musical talent, singing in her crib to entertain herself. The beloved pet of the family, her obvious favorite was her daddy: her first smile, first steps, first toidy on the potty, was for her "da-da"—which was her first word, of course. From her first breath, Earl adored this spritely soul who could heal the wounds left by the loss of his son. With Louise's birth, the spirit of the family changed from festering gloom to springtime freshness.

Another family move was welcomed as they were reunited with old friends in Southwest. Esther's singing talent prompted her selection as chorister at Yellow Creek Church. With a knack for memorizing, she acted in plays that were fundraisers for the PTA. As the depression began slowly easing its grip, Earl got a part-time job hauling gravel for the county. Helen went to high school in the small village of Wakarusa, making friends and excelling in her studies. Dresses were getting shorter, so she altered her school dresses. What she couldn't change was the therapeutic boxy shoes with the elevated sole. In her mind her shoes were the one marker of her debility. Erdene was the style maven of the family, and she fashioned Helen's black hair for Sunday morning church and school parties. Helen began to notice boys and always managed to be sweeping the front porch so she could wave to Emmert Herr when he went by on Saturday afternoons taking his sister to her piano lesson.

Because she was generally easy-going, Esther was surprised at Helen's vehemence against leaving Southwest—her cheeks flamed red, her angry voice bleated: "you can't do this to me, Mother. We haven't lived here two years. We're *always* moving. When I finally have friends where I fit in, you say we're moving again. The rest of you can go to Goshen. I'm staying here," she parked her legs, arms akimbo.

"I don't blame you for being upset Helen, but we've got to move to a farm with enough land to support our family. We don't have a choice. At least we'll be on Bashor Road close to Grandma. Goshen has electricity now, think how nice that will be. You have to take the good with the bad in life; that's just the way it is. We'll come back to Yellow Creek for church, so you'll still see those friends."

"There has to be a way for me to stay, at least until the end of the school year. If I can find a place to board, can I stay?"

"We don't have money to pay board, but I guess if you can find a way to work it off you can stay till spring. Daddy's not going to like it," Esther conceded. In February, when the family moved to Goshen they left Helen boarding with a friend, and a job at the high school for the remainder of the year.

Goshen High School was in another stratosphere from the provincial high school in Wakarusa. Helen sat with her face in her arms at the dining room table, "I hate it! I try to fit in, and it's like I have the plague," she bawled in her despair. "When classes change everyone swarms in a rush to get to the next class; the halls are like a maze. Today I tripped and *fell!* My books went flying. Everyone just walked around me. I'm there but no one sees me. The teachers are like professors—all business. They don't take time for students. Now I'm *failing;* I got a C on my geometry test. I can't keep up at this school. School work is the only thing I've ever been good at. Everyone always said I was smart, but I never have been smart. I'm not good at anything." She lifted her face, her expression puzzled and defeated, as if seeing herself in a new light: as someone lacking. That she didn't measure up had never occurred to her.

Esther put the iron on the cook stove and sat down, rubbing Helen's back, sweaty with spent emotion. Helen's future flashed before her eyes: she would work harder than anyone, yet not measure up; she would give every ounce of herself, but never be truly accepted. People would see *how* she was, not *who* she was. How can a mother's love repair that hurt? How can her words re-ignite that broken spirit?

"Helen, when you were a baby you couldn't move your right leg or use your right hand. The doctors told us you wouldn't walk. But *you* didn't know you couldn't walk, and Daddy and I weren't convinced. You endured hours of exercises and painful therapy. Daddy made a little walking stand with wheels that you pushed around. You wore shoes that caused painful stretching, but they straightened your feet. You were two years old when you learned to walk—not far behind schedule. Later you had a teacher who insisted you write with your right hand. You taught yourself to write with your left hand, and you have the prettiest handwriting of anyone I know."

"You think my handwriting is pretty?" she lifted her eyes balefully.

"Helen, why do you think the church has you write the minutes of council meetings? Your script is like the textbook. You've always gone to country schools with few students in each grade. There are many more students here at Goshen. I wouldn't expect you to do as well in the beginning. It will be the same when you go to college; competition will be even tougher. You'll figure it out. I've never known you to give up."

"I don't think I'll be going to college," Helen sniveled. "I'm already having trouble in high school."

"You can forget that talk. You *will* go to college; Daddy and I will see to that. Now, tell me one thing you like about high school. Let's find a place to start."

"I don't like anything about it," Helen moped, her chin in her hands. "I don't have any friends....I like the library; they have every book and magazine you could want. The librarian is nice."

"Then that's the place to start. Make friends with the librarian."

"Honestly Mother, I was thinking of friends my own age," the most sass Helen could muster.

"Remember, you're entering as a senior. These kids have been in school together for years. It's not that they don't like you; they don't know you. Is there a way to find other girls who've just moved in? They're feeling the same as you. *You'll* have to find a friend; they won't come to you."

"I've thought about trying out for the senior class play. They put on a big production—professional, with fancy sets and elaborate costumes. The play this year is "The Luck of the Irish". I read the playbook; I'd l-o-v-e to be in it." She left her tears at the table, jumped up, and with arms outstretched, glided across the floor. Caught by the acting bug, she spoke in muted voice: "Of course you have a pot of gold; every leprechaun has one."

Esther realized Helen had chosen her part and saw herself stage front. She could predict what Helen couldn't see: Helen's hitch-shuffle limp would interject a stark distraction. She would never get a part.

"There's no harm in trying out. You would meet people, even if you didn't get a part," she smiled her encouragement.

"You're right," Helen said, her innate aplomb restored. "I'm going to tryouts. Oh, I'll be so nervous. I'll need to practice. Who's gonna do my chores? There's practice every night after school."

"Don't worry about chores. If you get a part, Erdene and I can do the chores."

The next week Helen ran breathlessly into the kitchen, dropped her satchel, and hugged Esther. "I made it. I'm in the cast for "Luck of the Irish". I'm a prompter. It's not a real part but Mrs. McDonald said it's very important. I'll be at all the practices and cast parties. Sorry about dumping my chores on you, Mother, but the next month will be so busy. Part of my job is make-up and costume changes—lots of responsibilities. I'll get tickets for the family. Do you think the grandparents will come?"

Esther gazed at her chattering daughter in awe; she could hardly contain her pride. This was typical Helen: unafraid to try something remarkable, like play tryouts, then be perfectly content with a lesser outcome. No one wanted to be a prompter, but she had the assurance she would make that job invaluable. When the curtain opened, her imprint would be on every actor, prop, and cue—the safety-pin holding the production together. Her talent was in taking a nothing role and making it something.

A lot of Helen's social life focused on BY, the Yellow Creek Brethren Youth Group. As its elected president, she was a representative to the district cabinet—youth groups from six area Brethren Churches. BY met at least weekly for organized activities and parties, in addition to monthly activities with the six youth groups from surrounding churches. These get-togethers were a dating mecca; Helen dated young men but wasn't serious about any of them.

Esther needlessly felt sorry and protective of Helen during her teen years. A generation earlier, Esther had thrived with friendships; a social butterfly, she'd had her pick of beaus. Her hair and dress, partying and dallying with men, was a game of which she never tired. Being more serious, Helen was goal-oriented and good at getting things done. She wasn't interested in the coy frippery that came so naturally to her mother. In the spring of her senior year she began dating Paul, a fellow in her youth group. She thought him a dandy and a bit of a snob, but she liked having a guy at BY activities, band concerts, and other group outings.

In 1936, the year Helen graduated high school, Goshen was a city on the move. The depression was relaxing its grip. Large factories were becoming unionized, with wages increasing. Women were home where they belonged. Newspapers and mail were delivered daily, causing local and national events to become the focus of daily conversation. Streetlights had been installed and even some homes in the country had been connected to the electric grid. Sewer lines were completed inside city limits and extended out Berkey Avenue. Judd was sectioning off an area between the kitchen and bedroom for an indoor bathroom. Since Sarah had been sickly he was intent on making things nice for her.

The Fourth of July was a major holiday. The town was in a celebratory mood. Women styled their hair, wore their Sunday dress and a hat. Men wore starched shirts and seersucker slacks with a straw fedora. Helen, usually unfazed about appearances, was self-conscious. She had just spent two dollars at Marleen's Beauty Shop getting her hair cut and permed in the new style. She wore a gauzy dress with a wispy-veiled hat. She knew Grandpa would have a snide comment when the family gathered at Grandma Swiharts for a picnic. Judd roasted wieners, and the men cranked homemade ice cream. Everyone was groggy with too much food. Carl supervised sparklers for the children. Neighbors paraded from yard to yard, competing for the juiciest cherry pie and the best fireworks show.

Helen rode to the parade downtown with her uncles, Merle and Don, and with Merle's girlfriend, Margie. For Helen, the parade was exhilarating—reliable in its year-after-year sameness, yet fresh and new with reawakened patriotism. The high school band in maroon and cream uniforms always led with their high-stepping majorettes, flying batons, and John Phillip Sousa marches. Mr. Firestone, the mayor, rode in an open car, waving and throwing candy. Edgy show horses, stepping in nervous circles, were followed by veterans from WWI in their tight, moth-eaten uniforms. Helen swayed with the shuffling crowd, waving her small flag and cheering.

Next came the children, pulling decorated Radio Flyer wagons while their pets added to the noisy commotion. Accordion music accompanied the polka dancers, stepping and whirling, the ladies' skirts spinning. As always, closing the parade was Uncle Sam, walking on stilts while the band played "America the Beautiful". Tears filled Helen's eyes and her voice thickened as she sang the beloved song. Forgotten were the cold, the struggles and deprivations suffered in the depression. Goshen was the fair city—the good life beckoned.

* * * * *

"Yah Hoo! Watch out," Helen hollered as she drove in and out amongst the obstacle course of wheat shocks in the field.

"Slow down," Earl shouted. "This is not a racetrack. You're giving me a sick headache," he complained, taking several sniffs from his ever-present bottle of camphor. "You ladies have to get together. Helen, you need to slow down, and Mother, the car won't move unless you give it some gas—slow and steady on the accelerator so the car doesn't lurch forward, then stop. I guess you've noticed the car won't stop when you yell "Whoa". Now Helen, keep the speedometer about ten miles an hour and go in and out around the shocks, keeping about a foot away from them. Then back up the same way. Then I'll have you both take the tire off, patch the tube and pump it up." Teaching Helen and Esther to drive was taxing Earl's patience and aggravating his tendency for headaches. This was one task he could cross off the list in preparing Helen for college.

Earl and Esther were both preoccupied with finding money to pay for college. It was a sore trial for them to swallow their pride and beg for money. Goshen College was a small institution chartered by the Mennonite Church. It had a reputation for outstanding faculty and curriculum. The Christian emphasis and close relationship between faculty and students was a perfect fit for Helen. Plus, she could live at home and save on room and board. As with all educational institutions, the college had struggled during the depression, and while she met the qualifications for college acceptance, they regretfully acknowledged to Earl and Esther they didn't have the $105 per semester to loan for the cost of tuition. Most students who applied needed a loan. They did agree to help Helen get a job to assist in paying for tuition.

Neither of their families came from wealth. They went to several members of their extended families, some they hardly knew, only to come away empty handed. Finally, just before the semester began, Earl's great-aunt, Carrie Zeigler, a widow-woman, agreed to talk to Helen.

This is my life on the line, Helen thought as she drove to Elkhart to meet Mrs. Zeigler, a relative she'd never met. She walked to her front door, a bundle of nerves, though she had passed Esther's muster in her modest gray church dress with a simple necklace, a dark hat and gloves. The door was opened by a small stooped lady, her white hair in a U-shaped roll with crimped waves crossing the back of her head. Helen took her extended hand.

"Come in Helen. I'm happy to meet you," she led her to the parlor where a tea service and two chairs were placed in an alcove overlooking the street. The home was dark with oversized furniture and heavy draperies.

"I appreciate your invitation," Helen said, trying to still her shaky hands. Mrs. Zeigler sat, arranging her long skirt, then pouring tea, her movements sure and steady.

"Tell me why you want to go to college," she smiled warmly, her round glasses slipping down her nose.

"I think I've always been curious; I like to learn. Growing up, I usually had a book in my hand. When I was young, I played "teacher", knowing if I got the chance, I'd be one. I think it would be a challenge to help children learn—and I'd learn in the process."

"You know, I wanted a profession myself," Mrs. Zeigler rested her cup and passed cookies to Helen. "In my day that wasn't acceptable for women."

"Yes, my mother wanted to be a teacher. It wasn't possible for her either."

"It's quite likely you'll marry in the next year or so; you're an attractive young lady," she touched her napkin to her mouth. "They don't allow married women to teach—which is most unfortunate. My money for your education would be wasted, and likely you wouldn't have the resources to repay me."

Helen leaned forward, lifting her hand. "I don't think you need to worry about that. They wouldn't say it, but Mother and Daddy are afraid I *won't* marry. They want me to go to college so I can support myself. No, Mrs. Zeigler, I enjoy dating but I don't have to beat the men off," she chuckled. "I may marry sometime, but I'll be fine if I don't."

Mrs. Zeigler sat back in her chair. "I know the college curriculum is difficult, especially for women who've had poor schooling. Are you academically qualified?"

Helen nodded, "That's my main concern other than the money. In my senior year of high school, I moved from Wakarusa to Goshen, and at first I struggled. I graduated with A's and B's. I know I'll have to work, but I promise you I won't fail." In her fervor her cheeks colored, and she spilled a little tea in her saucer.

"I like your honesty and self-confidence, Helen. I'm going to give you the money. We'll start today with a check for the fall semester. I'm not financially independent. This is a loan, not a gift. I expect you to pay me back in good time."

Helen's hands went to her eyes, pressing back tears. "You can never know how thankful I am to you. You've made my dream come true," her voice was gravelly and choked.

"I wasn't able to go—you do what I couldn't do. That will make me happy." Mrs. Zeigler and Helen shook hands on their agreement, tears in both their eyes.

"You'll never regret this; you have my word. I can't wait to tell my parents. They'll be so grateful." Helen couldn't help herself, she twirled and step-danced around the room. "Goshen College here I come."

* * * * *

"How was Grandma last night?" Esther asked, putting the soapy plate in the rinse water for Erdene to dry.

"She doesn't act like herself, Mama. I made them chicken and noodles for supper. You know that's her favorite, and she hardly ate any; she said she wasn't hungry."

"She sure has looked peaked lately. Grandpa took her all the way to Michigan to a different doctor. I hope he does her some good."

Erdene lifted the dripping silverware into the drainer. "The new doctor gave her a purgatory or purgative; I forget what she called it. I know the bathroom was sure stinky after she was in there."

Esther looked worried. "She asked if I'd have the oyster supper this year. Now you know, if she can't do the oyster supper, something's wrong."

"She's at least sixty, isn't she? She's as old as Methuselah. Maybe it's just old age."

"She's an old sixty-one. That woman has had a hard life."

"I slept in the bedroom next to them last night. Before they closed the door, I heard her say, 'No hanky-panky tonight, Pop. I'm not up to it'. What do you suppose she meant by that?"

Esther's cheeks colored as she became preoccupied scrubbing the skillet. "Why I wouldn't know, Erdene. She seems to be losing ground though. I miss your good help around here, but we'll have you get off the bus at Grandma's anytime she wants you. You're a good help to her. Since you weren't here last night, you didn't hear Helen's good news: the college got her a job every night at the library—her favorite place. Somehow the government pays her thirty cents an hour. That's such a relief." Esther carried the soapy dishwater out to the garden.

"Jeepers, thirty cents. She'll get rich."

"Listen to you. Nobody in this family will ever be rich. I vow, this college is just right for her. I've never seen her so happy. I need to leave to get her at the library, she'll have lots of studying when she gets home."

Just before Christmas break, Helen was in the college library, watching the staff put away decorations from the Christmas tree. A few days later, she saw a few discarded trees piled behind the college furnace building. The Phillips family would have a meager Christmas. What surprise and joy it would bring their family to have a tree. After vacation started, Helen and Erdene went to the college, got one of the discarded trees, and secretly busied themselves making ornaments and decorations. Helen splurged and bought silver tassel. On Sunday evening when the family came home from church, there was the beautifully decorated tree in the corner of the kitchen, its pine fragrance filling the air. Six-year-old Louise was awestruck. Christmas joy buoyed their spirits as each discovered some small gift or treasure for other family members, wrapped it in newspaper and put it under the tree. Christmas morning was festive as they unwrapped packages of divinity candy, knit scarves, lace-edged hankies, and from Mother and Daddy, a warm store-bought sweater for each girl. When Grandma and Grandpa Swihart came for dinner, she brought an embroidered pillowcase for each of them. Surrounded by family love, they felt rich indeed.

When school reconvened, Helen found an official looking envelope from the college president in her mailbox. She had never met him; why would he send a letter to her? He requested she come to his office the next day. "Oh no." her hand flew to her mouth. It had to be the Christmas tree. Did someone see her take it? Were they accusing her of stealing? She read the letter over and over, but there was no hint. By nighttime she was stewing in her own juices. Looking back, it seemed such folly; she couldn't believe she had been so foolish. Her parents would be shamed beyond measure. Would her misdeed be published in the college newspaper? But worse, she feared being expelled, her degree in jeopardy. She couldn't bear to tell her folks, pacing through the night, rehearsing words to somehow minimize her appalling behavior.

By the time of her appointment, she felt like a knot of high-tension wires. She wasn't sure she would be able to talk, but she was determined not to cry. She would take her punishment.

Dr. Yoder was middle-aged and balding with wire-frame glasses. In an austere black stand-up-collar suit, genteel Dr. Yoder greeted Helen warmly, her hand trembling in his. She swooped to a chair before her shaky legs buckled under her.

"I have good news for you. You've been selected to receive the Laura Kindig Scholarship, a new award chosen for a woman who demonstrates good character, academic excellence, and financial need—you qualify in each of these areas. You are the first recipient. It's a high honor, Helen."

"Wha-a"...she garbled, choking on her words.

"Are you okay? You look pale. You shouldn't be surprised; you're an outstanding student and highly qualified. Mrs. Kindig was quite taken with your accomplishments, particularly since you've worked at the city library every evening. This scholarship money will offset this semester's tuition. Congratulations. You'll be an excellent teacher. I imagine this award will be beneficial as you search for a job." He stood up, shaking her hand.

"I can't believe it. I don't know what to say...please thank Mrs. Kindig for me," her eyes welled with tears, despite her resolve.

"Yes, she wants to meet you. We'll have a dinner for our scholarship recipients and sponsors."

"I still don't believe it. Thank you, Dr. Yoder." After leaving his office she doubled over, held her stomach, and laughed uproariously. She knew she'd never take a discarded Christmas tree again.

* * * * *

The other students and faculty were like her: poor, serious, intelligent, and hardworking. She fit in like a glove snuggles a hand. Students were encouraged to learn about the world, discuss new ideas, and express their opinion under the guidance of wise faculty. 1936 was a chaotic time: Roosevelt was re-elected to his second term and was implementing many new-deal measures. Prohibition had ended, a concern for teetotaling Mennonites and Brethren, who decried the scourge of alcohol. There had been several years of drought. The dust bowl was shifting east. That summer Goshen had several days when temperatures were over 110 degrees, destroying crops and gardens. Hitler had invaded Poland and Austria, and whispers about Jews being persecuted and imprisoned caused unease among this peace-loving, pacifist group. An unknown disease, causing paralysis and death had spread to Chicago, close enough to alarm parents, unnerved by pictures of children in iron lungs. Finally, the recession persisted with unemployment holding near 19 percent. Striking workers were endemic and union activity flourished. The Goshen Rubber Company just down the road from the college temporarily closed due to strikes. Helen passed the strikers every evening when walking to her job at the library. She was awakened to wrongs, inequities, and bigotry in their small provincial town. With a bit of the firebrand in her bones, Helen's independence aroused compassion and altruism.

Helen bolted down her wheat cakes, then grabbed a gunny sack on her way to the potato cellar. "I'm going to take some vegetables, potatoes, and a few jars of canned beef to the college today. The cooks are helping us make stew for the families of the strikers at Goshen Rubber."

Esther looked skeptical, "We really don't have extra, Helen. With the drought we'll be hard put to get through the winter. I'm not sure you should be there anyway. It seems there's always clashes between the strikers and management people. Last week there was a shooting. It's not safe."

"I know you're careful with our food stock, but you should see those hungry children, Mama. The fathers haven't worked for months. Their small homes have no garden plots. The little ones are hungry. If you saw them your heart would melt. They hang on to our skirts. For most of them the food from the college is the only meal they get. I'm telling you, those cooks at the college can take potatoes, onions, and a chicken, and stretch them forty ways from Sunday," Helen said while scrubbing potatoes.

"You're saying the college is financing food for these people?"

"There are several organizations working together and some churches have what they call a soup kitchen. They believe if your neighbor is hungry, you should feed them; if he is thirsty, you give him a drink. I'd say it's just good people doing good things. When going to college you learn there's a whole world out there," she lifted her arms, intent on convincing her mother. "It makes you look at things differently. I never paid attention, but now I want to learn all of it. Sometimes I could almost cry, Mother. I'm so lucky to be in college."

Esther looked thoughtfully at Helen, proud and happy for her, but her own limited experience clouded her ability to understand. "You learn about the world in your classes to be a teacher?"

"Sometimes, yes. But it's so much more. Special people come on campus to give a talk that anyone can attend. Why Mama, yesterday Rabbi Weinstein talked to us. Did you know there are Jews in Goshen? There's quite a large group; they have a synagogue. Recently they've been threatened, and some don't feel safe. The Ku Klux Klan burned crosses at some of their homes. The rabbi is concerned that Americans aren't aware of Hitler's treatment of Jews in Europe: their businesses are being destroyed; they're forced to live in walled ghettos; and they're imprisoned in camps. Roosevelt closes his eyes to it, and won't increase the number who can emigrate. Mother, why would people dislike Jews? The rabbi seemed perfectly nice, though it was hard to understand him."

"Oh Helen. I think you're getting too deep in this. I don't know much about Jews, but I know they don't believe like us. If Roosevelt doesn't want Jews here, I think he knows what he's doing. I wouldn't be talking about Jews if I were you. They're all rich and it's said they cheat in business, though I don't know that for a fact." Esther knew Helen's penchant for befriending the down-and-out, she didn't want her comments to fall on the wrong ears, jeopardizing all she was working for. "I think if you stick to college activities, especially if a professor is involved, you should be okay. But be careful what you say. Most normal people won't be so open-minded about feeding strikers and sympathizing with Jews. You keep that talk at the college and here in the kitchen."

"I'm careful. I don't want to get in trouble either. Thanks for giving our vegetables and helping to wash them. The cooks will be thrilled. Everyone is trying to share—it's a hard time all around. Any news about Grandma this week? I thought she looked poorly on Sunday. What does she hear from Clara and Edith?"

"Pop is still taking her to Michigan every week for a colonic treatment. Erdene says she is worn to a frazzle when she gets home, what with the long drive and all. Evidently Wilbur wrote a script for a big-time movie and never got paid for his work. I guess everything's not perfect in paradise. Clara's family likes Virginia. They went to visit Washington, D.C. I guess it's quite something. Clara told her it's too soon for them to come home, whatever that means."

CHAPTER 37

Sarah's Death

As Helen drove the family's 1936 Ford to her new school, she ruminated about the sudden change in the family's fortunes. Mr. Martin, an acquaintance of Earls, had struck it rich when he discovered gold in Alaska. He returned to Goshen to buy land and establish Pine Manor, a commercial farm with registered Guernsey cows—prize-winning livestock that were competitive around the United States. His new-found wealth and investment in Goshen made him a local celebrity. He hired Earl to be in charge of the calf barn. The family now rented a spacious home on his farm along South Main Street, where they boarded farm hands. Esther cooked and did laundry for the expanded household, and helped with the milking. Their home was no longer limited to family, but was more like a business operation, though some of the boarders were beginning to feel like family. While they weren't wealthy, they now had the trappings of wealth: steady work, a substantial home, and status in the community by association with wealth. Helen saw her parents' smiles came easier and their steps lighter when they moseyed among friends and family in town on Saturday nights. Erdene's weekend job as cook at Newberry's Five and Dime, the favorite eatery on Main Street, also lent gravitas to the family.

It was a sunny August day when she turned into the yard of the Jonesville School. Her grin reflected the day as she jauntily sauntered to the front door. "My first school," she said aloud, shivers welling through her body. Her hard work was worth her parents' tears on the day President Yoder handed her the Elementary Teacher Training Course Diploma from Goshen College. She knew she was luckier than most to have the job at Jonesville—a one-room school between Goshen and Wakarusa. Women teachers were pounding the pavement, even though they were paid less than their male counterparts. Her annual salary of $800 was a good wage and she was determined to repay Mrs. Zeigler by the end of the first semester.

She hurried up the steps and put the key in the lock. As the door shuddered open, a draft of hot musty air enveloped her. She meandered around the room, her fingers leaving their mark on every dusty surface. In front by the blackboard was an oval-shaped picture of George Washington. Beside her desk was a recitation bench that would seat eight students. She pulled down a world map which didn't catch, rewinding in a flurry of dust, breeching the quiet stillness. Each desk seated two students with a nook for books and papers under the desktop. In the middle of the room was a potbelly stove. Along the back wall were coat hooks, a shelf for lunch pails, and a cupboard with school texts and a few library books.

The slip-shod furniture and shabby floor planks looked beautiful to her. She took a determined breath, lifting her shoulders as she began a to-do list. As teacher she was also janitor: cleaning the dust and dead insects, washing the windows, and in winter, tending the fire and emptying ashes. The school year extended from October to May, though the older boys would occasionally work in the fields in the spring and fall, and girls would sometimes miss Monday wash day.

Helen had rented a room from the Nusbaum's, a couple and their two children who lived next to the school. They were eager to take this "green behind the ears" young teacher into their home. Helen respected Mrs. Nusbaum, also a career woman—the two becoming fast friends. In the evenings, when finished with schoolwork, she would join them in the parlor to listen to favorite radio programs: "The Shadow Knows" and "Little Orphan Annie".

"Miss Phillips" to her students, Helen settled into teaching as though born to it. She had twenty students, at least one in each grade. The youngest was timid six-year-old Marie, who cried almost daily the first month. The oldest, Chuck, a bull-necked hulking eighteen-year-old man-child was only two years younger than his petite teacher. Most students arrived at eight o'clock on a horse-drawn hack. The days were long, with morning and afternoon recesses and an hour lunch break. She taught seven subjects: reading, arithmetic, writing, English, spelling, history, and geography. The method of teaching was by rote learning. When younger children finished their assignment, they joined more advanced learners at the recitation bench, listening but not talking. Learning was reinforced when older children tutored younger ones.

Miss Phillips was nimble-witted and down-to-earth, generally not intimidated by the antics of the boys who drifted in a wave around Chuck. She had a shrill voice that she used to good advantage with strict, consistent discipline.

She saw Chuck with his arm raised, two fingers extended. "This is your second time, Chuck. You must not have enough to do. You may go, but when you get back do the next page of algebra problems."

"First grade, come to the bench with your reading books." Three little ones toddled to the recitation bench, taking turns reading short sentences and repetitive words in their self-important monotone. Carl stumbled on a word.

"Sound it out, Carl. What does the 'm' sound like?"

"Ma, Ma"

"Good. What does 'a n' sound like?"

"an, an"

"The word is...?"

"M...an"

"Is that a long or a short 'a'?"

"Ah..ah. A short 'a'," Carl answered.

"Very good. Barbara, you read next. You're learning the words so well; I want you to practice your expression and elocution."

"Run, Sam the man," Barbara read.

"How would you say that if you were yelling at your brother?"

Barbara looked up, raising her voice, "Run, Sam the man!"

"Yes, stories are more interesting when you read with expression." She looked up as Elaine, a sixth grader approached the bench.

"You're done writing your spelling sentences?"

"Yes. I didn't make any mistakes," Elaine answered.

"You take over then. I'll start second grade. Carl is working on letter sounds and Barbara on expression."

Miss Phillips walked to her desk, opening a drawer. "Oh-h!" she shrieked, retreating as a frog jumped out, sailing across to Elaine who yelled to beat the band, running around the room and scattering the first graders.

Miss Phillips looked at Chuck, fully engrossed in his algebra. "Class is dismissed early for recess," she announced.

"Come to the bench, Chuck," she sounded weary with him.

He clumped forward, his oversized feet stumbling, his head lowered to hide a snigger.

"I've had it with you, Chuck. You're determined to disrupt the class and try my patience. Last week you put soap in the well, and took all afternoon pumping it out. The week before you let loose a bag of grasshoppers that everyone had to catch. It's bad enough you misbehave, but Chuck, you're an example to the younger boys. They see what you do, and want to be like you. You're smart—the best math student in the school. I have no doubt someday you'll be very successful. For now, I have nineteen other students to teach. I can't let you continue to interfere with their education. What do you have to say for yourself?"

"I...n't ...ing to app..."

"You're mumbling. I don't understand." She stood and walked to him. "Look at me, Chuck," her eyes stared at him level-on. "You have one more chance—no more. My last resort will be to invite your father to school to observe your behavior. I'll not warn you ahead of time," her voice was steely.

Chuck's head jerked up, he half stood, "Please, Miss Phillips. Don't tell my dad."

"It's up to you then, isn't it? You've had all the warnings I'm giving you. Next, I talk to your parents. Now find that frog so we can start class again."

Miss Phillips often played with the children during recess. She had practiced marbles with her father, believing skill would enhance her standing with boys at school. One of the fathers had whittled and sanded a stick of wood, permitting the whole class to play softball. She had the whole group gather and place hedge apples around the outside of the school to keep insects out. Group activities allowed her to teach manners: how men treat ladies, and sportsman-like winning and losing. She didn't participate in the rough and tumble kick-the-can or crack-the-whip.

The girls, much more likely to idolize their pretty, young teacher, were satisfied to have her watch their games. The little girls played London bridge and drop-the-handkerchief. Older girls jumped rope, made a pretend house out of leaves, and wove clover for necklaces. That fall they gathered bittersweet, knowing Miss Phillips loved to decorate the classroom with it.

With all this play, Miss Phillips focused on Chuck. She ruminated and analyzed, not wanting to be overly harsh, yet not wanting to sacrifice her classroom to his unruly behavior. Could it be he misbehaved because he was self-conscious about being big in comparison to the other boys? Was he a "late bloomer" who hadn't yet grown out of childish behavior? She watched him continue his nuisance actions: throw stones at the girls in the privy, whisper naughty words so girls could hear, pull little girls' pigtails, and get the boys all incensed by cheating at marbles. Because Chuck was still in school at eighteen, she assumed educating him was important to his parents. She met his father on a blistery evening while he was in the field husking corn.

"I need your advice about Chuck," she told the tall man with elegant manners and a gentle voice. He assisted her to a seat on the back of the wagon as she explained his son's behavior and her uncertainty in dealing with him.

He nodded, lifting and replacing his straw hat. "Chuck is our only child so school is his main exposure to younger children. Maybe he's immature in the way he treats them."

"That's my idea, Mr. Grundy. It's why punishment doesn't seem the best way to handle him."

"Lately, when we go to town, he gives the young girls a lot of attention."

"Yes, he's been teasing the girls. I'm sure he's self-conscious about his size and acts out."

Mr. Grundy chuckled, "I remember when I was his age, I wasn't the easiest to get along with," he pulled back the corn shucks and threw an ear in the wagon.

"I would like you to visit during our lessons. This will tell Chuck you're concerned about him, maybe shame him a bit—but it's not outright punishment. I think he's smart enough to work out his behavior problems on his own. He's a good boy, Mr. Grundy. You and your wife have done a good job."

"I'll be there tomorrow morning, Miss Phillips, sure as shootin'."

"Give Mrs. Grundy my regards. I appreciate your help," she said as he assisted her from the wagon.

"I'll see you tomorrow," he called after her.

The next day Mr. Grundy quietly entered the school during math class, seating himself at the back of the room—good timing as Chuck excelled in math. Miss Phillips barely broke stride as she introduced him, "I'm glad to see Chuck's father, Mr. Grundy, visit our classroom. I welcome every parent to visit. All of you continue your work. Marie, would you take Mr. Grundy this textbook?"

When Chuck saw his father, the red seeped up his neck, even showing through his blonde hair. His eyes darted with swift intensity, he dropped his chalk and, after retrieving it, kept his back to the room. He became very diligent in working problems, eager to finish before Cindy. When he returned to his seat to complete the worksheet, he huddled over his desk, as if to close off the room. After handing in his paper, he glanced at his father with a pinched smile. Before lunch, Mr. Grundy quietly slipped out.

A result of his visit was that several parents came, this being a novel idea. Miss Phillips was welcoming, eager to update them on their child's progress, and encouraging their input.

Chuck seemed preoccupied in the next weeks; he was more serious about his schoolwork. He still cheated at marbles, but he more often let the younger boys be captain. He became willing to assist students in math rather than compete with them. He found subtle ways to help Miss

Phillips and paid less attention to the girls. His parents were pleased when notified he was making good progress.

One day Mr. Pratt, the superintendent, paid a visit to evaluate Miss Phillips. She conducted the regular lessons, aware the children were intent and watchful of the well-dressed stranger. From the recitation bench she observed young Jerry contorting his face, sticking out his tongue, and wiggling finger-ears at Mr. Pratt, who was trying mightily to keep a straight face.

"Continue reading, Carl." She walked back to Jerry, turning him in his seat. "You're not finished with your spelling, Jerry. Put "wagon" in a sentence. Work on your cursive. You can do it more neatly."

She returned to the first graders where Marie was reading in a sing-song voice, no longer too shy to read aloud. "Very good, Marie. I can tell you've been reading to your mother at night. Barbara, next please," as she looked to see Jerry making funny faces again. This was a dilemma: she could be penalized for being too strict *or* too lax. She wanted to wallop him.

She walked to his seat, squatting, and taking his face in her hand. All eyes were on her. "Jerry, you're being rude to our guest. I'm disappointed in you. You usually do your work without misbehaving. Do I need to put you in the corner, and everyone will go home and tell their parents we had a visitor and you sat in the corner? Because I will do that. I can't allow you to be unkind to a guest. It's your choice; what shall we do?"

"I'll behave," Jerry mumbled, his head bowed in shame.

She dropped her hand from his face. "That's a good choice. I don't want to come back here again. Get busy on your sentences." The rest of the hour passed without incident, but Miss Phillips was tense. She felt everyone's antennae roving the room, anticipating another scene.

When Mr. Pratt left, he shook her hand. "You're doing a good job, Miss Phillips. I'm glad I hired you."

Helen's weekends with family at Pine Manor Farm were a highlight. Since she had never lived apart from family, she was surprised she got homesick for the daily chit-chat and goings-on. At first, the men boarders seemed like intrusive trespassers; she missed the decorous meals of old. But her family had warmed to them, and mealtimes were filled with boisterous levity. Esther went to extra trouble, baking every day. The men raved and complimented her. She coyly blushed and tut-tutted, but she thrived on the accolades. Everyone took a shine to Tony, a stocky Italian with a gregarious personality and a head of black curly hair. He called Esther "Mama" and taught her how to cook pasta and make spaghetti sauce. He brought a cosmopolitan flair to the supper table. Walt, one of the other boarders, was his foil. With a jaunty smile and amiable good will, he innocently "pulled Tony's chain". The girls were a rapt audience, especially seven-year-old Louise, and the men played this to the hilt.

In the blink of an eye it was Christmas, bringing parents, grandparents, and community to the school for the special program. Miss Phillips wanted a play in which every child would have a part. Neither the city nor college libraries had one which satisfied her; she would have to write it herself. As Christmas would be spare for these families, she reiterated the proverbial theme that trinkets and gifts don't satisfy, but kindness and charity reveal the true Christmas spirit. Cindy and Chuck, being the oldest students, had the part of the parents. When children weren't on "stage", they sang in the choir. Chuck became "Boy Friday", closing off a corner of the classroom with a blanket-curtain to make a stage. English and art classes were in charge of invitations. The fourth-grade class was working on fractions, so they figured the recipes for cookies and punch. All students helped with decorations. It was a standing-room-only crowd with Helen's extended family in attendance. The program was a blowout success with little Marie tearfully hiccoughing her part; a Christmas play that brought a lump to the throat; spilled punch; and young Jerry making faces when saying his part. Earl brought Mrs. Zeigler, who was honored with a speech of appreciation and Helen's check repaying her loan.

* * * * *

"I made your favorite, Mother: mincemeat pie." Esther cut a small wedge for Sarah. "I ground some of the beef and potatoes for your supper. Erdene will heat it when she comes after school. Here, have a taste," Esther offered.

"Mincemeat pie. I haven't had that in ages. I do want a taste. There's coffee left. Sit and have coffee with me, Esther. She pushed the pie around her plate. A shadow darkened her brow. She winced, holding her abdomen as she reached for the sugar.

"I see you holding your stomach. Are you in pain?"

"I feel so bloated and stopped up. It's getting so I can't eat. Food doesn't go through. Sometimes I just chew food, then spit it out. I don't want the grandchildren to see my manners, but I can't swallow it. I've wanted to talk to you. Don't say anything to the family, but last week Dr. Williams, the Wakarusa doctor, told us I have a tumor in my colon. Evidently this has been my problem all along, not dyspepsia like the Centerville doctor thought. This doctor doesn't recommend surgery."

Esther reached for Sarah's hand, instantly understanding her hollowed-out cheeks, pasty pallor, and the steady deterioration of her mother's health and vigor.

"Oh Mama. Did he say it's cancer?"

"No, he didn't say cancer, but a tumor may not be much better. Pop wants to take me to a doctor in Ft. Wayne, but Esther, these long trips and treatments are so hard on me. Try to talk Pop out of it. If I don't get better, so be it. I know Heaven will be my home," her eyes were soft on Esther, her touch gentle.

Esther looked desperately at Sarah, "I've never imagined our family without you at the center of things. You keep us all...anchored." Esther's eyes filled with tears.

"He didn't say I can't get better, but he's not proposing surgery or other treatment. This is why I'm telling you; I want you to help me make plans. There are two things I want before I die, and I need you to arrange it. I want to be with Will, my brother, while I'm still myself. Also, I want to see Clara again. Unfortunately, Edith is too far to bring home."

"I'll tell Pop you want to stay with Dr. Williams, not the doctor in Ft. Wayne. We all want someone who can make you better, Mother. You can't give up. I'll never stop praying for God to heal you. There's more power in prayer than all the doctor's treatments and medicines. I'll call Will and Clara tonight and write a letter to Edith."

"I hate for you to make long distance calls, but I just can't do it. Will has been my one constant, the family I've felt closest to all these years. I have such tenderness for him; I want to see him one more time."

* * * * *

Helen and Walt, one of the herdsmen boarding with the Phillips, were crossing the highway to get to his car parked beside the Pine Manor milking barn. They had a date to go to a class play at Wakarusa High School. Helen, who had rarely seen Walt in anything but barn coveralls, was pleased to see he looked quite dapper in dress clothes.

"I have to say, going out with you feels weird," she said as he took her arm, guiding her across the busy road.

"Why does it feel weird? You know me."

"Exactly. You live at our house and eat with us. I feel like I'm dating my brother," she grinned at him.

"Well, I think we have a leg up. It's our first date and we already know each other. Oh, shoot," he hurried toward the car.

"What's the matter?" she heard distress in his tone.

"Someone let the air out of all the tires. What a how-de-do," he said, running his hand through his long sandy hair. "It's the guys in the barn. They warned me they would play an April Fool's joke on me. I'd say they got me good. I'll bet Tony was the shyster behind this. I'm sorry, Helen."

"Don't worry, it wasn't your fault. I'm surprised at Tony. By the time you get the tires aired up it will be too late to go to the play—your tickets are wasted," Helen said.

Walt smiled, shaking his head. "Tony's not mean. He didn't know we were going out or he wouldn't have done it. While I'm airing up the tires, you can think of something else to do."

"We could go for a ride and end up at the Olympia Candy Kitchen," Helen said later.

"I have another idea. I'd like to go to Jonesville to see where you teach," Walt said.

"You want to see Jonesville?" Helen was surprised; men seldom showed much interest in her job.

"The stories you tell about your students when you come home are funny and interesting. I'd love to see your school so I can place your stories in my mind. We could go to your school, then get ice cream after." That's what they did. She showed him the children's work and described her typical days. They sat at desks in the shadowy school until they realized it was nearly closing time for the Candy Kitchen. Though their first date was spoiled by the April Fool's trick, they both thought the evening a success.

"Since we missed the play, can we do our first date over so I can get it right next time?" Walt asked.

"It wasn't what we planned, but I had a nice evening. You let me talk about my favorite thing. Yes, I'd love to go out again," she answered.

* * * * *

The week Will and Elma came to Goshen on the train was like a spring holiday for the extended Swihart family. Everyone eddied in and out of Judd and Sarah's home, not wanting to miss the rousing good times and the aura of good fellowship.

Will, a robust fifty-eight years, had a little potbelly, ruddy cheeks, and a pate with a fringe of gray. The couple's energy and hardiness glared a stark contrast to Sarah's gaunt and shrunken body. Melancholy settled over him as he held his fragile sister close in welcome.

"There's my girl. How good to see you. How is it that I'm an old baldy and you have a full head of hair with hardly any gray?" he teased.

"Probably because you spend more time preening your wispy few stubbles than Sarah spends on her whole head," Elma folded Sarah into her tiny body.

"You don't know how I've been looking forward to a whole week with my little sister. They say guests are like fish—after three days you'll want to send us home."

Sarah and Judd greeted them warmly, "That would never happen."

"If you two want to wash up, supper is ready. I'm sure you're famished after your long trip." Esther had prepared beef and noodles with mashed potatoes.

Will and Elma were impressed with the changes in Goshen. "Having your streets paved dresses up the town. I'm guessing they put sewer pipes in when they did that," Will commented. "That sure is a nice bathroom you put in, Judd. You take good care of my sister. Elma will get spoiled. She won't want to go home to our old stinky privy."

"Things happen at a slower pace in the country. I saw your Kline's Store had a lady mannequin dressed in slacks in the window. We don't see *that* in Pioneer, Ohio," Elma chuckled.

Erdene piped up, "Last weekend I went to Klines and tried on slacks. They have pretty blouses to match. It's getting more common to see women wearing pants."

"Erdene, if I see you wearing pants, I'll kick you all the way to town," Judd bellowed. "I'm the only man in my family who isn't a minister, but I know what the good book says, and pants don't belong on a woman," he huffed.

Erdene's face flushed red, she lowered her head as a pall settled over the group.

"Elma, you can pass the fruit to go with the cake," Esther requested, attempting to gloss over the strained silence.

Will leaned forward on his elbows, a genial smile on his face. "Erdene, I've heard it said you can never understand the fashion industry. It's because they're too "clothes" minded," he chuckled. "I think Judd is saying clothes shouldn't be important to us. Esther, isn't this one of those cakes that has twelve eggs in it? It's delicious."

"They call it angel food. It's good when making noodles—you can use the yolks from the cake in the noodles," Esther was thankful to Will for distracting Judd's outburst.

Earl smiled at Will, "Do you remember what you did to Esther and me the first night of our honeymoon?"

"It's hard to tell with Will," Elma grinned. "My guess is, it was risqué."

"Now Elma," Will looked abashed.

Earl started laughing so hard he could hardly talk, "You brought a broom to our bedroom so Esther could hide behind it when she undressed," he guffawed.

"We have laughed about that so many times," Esther chuckled.

"That sounds like Will," Elma nodded.

The week passed in a blur. Will had never seen a huge commercial farming operation like Pine Manor. He was blown away by the prize livestock and the logistics of the feeding and milking operation. One day they took the ferry boat to Blosser's Island for a picnic. Elma and Erdene outdid themselves, planning special meals from the bounty of Sarah's larder. There was a wiener roast, homemade ice cream, and pies and cakes at every meal. One evening Walt and Tony joined Helen and Erdene. Though neither of them was Brethren—the family "true religion"—they were welcomed to the nightly hymn sing.

Will and Elma's visit invigorated Sarah. Unspoken was the knowledge that this reunion would be Sarah's last. Will's nature didn't brook sadness; days were filled with laughter, joy, and quiet celebration. A smile never left Sarah's face. Throughout her life her greatest pleasure was being with family, and this week was the epitome of family togetherness. She sat peeling potatoes with the ladies, watching with delight as Judd gave pony rides, and taking short walks with Will.

The highlight of the week was a surprise Will had planned: their sister Juda, and her husband Josiah, joined the family get-together. Sarah and Juda had stayed in touch with occasional letters and rare family reunions, but due to distance and family responsibilities, neither Will nor Sarah had restored their childhood bond with Juda. Love overflowed in their tender greetings. No eyes were dry as the family drifted away from the front porch, leaving the three siblings to piece together their lives.

The drone of their voices waxed and waned through the afternoon in time with the squeak of the porch swing. "Ladies, we've chewed on everything till it's gravy," Will chuckled. There was a paucity of shared memories. It became comfortable to tell their stories—the good and bad of it. How humbling it is when aged people look back on their life unfolded, at the paths taken and denied—at the richness of the journey. One sees in vivid color how the innocence of youthful dreams is usurped by life in the raw. There you are, flayed open for the world to judge. Certainly, this can only happen in the safety of those who love from the soul.

Juda had raised her four children in the city, had known a modicum of wealth and status, and was secular—even cynical. Her dreams were dwarfed with regret. "I had so many dreams, so much I wanted to do. I loved working at the department store, and I was good at it. Josiah was my boss of course, and he really encouraged me. After we married, I learned he had a very traditional view of a married woman's place—which was to stay home. Of course the war intervened, that wasn't his fault. I became active in women's rights groups. One day he came downtown and pulled me away from a rally, afraid he would lose his job if I made the newspaper."

Sarah laughed woodenly. "I don't think I ever *had* dreams; I didn't have time. I was glad to get through the day, and if I was lucky, I got a little sleep. Now Judd had dreams—maybe my dreams were for him. I think he has accomplished what *he* wanted, so I guess that makes me happy."

"It's interesting to hear you two talk. I think I was afraid to dream to the point Elma thinks I lack ambition. She always suggests things for me to do, and I don't follow through. Likely I'll never do more than run a small truck farm. We get by, but I should have done better by Elma."

"I wonder," Juda mused, "if anyone looks back on their life and doesn't wish for more?"

Sarah was thoughtful, "These last months I've done a lot of looking back. I feel certain I won't get better; I'm sure Esther told you about the tumor, Will, and you told Juda." They both nodded, taking her hands. "If I'm truly honest, I do have regrets. I've lived through my children and my husband. My family is my greatest joy, though my failing is I often haven't conveyed my values to them. That's very disheartening...so what was the point? My garden has always been a joy to me, but I regret...too few joys. Maybe I was so busy and tired I didn't see them. I wasn't as brave as you, Juda. I was more traditional like Josiah in believing a woman's calling is to her husband and children. Looking back, that seems...trifling."

Will smiled, "If there's anyone who has done right by her children and husband, it's you, Sarah. When I think of all you went through in childhood, I'm amazed at your accomplishments."

Juda nodded.

"I don't see much point in regret—didn't we each do the best we could with what life gave us? Having you two here this week is a dream I couldn't have hoped for. Whatever future I have, I'm at peace."

* * * * *

As vitality ebbed, Sarah sought to capture and treasure the vignettes of life that bubbled up in her household: Judd's tender kiss; custard that tasted good; conversations of memories past; and awakening from a nap clear-headed with dulled pain. Since she was bedridden, the family lovingly and quietly flowed in and out of her bedroom. The house at Pine

Manor was full, so Helen moved to Grandma's house at the end of the school year. Clara and her sixteen-year-old daughter, Ruth Evelyn, came from Virginia. Sarah meandered in and out of their conversations, smiling and occasionally joining in. She knew the time for her mind to be clear would soon end. She needed more laudanum to get through each day. In her quiet way, she began to say her good-byes to her large family.

"Grandma, I have some warm chicken broth," Helen said, lifting the invalid cup to her mouth. I've got toast to dip in the broth."

"That tastes good," she said, smiling at Helen. "It's nice to have you staying here. I'm proud of you. You've done well, my dear."

"Thank you, Grandma. I enjoy teaching. I believe I was cut out for it. It's a lot of work, but I rarely get tired or frustrated."

Sarah patted her arm. "I think you could have been a nurse too; you're taking such good care of me," her shaky hands tipped the cup to her mouth. "Are you still keeping company with the young man who boards with your folks?"

Helen's cheeks turned pink, "Yes Grandma, Walt and I see each other most weekends."

"Your mother thinks a lot of him. Do you think he could be the one?"

Helen squirmed and giggled, "Grandma, you know Mother and Daddy would like anyone who took a shine to me. I haven't known Walt long enough. How did you know Grandpa was the one? Did you fall in love right away?" Helen, genuinely curious, was putting Grandma on the spot now.

"Oh Helen, that was so long ago," her eyes peered the distance as she reminisced. "Grandpa was from a good family and we both went to the Dunkard Church. That's what was important then. I really didn't know Grandpa well when we got married; we lived so far apart. It's better these days, with cars and all. You learn to know each other better," she rested, catching her breath. "Don't rush into marriage, Helen. It's for life, and that's a long time."

"I always thought if I married it would be a Brethren man. That's mostly who I've dated. Walt belongs to the Apostolic Christian Church—it's quite different. That's a big worry. He lost his mother when he was young, so his childhood wasn't the best. Oh Grandma, what am I getting myself into?"

"Is he a good sort? How does he treat you?"

"That's what attracts me: he always puts me first; he has a gentle kindness; and he doesn't blow his own horn. Daddy says he's hardworking. I like that he lets me be independent. So many men think it's their right to control their women. I'd rather be single than live like that."

"Good for you," Grandma nodded. She seemed thoughtful as if questioning how much she wanted to share. "Grandpa is of the generation to believe he should make decisions. He didn't care which church we attended—he told me to decide. But when we were young there were issues with the children. I wish I had put my foot down. I believed what the church taught us: wives be submissive to your husband. That's all I knew. Helen, there's so much you can't know when you marry. Find someone who makes you feel your life would be barren without them. You've made good decisions in your life; you'll likely make the right decision about marriage."

"Thanks for your advice, Grandma. I think I'm lucky: Mother and Daddy and you and Grandpa have been happily married. I'm sure it helps to grow up around successful marriages."

"No marriage is perfect, but I've loved your grandpa every day I've lived with him." Her brows furrowed, "well, most days," she smiled.

"I've always loved our talks, Grandma. Even when I was young, you seemed to care about my opinions."

"I learned that from Edith. She always said women must treat each other with regard if we expect to gain standing among men."

"The broth is gone. Would you like some mashed banana?"

"No, I've had enough. I'll take a nap now."

* * * * *

He saw the view as if looking from above: they were sitting on an upturned tree, Judd holding Sarah. "I'm not being a good girl," she said demurely. "I like you like this, my sweet. I'm going to bring blackberry wine each time I visit. This is what I want for us—to court like other couples. I'm going to visit more often. With winter coming, I may get snowed in—now that might be fun."...."You've planned a perfect day for us, Judd. I haven't had so much fun in a long time."

Sarah coughed, gasping to get her breath. Judd jerked awake, pulled from his youthful reverie. He jumped from his chair, holding a hanky to her mouth.

"That's my girl, cough it up." Judd had hardly left Sarah's bedside the last few days. As Sarah's body weakened, so Judd seemed more shrunken and insubstantial. He sat beside her, holding her head to his shoulder, insinuating his strength to restore hers.

"Oh Sarah, I was dreaming of us when we were young. That Sunday in the woods after Amy and Art's wedding—we'd been apart so long. When I saw you then, it was like a spring rainstorm after a drought; you made me come alive again. That's what you do for all of us. You somehow know where we're needy and you fill that place with love. Then we go back to our lives replenished until the next time. It's a gift you have, my dear. It's why we all come to you. How are we going to live without you caring for us?"

"Judd, I know for certain who will take my place: it will be you. I have no question. It may be that women naturally have softer edges, so tending a family falls more easily to us. You're every bit as capable. When I'm gone, *you'll* see whose eyes are sad, who misses Sunday dinner, and whose step is slow. Then you mostly listen; you can't judge. This is your job now. It will be hardest the first weeks after I'm gone. Keep the family close. Open your heart to God's comfort; don't countenance despair."

"So many hard times," Judd mused.

"It wasn't easy for us, but I've never regretted one minute of loving you Judd, all these years. You've given me your best: the dangerous logging in the dark, clearing roads after winter storms when everyone was home by the fire, think how many injuries you've patched up from training horses for extra money. You made your living with your exceptional mind, as I knew you would, but your hands are always calloused and cracked because that, too, is who you are. You say I'm the family stalwart, but that's who you are for all the county employees."

"I wanted to give you everything, I didn't want your life to be so hard. I couldn't even find a doctor to make you better," Judd rested his elbows on his knees, his hands over his eyes.

"No one could have tried harder than you. Like everyone, we were caught in hard times. Sixty-five years old; it seems the years slipped by with hardly a chance to mark them as they passed. Like a rushing river, the joys and heartaches mingled together, me just doing what I had to do." She turned to Judd with a hint of a smile, "I thought my life would be more noteworthy. You know, something that dazzled. I could look back and say: 'there was the time...we sure laughed at that...don't forget the day....' Where were the...mountaintops? Was my life all...muted? God put us on earth for a reason—and here I am; I'm not sure I delivered on my reason." Sarah's hand held her abdomen, acknowledging the pain. "Well, I'm too tired to get in a dither about it."

"It's because you had all of us on *your* shoulders. You helped us reach *our* mountaintops, staying in the background and urging us on. Not a one of us ever slipped off your shoulders. It's not a wonder you feel life passed you by—you were under the pile of us."

"There was never a day I didn't love you, Judd. I'm glad I'm going before you; I wouldn't want to live without you. I know you'll be okay. Let the girls look after you. We'll be together again, in a better place. She kissed him softly, "There's nothing more I need to do. I'm ready to go. I don't want to live like this. I'm going to let Esther give me the pain medicine as often as the doctor ordered. Will you go get her, Pop?"

Judd went to the kitchen where the ladies were cleaning up after dinner. "Mother wants you, Esther. She says she's ready to go," his voice thick and cracking. "She wants medicine so she can rest."

Esther nodded, her eyes welling over. "I'm glad she's finally ready. She's suffered enough, but she wanted to do it her way. Nothing has ever been easy for her—death is no different. Now at least, we can take away her pain."

Sarah swallowed the pill, noting Esther's tears. "Don't be sad, Esther, this is my time. I'm at peace; I'll be with my mother again. Go to my top dresser drawer. When Juda was here we decided we'll both meet Mother wearing her pearl combs. You know I've treasured Mother's comb all these years. I want it with me when I go to my rest." Her smile was weary, "I've missed my mother all my life; I'll be so happy to see her."

The large extended family milled about the house over the next two days. They sang, played with the children, and prayed with somber reverence. Sarah never woke again. That each family member felt they the most bereft, that she had loved them especially, was her gift to them. As she peacefully slipped the bonds of earth her loved ones were comforted with the assurance that this beloved woman would go to her heavenly reward.

Sarah's body was viewed in their home by hundreds of friends, family, and neighbors—the couple's reputation well established in Goshen. During her funeral, people stood in the aisles in the overflowing church. Judd remembered Sarah's last words: "I thought my life would have been more notable, more of it remembered". *Well, my dear, I believe your life has been remembered.*

The family was surprised the doctor wrote "Colon Cancer" for the cause of death on Sarah's death certificate. "I guess her tumor was cancer after all," Esther said to Clara. "I wish we had known so we could have taken precautions."

The days after the funeral were like a crash landing. Esther felt her body was whipped and battered, physically from caring for her mother, and mentally from the depletion of grief.

It was decided Erdene would spend time with cousins, returning to Cleveland with Esther's sister, Ruth's family. Judd was at loose ends, mowing the lawn and cleaning eaves, but after a few days he returned to the respite of his work at the county highway department. When the cleaning was done, Clara would return to Virginia. Esther's life would resume a new normal—without her mother.

They felt an urgency to sanitize the house with Clorox water and get rid of Sarah's clothes. Esther was emptying Sarah's dresser drawer when she found a small sack containing what seemed to be wood ashes. Underneath the sack was a black and white speckled secretary notebook, the pages ruffled and yellow, the penciled handwriting faded.

If someone told me I'd be writing like this I would have thought them crazy. I think I am crazy in love! I feel compelled to write my feelings—better that than gush them out to you, Sarah, and make a fool of myself. Isaac, old boy, you've fallen like a ton of bricks.

Esther gasped; her eyes ogled the words. Had her mother been unfaithful? She skipped ahead through the pages.

I ate beside you at youth group. You smiled, but pretty much ignored me. That's okay, I can be patient. It was enough to sit beside you and hear your sweet voice singing....

The best day of my life! Our first kiss. I remember every touch, every sound, and every sensation. I'm in love! My heart feels as big as the sky. Sure, we hardly know each other, but this is right. I have a good feeling about us. Oh Sarah, you make me so happy....

I went over to Miller's tonight. Thought they might chase me off, but they were very nice and invited me in. We visited with them then sat on the porch swing. I didn't even hold your hand. I'm not going to mess this up....

Tonight was monumental. Now I can see us making our future together—we agreed we want to work toward this. I made a campfire and we talked for a long time about our feelings. Sarah has worried that her insecurities will drag down my happiness. I just see how we complement each other. WOW! This is huge.

As much as Esther was curious, as much as she wanted to read every word, she had the niggling feeling she was intruding on something private and precious to her mother. Now was not the time. She closed the journal—obviously treasured by her mother. It almost felt sacred. She would keep it safe as her mother had all these years—just a touch away from her life. As Esther scrubbed and mopped she couldn't get the journal and the ashes from her mind. *Oh Mama, why couldn't you tell us the story?* That she couldn't part with the remnants of this time in her life revealed how consequential it was. In her youth she had loved another. How did that story end? Her mother was organized and circumspect—it wasn't an accident the journal was found. Esther wasn't sure what to do with Sarah's secret, but she knew she couldn't leave it for her father to find. For now, she would keep it safe as her mother had all these years.

CHAPTER 38

Erdene Polio

"Mama, come! Hurry, it's long distance from Aunt Ruth in Cleveland." Esther ran from the garden into the house, grabbing the phone. Ruth calling long distance could only mean trouble.

"What is it, Ruth?" her voice was breathless.

"Esther, you have to come right away and get Erdene. It's terrible here," her voice choked. "They hadn't seemed quite right for a few days, but I had no idea...they all got sick yesterday. We took them to the doctor today. They have high fevers. Esther, all my children are in the hospital! Dana can't move his legs—they're paralyzed. They're saying it's infantile paralysis. They seem to think we picked it up when we came to Goshen for Mama's funeral."

"Oh, my dear, the poor things. They were fine just last week. How's Erdene?"

"She's been running a fever for two days. Just like my kids, she aches all over. Vail and I need to go to the hospital. The nurses make us cover with a gown and mask when we're with them."

"We'll leave right away. I'll be praying, Ruth. Tell Erdene we're on our way. I don't want to run up your bill, so I'll go now. Bye."

Sixteen-year-old Rosemary could recognize an emergency. "Who's in the hospital?" her voice was panicky.

"Ruth's children are sick. Go get Daddy in the calf barn. Tell him we have to leave for Ohio NOW! We won't be able to milk tonight. Tell him there's no quibbling about this—Erdene is sick. We need to get her back here to a doctor. Go now, Rosie. Careful crossing the road," she yelled after her.

She grabbed the phone again. "736" she called to the operator, unable to quell the shaking in her voice. Helen was spending the summer with Grandpa Judd. She was probably in the garden. "Pick it up, Helen," she begged.

"Hello?"

"Helen, it's Mother. Daddy and I are leaving for Cleveland to bring Erdene home. They think she has this disease that cripples people. Ruth just called. Dana, Winston, and Beverly were all put in the hospital today. Dana's legs are paralyzed. It seems to be contagious, so Pop needs to keep Rosemary and Louise at his house until we know what's happening with Erdene. It will be nearly morning till we get home. Poor Pop, he sure doesn't need anything else to get him down."

"I don't believe this. What's the matter with Erdene?"

"She has a high fever and is achy. Get the girls' clothes together; I don't know how long they'll be at Grandpa's. I have to get things together for the trip. I'll call you in the morning."

"Be careful, Mother. I wish you didn't have to drive at night. You don't think this was caused by Grandma's cancer, do you?"

"Nobody knows these things. Remember, Ruth Evelyn was sick and couldn't go to Grandma's funeral. Why some get sick and some don't is so unnerving."

"Tell the girls I'll be there before supper. Call when you get home. Be safe, Mother," Helen hung up the phone.

Earl and Esther returned home in the middle of the night after an arduous trip. Uncertain how the disease spread they never entered Ruth and Vail's house, just helped Erdene walk to the car. She complained of headache, and her cheeks were ruddy with fever. Worse were the aching muscles and joints that prevented comfort and rest. The return trip felt like forever. Earl eyed Esther in a frozen glance when Erdene was unable to walk into the house.

There were many cases of the disease in Goshen. Not knowing what caused it or who would be affected caused everyone to be fearful. The doctor had few answers the next day when he saw Erdene. "Some people only have mild fever and aching, some lose muscle strength temporarily, and some permanently. In some, one limb is affected, and some are totally paralyzed. It's contagious, so have as little contact as possible. Massage her legs vigorously several times a day with a mixture of ether and alcohol."

1940 was a long hot summer in Goshen. People mostly stayed home. No more socializing on Main Street on Saturday nights. Earl and Esther massaged Erdene's legs conscientiously. Earl carried her around the house. She was one of the lucky ones. After three weeks her legs slowly regained strength and function, and after several months she felt no lasting effects of the disease. No one else in the family got sick. In Cleveland, Ruth's children, Beverly and Winston recuperated also, but Dana, the oldest, was left a paraplegic.

Meanwhile, Helen and Walt's friendship cruised along, one day bumpy, the next, spicy and smooth as a downhill coaster ride. Helen rued the ardor the handsome farmhand stoked in her. She was affronted to admit the pleasure of his company, but she couldn't help herself from greedily sidling back for more. She would rather not have noticed that shirts in his size stretched to accommodate his muscular heft. This didn't fit her self-image as a proper, restrained young lady.

The reasons for caution seemed valid. His childhood was very different from the sheltered one she remembered. His mother died when he was young. Stories from his childhood seemed harsh and even cruel. Her faith and the Brethren Church were pivotal in her life. Walt's family attended the Apostolic Christian Church, whose practices seemed strangely foreign to her. By now she was fast friends with Walt's sisters, Gerry and Ann. The two sisters were to be wed to two brothers in a marriage negotiated by Apostolic minister. The two couples could be together at church functions but weren't allowed to date before marriage. Helen noted that church members were close-knit and almost insulated from society. This threw up red flags from her family's experience with Aunt Edith's membership in the Lemurian Cult, renouncing family ties, and moving to California. This was still a raw, seeping catastrophe within the family.

Another concern was fear of losing her career, income, and independence. She loved her life. If she married, she could no longer teach. Plus, most young men she had dated put a damper in her style. They held her arm as though she were an invalid. Her fear was that some well-intentioned man would marry her out of pity, then try to "take care" of her. At least with Walt that wasn't a problem; he acted oblivious to her gimpy leg. They often took long walks. The first time they went hiking he had whittled walking sticks for both of them. He let her set the pace, and if she slipped or lost balance, recover on her own. He seemingly had no need to thwart her independence; maybe by living with her family he had observed their ignorance of her limitations.

"Well, look at you, lady," Walt whistled, his eyes popping open.

"That's debatable. My grandpa wouldn't call a woman wearing pants a lady. I figure we won't run into him today."

He gave her a quick peck on the cheek. "So, we don't want to go near Berkey Avenue. How about following the river at the Mill Race? There's plenty of fall foliage there. Do you want to wear rubbers? I've got our sticks in the car."

"Really Walt, what do you think? Pants are pretty brazen for me."

He gave her a raffish grin as he opened her car door. "I think you should wear whatever you want, my dear. You'd look smashing in whatever you put on. At least now I don't have to worry about your skirt getting caught in the door." She couldn't resist a half-smile as she pleasured in his compliment.

They walked briskly for over an hour. On every outing Helen had an agenda. Today she gathered milkweed and searched for chrysalis for a butterfly project for her fourth graders.

"Let's take a break, girl. I'm going to rustle up a nice bed of leaves, so you don't get your new pants muddy. What does brazen mean anyway, Helen?"

She plopped down in the leaves, her eyes sparkling up at him. "You saying you're rustling up a bed for me is *brazen."*

"Aha. There you go. We're a good pair then—two brazen degenerates." He knelt beside her, tipping up her chin and nibbling her lips while fall leaves floated around them. He coddled her in his arms, his fingers petting her wind-blown black hair. "This is nice. We're all alone here."

"Only the squirrels can see us, and they won't tell," she chuckled. Their kisses were ardent, their embrace urgent, their bodies straining to seek and mesh. Walt groaned, resting back on the ground, his arm encircling her. His voice was husky, his eyes teasing, "My dear, you're a lover like you do everything: you go for broke. I love it," he laughed.

She got up with a jerk, clearly offended. "I'm *NOT* a lover," she said adamantly. "You make me sound like a hussy, and I'm not that way," she said piously.

"You sure were close to me, and we're both just now catching our breath."

"Don't get any ideas about a lover or I'll just leave. I don't like the sound of it." She looked around, then down at him. "Are we lost?" she asked, her head-of-steam evaporating.

"No, we're not lost," he flicked her nose with his index finger. "Come here sweetie. I won't get us all hot and bothered again. Cuddle, I'll make a chair for you. This is how Manny and I kept warm at night when we were kids.... Boy, I could take a nap," his breathing slowed.

"I can't believe you could sleep now," she said, aghast.

"You couldn't?"

"Goodness no, I'm too worked up."

"Then I may as well ask you a question and get you more hyped. Tony has a friend in Chicago. In two weeks, he and Diane are going for the weekend, leaving Friday evening and returning Sunday. We'll stay with his friend and girlfriend in separate apartments. He's planning a boat ride on the lake and a visit to a big museum. He invited us to go along. I'd like us to go; I've never been to Chicago."

Helen turned to face him, a smirk on her lips. "Do you have illicit intentions like you would with a lover? Hmm, Walt? You know how Italians are. We'll be with them."

"I promise this is on the up-and-up. If you agree, I'll talk to your mother. I know I tease you, but I want to do right by you, girl. You make me happy. I don't know what I'd do if I couldn't tease you, but I sure don't want to mess it up for us. I'm not going to shoot myself in the foot by having my way with you."

Helen looked away, her voice soft, "I wonder if you just take pity on me." *WHOOSH...it was out. She had voiced it.*

His frown was quizzical, "Why would I pity *you*? You have it backwards—you with your big words, college degree, and professional job should pity *me*," his voice rose with feeling.

They were quiet. Only the singing birds broke the silence.

"If we're to make anything of this, we both need to forget thoughts like that—for good. We're who we are. If we can make each other happy, that's what counts," he said huskily.

Her heart warmed to his common-sense wisdom. She still had qualms to work out, but they had crossed a threshold of honesty and trust. It felt huge to her.

She leaned forward, a lingering kiss on his lips, "I'd love to go to Chicago with you. I agree, it'd be good for you to explain the particulars to Mother. It helps that she likes Tony."

CHAPTER 39

Love and War

WWI left an unfortunate history for conscientious objectors (COs) who were members of the three recognized peace churches: Brethren, Mennonite and Quakers. They believed God created every person, adhering to the commandment "thou shalt not kill". They hadn't participated in Indian extermination or fought in the Spanish-American War. Nonresistance was a tenet of their faith. During WWI there was no option other than military service for conscientious objectors. Often these men were harshly treated, imprisoned, or required to pay large fines. In 1935 representatives from the peace churches met with government Selective Service System officials to devise a legal alternative to military service. In 1941 Civilian Public Service (CPS) was established. This was not to say President Roosevelt, the military hierarchy, or the American public were supportive; they believed it the coward's way to avoid military service. The law stated that COs could apply to their local draft board requesting IV-E status. If granted, there was often a grueling appeal process to verify the authenticity of the request. They were then sent to a work camp for two years of unpaid "service of national importance" on jobs such as fighting forest fires, attendants in mental institutions, soil conservation, or dairy testing.

Two years earlier Hitler had been elected in Germany. Insidiously he removed democratic rights from Jews, confiscated their property, and imprisoned them in concentration camps. In 1939 he invaded Poland, prompting France and Britain to declare WWII.

Hitler's actions did not cause an uproar of moral outrage in the U.S. Most people had little association with Jewish individuals. They thought them rich and stand-offish. Many assumed German Jews who were in trouble likely brought it on themselves. Early in the conflict, most agreed the U.S. had no business interfering in Germany's internal affairs.

For a small group meeting in the basement of the Yellow Creek Brethren Church, the topic was monumental, keeping them awake at night. For several months, Walt had been attending church with Helen.

They were carefully nurturing the fly-away tendrils and deepening roots of their love. Walt had been promoted at Pine Manor, earning significantly more than Helen. They were in a committed relationship. Several in the youth group were dating, some were engaged. They were Walt and Helen's best friends.

All men between eighteen and thirty-five were required to register for the draft. War was an unwelcome intrusion clouding their future. They respected their minister, Rev. Sam Miller, who was knowledgeable about the new Selective Service Act.

"I want you men to listen to your heart when making the decision about registering for service. What is right for one person may not be right for another. If you request 1-A classification you'll be inducted in the military along with most young men in the U.S. If you request IV-E status, you claim to be a conscientious objector, choosing service in Civilian Public Service. The Brethren Church has always been a peace church; that's one reason our Brethren ancestors emigrated to this country. They didn't want to fight in wars against their conscience. With this new Selective Service Law, we have a legal option other than military service. It doesn't mean we don't love our country or we're not patriotic. It means we don't believe it's right to kill another person, even in war."

"I've read that Hitler's army is imprisoning and killing Jewish people. Can it be right to refuse to take arms against soldiers who are killing innocent people?" asked Elmer, his face serious.

"There you have the age-old dilemma about fighting wars," Rev. Miller nodded. "Our church believes there are better ways to solve problems—kindness and diplomacy is preferable to hate and revenge. We must pray for President Roosevelt, Hitler, and other world leaders."

"The fellas at work are all gung-ho to go to war. I sometimes think they *want* another war. If I register IV-E, it's not because I'm afraid to go. But I hate to think of the heckling I'll get when they find I'm a CO. I'm more worried about *that* than going to war," Paul spoke with intensity. A general murmur arose: everyone had experienced derision when explaining their anti-war stance; war mania was pervasive—heroes go to war, cowards stay home.

Helen raised her hand, "Where will COs do their service? Will they work at home or go to Germany, the same as enlisted men?"

Rev. Miller restored quiet. "That issue hasn't been worked out. I doubt COs go to Germany. Neither can I imagine men staying in the comfort of their home. You remember the CCC—Civilian Conservation Corps that Roosevelt established to create jobs during the depression? There are over one hundred of those camps around the U.S. I believe they're considering putting men in these camps. More important will be to find jobs for them. Everyone hopes the German people will solve the problem by getting rid of Hitler."

Walt spoke up, "I grew up in the Apostolic Christian Church. They're conscientious objectors too, but their men go to war as medics. They don't carry a gun. Is that an option for Brethren men?"

"A few denominations send their men as medics. I don't know the conversations of the early Brethren as they decided our policy. Maybe they didn't want to place a young CO in the heat of battle, forcing him to act in a way he may later regret. That's an option that may be best for some of you. Some denominations speak of a "just" or an "unjust" war. Many in Germany would say Hitler's war is "just". The newspapers have been informing us about the eugenics issue: that some races, such as Negroes and Jews, are defective and inferior to the white race. Brethren believe all are equal in the sight of God. I don't want to influence your decision. I want you to know the beliefs of the Brethren Church." The questions and discussion continued into the night. Rev. Miller's belief that they needed to prepare for war was sobering and frightening. Did they even care what was happening in Germany? Could they kill another child created by God? Were they afraid to go to war? Could they bear the ridicule of everyone who believed they took the cowardly way out? At the core of their soul, what did they believe?

* * * * *

Esther's days returned to the mundane. Erdene, recovered from infantile paralysis, returned to her new job as head cook at Newberry's Five and Dime Store. As Esther milked cows and put out hearty meals for the boarders, her mind wrestled with the secret journal found in her mother's bureau. She became convinced Sarah meant for her to find it.

One afternoon when alone in the house, she went to her bedroom and read Isaac's diary. It was like a play with the curtain opening to a hidden life. Isaac and Sarah had a magically fed energy, their bountiful love swelling on the breezy cadence of his affection—her mirrored reciprocity, a savory repast. Esther's tears blotted the pages. *Where is the woman I knew—the yoked-to-the-grindstone, weary-wracked gentle soul? When was that free spirit squelched? When did the breathy sparkling orange in her days become monotonous gray? WHAT I WOULDN'T HAVE GIVEN TO KNOW THE WOMAN IN THE DIARY.*

As summer melded into fall, Helen was wrestling with her own dilemma. She and Walt had been keeping company for over a year. Every way she knew him was positive. She remembered Sarah's gold standard: she knew her life would be barren without him. The niggling differences wouldn't let her mind rest. The war in Europe seemed to jump-start every one's plans for the future.

Home for the weekend, Helen was helping Esther make meatloaf for supper. Her voice was shaky; she wasn't used to confiding in her mother. "I've got to make some decisions about Walt. How can I know he's "the one"? Did you have questions about marrying Daddy?"

Esther smiled, remembering her youth, "The first time I saw Daddy I was taken with him and it never changed. I think that's unusual though. I've heard of nervous brides-to-be. Do you think Walt is going to ask for your hand?"

"He acts pretty certain about our being together. If I'm not going to marry him, I need to break it off."

"Can you see yourself living with him the rest of your life?"

"I can. I'm happy when I'm with him, and can't wait to see him when we're apart. He treats me like a queen. I'm his "little brunette". Then I think about his dad who drinks too much; cranky Aunt Lillie who raised him so harshly; and the strange beliefs of the Apostolic Church. These things make me uneasy. He's not religious in the…customary sense, but I can't think of anyone who is more decent or Christian than he is. Walt is everything he shouldn't be: his father was sometimes abusive, yet he is gentle; he had poor schooling, yet he has lots of common sense; his exposure to church was patchy, now he never misses. I just don't know, Mother. It seems if I loved him enough, I wouldn't have these doubts."

"Have you two talked about church?"

"We've been talking about it because of the war. He asks questions about registering as a CO. This is why I need to make up my mind. It would hurt my conscience if he registered differently because of me."

Esther lifted her hands out of the meatloaf as though startled. "Oh," she said, her eyes wide. "I'll be right back. I have something that might help you."

She went to her bedroom and returned with Isaac's journal, placing it in Helen's hands. "I found this journal in Grandma Sarah's dresser. You and I are the only ones who know about it. Now I understand why she wanted me to find it. Grandma was in love with the young man who wrote this diary. I think it was before she met Pop. Read their story. Theirs was such a tender, joyful love. You won't recognize your grandma, Helen. If you and Walt feel toward each other the way Grandma and Isaac felt, you'll have peace about getting married. I see it now. Grandma left this for you."

* * * * *

"Esther, I think you'd better come. I don't want to bother you in the middle of the...."

"What's wrong, Pop? Are you sick?"

"I've had this pain in my gut for a few days. I made a hot pack by boiling up some flax seeds and put it on my stomach, but heat doesn't seem to be helping," Judd's boisterous voice was weak and shaky, his breath came in gasps.

"I'm coming right away, Pop. I'm taking you to see Dr. Young." Esther had seen her dad a few days earlier when he seemed in good health. She couldn't believe the change in him.

"I knew you'd drag me to a doctor. That's why I didn't call sooner."

"I'll be there in a few minutes."

Upon arriving at Dr. Young's office, the emergency took on frightening momentum. It didn't take Dr. Young long to realize Judd was seriously ill. "You've got to go to the hospital, Judd. You're in bad shape."

"Doc, can't you just give me some pills?"

Dr. Young touched his arm. Judd was his friend. "You have to have surgery. I think your appendix has ruptured. Without surgery you'll die," his eyes were soft but unflinching.

Esther choked back the gasp bubbling from her throat. It was inconceivable her indomitable father could be so sick.

"Whatever you say, Doc," even Judd was shaken by his words.

At the hospital it was controlled chaos; only minutes until Judd was prepped and taken to surgery. A foreboding fear silenced family members as they rushed into the hospital's small waiting room, in disbelief that their invincible family patriarch was fighting for his life.

Minutes became an hour until Dr. Young walked into the waiting room, his shoulders bowed, his eyes tear-filled. The children gathered around him, his demeanor telling the outcome. "Judd has passed from labor to his reward. He died on the operating table. His gangrenous appendix had ruptured; his abdomen was full of infection. I don't know how he stood the pain. Had he come when he first felt pain, a simple surgery would have saved him. But that wasn't Judd's way now, was it? I'm sorry I couldn't do more. I lost a friend on that table. He was a good man."

* * * * *

"Put on your wooly duds. We're going sledding on Buzzard's Hill." Walt phoned Helen on a blustery Saturday morning following a four-inch snowfall.

"Buzzard's Hill?" Helen questioned.

"It's the nearest thing to a mountain in these parts, just south of New Paris." Walt's excitement was contagious, "I've never seen you scared, but this might give you a fright. I borrowed a toboggan. We'll show 'em how it's done."

"Sounds like fun." Helen was always enticed by adventure. Give me an hour. I'll be bundled and ready."

Two hours later, standing at the peak of Buzzard's Hill, her stomach was doing flip-flops. "Oh Walt, that's a long way down." She grabbed his mittened hand, her breath steamy puffs.

"Let's go over to the shorter hill first, till we get the hang of it," Walt suggested. Down they went, their breath grabbed by the wind, tears pulling sideways on their cheeks, hitting bumps and catching air, just this side of dangerous. At the bottom, Walt rolled them off the toboggan to prevent hitting children who were oblivious of their surroundings. Helen lay in the snow, belly-laughing. "I love it!" she screamed, reaching for his outstretched hand, pulled into a bear hug.

"You're a wild woman," he hooted. "I *knew* you'd like it." They shuffled up to the high peak, her stomach doing cartwheels. "Are you sure you're ready?" he asked. The adventure pulled her down from the peak, the terror held her back. As usual, she went with adventure. They settled into the toboggan, she, cradled between his arms and legs. She yelled, "We better go, or I'll lose my nerve."

"We're off!" They flew, the sun-sparkled snow whizzed by, her laughter paralyzed, caught in her throat. *This is right, her heart spoke. Though she was flying along she felt suspended in time, her world silent and clear. This is what I want. I want his decency, the safety I feel with him, the glorious adventure. Like Sarah and Isaac, we're right for each other. She felt buoyant and assured.* They slowed to a stop; he took her hand. "Wow," she said tentatively, her thoughts lingering on marriage.

"Are you okay? Did it scare you too much?"

"I'm fine," she enthused, her eyes searching Walt's face as if seeing him the first time. "I'm perfect. Let's go again," she rushed ahead.

Later they stopped for cocoa at Lehman's, a little cafe in New Paris. Helen, true to form, having made "the decision", was ready to dot the I's and cross the T's.

"Look at all these people drinking beer, just in from sledding. As cold as it is, you'd think they'd want a hot drink. You don't often drink beer. Do you like it?"

"I guess it's okay. You know I'm not much of a drinker. Apostolics aren't against drinking, so I grew up with it. I didn't like the way it affected my dad. Then when I moved to Gawthrop's, their Brethren Church was opposed to alcohol. Carl and Chloe were like parents to me—

good people. Back then I decided it was something I didn't need. Why do you ask?"

"Oh, no reason. To be honest, I have a hard time with people who drink routinely. I think it can become a habit."

"You're probably right. I think my dad has trouble controlling it."

"Are you still a member of the Apostolic Church?"

Walt leaned forward, his hand to his mouth as if whispering, "You have a lot of questions, my dear. Is this a test?"

She laughed, realizing she was grilling him, "I *am* being nosy, aren't I? You've been going to my church for a while, so you know my beliefs. I don't really know where you stand on some things. It's important to me."

"Although my family went to the AC church, their beliefs never "jelled" for me. I never wanted to join the church. What they believed didn't seem to relate to the way they lived day-to-day as the Brethren beliefs did for you growing up. When I lived with Gawthrop's in my early teens, I often attended their church. They raised their children with high standards, and I was like one of the family."

"It means a lot that you take me to visit them. They're good folks. It impresses me that you lived with them only a few years, yet they've had so much influence on you," Helen said.

"Yes, they did. I like going to Yellow Creek with you. Rev. Miller is the best minister I've known. He's helping us guys figure out the draft question. I know the Brethren way is CO status, but he doesn't say what is right and wrong; he supports the decision we make. I think churches should be more open to different views, not just say what you can or can't do."

"I'm glad he's including us women in these meetings. It's informative, plus it affects us too."

"I *hope* it affects you," Walt drawled with a teasing smile, causing Helen's cheeks to color. "I teased you about this being a test, but you're right, we need to talk about these things. I'm pretty close to registering as a CO."

"Will your dad be against that?"

"I don't know. I don't think it's his decision to make."

"I'd hate to get off on the wrong foot with him. Do you think he'd hold your decision against me?"

"Helen, we're going to have to give ole' Sam a long leash. All my life I've tried not to rile my dad—kept my distance, really. You can see, he was born with that harelip. I figure he was bullied all his life. He's an unhappy person who drinks too much. But he's my dad. If I had his life, I might be worse than he is. He kept our family together; that couldn't have been easy."

"I'm glad we're talking about this. To tell the truth, I'm almost afraid of him. He seems like anything could set off his temper. Because of his...deformity, I can't understand when he talks. If it wasn't for that, I think I'd do okay. I grew up with the same thing, people made fun of me too. I get that." Helen's voice was dead earnest, her eyes filled.

"I don't want you to be afraid of him, my dear. Since you first met him, I've thought you handled him well. Keep doing what you're doing. He told me awhile back I had myself a winner; he didn't understand why you're wasting time with me," Walt smiled.

Helen's eyes shone, "He said I'm a winner? If he said that, then I think we'll be okay. I can handle him."

"I know you can. You're good with people. Besides, if he ever does anything that upsets you, that's it. I'll never let anyone in my family come between us, and I trust you'll do the same. It's good we talk about this, but I don't think it will be a problem." He looked at his watch. "We have Fern's birthday party tonight. I'd better get you home."

"You're right. I'm a Buzzard's Hill survivor. I haven't had so much fun in a long time," she said proudly.

"I have to say, you're a spunky one," Walt chuckled.

* * * * *

Esther reached for Earl's hand, cozying up to him in bed. "Be sure you get home in good time tomorrow night. Walt wants to take us to the Candy Kitchen after supper."

Earl's smile stretched across his cheeks. "Well, well. We don't have to be smart to know what *that's* about," he mused in the darkness. "I never would have guessed Helen would find a young man so well-fitted. You couldn't have picked better yourself, Esther. By George, we must be getting old to be having a married daughter. Pretty soon I'll be a grandpa," he chortled.

"Careful. We don't want to get the baby buggy before the horse," Esther laughed at her own joke. "You're right, I've liked Walt from the beginning. He's a gentleman. He won't hold her back; he likes her independence. Do you think you men will have the new church finished by summer? I'd love for her to have the first wedding at Yellow Creek's new church. I'd better settle down. What if he just wants your advice about something at the cow barn? Wouldn't we be the fools? Oh Earl, I'm too excited to sleep."

Helen was finishing up her week at the Clinton Community School, waiting for Esther's arrival to take her home for the weekend. She had been promoted to a larger school and this year taught only second and third grades, having twenty students in each class. This school required a higher level of professionalism. Helen wore a veiled hat and a Sunday dress to school. Her svelte form was enhanced by a rubberized girdle with garters attaching rayon hose to smooth her legs. How she would have liked smart shoes, rather than the tie-up block heels she had to wear. It had been a long week. She'd finished putting together the Christmas program, satisfied each student had a part. Now she was preparing for a meeting she had requested with Miss Kreider, a professor at Goshen College who had agreed to help her with Joseph, a student with severe stuttering. She was shocked when Walt walked into the school, holding a bouquet of yellow roses.

She jumped up, "What a nice surprise. Are you going to be in second or third grade?" she teased.

"You don't know how much I wish I had a teacher like you when I was young," he handed her the roses while kissing her cheek. "I asked Esther if I could pick you up tonight. Your dad is covering for me in the milk barn. There's always someone listening to the radio or reading the paper in your folks living room. I figured this was the best place to get you alone."

"The roses are beautiful. You know yellow is my favorite color." She blushed, her eyes hooded, "Is this a special occasion?" knowing Walt would do this only to propose.

He was serious and intense, his feelings spilling from his eyes. He leaned forward on the recitation bench, his elbows on his knees. He held both her hands, his voice thickened with emotion. "It would make me so happy if you would be my wife, Helen. More than anything, I want to spend my life with you. I wouldn't have believed I could love someone so much. When I'm not with you, I think about the next time we'll be together."

Helen's head bobbed, her eyes tender, her smile as big as the sky. "I feel the same, Walt. Grandma Sarah said I should marry someone only if my life would feel barren without them. Already you feel like the other half of me. I'll do my best so we can be happy together."

He pulled her to him, they kissed deeply and longingly. This moment held a binding promise. He sat down with her again. "I'm not so good with words, but I need to say a few things. I want to make a good life for you. This is what I've been thinking: the conflict in Germany is heating up. I'm going to register as a Conscientious Objector. If we go to war, I'll have to leave for two years. If you agree, I'd like us to marry before I leave. I'm hoping if most men go to service they'll allow married teachers to continue teaching. We could save some money. After my service term, I'll take up farming. When I worked for Gawthrops, I learned to know the man who hauled their milk to the Goshen Milk Condensary. I rode his route and learned the basics from him. With milk hauling, you buy your truck, and own the business. The farmer pays a fixed amount for every one hundred pounds of milk hauled into the milk plant. With farming, we'll start small, renting farmland and growing a dairy herd until we can buy our own place. I want our kids to help run the farm like I did. It teaches responsibility. You won't be doing outside farm work, Helen. It wouldn't be safe for you."

Helen laughed, "I declare, Walt, you have our next fifty years planned. I'll want to help. Don't you think *I* need to be taught responsibility?" she teased.

"There will be plenty of work for you. It'll be a partnership in everything. You just won't be driving tractor or working in the barn."

"If it's allowed, can I get a teaching job?"

"That should be up to you. When we buy our farm, we may need you to teach."

"I like that we're partners. My parents made decisions together, and I think they have a good marriage," Helen said.

"I plan on doing right by you, Helen. I'm saying all this because I never saw an example of marriage till I was a teenager and lived with Gawthrops. I want our marriage to be like theirs. They were kind and respectful to each other. Chloe didn't do barn work or drive a tractor, but she had her say in their decisions."

"I appreciate your views on this. I think Carl and Chloe are a good example for us."

"I sure don't know what's ahead, but I promise you this: I'll do my best to care for you and give you a good life." He smiled, tipping her chin, "If things get bad and we starve, I'll starve first."

* * * * *

Walt and Helen were driving home from a required marriage counseling session. "My mother thinks these sessions are a good idea," Helen said.

"Rev. Miller is a nice guy. He's so down-to-earth. I was dreading these meetings but it's not so bad. At least you haven't backed out yet," Walt reached over to ruffle her hair.

"I still have three weeks," she grinned. "I'll be glad when school is out. I never realized there was so much to planning a wedding."

"I thought our answers to that marriage test were mostly in agreement. Don't you think that's a good sign?" Walt said, proud-like.

"I was surprised when you said you wanted six children," she said.

Walt screeched, "I couldn't believe *you* want six. What are the chances? We *both* must be nuts."

"Only if we can afford them. I always wanted a passel of kids. Which reminds me, I have my doctor appointment tomorrow."

"You're not sick. Is something wrong?" he asked.

"I'm being fitted for a diaphragm, so I don't get pregnant right away. This is what most gals are using for birth control. I want children, but I don't want them willy-nilly. I want to plan."

Walt was quizzical, "How do you know about things like that? I only heard about rubbers."

"Girl talk, my dear, girl talk. Fern and I are both going to the doctor this week. By the way, I about jumped out of my chair when you said you get silent when you're angry. Now that you mentioned it, I've noticed that." She turned to him, her feathers ruffling, "Walt, I *hate* a pouter. When my school kids pout, I can't work with them if they go into a shell. I want to shake them."

"That's better than yelling, which is what you say you do. I grew up in a house of yellers and I don't want a repeat of that."

"It's better to get it out and be done with it," Helen said with certainty.

"By George, this sounds like something we need to talk about next week. How is your dress coming?"

"All the dresses are done. I can't tell you, but they're so filmy and elegant. I love my dress. It's soft lace over a satiny layer. Daddy just bought me a long net veil. He said since I bought my dress he wanted to get me a veil. I hope I knock your socks off when you see me," she smiled.

"My dear, you did that a long time ago."

Helen remembered the journal and the tender romance of Isaac and Sarah. "You know, what's really important is if I'm still knocking your socks off in fifty years. For so many couples the romance dulls along the way. They get bored with each other."

"I guess it's up to us to keep the spark going. I know I sure am ready to tie this knot and get on with the romance."

Helen scooted over beside him in the seat, laying her head on his shoulder, "So am I, Honey."

"I can't imagine life with you ever being boring, my little wild woman," he said.

CHAPTER 40

Married

The wedding was on a blue-sky summer day. Yellow Creek Church, modeling the Brethren ethic of simplicity, smelled of newly-sawed wood and fresh paint. Only glowing candelabras and baskets of flowers saved it from being plain.

Fern, Helen's best friend, and Erdene and Rosemary were attendants. Their long dresses had a shirred bodice and puffy lace sleeves. Little sister, Louise, was the junior bridesmaid.

Esther ran through the church basement to the kitchen to make sure the three-tier wedding cake was in a cool place. She hustled to the room where the men were gathered to be sure they could hear the music prompt for their entrance. Back downstairs she pinned Helen's veil and straightened her pearls, then stood back, gazing at her eldest daughter. Her hands lifted to her mouth, "Oh Helen, you look so nice. There couldn't be a prettier bride."

"Do you think Walt will think so?"

She hugged her carefully, "I know so. Walt is a lucky man."

"Thanks Mother, for helping make my wedding perfect."

"Oh Pshaw, you did all the work." Esther handed her the fragrant bouquet, "There's our song: "Oh Perfect Love". I'll put on my hat then we'll go upstairs. Louise, you carry the veil."

Vows were repeated. Walt placed a gold band with small diamonds on her finger. There was scripture and music, then Rev. Miller pronounced them Mr. and Mrs. Walter Steffen.

As they were organizing after the recessional, Esther said, "At least I didn't cry."

"You didn't?" Earl sounded skeptical.

"Not so I had to use my hanky. Why Earl, I believe you're a little teary now," she dabbed at his eyes.

"Tears of joy," he allowed. "I hope they're as solid as we are after twenty-three years."

Esther looked at him tenderly. Indeed, Earl's comment on this day was well spoken: their marriage was as strong and enduring as a great oak tree, giving shady sustenance, its roots deep. They'd had their missteps: fleeting angers, hollowed-out despair, days when every breeze came near to thrashing the spirit, and precious little of glittering gaiety or spitfire humor. There was though, the comfortable nothings, the reaching out in the dark, knowing the thought without a word spoken, and the succor of twinned souls who lifted the chin and walked the walk. Yes, Helen and Walt would do well to follow after.

Later that night the couple was on their way to the Alderman Hotel on Lincoln Avenue in Goshen. Helen was on a wedding high, wound up like a spinning top, prattling on about the day. "Mother told me she heard Mary McDowell tell Hazel it was the prettiest wedding she's ever attended. That's high praise from Mary. Didn't Hazel do a good job with the music?"

"I liked the song she played when you came down the aisle. It brought a lump to my throat, seeing you with your dad. The Apostolics don't have music like that. Your mother always comes through with desserts. That cake, I wanted to cut off a whole slab, not just a couple bites. By the time we're home from the honeymoon, the cake will be gone."

"Don't worry, my mother takes care of you. She put a container in my suitcase while I was packing. 'Here's a bedtime snack for you and Walt—unless you're otherwise occupied'." Helen laughed. "Now that's racy talk for my mother."

Walt cupped his hand to his mouth, calling out: "I love you, Esther." He grinned, "Will we be?"

"Will we be...?" she queried.

"Otherwise occupied?"

"I would guess, yes."

"Good answer. This hotel room and meal Gerry and Harold gave us for a wedding gift is very generous. I didn't know Gerry had a romantic bone in her body."

Neither Walt nor Helen had stayed at a hotel or enjoyed such luxurious dining: a four-course candlelight dinner. They oohed and aahed over black-coated waiters, linen napkins, and the silver tea service. It was no secret to other diners they were newlyweds.

In their room they wrapped in fleecy towels and filled the tub full. Helen came out of the bathroom in a new lacy nightgown, her hair loosened from the style arranged for the wedding. She was curiously eager, but shy too. Walt lifted the sheet, pulling her against him.

"I'm sure you didn't forget the gizmo you got from the doctor, but just in case, I came well prepared."

"I'm good," she nestled into his neck.

"I know you're good," he kissed her. "You're also beautiful, and kind, and smart, and you're my wife." His hands reached out for her. "But I think you have a little naughty in you too," he teased.

"At least we're legal now," she said primly.

The next day they had a lazy morning before starting their trip. They were innocents, savoring the magic of unbridled passion and sumptuous gratification. Honeymoons are for discovery and new-found intimacy: unrecognized habits and dubious oddities; possession and satiation. Helen had bathed and was dressing while Walt waited in bed, pouring over a map. She glanced at him, "What are you smiling about?"

"Am I smiling? I'm enjoying. What are you smearing? Why do you shave and wear those underarm pads?"

"It's Mum deodorant—so I don't smell like body. The underarm pads keep my dress clean. It's considered good grooming."

"Men sweat more than women. You'd think men would wear deodorant and underarm pads too."

"Some women think sweaty men smell "manly". Honestly, some of the men at school are hard to be around, they smell so bad. I think deodorant is only advertised in women's magazines."

"Helen, you'll have to tell me these things. Men don't talk about it. I sure don't want you to think I smell bad. If you don't care, I'll use your Mum. Look at the map here. I thought you would like to stop at a horse farm in Kentucky. If we do, it will probably take three days to get to Virginia. Is that alright with you?"

"I'm on my honeymoon. As long as I'm with you, I'm happy."

They had never seen mountains, certainly never driven them on less than perfect roads.

They toured a white fenced horse farm and rode horses into the mountains. "I wish Mother could see these beautiful horses and the green mountains. She wouldn't believe the fancy horse barns and sculpted fields."

"I like Esther plenty but I'm not sorry she isn't with us. When we get to Lexington tonight do you want to call your folks?"

"My land, I'm not going to phone on my honeymoon. I'm just saying this would be a thrill for her. She only went to Uncle Will's home in Ohio on *her* honeymoon."

Every day brought new beauty. They slowly meandered the road through the mountains, stopping at overlooks and hiking trails. "Count them, I can see four different mountain ranges. I wonder how far away it is?" Walt questioned.

"I understand why they're called Blue Ridge; they really are hazy and blue."

Their most lasting memory was a tour of a Virginia antebellum plantation. They'd not had firsthand exposure to the Civil War and slavery. Their eyes were opened to injustice and bigotry not known in provincial Elkhart County. "Walt, look at this slave cabin with the paper walls. Here's a picture of them picking cotton with young children dragging large bags of cotton. I never realized it was a crime to teach slaves to read. I'm going to completely change my sixth-grade unit on the Civil War. The children need to learn this."

* * * * *

Walt and Helen settled in a white frame duplex on Indiana Avenue, across town from Walt's job at Pine Manor. As a married woman she was not permitted to teach, so she got a job at the Bag Factory where she could walk to work. In the evenings, the couple took walks and played Parcheesi. They attended Yellow Creek Church where Walt was now a baptized member. Many in the youth group were newly-weds. Their social life was active with showers, weddings, and bellings. Helen was pleased to be warmly welcomed by the Steffen clan. Gerry and Harold, and Ann and Lester, Walt's sisters and their husbands, became close friends. She spent time with his dad, Sam. After Sunday church they often went back to Esther's for dinner. One Sunday in December they ambled through the snow as far as Goshen College, enjoying the winter quiet of snow-covered trees and the muffled tires of slow-moving cars. When they returned to her parents, everyone was sitting in the living room, listening to the radio.

Earl jumped up to get chairs, whispering, "The Japanese bombed Pearl Harbor in Hawaii. Evidently many ships in the naval yard were destroyed with possibly hundreds of sailors killed. Not much is known. They're afraid there will be other attacks in the U.S. They're calling congress together to decide about declaring war. This attack changes everything."

Pearl Harbor ripped the blinders off everyone who sought to be oblivious to cultures who found glory in suicide missions, and countries that marched Jewish families to cremation ovens. Many choose ignorance and isolation to staunch the hatred, bombast, and bigotry from leaching into their safe world, an ocean away from war.

For the next year, the couple recused themselves to a quiet life in their little home. They coveted their time together, knowing it wouldn't last. Life in Goshen focused on the war effort. Almost daily, uniformed men and their families gathered at the train station—with a band trumpeting patriotic songs as men went off to war. Some left high school to join the army. Mothers and sweethearts stitched blue-star banners, hanging them in their living room window—a request for prayers for their loved ones. The mostly rural population of Elkhart County had a significant number of "peace churches", but the pacifist stance was viewed askance. Walt and other Brethren men kept a low profile to avoid trouble.

In January 1942, Helen was asked to teach at Clinton Community, her previous school. She was thrilled to be back in the classroom, now with a male teacher's salary.

The same month, Walt received his notice: in two weeks he was scheduled to report to Lagro, a small town in Central Indiana for his Civilian Public Service assignment. He would be assisting in the development of the Salamonie River and Francis Slocum State Forest. They bought him a warm coat, high-top rubber boots, and overalls. Helen invited Sam Steffen and the family for supper. The young-married class at Yellow Creek had a farewell party. Walt and Helen went to Milford to say good-bye to Carl and Chloe Gawthrop. He packed writing paper, stamps, and their wedding picture. Then they were out of time.

They were quiet and pensive during the drive to the train station, lacking in small talk and last-minute reminders. They didn't know if he would get leave during the two years, or if she would be allowed a visit.

A group of servicemen and their families were also waiting at the station. "As bad as I feel about leaving you, I feel guilty about staying in Indiana and not shipping out to Germany."

"I know you believe in the CO stand. You shouldn't feel guilty."

"I just want to do my part for my country. I hope my job in Lagro is worthwhile. These army men here act so excited and proud. I don't feel that way."

"Well, I'm proud of you and I always will be. You know how your stomach acts when you get upset. You can't be worrying about this."

"All aboard," the conductor yelled, leaning out the door of the train. Steam chugged from the engine.

"I guess this is it." Not one to show affection in public, he held her tightly then softly kissed her lips. "I sure am going to miss my little brunette."

"Take care of yourself. I love you, Honey. I miss you already."

And he was gone.

* * * * *

CPS Unit # 006-01 Lagro
Camp #6
February 12, 1942

My Dear Walt,

I liked the words of this valentine. You truly are the light in the window to my heart. I'm sad for all couples who are separated on this Valentine's Day. War is a terrible thing.

I was glad to finally get your address. Lucky you (ha) to be one of the first sent to Lagro. It sounds like the old CCC barracks are in pretty bad shape. At least you like carpentry work. I'm not surprised by the lack of tools, food, heat, etc. The government isn't going to spend money on COs. We're lucky you're allowed a choice for service. I'm glad you're happy with your new coat. Maybe you should wear it to bed.

I have a new roommate. Jim Schrock was called soon after you left. He's doing his CPS in Tiffin, Ohio. Fern and I decided to double up and save on rent. She got a job at the Bag Factory sewing army uniforms. It's great having her here.

The lack of men is becoming apparent. All businesses need workers. Even elderly women are getting jobs. The Goshen Defense Plant is hiring women at the same salary they paid men. They even have childcare provided by nurses.

The city of Goshen is going all out to support the war. There's a big push to buy war stamps. They have a goal to sell enough war stamps to buy a fighter plane. That's amazing for such a small town. I try to do our part. We take our kitchen grease to the grocery where it's collected to manufacture explosives.

Daddy says something strange is going on at Pine Manor. You know how Mr. Martin was always sniffing around and bossing everyone. The last few weeks he has hardly shown his face. The supervisors can never get ahold of him. Daddy thinks something is up. I miss you so much. You are in my thoughts minute by minute. Don't hammer your finger. I pray that all goes well for you.

I Love You Forever,
Helen

The war was the elephant in every living room. It controlled lives. It took time, money, food, and peace of mind. Everyone knew several who were serving. Helen wrote to her cousin, Junior, Clara's son. Letters from the front were gold currency—even though location and every detail was blacked out.

War bonds were sold for the duration of the war. Goshen Penn Electric and Switch Company, where Sam Steffen worked, bought $100,000 in war bonds; challenging the citizens of Indiana to exceed all forty-eight states in contributions. Helen and all the Steffens and Phillips went door-to-door, organizing contests to sell war bonds. They wanted to make Sam one of the leaders in sales. Both families gave part of their sugar ration to Esther, whose molasses cookies sold for a good price. What a celebration when President Roosevelt announced at a fireside chat that the small State of Indiana topped all forty-eight states in sales of war bonds. The families celebrated with the rest of the state as if they had won the war themselves.

Goshen, along with cities around the country, established a rationing board. As many of the ration cards and stamps were distributed from schools, teachers were encouraged to assist. Lines were long so Helen stayed when possible. Everything was in short supply. Families received a ration book for such staples as: gas (three gallons/week at fifteen cents/gallon), canned goods, coffee (one pound/five weeks), sugar (one-half pound/week), Karo syrup, meat, and such items as shoes, boots, and tires. Even with a card or token, some articles like gas and soap powder were not available. When gas *was* available, a car was always filled with neighbors when making a trip to town. Most often people walked. If the family car broke down, the junk yard was the best place to find parts. Nighttime activities were curtailed as car headlights were darkened.

Every home had shades or blackout curtains. Air raid drills in the schools and homes had everyone getting their gas masks and going to the basement where water, food, and blankets were stored. Initially the sirens and drills were frightening, but after several weeks and no bombardment, families played games and read stories by lantern light in their safe cubbyhole in the basement.

* * * * *

March 16, 1942

Dear Helen,

I have to believe no news is good news. I didn't hear about the March 13 tornado till the 15th. We're remote here. The camp director told me a big tornado ripped through Goshen killing 2 and injering over 50 with many homes destroyed. At first, I about went crazy then Merle reminded me that if something had happened to you, I'd have been first of kin to be notified. I wonder how close it came and if you were afraid. Glad Fern is with you. I know I'll hear from you soon.

We have 20 men here now, desent men to be with. We are tearing down one of the barricks to get wood to repair the others. A slow go of it. The more men with different skills, the better we get things done. We have someone to cook now but food still not plentaful. We get packaged food from the army. It's ok. Not much to do here except work. Went to Lagro one Saturday but not much of a town. What I wouldn't give to hold you close and just talk to you for an hour. That seems like a far-off dream. I think of you so much and love you with all my heart.

Certified member of Lagro Lonely Hearts Club
Your Walt

Women on the home front were as busy as their men at the battle front. Many worked at new wartime industries. The Studebaker Wagon Company in South Bend, owned by Grandma Sarah's Zumbrun family, switched to manufacturing airplane parts. With spring weather came Victory Gardens. Anyone with a small plot of land planted potatoes, carrots, lima beans, red beets—anything that would feed service men. Every child hoed, pulled weeds, and watered. Every week a county truck came by to collect vegetables, taking them to a cannery, where they were shipped to army bases around the country. After gardening, the women met at Red Cross Community Centers and churches to make comforters and padded dressings. They cut sheets to roll into bandages. While it felt like "war mania", there was an esprit de corps in which men, women, and children were indispensable to the war effort. Though it was bittersweet, most people couldn't resist the draw to the Saturday movie show to watch footage from the war front which preceded the movie.

CPS Unit # 006-01 Lagro
Camp # 6
April 1942

My Dear Walt,

I'm so excited to share my good news with you. I just got home from seeing Dr. Young. He confirmed my suspicion: we are going to have a baby! He thinks it will be in September. I have been feeling queasy for a few months. I've had all the signs: morning sickness, fatigue, and growing tummy. Our timing is good—I'll be able to hide the pregnancy till the end of the school year. I guess my teaching days will be done for a while. Don't worry about me.

Dr. Young says I'm doing perfect. I'm just sorry we can't be together, but many couples are in the same situation. We all get through it.

Now there are four of us living here; Alice and Lucille Malcolm moved in. They are sisters, also teachers. It's a little crowded but we all get on well. Fern knew them. Now we're actually making money on rent. Makes it worth it, getting up early so we can all get through the bathroom. The tornado was on the east side of Goshen which had most of the damage. We went to the basement, but not much damage here. Daddy and Mother are in such a dither. You know how they worry. The rumor is that Ernest Martin is going bankrupt and Pine Manor Farm will go to the bank. I can't blame them being upset. It's Daddy and Mother's jobs, plus they'll lose their home. Of course, you won't have a job either when you leave the service. At least there are lots of jobs open now, though nothing as good as Pine Manor. We're doing fine as far as money goes. We'll have plenty to pay baby bills. Dr. Young said I will be in the hospital five days. The hospital bill is $30 and doctor bill is $8 which includes all checkups. I've saved rent money plus my salary. Your little family sends all our love forever.

We are healthy and well. Just lonesome for you. I hold you close in prayer.

Your Helen

* * * * *

Camp # 6
Lagro, Indiana

September 1942

Dear Helen,

Thank you for your letters, they sure do help. Things have settled into a routine here. We have 46 men now, maybe all we'll get. They are from all backgrounds, quit a few are farmers but there are teachers, book keepers, bisness owners, preachers, and college fellas. About any problem we have, someone can fix it. A newspaper man has started a weekly camp newsletter that we all enjoy. There's a men's chorus and classes on car mechanics and typing. We have a Bible study. We grow a lot of our own food so we all work in the garden. Several of us do field work for ladies in the neighborhood whose husbands are in the army. Several evenings I go to a farm and milk cows after our day work is done.

Our camp is in the Francis Slocum State Forest. The Salamonie River often floods and soil washes away deep gullys. We're building up the land to prevent erosion, constructing terrasses and ditches. Then we plant grasses and pine trees. We're building a fence all around the state park to keep farm animals out. It's good fisical work and I have no trouble sleeping. I hope people think we're making a difference. That's why I help neighbors as much as I can.

Do you remember Merle Weaver? We met him when I went with you to a district cabinet meeting at Union Center Church. He's here at Lagro—the only person I know.

How is my little mother-to-be? Not being around you, its hard for me to imagine you walking around with a big stomach. I bet you have the cutest potbelly in Goshen-ha! Have someone get the box camera out. I sure do miss you. That part doesn't get a bit easier. I got nice letters from your mother and Louise last week. Tell Louise that at 11 years old she has better penmanship and spelling than I have. I'm surprised how much I miss that little dickins. She is my buddy. Tell everyone I really appreciate their letters, especially with stamps costing 3 cents.

Take care of yourself and obey Doc Young.

Your Papa to be,
Walter

* * * * *

Yank. Yank. Yank. Yank. Esther pulled so hard on the weeds that when the roots released she fell backward on top of a row of beans. She was frustrated and disgusted. At least pulling weeds was a good way to vent the energy smoldering in her head and roiling in her body. Earl was so discouraged and dour. She didn't blame him. Life refused to let him get a toe grip. Whenever fortune smiled and he got a hold on success, it was pulled out like these weeds—leaving a hole. The farm they were meant to have, his parents lost during the depression; the Yoder farm was too big; the farm at Southwest, too small; the owner decided to move to the farm on Basher Road. As hard as Earl worked, things didn't fall into place for him. She could see farming wasn't his strong suit; he didn't like the pressure of daily decisions. Pine Manor had been a good fit. Working under a supervisor scaled back the pressure. With his methodical temperament, he kept a steady hand on the daily routine of the calf barn and worked well with cow hands. She looked up to see him crossing the road. Strange for him to come home in the afternoon. Esther stood to greet him.

"Well, it's over. Bill Plank from the bank came to talk to us. They're going to sell as much of the livestock as they can. What hasn't sold in a month or two, they'll sell at auction along with the land and farm equipment. With all the money Ernest Martin had, it should have been successful. He spent too much buying a registered herd and traipsing them around the country to competitions. Such a foolish waste. Bill says Mr. Martin is at least cooperating with them now. Esther, he's penniless. Can you believe that?" Earl lifted and resettled his hat. "He'd like me to stay till the auction; then I'm done. I can take what time I need to look for a job. Here I am, forty-six years old and I'm starting over. I'll be wearing out the shoe leather."

"A job is the priority, Daddy. I'd rather you not go back to contract rental farming. We had a four-year run of good luck. Let's try to keep it going."

* * * * *

"I'm glad babies are born in hospitals nowadays," Esther said, her voice anxious with the drama of Helen's pending delivery. They had just come from Dr. Young's office: "Take this gal to the hospital, Esther. You don't need to take her on a bumpy ride over the railroad tracks," he teased, reminding her of the wild ride he gave her before Louise was born.

That evening at four-thirty Earl made the call to Lagro. Surprisingly, the camp director called Walt to the office phone. "Walt, I didn't think I'd get to talk to you. Can you hear me?" Earl felt the need to yell since the call was long distance.

"Hey Pop, what's happening?"

"Esther just called from the hospital. You have a perfect baby girl. Mother says she's a nice size and wide awake. You're not to worry. Everything went fine."

"Oh, wonderful news," Walt heaved a big breath. "A baby girl," his voice was awestruck. "How did Helen get along? Is she okay?"

"She did real good. She called Mother early this morning. Course Mom high-tailed it over there. They went to Doc Young's this morning and now it's about five o'clock."

"I can't believe I happened to be near the office. Actually, I'm just getting back from the doctor in Wabash myself."

"My lands, Walt."

"He tells me I have a stomach ulcer. Don't say anything to Helen. She'd just worry and there's nothing she can do. I HATE THIS. I'm not earning my keep, let alone giving service to the country. The blood test showed

I'm anemic," his voice was frustrated. "They want me to stay in bed—can you imagine," he hissed. "My diet is very limited. I have to take cream and antacid every hour. Instead of ME working, the cooks are going to have to go out of their way FOR ME. That's the LAST thing I want. Anyway, enough about that. I go back to the doctor in two weeks. I sure hope I'm better, but he wasn't encouraging. Doc says I worry too much. Maybe since the baby's here I'll be more relaxed. Did Mother tell you the baby's name?"

"I guess she forgot. She was all wound up."

"Her name is Janice Helen, continuing the tradition of using the mother's name."

"That's real pretty. Thanks for making us Grandpa and Grandma."

"I need to get off the phone, Pop. Tell Helen I'm sorry I couldn't be with her. Thanks for all you're doing to help. Tell her I sure miss her," his voice was nostalgic.

"Take care of yourself, Walt. Do what they tell you."

"I don't think I have a choice. Thanks Pop, for calling. You sure have made me happy. Don't mention the ulcer; I'm in hopes it will clear up. Tell Helen I'll get a letter out. Bye."

* * * * *

"Listen to this, Mother. Mrs. France chose this for my recital piece. It's "Etude in D Major"." Louise played through the piano piece as Esther pumped her treadle sewing machine, stitching together rag blocks for a comforter for the Red Cross. Life in the Phillip's house was back to normal now that Helen and Janice had returned to the duplex.

"That's very nice. It will take a lot of work. Mrs. France puts a lot of stock in you, Louise. I don't know where you got your talent on the piano, but you sure were born with it. I've never seen anything...."

"Hullo, ladies," Earl called. "That's pretty, Louise. With the windows open I heard you playing clear out on the street. I have good news, Mother," he hustled over to pat Esther's shoulder, his high spirits ripening his cheeks. "I got the job at the Milk Condensary. I can start on Monday. I'm lucky. A lot of men were after that job. I think Ike Roth put in a good word for me."

Esther jumped up from the sewing machine, her face glowing with pride. "Oh Daddy, good for you. Now we can check out that rental on Plymouth Avenue. Louise, maybe you can go to Model School where your sisters went. I'm so proud of you," she reached tall to kiss his cheek.

Louise, knowing her daddy was wrapped around her finger, was not one to miss an opportunity. She sang as she played the ice cream advertisement: "When they say it's hot and steamy, ice cream is so cold and creamy." She danced toward Earl, "We need to celebrate Daddy's new job. The Candy Kitchen makes ice cream on Friday. Please, Daddy?"

"Good idea, Louise. Get your hat, Mother. Let's celebrate."

* * * * *

"What can be so important that Walt wants me to be here for a long-distance call? His letter was very explicit." Helen was pacing, jiggling Janice, who was picking up on her anxiety.

"He would never have me take Janice out in this nasty winter weather unless it was an emergency. What must have happened? I feel like a train wreck. Do you realize I haven't talked to him in almost a year?"

Esther treadled away on her sewing machine, her default activity in wartime stress—which seemed a constant. She pretended calm, "Oh Helen, you never know what the government is doing. He's to call at two o'clock, so you don't have long to wait. Let me hold the baby so you're ready," she stood from the sewing machine.

They both jumped at the shrill long-short-long-short ring. "That's it," Esther said, her shaky voice giving lie to her calm.

"Hello?" Helen yelled.

"Helen? Can you hear me?" Walt yelled as well.

"Pretty well. What's wrong, Walt?"

"I'm coming home, Helen. They're giving me a medical discharge."

"What's wrong with you?" she screeched.

"I have a stomach ulcer that's bleeding. I've been trying to heal it with diet and medicine for a month. The doctor told me it's not healing. I'm still anemic."

"Then you come right home. If its diet you need, we can do that. Maybe we can get special rations," she nodded her head.

"I'm so disgusted about this. You know everybody will say I can't hack it," his sullen anger communicated across the phone line.

"You can't help you got an ulcer."

"What's that?" he yelled.

"You can't help that you got an ulcer. You didn't have it when you left," she asserted.

"Tell that to the guys fighting in Germany. I'm a washout. Everyone's been real nice, but I'm just a problem down here. They want to get rid of me. We're so far in the boondocks, they're afraid I'll start to bleed and not stop. They don't want a CPS casualty. That's a laugh," he muttered.

"Honey, you need to get home. Even if you got an ulcer in the army, they'd send you home. You can't live with a bleeding ulcer."

"I got my train ticket when I was in Wabash this morning. I'll go through Ft. Wayne and get to Goshen at nine thirty this Friday night."

"I know you're disappointed but be careful. I don't want anything to happen to you," her voice thickened with tears.

"I've been thinking, it wouldn't be fair to kick Fern and the ladies out of the duplex, so if you can check around for a place for us, that's what we should do. I can't work for at least a month."

"Get home, Walt, and hold your baby. That will heal your ulcer."

"I think you could be right. I hate being away from you. I never adjusted to it. Be sure to have milk, cream, bread, soda crackers, and graham crackers. I eat something every hour and soak everything in milk. No fruits, vegetables, or solid food."

"I'll be at the train Friday night. I can't wait."

"Bye, see you soon."

CHAPTER 41

Second World War

Oh, the inexpressible comfort of melding the dreams of past months: silkened skin of familiarity, embedded in memories that resumed second nature with a seeking caress. Walt groaned with contentment and desire, instantly recalling and responding to their language of love. Helen took his large work-roughened hands in her small ones—the left, soft from baby oils; the right, rigid and contracted; her hands a haven for his.

"I understand your disappointment and even humiliation, but Walt, I don't understand your shame. You're ill."

"Even though we were isolated in a forest preserve, I know the evil and inhuman goings-on in Europe. I have an inkling of our servicemen's lives. I'm like every American man: I want to protect my family, my home, and my country from the Nazis. We've got to stand for what we believe. Twice now, people will think I copped out, once as a conscientious objector and now with an early discharge. I'm ashamed to face people."

"The people who know you won't think you copped out. Others may think you're unpatriotic. Because they have loved ones endangered or even killed, they might be angry and say hurtful things. They're background noise. You can't blame them or listen to their words. You don't know their story as they don't know yours. Hold your head up. I know your decency, Walt. You'll find a way to serve your country. Tomorrow we'll see Doctor Young. We also need to get you a gas mask for the air raid drills."

The next months flew by in a flurry of domesticity. Walt stayed home for several weeks, religiously following his small hourly feedings of milk and soggy crackers, warm milk bread, cream of wheat, applesauce on toast, and cornbread and gravy. They moved to a small house on Lafayette Street, an area swarming with young mothers and children. After several weeks, Walt's ulcer was no longer bleeding. His energy returned as his hemoglobin level normalized. After another month he was allowed to take a job at the Goshen Milk Condensary, close enough for him to walk to work. Despite their intention to space their babies, according to Walt, Judy, their second daughter, "came up from the woods" when Janice was thirteen months old. Helen easily embraced a second child with her casual mothering and laid-back rigor for housekeeping.

The family hunkered down, as did everyone in the war years. It was no disgrace to have nothing, as all were equally deprived. The pervasive sense, "We're in this together", was universal. When families were putting a gold star on the banner in their front window, indicating their serviceman was killed, everyone else wanted to be worthy of that sacrifice. The Goshen American War Dads dedicated a Scroll of Honor Monument, the list steadily increasing to 1,500 names.

Older children were as engaged as the adults. "I'm tired of cottage cheese, especially dry without syrup," Louise complained. "What I wouldn't give for a wiener."

"You should be thankful you have something to eat. Children in Europe are starving. We're fortunate to have a barn so we can keep cows and pigs. It would be tough for us and Helen's family if we didn't have milk."

"Daddy, I'm going out in the field this afternoon to gather milkweed pods. Do you want to help me?" It was lunch time on a busy Saturday and thirteen-year-old Louise was running on with her usual nonstop commentary. "We're having a contest at school. Whoever gathers the most bags of milkweed pods gets a new book at the library. Since we're surrounded by fields, I have a good chance of winning."

"When will the Victory Wagon be by, Mother?" Earl asked.

"They're usually here by three o'clock. Louise, don't forget your sunbonnet when you go to the field."

"I'll help Mother dig vegetables, then I'll come help you." Earl said.

"Why are you collecting milk pods?" Rosemary asked.

"They make life jackets for soldiers. They take that little white fluff out of the pod and dry it. Two burlap bags full will make one life jacket. I'd much rather gather milkweed than go door to door picking up tin cans. The houses are so far apart out here. After I get the can, I have to take off both ends and mash it. That takes lots of time."

"Helen gave me her tin cans for you, Louise, so evidently no one is gathering on her street. When we go to her house, take a gunny sack and collect on her street."

"Mother, I want to look for a pattern and material for my wedding dress. Can you go with me to Plauts? I don't know anything about bridal material," Rosemary asked.

"After I dig up vegetables, I have to make a double batch of cookies to exchange for blue stamps. By the way, Pop, can you get more molasses from Henry? You mentioned he's running out. I sure can't make cookies without sugar, lard, *and* molasses. I found a new recipe that uses beaten egg whites and cream instead of sugar and lard. I'm eager to try it. Rosie, can I meet you when we go to town tonight? I'd love to look at material with you."

"Dean and I have a date, but I can have him meet me downtown a little later. We're meeting Erdene and Art so it shouldn't be a problem. I think Erdene is getting serious about Art. What do you think, Mother?"

"Oh, they're lovebirds all right. I have my ways of knowing," Louise nodded with a sly grin.

"Well, I'd be the last to know," Esther chuckled.

"I'm going to wash my hair before we go to town. Is there plenty of water?" Louise asked.

"Go easy on the water; it's been dry lately. The cistern is probably low, and we all want to wash our hair," Esther reminded her.

* * * * *

"What are you doing? Jannie, get back from the fire!" Helen yelled as she rushed out the back door of the house. She grabbed both toddlers away from the back stoop where flames and wispy smoke shrouded the old wood steps. Encumbered by a nine-month pregnancy, she ran into the house for a bucket, filled it with water and doused the fire, stamping it with her shoes. Four-year-old Janice, still holding a box of matches, was screaming, frightened by all the hullabaloo.

Walt, returning home from work, came rushing around the corner of the house. "What's burning?" he yelled. "There's smoke clear out by the street."

"You *would* come home right now," her voice was piqued as she bent to inspect the scorched wood.

Recognizing a narrowly missed catastrophe, he was furious. "Where were you? The yard is full of smoke. I smelled it out by the street," he hollered.

"I was in the bedroom sewing. I didn't smell it."

She squatted before Jannie, grabbing the matches from her. "Never, never touch matches. Matches hurt you. Where did you get them? Tell Mommy." The little girl collapsed onto the ground, sobbing, unused to the anger and yelling of her parents.

Walt picked her up, coddling her, "You're okay, sweetie." He put his arm around Helen, "This is our fault. We've got to do better than this," he said.

"I feel like an irresponsible mother. How could I have left matches where a four-year-old could find them? I can't imagine how she lit matches and caught the wood. Come, Judy. Let's go in and have a snack with Daddy. I'm going to find a tin box that can't be opened and put our matches away. Walt, I called Mother to come; thank goodness she didn't see the burning steps. I think the baby will come tonight. That's why I wanted to finish sewing new diapers."

"If your mother is coming, we'd better clean up around here. Jannie, Judy, come help Daddy pick up toys in the living room. Helen, you'd better get a bag packed in case you have to leave in a hurry. We should wash that sink full of dirty dishes."

The next morning Walt staggered into the house as Esther was awakening. Her hair was plaited and her eyes sleep-swollen. As she wrapped in her robe, a wave of chills rolled down her spine. Something was wrong. Walt's face looked hollowed out and weary, a haunting sorrow spilled from his eyes.

"Helen got along okay. They said she'll sleep off the anesthesia, so I came home."

"I'll make us some Postum. You look exhausted."

"We have a little girl, Nancy," he smiled, "the sweetest little blue-eyed blond towhead. She has what my dad has: they're calling it a harelip and a cleft palate. I guess it tends to run in families."

Only Esther's unwitting intake of breath betrayed her concern, her face remained composed. She brought the Postum to the kitchen table, bathed in the soft light of early morning.

"Evidently when a baby has one abnormality, the chances are higher for others. They're checking her closely. So far her heart seems okay, and she's alert and looking around."

"They do so much for babies now. Did they say they can fix it?" Esther asked.

"They want us to take her to Riley Hospital in Indianapolis."

Esther nodded, a wry smile, "Like mother, like daughter. That's where we took Helen. Look at her now, Walt. There's nothing she can't do. Nancy will be the same. They'll fix her up you won't believe," she declared with the confidence of a mother who has been through such an experience.

Walt looked somber, "It's pretty noticeable. It's going to be hard. What bothers me is that people won't give her a chance, or they'll be unkind because she looks different. A little kid shouldn't be saddled with that."

"Oh Walt, that's just the way I felt when Helen was born," Esther said in a calm, matter-of-fact tone. "What I've learned: when God gives a child a burden to bear, He gives something special to them—a trait or personality that will help overcome the obstacle. Helen is the perfect example. I worried so much about her, but she was a determined soul, and she didn't let unkind people bother her—she brushed them off." She paused, remembering, "I'll say too, when Helen was born, I felt such a weight from her disability, like everything was on me. I think I closed out Earl a little bit. I won't say it'll be easy, but God walks the journey with you. I can vouch for that, Walt. Earl and I didn't feel alone in the hard times. My mother, Sarah was a life saver, and you know we'll help. That's what family is for."

Walt was overwhelmed, the misfortune too fresh to see a silver lining. "I should have your confidence and faith, but it seems like a lot right now. Just feeding her will be huge, they said. The roof of her mouth isn't there, so the milk comes out her nose. She chokes. Those nurses, they didn't see me watching them. Who will care for Jannie and Judy when Helen spends her time feeding Nancy? How will I work and get us to Indianapolis? How will we pay for the surgeries and hospital bills? What if she has brain damage we don't even know about yet?" he worried.

She took his hands, her eyes filled with tears, "Those were my exact questions when I had sick babies years ago. You start one day at a time, doing your best that day. And that's how you get through it. Remember you have a wife who has been plodding through struggles for twenty-seven years. You'll do it together and you'll be the better for it in the end. Now, I'm going to fry some eggs."

Walt spent the morning with Jannie and Judy, diapering, bathing, and brushing their soft brown curls. He never wearied of time with his family—reading stories, playing, and tussling on the floor. He never could fully comprehend the wonder he felt for his wife and daughters; perfection beyond anything he ever imagined in life. And though baby Nancy's problems seemed huge, he guessed their little family was up to it. He was comforted that their extended family was appended to the five of them when it came to caring.

He took the girls to Esther's, knowing he needed to be with Helen. When he went to the obstetric ward, she wasn't there. The nurse told him in a hushed tone that she'd been moved to a room where she would have privacy.

Arriving at her bedside, they each reached for the comfort of the other. In their marriage they had become tethered, like a graft that took—growing out lush and green. This melding never just happened, nor was it put into words, unless you count a belly laugh, mumblings in the night, or eyes that spilled out a thirsty draught feeding the soul. Whatever the ineffable something, it was locked in for both. Yes, they would have hard times, harsh words—or worse, no words. They may come to the edge of giving up, but they would never arrive at that point simultaneously. All this was bundled in their embrace. Some couples never have this certainty; for Walt and Helen, married less than five years, it was a gold bond apprised to their marriage certificate. Anyone could see it.

* * * * *

"Did the nurses tell you how they fed her?" Walt was helping Helen with the first feeding after coming home from the hospital.

"They said use longer nipples. They sent a couple. I fed her once at the hospital. You have to sit her up straight with the nipple on the side of her mouth, aimed down, so gravity directs the milk to her throat. It will come out her nose every time she swallows, but she gets some of it."

"Do you want me to hold her or hold the bottle?" Walt asked.

"I'm the one who's going to be doing it, so I'd better learn to use the bottle."

"Okay, come here, Pumpkin. We're new at this so be patient with us. I can tell she's hungry."

"It just doesn't feel right on the side of her mouth."

"Hold her forward so she spits it out," Helen said when Nancy gagged and choked.

"Sorry, cough it out," Walt said lifting the little tyke to his shoulder. Nancy caught her breath and wailed her baby frustration.

"Maybe I need to sit her up more. We've got milk going everywhere but down her throat. Here we go." Walt repositioned her. "When she sucks she pushes the nipple to the center and milk comes out her nose. I wonder if she swallows any?"

"Whoops, she's choking again. Poor thing. We'll figure it out, Sweetie. That's all right," Helen patted her back. "Cough it up." Walt said, standing and bouncing Nancy, her little face red and damp.

"We should check the girls. We don't want them torching the steps again," Helen said, peeking in the living room.

"Do you think we could hold milk in a straw and dribble it in her throat? There has to be a better way. I don't see how you're going to feed her by yourself, Helen."

"Let's try the straw." She went to the cupboard. "It can't be worse than what we're doing."

"Look, her little tummy is all hard from the air she's swallowed. I should burp her, or she'll get a tummy ache," Walt held her to his shoulder, patting her back.

"Do you think the people at Riley would know how to feed her? They see babies with this more than the nurses here do. I hope we get an appointment before she starves."

Helen put milk in the straw, "Hold her hands, I can't see where I'm putting the milk.... Oh dear, that didn't work." They both jumped up as Nancy struggled to catch her breath, unable to even cough or cry. Walt pulled Helen into his free arm, helpless tears sliding down both their cheeks.

"Do you want me to try?" he asked softly.

"Yes. Don't worry, I'll get a grip. It makes me so sad for her. I'd better reheat some more formula."

"Yeah. I'm going to try bending her forward and tipping up her chin. It seems she chokes with any reclining. Let's try again, girlie." Milk gushed everywhere but she took a few swallows before twisting her head away.

"Take it out. She can't breathe," Helen said, sopping up the milk coming from her nose and mouth. I believe she got some that time. She wants more, Walt. Look at her little mouth," Helen said gently.

"Oops. Didn't work that time," Walt lifted her as she choked and cried.

"I wonder if it comes out the nipple too fast." Helen suggested. They tested both nipples, finding one dripped twice as fast as the other. It seemed to go better after changing to the slow nipple. Nancy became sleepy and satisfied.

"I wish I knew how soon you can give babies rice cereal. If the milk was thicker she would get it easier," Helen suggested.

Nancy gave a hearty baby burp, spitting up into the burp pad. "Don't spit up, little one. You worked too hard to get it," Walt said, carrying her to her crib. "You'd better check out the living room, Helen. The girls have redecorated the walls in here."

"I knew it was too quiet," she said, going to check the damage.

* * * * *

"Wow, Helen, look at this headline: **MAY 8, 1945, A DAY TO REMEMBER,"** Walt passed the paper to her. "They made a special edition of the paper for V-E Day. It sure as heck took long enough for those Krauts and Japs to give up. Remember back at the beginning, no one thought this war would last five years. It says here some Japanese still haven't surrendered. I hope they don't drop any more bombs. Too many people have died already. Here it says forty-four men, just from Goshen, with eleven prisoners of war. I wonder if they'll ever get home. Truman pronounced Sunday a day of prayer. I never thought much of Truman, but he's looking better. I wish he'd clean up his language."

"What time did Mother say they'd be by?" Helen asked.

"One o'clock. Are you going with us to the parade?"

"No, I don't want to take the baby out—everyone stares. I've got wash to do. It'll be a wild celebration. The girls will have fun. Put the yellow dresses on them. Those feed sacks weren't very pretty, but at least they're new. Mother won't believe I finished them already; you get a lot done when you're up at night."

"Come here, girls. Daddy will wash your face and brush your hair. Jannie, did you know Mommy made you a new dress to wear to the parade. We have to hurry. Grandma and Grandpa will be here soon. Judy, give the rattle back to the baby."

"Be sure to take their bonnets. The sun is warm today," Helen reminded.

* * * * *

Helen was bathing six-month-old Nancy in the kitchen sink, her mind organizing her day to complete tasks in preparation for the trip to Riley Hospital. Feeding her away from home was her main concern, as it was time consuming and messy. She would have to take enough boiled water, evaporated milk, pablum, cereal, and Karo syrup for five feedings.

"Ah-h-h!" she screamed, dropping to her knees to reach for Nancy who had slipped out of her arms, falling to the kitchen floor. Nancy bellowed her hurt and fear, her wet body making watery circles on the dirty linoleum.

"Oh no, come Sweetie." She was unable to lift the kicking, slithery baby with her left hand. The stress of caring for three little ones, compounded by sleep deprivation, coalesced in heart-wrenching recrimination. Jannie and Judy came running to the kitchen, frightened by the mayhem. Their little hands helped gather Nancy in her arms. *What kind of mother would drop her baby? Why hadn't she wrapped Nancy in a towel as usual? Would she ever measure up as a good mother? Would the Indianapolis doctors see bruises?* Jannie's soft little hand patted her mother's cheek, "Don't cry Mommy. Don't cry, Mommy."

The next morning Esther came in the early darkness to watch Jannie and Judy. She brought cookies and a pack of Blackjack gum to alleviate car sickness. This trip weighed heavily on all the family. Nineteen forty-five Indiana was provincial. Many people had never been far from home. Though they didn't verbalize it, Walt and Helen were intimidated by the 150-mile trip and driving in Indianapolis traffic. To save gas and rubber for the war, the defense department had established a victory speed limit at thirty-five mph, making the trip five to six hours long with feeding stops. They had been protective of Nancy, seldom taking her out in public. How would people treat their beloved baby whose spirit was spontaneous and spritely. Most of all, they were in awe of the university hospital and doctors. These men held their daughter's well-being in their hands. Though they weren't worldly-wise to the medical profession, they would jump through every hoop to advocate for their baby.

The Riley waiting room was an enclosed long narrow outside entryway with a brick wall and cement floor. A large stained-glass window was at the far end. Patients and their families sat facing each other on benches along both walls. In the narrow center were patients in wooden wheelchairs with breathing apparatus, and restless, whining children harboring painful memories of previous visits.

Walt and Helen walked into clinic as clear-eyed innocents, sucked into a maelstrom of crying, misshapen, bandage-covered children—a place unique and never otherwise seen. Notified that the wait would be one to two hours, they shuffled to find a seat, hoping to blend unnoticed into the chaotic assembly. Who would have known there were so many children with problems? Some children had no muscle control—they couldn't hold up their head. They made noise but couldn't speak. There was a whimpering baby whose head was too small who didn't move at all. There was a toddler whose head was twice the normal size. There were children who had been burned, with scars shiny and twisted, and some with fresh scabbed burns that were still oozing. All the children had some form of facial deformity. Prior to this visit Nancy's lip had seemed glaring. Just now, Helen said a prayer of gratitude. Some of these children would live a short time. Some could not be repaired. How fortunate that their baby could be fixed. It wasn't uncommon for doctors to recommend institutionalizing handicapped children, so a few children were there with professional caretakers. Helen wondered if these children had parents. There were several Negro families, a curiosity to the couple from Goshen, a town where Negroes were refused overnight lodging. The atmosphere was one of casual acceptance of bodily infirmities. Some seemed to be "old timers", cackling and visiting as friends. The adults assisted all the children, sharing snacks and wiping noses and drool as necessary. Children mulled about and played, accommodating each other's limitations. Everyone there was accepted in the club.

After a long wait they were ushered into a small room. A nurse weighed and measured Nancy. Finally, portly Dr. Amos with his small round glasses and fringe of gray hair, his starched white coat and formal manner, entered the room. A young medical student accompanied him. They nodded to Walt and Helen, sycophants in this alien world. Nancy, having had her fill of strangers, wailed her displeasure at their fingers probing and poking.

After the examination, Dr. Amos questioned the student, "What is your diagnosis?"

"A cleft palate with fissure involving premaxilla through the uvula. Protrusion of the premaxilla and visible alae with significant cleft likely to require bone grafting. Externally there is a unilateral complete harelip," he replied.

"What are the primary problems with these infants?"

"Malnutrition and dehydration with repeated secondary infections such as pneumonia. Also, failure to thrive because of difficulty feeding," he answered as though quoting from a textbook.

"How do you propose we treat this baby?"

"This is a significant deformity. Growing up, she will require repeated surgeries to improve esthetic results."

"Do you observe anything unusual in this baby, Dr. Flora?"

"Absolutely. This baby is right on the mark with her six-month weight. She is active, standing and bouncing on her mother's lap, and pulling herself around. Her eyes are bright, her hair shiny, good skin turgor—obviously well fed and hydrated. She babbles like a normal happy six-month old. She's clean and well cared for. Generally, babies with this deformity are in the lowest percentile for weight. They are anemic, listless, lacking in energy, and they lag developmentally. They're often sick. This baby is highly unusual," he nodded to Dr. Amos.

"Very well, Dr. Flora." Dr. Amos now acknowledged Walt and Helen with a smile. "Mr. and Mrs. Steffen, I commend you. You have found some way to keep your baby fed. You need to share your secret with us. Are you using one of those new flanged nipples?"

The struggle and frustrations of the past six months were forgotten as Helen received accolades from the doctors. "We don't use a nipple, Dr. Amos. We gave those up long ago. We tried everything. I decided to thicken the milk, slowly adding pablum and rice cereal to her evaporated milk. Thickening the formula helps prevent choking. Sideways positioning is important. I feed her with a turkey baster with a tube on the end—a lot comes back out. As she gets older, she has learned how to direct the tube with her tongue. She collects a little milk, then swallows. We learned we needed to make a longer tube so we can squeeze it closed when she swallows, or milk trickles down her throat and she chokes. She swallows air, so we sit her up to burp frequently, or she spits up. Walt and my mother have learned to feed her. It's time consuming. It takes hours every day."

"You can't imagine how pleased we are to see an infant with such an extreme deformity who is healthy and thriving. This is a good time to explain Riley's program to you. Nancy's impediment is something that can't be treated by your local doctor. Riley is at the forefront in treating maxillo-facial deformities. Our doctors learn from doing research and surgery; Nancy will benefit from the care of some of the best doctors in the country. You have to agree to follow our treatment plan and return for periodic check-ups in exchange for medical care. Mrs. Steffen, if you wouldn't mind, I would like Nurse Williams to observe a feeding. Dr. Flora, clear the conference room for them and get as many med students and nurses as you can to observe. This may be your inclusion in your first medical journal article. We have much to learn from this patient."

Now speaking to Walt and Helen, "We can't do the first surgery to close the palate until the baby is near eighteen months. We would like to see you again in three months. You're doing a remarkable job; keep up the good work," he smiled as he left the room.

Walt hugged Helen, both of them smiling ear-to-ear from the positive feedback from Dr. Amos. This was one of few successes of past months.

Walt thought Helen exhausted and sleepy on the way home from Indianapolis. Her eyes were closed but her mind was hyper vigilant, her thoughts racing. This day was a "life-at-the-crossroads" moment for her. In the future when life experiences tried to pound her down, she remembered the day she taught the doctors and nurses at Riley. The validation she received sealed her self-worth like a light switch in her brain. She had been proven competent. Never again would any powerful person intimidate or demean her. She knew she could figure out problems, finding answers without deferring or being subservient to anyone. This assurance, embedded in her spirit, was a genetic gift passed from her grandmother Sarah and her mother Esther. She felt suffused with their resolute, unflagging essence pulsing through her veins. With certainty, she saw the model for mothering her daughters—it became essential for her to convey this gift to *her* daughters. Whew! The import of this staggered her.

She smiled, thinking of her three daughters: Jannie, the typical firstborn, wanting to take charge, be responsible, and go by the rules; Judy, the second born, usually content to follow her sister, but having a more curious, adventuresome disposition; and Nancy, her independent baby, cheerfully sitting back and observing, then content to do her own thing. She was awed by her responsibility to teach her girls this inheritance: they have unlimited potential; they must strive to be the best, and they should never settle for mediocrity. That day she determined to begin demonstrating this heritage.

Over the years, trips to Riley Hospital had a significant impact on Helen. Even the logistics of the long trip and big-city driving, made her more independent and resourceful than most women. She became adept at checking and adding oil, changing tires, and adding water to the radiator. After several trips, she was one of the "old timers" on the Riley waiting room benches, befriending all the other dressed-for-Sunday, bald, cleavaged, nappy-headed, bejeweled, dirty, duck-tailed, snot-nosed, turbaned bench warmers. They were joined in heart by a great equalizer: a beloved child who needed a hand-up. Her tolerance for "things not Goshen" magnified as she grew to appreciate and care for these families. She was one of the lucky ones, her baby would be fixed, unlike children whose absences were noted at every clinic visit.

* * * * *

"I'm glad you came with me, Mother. Nancy doesn't sit still for a minute. You'll be worn out; she'll crawl all over you. Do you think you can watch her *and* follow the map? Walt marked our trip." Helen and Esther were on their way to Indianapolis in the still dark morning shortly after Nancy's first birthday. This was Helen's first time driving the entire trip, and she wasn't looking forward to it.

"I think so. I usually follow the map for Daddy. I've been looking forward to having you to myself for a whole day, Helen. We rarely have time to visit."

"I'm hoping the ride will lull her to sleep. We always have to wait at the clinic, so it will be late when we get home."

By afternoon it was their turn to see Dr. Amos. Holding a screaming, squirming baby while the doctors tried to focus their flashlights to measure her palate was difficult at best. Helen was sweaty, her heart pounding as if she'd been in a race. After a short time, they brought in another doctor who repeated the exam. Helen wished she understood the discussion, but the medical jargon was like a foreign language.

"Mrs. Steffen, this is Dr. Famy. He is the orofacial surgeon who will operate on Nancy's cleft palate. Her mouth is of sufficient size to operate now. We'll schedule her later this week after we do tests to assure there is no other physical impediment that would postpone surgery. It's uncertain if she'll need one or two surgeries to close the cleft. Plan on her being here three weeks. She can't return home until the stitches come out at two weeks post-op. If you return to the desk where you checked in, and follow the yellow line through the tunnel, you'll come to the hospital admissions office."

"What?" Helen shrieked, clutching Nancy to her chest. "Are you saying I have to leave her? But I didn't know!" Her voice was desperate, her eyes frantic. "I didn't prepare. I didn't bring her jammies...she can't sleep without her monkey...she won't understand," tears welled in her eyes. "Can I come back to be with her after surgery?"

"Mrs. Steffen, you needn't worry over that. It's easier for children if the parents stay away. We have excellent nurses; she'll get the best care. Riley is one of the premier children's hospitals in the country. You'll receive a call when to come and get her."

That night observers would have seen two poised, well-dressed women walking to their car. They wouldn't know the ladies were still hearing baby screams in their minds, and that when they got in the car they collapsed in each other's arms, hearts riven. It was the first of several long trips back to Goshen, an emptiness where little Nancy belonged.

* * * * *

This was their life now, and Walt thought it high time to move ahead and take on their future. They rented a house in west Goshen on Bashor Road as the first step in building their farm. This home, a few miles from Grandma Esther, had several acres, a cow shed, pigsty, and chicken house. They settled into a cozy ebb and flow, couched in the nests of the extended Phillip's family and the Yellow Creek Church community.

Earl and Esther's family was growing exponentially. With Rosemary and Erdene's marriages, there were soon cousins for Helen's three girls. During these middle years of Esther's life, she was the fulcrum around which her family revolved—and she thrived. She, with her daughters and their children, were often together, sewing, putting up fruit and vegetables, or playing with the children at Rogers Park. Esther was the go-to babysitter and baker of everything good.

The Yellow Creek community, with pious intent, held fast to its toe-the-line scruples; after all, right is right and wrong is wrong. With two Sunday services, prayer meeting, ladies aid, young-married class meetings, and council meetings, the couples—with few exceptions—believed, breathed, and moved with one accord. They fed the sick, straightened out the doubters, pledged their tithe, and prayed for missionaries to convert the heathen. They walked the walk of all good Brethren.

The Steffen family dynamic gentled into an idyllic, charmed life, the girls coddled and cossetted, especially by their daddy. Walt and Helen continued to be comfortable with benign laissez-faire parenting. Others may have observed socks with holes, shoes a size too big trailing barnyard debris, but if a few stitches were dropped in the woof and warp of the Steffens' lives, the parents didn't notice. Helen, preoccupied with the project of the day, allowed the girls to roam with few limits. They became scrappy and independent. This languorous inattention was interspersed with meteoric pandemonium when something went wrong. Then, anger and fear erupted in a spouting flume of screams, hair pulling, threats, and punishment; after which the flumes slowly and darkly emptied of force, receding to the accustomed harmony—though leaving everyone a bit buggered around the edges.

"Girls, come see the surprise Daddy brought home," Mommy called as Daddy unloaded calves from the car.

"Baby cows." Judy shouted.

"Count them, Jannie. How many calves do we have?" Helen asked.

"One, two, three, four, five, six baby cows."

"What color are they, Judy?"

"White and black."

"They're called Holsteins, registered Holsteins. The best cows you can get," Daddy said proudly. "You girls can each name one of the calves."

"I want to name the black one "Blackie"," Jannie said.

Little Nancy pointed to a calf: "Nae Ehie."

"That is sweet of you, Nancy. You named her after Elsie, the sick lady we visited today," Mommy stroked her spikey hair.

"Do we have to feed the chickens *and* the little cows?" Judy asked.

"I should say so. My girls are going to be farm girls," Daddy answered. "These calves will put food in your mouth."

"Girls, kiss Daddy good-night. It's bedtime. The baby calves want to go to sleep in their new home."

Later, Helen and Walt relaxed as he ate his warmed-over supper. "Today I was talking to Fred Jessup, one of the milk haulers. He's thinking of retiring next year, and will be selling his milk route. He just bought a new 1947 Ford truck with a good insulated bed."

"Walt, that would be perfect. In a year we can save a good down payment. I'm sure the truck is expensive. Do you know Fred? Will he want top dollar?"

"I like him, and I trust him. I told him today to give me first right of refusal."

"This is great news. I love the cute little calves you brought home."

"They're good stock, Helen. I'm thinking we should get a few more. In two years, they'll freshen, and the milk checks will pay off the milk truck. That's the plan anyway. How was your day?"

"Oh, the usual. We made cookies and took them to Chloe and Elsie from church. I tell you, those girls try to shame me. Janice was embarrassed that the cookies were kinda' overbaked. I told her you *like* burned cookies. She said, 'Well I like soft cookies and I think Chloe does too'."

Walt smiled tenderly, "You told her I *like* burned cookies? That's because only burned ones are left. That girl is a hoot. It's hard to believe she'll start school in the fall."

Helen laughed, "Her teacher will have a challenge. Tonight, I read them the chapter about Abraham and Isaac from the *Bible Story Book*. We're going to have to censor those stories, Walt. Judy was pulling her hair and teasing. Jannie fought back and yelled, 'If you don't quit, Mommy will take you to a mountain and chop off your head like Abraham did.' I guess she missed the end of the story. There's too much violence in some of those Bible stories. They're not true anyway."

"Careful you don't repeat that at church, Helen. That reminds me, I forgot to tell you what Judy said last week when Jannie spilled a glass of milk: 'you're bad, Jannie. You're going to burn in Hell'. Now who at church would say that to little kids?" Walt sputtered.

"I hate to say it, but some of those people believe in threatening kids with that. If we keep hearing things, I'm going to have to say something."

"You'll open a can of worms, Helen. Maybe when something like that comes up we should tell the girls there are different ways of thinking about some of the Bible stories. They like the *Little Black Sambo* story. I think it's good for them to hear about a Negro family."

"That's kind of violent too; the tigers turn in to butter."

"I see your point. The stories I like best are the *Uncle Arthur Bedtime Stories*. It teaches values to children. They suffer a consequence when they disobey. Did you ever think there would be so many quibbles in raising children?"

The next afternoon the girls were helping Mommy in the garden when she went into the privy. For an unknown reason, whoever built the privy nailed a stub of wood on the door which, when turned sideways, locked the door from the outside. The little girls thought it a great joke to lock their mother inside the privy and weren't convinced her increasingly loud and angry pleadings to open the door were to be taken seriously. What fun this was to hold Mommy hostage in the hot, stinky privy.

"Jannie, let's get our instruments and sing to her," Judy piped up. They ran into the kitchen ignoring her screams and threats: "Open this door NOW or you will be spanked within an inch of your life! Girls, I mean it. Open the door."

In the kitchen they set out the sugar and flour to reach their "band instruments": cymbal pan lids; a metal skillet and large spoon; and a slaw colander and spoon for Nancy. Always intent on developing their self-worth and pride of family, Helen wrote a song which the girls learned for one of their recent music projects. They proceeded to march around the privy, singing the family song, accompanied by the "band instruments":

We are the Phillips' triplets.
The hearts of Sarah, Esther,
Mommy lead our way.
We are tiny but tough
With all the right stuff.
On any old day we'll have our say:
One for all and all for one.
Go Jannie (Bang!)
Go Judy (Bang!)
Go Nancy (Bang!)

Such smart-stepping hijinks. Around and around the privy they went. Finally, the quiet from the privy was resounding, a greater impediment to fun than the screaming, which was more familiar. As with all children's games, eventually little ones weary. The first nagging doubts and thoughts about spanking took form. Plus, little Nancy was missing her nap and her Mommy. Jannie and Judy disappeared into the house.

"Come out, Mommy," Nancy begged, leaning against the privy door.

"I can't get out, Honey. Go in the house with Jannie and Judy. Climb on Mommy's bed and take your nap. Go ahead, Honey. Mommy will be okay."

Going into the kitchen, Janice and Judy spied the five-pound sacks of sugar and flour—immediately enticed to another activity. "Let's play baby doll with the bags. There's one for each of us." They were off and running—Mommy forgotten.

"I'm going to dress my dolly," Judy said, carrying the sugar into their bedroom.

"Me too," Jannie said. "Look, my panties just fit my baby. Her name is Betsy."

"My baby is Bonnie. I'm going to wrap her in a towel. Look, Nancy's asleep on Mommy's bed. We'd better go to the living room or we'll wake her."

"I'm putting this barrette on Betsy. Oops, I made a hole. It's not too big."

"You're dusty all over your face. I want powder too," Judy laughed, patting her hands in the spilled flour.

"Let's rock our babies in the living room," Jannie settled in the rocker, holding her baby to her shoulder.

"Bonnie has to go potty," Judy said. As she hurried to the kitchen she stumbled, dropping, and breaking the bag of sugar.

"You broke it," Jannie said. "All the poop is coming out," the girls laughed uproariously, then began realizing the mess they were making.

"We have to clean it up. I'll get a rag." Judy pushed a chair to the sink.

"We need a broom," Jannie said.

"Maybe we should take it outdoors and hide it, so Mommy doesn't see it," Judy whispered.

"Oh-oh, Daddy's home from work. He'll see it. Let's hide behind the couch."

"I'm home. Where is everyone?" Daddy called as he came in the back door. "What in the world...."

Of course, a tell-tale powdery trail led behind the couch. "Girls. Where's Mommy? You kids have made one heck of a mess." Daddy's good humor was rapidly going south. Their woeful demeanor was a give-away indication of disobedience.

"Mommy's in the privy. You go get her, Daddy," Judy suggested.

"Why is she in the privy?" Daddy asked, going out the back door as the two girls went out the front, thinking to hide in the bushes. A few minutes later they saw Mommy in the car, zooming out the driveway, spitting stones.

Daddy barreled out the front porch, yelling, "You girls get up here, NOW!" He grabbed the girls by the arms as they stumbled from behind the bushes, sitting them on the porch steps. His voice was shaking, "I can't believe you girls would treat Mommy like you did. Now listen to me: it's our job, yours and mine, to take care of her. She does so much for us. We can never do anything to make it harder for her. She has a bad foot and a bad hand. I never thought my girls would be unkind to Mommy, but you were today." Both girls were fully contrite, whimpering and blubbering their shame. "She's so angry with you she can't stand to be around you, and I don't blame her. Now we're going to clean this terrible mess you've made and then we'll see how well you two like being in the privy."

* * * * *

Esther relaxed in the warm bath. Tonight would be quite an affair. Her daughters were hosting a dinner for her fiftieth birthday at the West Goshen Church cabin. It would be a large group: her brothers and sisters; their Yellow Creek Sunday School Class; their Domino Group; and dear friends, Abe and Cleota Roth. As the twice-elected mayor of Goshen, Abe would bring status to the party and would likely have a short speech.

She dusted herself with talc and shimmied into a one-piece brassiere and corset, snapping all twenty hooks and eyes down the front, then tightening and tying the crisscrossed strings. Since the war ended, her daughters had updated to a bra and rubberized girdle, though in Esther's opinion, no proper lady left the house without a full whale-boned corset. She put on her new dress and string-up shoes, viewing herself with approval. She removed the metal clamps that crimped her gray hair in waves around her face, then coiled and pinned her hair in a French twist.

She looked in the mirror, smoothing out the wrinkles on her face—fifty years' worth. She felt so fortunate. She and Earl had molded the life that worked for them. They were devoted to each other and their enlarging family. Their home on Plymouth Avenue was sedate, orderly, and without drama. Conversations were in earth tones and tepid voice. Never one to speak of unseemly or private matters, when Erdene, about to deliver her first baby, had the temerity to ask how she would know she was in labor, Esther's response was curt: "You'll know." She choked the first time she used the word "pregnant", though new babies were frequently discussed.

Their property was immaculate and well-tended: flowers bloomed, the lawn stayed freshly mowed, and the garden flourished. Her days were predictable: on Monday she washed and starched clothes in the pump house out back, hanging items on the line to dry. Tuesday she ironed the dampened clothes in the prescribed order: collar, shoulders, sleeves, then around the bodice. Wednesday, she went to Ladies Aid or Women's Club. Thursday, she worked in the garden. Friday, she sewed and mended, and Saturday she went to town, bathed, washed her hair, and prepared Sunday dinner. She admitted being a gadabout, caught up in family and church activities, always arriving with something freshly baked.

Louise, a recent high school graduate with an active social life, was attractive and capable, bringing spirit to the house. She transcribed shorthand and typed sixty words-per-minute despite long lacquered fingernails. She wore bright red lipstick, molded plastic cups in her brassiere, short swinging skirts, and spike heels. She was the fashion maven of the family, cutting hair and giving Toni hair permanents. As with all Esther's daughters, she designed and sewed her own dresses. She and Helen had achieved local renown for giving "readings", memorizing, and acting out a long humorous or religious monologue which they presented before women's clubs and church groups. Esther was often invited, basking in the reflected glory of her talented daughters.

As the oldest Swihart daughter living in Goshen, Esther felt responsible to keep the large family intact, organizing summer picnics and the New Year's Eve oyster supper. These occasions were rambunctious and entertaining with state-fair-worthy food, a four-part harmony hymn sing, prayers, and the current fallen angel and black sheep warmly embraced. After Judd's death, Esther felt less burdened to measure up to her more conservative Dunkard brothers and sisters. She knew her family would celebrate her fiftieth birthday party with alacrity.

She went to the living room, shaking Earl who was lying on the couch, an ice bag on his forehead. "Daddy, it's time to get ready. I laid out your clothes. Is your headache better?"

"A little better. You look nice, Mother. Your new dress is just right. No one would ever guess you're fifty years old. If you look in the refrigerator, you'll find a corsage that will match your dress. I followed Louise's instructions," he smiled, patting her shoulder. "I'll have a hard time looking as good as you."

"Oh Daddy, now you're being silly," she flushed, smoothing her hair as she followed him into the bedroom.

* * * * *

"Jannie, we have to get you ready for first grade. We need to work on your colors and numbers. I don't want Mrs. Wetzel to think my child is lagging."

"Yea! I get to go to school," Jannie yelled, jumping on the chair to get the bag of school supplies.

"I'm going too," Judy piped up as the two girls tussled to pull items from the bag.

"You have to stay home. You're not old enough," Jannie grabbed the bag from her.

Never one to be left behind, tears pooled in Judy's eyes, "I always go with Jannie, Mommy. I'm going to school too."

"You'll go to school next year, Judy. I need you to stay home and be my helper. Jannie, you tell Mrs. Wetzel your name is Janice, not Jannie. We need to quit calling you a baby name. I wish I had taken the school supply list when I shopped at Newberry's on Saturday." She mumbled absentmindedly as she sorted through the bag: "I got colors; I forgot an eraser; I got one pencil instead of two; I'll have to paper-clip stationary together for a notebook; and I'll have to find a box for a pencil box." Her head lifted at knocking on the front door.

"Hi Betty, hi boys. Come in," she greeted the neighbors from across the road. She looked down at three-year-old Nancy, who was holding Betty's hand.

"Davie saw Nancy playing on the road, Helen. She was lying down, and the cars were swerving around her," Betty said, handing Nancy to her mother. "I declare, you can't take your eyes off them for a minute, can you?" Betty said, as though her apology was needed.

Helen scooped Nancy into her arms, "You're a naughty girl; how did you get out of the house?" she scolded.

"Mommy. 'top, 'top," Nancy wiggled. "You 'queezing me."

"Can you come in for a cookie and a cup of Postum? We're getting Janice ready to start first grade tomorrow. Somehow Nancy slipped out the door."

"Thanks, Helen. I'd better get back. I'm canning peaches today. Maybe when the kids get in school we can visit."

Helen closed the door after the neighbors. "How many times have I told you to stay away from the road?" she admonished, squatting down to shake Nancy. "Listen to me. You never, never go near the road. Do you hear me?" she yelled over Nancy's indignant screams. She clutched Nancy to her, ruffling her blond hair, "Oh Sweetie, I couldn't bear if anything happened to you. Now Nancy, stay beside Mommy. We're going to help Janice study the colors. You hold them up so she can say the color, then put it back in the box. Stop!" she yelled, grabbing two broken colors. "Nancy, you're driving me crazy. Now Jannie has to start school with broken crayons."

"Land sakes, now who can that be?" Helen jumped up again at persistent knocking at the door.

"Why Pastor Light, what a nice surprise. Come in. Sorry about the mess. We're getting Jannie ready for first grade. Can I make you a cup of Postum? Walt can't drink coffee, so I don't keep it around."

"Thanks Helen, that would be nice. Is Walt's ulcer still acting up?"

"Oh, it comes and goes, but he has to be careful what he eats."

"He's such a strong, muscular fellow; it's too bad his stomach is puny. I'll keep him in my prayers. I want to talk to you about the Chicago girls you brought to church this summer. They created a bit of a stir for some people."

"Tawana and LaShondra. They were a joy to have in our home. The girls loved them. We were sad when they went home."

"When you introduced them at church, you said they came as part of the Fresh Air Program. How did you learn about that?"

"My friend from the Goshen City Brethren Church told me. A group of ministers in Goshen got together with some Negro ministers from the slums of Chicago and brought a bus load of kids. They thought it would be good for inner-city children to spend time in the country, and for white country children to learn to know Negro children. Since there aren't Negroes in Goshen, we wanted our girls to know children who are different from them. It was a good experience for our family. Tawana and LaShondra say they want to come back next summer and stay a month. I hope they do."

"I'm glad we have people in our church who help us look at things in a new way. As you would expect, we've had some negative feedback. Because Negroes aren't legally allowed to stay in Goshen hotels, these people extend that prohibition to private homes. On the other hand, I've had two families who would like to have African children in their home next summer. Helen, I think if we handle this right, it could be a good growing experience for our church. I'm going to join the Goshen ministers' group. When spring comes, maybe we can have a meeting where you tell your experience. I may want to do a sermon," he said thoughtfully. "What do you think, Helen?"

"That would be great. I'll do whatever I can to help."

"Thanks for the Postum. I'll be in touch. Bye girls. I hope your first day of school goes well, Janice," he said, going out the door.

Helen grinned, pumping her arm, "Yes!" she said, elated.

* * * * *

"Come, Judy and Nancy. As soon as Janice gets home from school we're going to take Daddy to pick up the new milk truck." Helen was suffused with pride: Walt was realizing his dream to own a milk route and start his own business. "Do you have the checkbook?" she asked as they all piled into the car. For days, the little girls had sensed the family excitement over the purchase of the red truck with the big-box insulated bed on the back.

Helen wrote a check while Walt shook hands with Fred Jessup. "Who wants to ride home in the back of the new truck?" Daddy asked, his smile near to filling his face.

"Me, Me, Me," the little girls lifted their arms. This truck would become the second family "car" with the children riding in the big bed, everyone oblivious to the danger of steel ten-gallon milk cans as projectiles in the event of an accident or roll-over. Daddy lifted each girl atop a milk can. "Have fun," he yelled as he closed and clamped the lock on the big door.

"Oh-h-h," the girls caught their breath tremulously when they were penned in the pitch-dark enclosure. Startled and afraid, little Nancy screamed.

"Don't cry, Honey. Reach out and find my hand. I'll take care of you. Judy, find my other hand. Let's sing a song and we won't be afraid." Janice, the six-year-old caretaker started singing, "Jesus loves me, this I know". Though the little voices were soon drowned out by clanking cans knocking together, they bravely sang until the truck stopped at home and Daddy opened the big door. Relieved, they slid off the milk cans and jumped into Daddy's arms.

"Was it fun?" he asked. Still shaking, Nancy ran to Mommy with a fresh rush of tears. "I skeered," she shuddered.

"It was too dark and noisy," Judy complained.

"It was okay," Janice said halfheartedly, with a long face.

The girls never missed a chance to ride in the front with their Daddy, watching him carry the one hundred-pound cans, usually one in each hand. While riding the route, they tuned in to talk radio, Daddy listening to the girl's ideas as if they were the smartest bureaucrats in Washington. Not only was their opinion important, he wanted them to think logically and reason carefully. His affection and pride was apparent as he introduced them to the farm customers and employees at the milk condensary: "This is my little Jannie. She's my good helper."

The best part of going with Daddy on the milk route was stopping at the South Side Soda Shop, being warmly greeted by Junior, and hopping on a stool at the soda fountain. Nothing said love like shooting the breeze with Daddy and Junior, while lapping up a butterscotch sundae.

The trips the girls took with Mommy to Riley Hospital in Indianapolis became part of the thread of normalcy. Everyone was tense and cranky, uncertain what would happen to Nancy, who, upon seeing certain landmarks, would realize the destination and cry for the duration of the trip—a mewling fretfulness as she reached for her mother: "Mommy... Mommy... Mommy... home... Mommy." Silent tears trailed down Helen's cheeks, her hand leaving the steering wheel to grasp Nancy's little hand.

"Pretty soon we can get out of the car, Nancy. Honey, sit by Janice. She'll tell you the *Yertle the Turtle* story. Show her the pictures, Janice."

"Mommy... Mommy... go home." It was a long, tough day. They waited two hours to see Dr. Amos. When he examined Nancy's mouth, he found what Helen suspected: the last surgery had not completely closed the roof of her mouth.

"Mrs. Steffen, I'm feeling a sizeable fistula on her palate. I hoped it would have healed better. We need to take her to surgery as soon as possible. We'll have to do a bone graft this time."

Helen's voice shook as she battled to hold her screaming daughter, "She'll be home by Christmas, won't she?"

"No, this will be considerably more extensive. We'll do it in two stages, leaving the stitches in longer this time."

Helen hugged her daughter. This she hadn't expected. She and Walt had prepared this time: they had packed a small bag with Nancy's pajamas, blanket, and monkey. They had included her favorite books and a treat for each day. It had not occurred to them she would be gone a month, that she wouldn't be home for Christmas.

Every time Helen left Nancy at the hospital, she thought she would die—two frantic broken hearts, a cataclysm of desperate pain. What could she say or do to help a little one who couldn't understand, who only knew separation and loss? She left the older girls with a nurse, and took

Nancy to Riley to the large, functional ward with white iron cribs. A nurse in a long, starched dress met her, pulling frantic Nancy from her arms. On this day, the esthetic benefit of surgery was not worth the gouging pain.

The days of Nancy's homecomings were joyful—the rightness of everyone together again. Janice and Judy made little gifts. They hung on her and babied her. She was the focus of their play. Grandparents and cousins all came to welcome her. But Nancy was withdrawn, skittish, and shy of people. Her little mind reverted to strangers in a fearsome place, pain, bandages, and people covered in white staring down into her crib—things a little tyke doesn't forget.

CHAPTER 42

Byler Farm

America burst its britches after WWII. By 1947 the men were home and the economy was booming. There was penicillin and streptomycin. Esther got new kitchen cabinets with doors, plastic covered chairs and table, and a toaster. Now she had a proper kitchen. There were babies, babies, and more babies as families were united. Helen stretched her pregnant abdomen over the shelves as she reached for new choices in the grocery store: boxed cereal called Cheerios, bananas shipped from the tropics, and frozen orange juice from Florida. Goshen had daily mail delivery, a grocery truck with bread and milk, and women's dancing legs smoothed by seamed nylon hose.

An upsurge of religion sent families to church in record numbers. Required to run the daily milk route, yet committed to his spiritual growth, when Walt passed Yellow Creek Church on Sunday, he took off his milk apron and slid into the last pew, attentive to the sermon, before finishing the route. People not only prayed together, they shared the proud certainty that the good old U.S.A. was the greatest country on earth; enough that they supported President Truman in funding the Marshall Plan to rebuild Japan and Europe and send troops to keep the peace on the Korean Peninsula. Family, country, and character were the bywords of Goshen in the 1950's.

The Steffens were a typical upwardly mobile young family. They were renting the prosperous eighty-acre Byler farm. The big brick house, which was down a long lane, had five bedrooms and indoor plumbing. Here they would start their farming enterprise with the eight heifers who had calved and were giving milk. Helen proudly carried on the tradition of her mother and grandmother: putting food on the table, tending the garden, canning, butchering, and sewing clothes for the family. She supervised the jobs of seven-year-old Janice, six-year-old Judy, and four-year-old Nancy: shaking straw for bedding the cows, feeding baby calves, slopping pigs, feeding chickens, and after dark, bringing in the cows. She didn't think about a work ethic, it was just what needed to be done.

For Helen, this was the idyllic life she dreamed for her family. They could look out their window across the field and see the farm her sister Rosemary shared with her husband and two young daughters. Less than a mile away was Grandma Esther's house. If a grandma was meant to spoil, Esther did her best, especially in the home-made cookie department. All the sisters lived close, a bevy of cousins for the Steffen girls to play with.

Esther's daughters' families were part of the Yellow Creek Church community. The same passel of children learned the Bible stories and misbehaved in Sunday School. The underlying sense being that love was constant and unconditional in the cocoon of family and church.

* * * * *

"How was your day, Pop?" Esther asked, emptying his lunch bucket from work.

"Same old thing. My feet get so tired from standing all day."

"Sit down, Daddy. I'll rub them for you," Esther removed his socks and massaged his feet.

"Walt had Janice on the route with him. They sure give those girls a lot of leeway. Walt gave her two milk samples and let her strut through the plant to the lab. Of course, Dorothy and the girls made over her—'such a good helper' and all. Esther, what if she had dropped those samples or got lost in the plant?"

"I know Earl. Walt and Helen are loose with the discipline," she frowned as she rubbed lotion on his feet.

"That sure feels good, Mother. You are the best at relieving foot pain. One thing about Walt and Helen: those girls know how to work. I sure hope Walt gets a boy this time around. He's going to need real help."

"Helen surprises me sometimes. Usually the girls get by with murder, but the other day she was braiding Nancy's hair. Land sakes alive, she can make the prettiest French braids with her crippled hand and stiff fingers. Helen yelled at Nancy for calling her "Mom". Neither can they say swear words: shut up, gosh, darn, and golly. I almost laughed! Earl, I bet my eye tooth those girls won't swear or call Helen "Mom"."

"Is Judy still washing out her sheets?" Earl asked.

"Oh yes. With a little effort, Helen could train her to quit wetting the bed. After all, she's in school now. But she punishes her every morning by making her wash her sheet in a wash tub and hang it over the back fence, all the while throttling her with guilt. You know that little girl can't get the sheet clean. Her bed must reek."

"Thank you, Mother. My feet feel better. How's your bursitis today?"

"Oh, it's kicking up. That's what I get for ironing all those tablecloths from Louise's wedding. The wedding was a lot of work, but it sure was nice. My goodness, all those pews you moved to make a center aisle. I know things have been tight, but I'm glad we didn't scrimp on any of the girls' weddings. We went out on a limb with that cake; I've never seen anything so elaborate and fancy. I sure was glad when they got it cut and on the plates," she chuckled.

"Louise chose well with Harley; they'll be happy," Earl's voice evidenced his fondness for his youngest daughter.

"They'll be home from their honeymoon in two days. I'm guessing people will show up for the belling on Friday night. We need to get some favors. What should I get?"

"Everyone always likes ice cream in the paper cups. Boy, if you'd serve your molasses cookies, everyone would think they hit the jackpot."

"That's what I'll do then. We'll need a double recipe". Her eyes fell tenderly on Earl, "It seems pretty quiet around here, doesn't it?" She stood, kissing his cheek before washing her hands, "Do you suppose we'll get lonely, just the two of us?" she teased.

"Mother, I'll never be lonely when you're around," Earl said, tying his shoes. Thus, they nestled in the comfort of quiet order and unspoken wonderings, the familiarity of sameness—a life lived in the back seat.

* * * * *

"It's time. I'm taking her to the hospital," Walt phoned Esther, his voice tight with suppressed concern.

"I need to watch the girls. Walt's taking Helen to the hospital," Esther scurried to the bedroom. "Let's see, I'd better take my overnight case. I might need my medicine. Earl, I made that tuna casserole for you—just heat it. Open a jar of peaches to go with it. The cookie jar is full. Dear God, I hope this baby is okay. They've hired Gladys, the baby helper, but I don't know when she'll come. I won't leave you alone too long."

The next morning when Walt came home, the three girls bombarded him with questions. "We have a new baby sister," his voice was tender with pride. "Her name is Susan. She has lots of dark hair. Judy, I'll bet you can put one of your barrettes in it. You girls will be Mommy's helpers." He turned to Esther, "Everything went like clockwork. Helen will be in the hospital three or four days. Doc says we should give her a rest 'cause she won't rest after she gets home. I'll take Nancy with me on the route today." His face glowed, "Four beautiful little girls, Esther. I'm a lucky man."

She handed him a plate of eggs, "I'm thankful everything went well. Janice, Judy, get your wraps on. It's a long walk down the lane. You can't miss the bus this morning."

"Girls, give Grandma a hug and thank her for spending the night with you. We appreciate all your help, Grandma. We couldn't get along without you."

"We had fun, didn't we girls? I'll bring a tuna casserole for your supper and check in to see what you need for tomorrow."

Baby Susan came home bringing springtime. She was an alert, content little tyke who thrived on the chaotic over-attention of the Steffen household. Gladys, a distant aunt, was used by the Swihart family as a live-in nursemaid when babies were born. She was inundated with help from the three girls, all vying to care for Susan.

Janice and Judy were complaining about Gladys in their upstairs bedroom as they prepared for bed. "Hah, Hah. I have a secret," Janice purred in a smart aleck voice.

"You do not. Nobody in our family is allowed to have secrets," Judy snooted smugly. Janice's voice turned to a stealthy whisper, "Truly I have a secret. I can't tell you 'cause you'd tattle to Mommy."

"I wouldn't either. I never tattle on you, Jannie." Becoming convinced Janice really had a secret, it was imperative that Judy be in the know.

"You *promise* not to tell? I could get in big trouble."

"I promise—cross my fingers, hope to die," Judy held up crossed fingers. Janice ran to her dresser, reached under her clothes and brought out two unopened packs of Beeman's gum. Judy's eyes widened—an amazing secret. This was real loot.

"WOW! Where did you get that?"

"I got it out of Gladys's suitcase. You can't tell, Judy. You promised."

"You rummaged in her suitcase? You'll get a spankin' for sure."

"No, she'll just think she lost it. I'll share a stick with you. We can taste a little of it tonight and leave it on the bedpost so it's still fresh in the morning. We can't let Mommy see us chewing," Janice said as she tore open the pack of gum.

"Just a minute, I have to pee," Judy jumped out of bed, took off her panties, and squatting over the floor register, proceeded to pee.

Janice was aghast, "What are you doing?" she sucked in a yelp.

Done now, Judy shook her bootie and put on her panties. "What's the problem?" she asked nonchalantly. "It's a hole in the floor. You stole. I just peed in the register."

Janice looked down the black iron grate, "But Judy, it will leak on the living room ceiling." She shook her head and scrunched her nose, "Plus, it stinks."

"Oh, it doesn't smell that bad. Besides, I don't pee in the register every time—only when I don't want to go downstairs."

"Janice, Judy. You get down here. NOW!" Mommy was yelling from the bottom of the stairway. Her voice was spitting fire. "And bring the gum you took out of Gladys' suitcase."

Two pair of eyes flared with fear. Janice looked at the gum in her hands, then frantically searched for a hiding place.

"She knows you took it. We're in big trouble," Judy whispered.

"We don't have any gum," Janice said, and with a long face she dropped the two packs down the register. "If you snitch, I'll tell her you pee in the register, and you'll be in more trouble than me. Let's go now," she grabbed Judy's arm as they walked toward the stairs. "Get that guilty look off your face."

Many might have said the Steffen household was run like a poorly greased machine. They went without what many considered essential. Yes, they were poor, but what people couldn't see was how they allocated money: paying cash for the new Allis Chalmers tractor bought after moving to Byler's farm. Truth be known, the shabbiness was really an unspoken belief in a life of simplicity and lack of pretension. Had people known their income was nearly nine thousand dollars, significantly greater than the average Goshen family, they would have been astounded.

Walt was up at four o'clock, milking the ten cows by hand. This was his time to think and plan: how could their money be budgeted so they could buy a farm? Helen was up with the baby at six o'clock, and when Walt came in at six thirty, his warm breakfast was ready—unless she got side-tracked by the dress she was sewing or the Christmas cards she was making. At seven o'clock, Walt left on the milk route. For Helen and the girls, summers were spent working outdoors: tending the big garden, pulling weeds out of corn fields, mowing the hilly yard with a push mower, canning produce from the garden, and bringing the cows from the pasture in the evening. A lack of strict supervision allowed work to mingle with exploration.

The highlight of the day was at noon when Walt got home from the milk route. Though he had lifted thousands of pounds of milk that morning, he still had a jocular air and a spring in his step. It was obvious he adored his ditzy little wife as he bounded in the kitchen door with lusty eagerness.

"Where's my little brunette?" he called, rushing to the sink where Helen was peeling potatoes, encircling her in his arms and nuzzling her neck. "Do you need a little break, Mommy?" he teased as he glided her into the bathroom and closed the door.

Seeing Daddy come home, Janice and Judy came in from the field; they *were* ready for a break. The girls were lean and scrawny. Now they were hungry.

"Where's Daddy?" Janice asked.

"Daddy's kissing Mommy in the bathroom," Nancy said, concentrating on her library book.

Judy was always the hungriest, "Is dinner ready?"

"She's working on it. I stemmed the beans," Nancy said as Helen languorously sidled out of the bathroom, flushed and nattering, straightening her dress and finger-combing her hair.

"Hey Jannie," Walt said with hearty cheerfulness, "The cornfield looks good." Helen went back to the potatoes, lowering her voice, "Walt, you're going to have to stop that. The girls are getting to an age...."

"Aw Sweetie, what would I think about all morning if I couldn't come home and snuggle with my little brunette?"

No matter how busy the family, most meals were leisurely and enjoyable. Food was home grown, simple, and plentiful, often covered with gravy. They took turns saying the prayer, as this was a desired assignment. The one who prayed "had the floor", so each girl got to show off a bit, requesting divine guidance for school homework, friends, elderly and sick, the cat with no name...ad infinitum.

Occasionally a spark was lit during a meal—with a leaden pall or even fireworks. In some ways, Helen was the go-getter of the two. Sometimes she couldn't seem to stop goading: "Do you think you should call on some new milk customers tonight?" she asked in an artificially chipper voice.

"No, I'm not going to go out and hit on possible milk customers tonight," Walt answered, his dander striking a quick smolder.

"If it would help, I could ride along. Yes, I'll go with you. Mother can watch the girls."

Walt grimaced, gritting his teeth—his voice a deadly monotone. "Helen, I got up at four o'clock to milk. As soon as you get off my case, I'll go out in the field and mow clover. Just before dark I'll come in and relax a few minutes before going to bed. I'll do the same thing tomorrow. So no, I'm not going to call on farmers tonight, and no, it wouldn't help if you toddled after me to sweet talk a potential customer."

"I know when you bought the route, Fred Jessup said he went out every couple of weeks to visit with farmers to see if someone was unhappy and ready to switch milk companies."

"Well good for Fred Jessup," his voice was scathing as he left the table and stomped out of the house. Walt could brood for days over such a conversation. His dark mood lowered a pall over all attempts by the rest of the family to tease, joke, or tell a funny story. The truth was, he needed

Helen to nudge him to "schmooze" with farmers. He knew it and she knew it. After a few days, she presented his favorite meal, a beautiful cornbread, served with maple syrup and tomato gravy—her gesture an eloquent unspoken apology. A few days later he'd make the rounds to farmers.

"Who cut holes in my hat?" Walt yelled. "Girls, get out here." He was livid, grabbing the girls as they shied back, fearful of a spanking. Walt shoved his hat in their faces. His old Sunday fedora, relegated to a work hat, had diamond-shaped holes cut all over the crown of the hat.

"Which one of you did this?" he hollered.

"Not me," Judy shook her head.

"I didn't do it, Daddy," seven-year-old Nancy promised. "I don't cut good."

Generally obedient, Janice knew she shouldn't be charged, "It wasn't me, Daddy. I didn't know where your hat was."

"Someone cut holes in my hat. I'm going to find out who did it," he threatened. The girls fell over themselves, chiming as one: "It wasn't me;" "I didn't do it;" "I'm telling the truth;" "I never touched your hat;" each was certain the other two were guilty.

At the end of his patience, Walt grabbed Nancy by the shoulder and whacked her hard, three times on her bottom. "There, I guess you learned a lesson—no more cutting holes in anything." His anger spent, he dropped Nancy to the grass and stomped into the house.

"Walt, I think you spanked the wrong girl," Helen said, gathering up the wailing child who still sputtered her innocence. "Nancy couldn't have cut holes that well."

"Oh, I know she didn't," Walt acknowledged breezily. "I cut the holes myself to make air vents. I taught them a lesson in case they think about doing something like that," he said going out the kitchen door.

"Walt Steffen, I'd like to kick your butt to Goshen and back," Helen mumbled under her breath as Walt walked toward the barn.

Nancy's bawling stopped in its tracks; "you said a bad word, Mommy," she said.

* * * * *

Walt seemed tough and invincible so it was shocking when Doc Young told him he had Yellow Jaundice and would need to quarantine. Accustomed to glitches in her life, Helen cut to the chase, "Jaundice is your liver, isn't it? Will you get better? That's all that counts."

Fearful of permanent liver damage, Walt was isolated upstairs, on bedrest for several weeks. Everyone stepped up: Esther and Helen did the morning chores. Esther milked and Helen washed udders and fed animals. Sam Steffen milked in the evening with the girls helping. They soon learned to keep a distance from Sam who, with great accuracy, spit his stream of tobacco juice at their toes.

It was a long two months until Walt slowly resumed the farm work, then the milk route. Fortunately, there was no long-term liver damage. Life-threatening illness can be a great teacher. Walt had rarely been sick, even with colds or flu. Still a young man, he had taken for granted his strong, healthy body. He quickly realized the family business and income was solely dependent on his well-being. A healthy lifestyle became important, he trained a back-up driver for the milk route, and was especially cautious around farm machinery. The illness reinforced his value in family, not things.

CHAPTER 43

Move to New Paris

"Look at this: All three of you got a C. There's no reason for anyone in this family to get a C on their report card. You aren't working to your potential. This is the *worst* time to let your grades drop—before moving to a new school. Your new teachers will think you're dumb as bricks."

This was Mother's memorized-by-heart tirade at report card time. Likely her daughters weren't the prodigies she convinced herself they were. Grades were huge in the Steffen house: for Mother, because she always got good grades, and for Daddy, because he regretted his limited schooling. Unless the girls got all A's, they weren't working to their potential. And if any daughter was marked "needs improvement" in Citizenship, it indicated gross misbehavior, warranting a meeting with the teacher to assure it wouldn't happen twice—and it didn't.

Even the C's on report cards couldn't stifle Walt and Helen's enthusiasm when they took Earl and Esther to see the farm where they were moving. It was five miles south in the country outside the little town of New Paris. They had made a hefty down payment on the twenty-four thousand dollar property. The one hundred fifty acres couldn't have been more beautiful: the land was flat and gently rolling with a meandering creek flowing the length of the farm through a woodland of oak, maple, and poplar trees.

Walt was giddy with joy. "The house and barn are over seventy-five years old. It's on a dirt road so it'll be dusty, but there shouldn't be much traffic." Walt's pride as they entered the big red barn was evident, "Look at the hewn timbers in this barn, Earl. We have nice big hay mows and a grain bin on this top level, then the milking stable and loafing shed are on the lower level. There's a nice big calf barn down in the barn yard. The creek will be nice for fishing and ice skating. Grandma, there couldn't be a better place to raise kids. Come along. Look at the storage shed and corn crib—a place for my new tractor. It's perfectly set up for a big farm operation."

The large wood frame home was shaded by seventy-five-year-old maple trees lining the driveway. It looked neglected: paint was peeling and the porch steps around two sides of the house were sagging. Her enthusiasm undampened, Helen admitted, "The house isn't nearly as nice as the farm buildings. It will need attention. They just recently put in electricity for a hand pump to bring in running water. The kitchen isn't much." Esther saw the cracked linoleum and lack of kitchen cabinets and appliances, wondering how a family could live here. The girls raced around the vacant house, their voices echoing in the cold emptiness.

"Where's the bathroom, Mommy?" Nancy asked, opening the only closet door.

"We won't have one for a while. We'll have to get used to a privy again."

Even little girls who were country bumpkins could be spoiled by the finer things. "I think we should stay where we are. I like our nice house with a kitchen and bathroom," Judy said, leading the group upstairs.

"Do we get to choose a room?" Janice asked, checking out the three upstairs bedrooms.

"You'll all have to sleep together in this room. There's no heat in the upstairs except what comes through this register from downstairs. Eventually we'll have to get a new furnace. At least it'll soon be summer."

Esther walked through the house with Helen thinking of curtains she would sew to bring some class to this old farmhouse. She noted the gray coating on the flower-splashed wallpaper. "Helen, you go to Stiver's Hardware and get wall paper dough. The two of us can have this wall paper cleaned in a few days. Obviously, the previous owners never did spring cleaning. Daddy and I are so proud of you and Walt. Here you are, only thirty-three years old and you're buying a large farm. It's amazing what you've accomplished."

Earl and Esther's motor mouths were going sixty per on the way home. "What do you think, Daddy? Did they bite off too much? Can you imagine owing someone nearly twenty-thousand dollars? What if there's another depression like in '29?" she worried.

"No, I'd never put myself in debt like that—too dangerous. I have to say, if anyone can do it, Walt and Helen can."

"Just look where they've come in these few years: Helen told me the milk route is paid off; they have a new tractor that will speed through those fields; and Walt already bought some second-hand implements."

"They're probably going to have to borrow more money to get electric milkers to milk sixteen cows. That's what they'll have fresh by fall, Walt says. Now they call them milking parlors. Walt said he'll sell Grade A milk—good money there," he knew from working at the milk condensary.

"The house is barely livable," Esther despaired. "Even the girls said they want to stay at the Byler house," she became silent, deep in thought.

"You know what the difference is, Daddy? I walked through that house and saw all that was missing. Helen sees possibilities, what it can become. Maybe you and I should start to look at things differently, at potential, not just what can go wrong." Her voice became tremulous, her eyes misted, "Wouldn't it be nice to have a little place in the country with a few acres. Earl, you could get a few white-faced Herefords like we had when we were first married. Remember how we enjoyed them and the little calves? We could get enough chickens to keep us in eggs. Oh Daddy, do you think it would be possible?" she asked wistfully, knowing whatever she asked, Earl would jump through hoops to give to her.

The move to the Weaver farm was when Helen started losing control; that is, if she ever had it or wanted it. What bliss for children: finding worms; fishing with bamboo poles; picnics in the woods; swimming in the cold creek; the birth of baby calves; snakes; sledding down the barn hill; snapping turtles; mice in the grain bin; making a tree house; or building a winter igloo. The girls were only limited by their imagination as there was little supervision and few rules, rare punishment, and little concern about dirt. Helen didn't see herself as negligent so much as instilling her belief that children were wise and could make their own fun. They were a few miles from New Paris, a town of less than eight hundred people with a blinking red light at the main intersection. Being remote, the sisters were a fraternity of three, with four-year-old Susan trying to keep up. They were alternately harmonious or fractious, always dancing around the edge of chaos.

"You girls watch Susan," Helen called as she started the half mile walk to the elderly neighbor's farmhouse. "I'm going to help Mrs. Lantzer wash windows. I'll be back by dinner time. Don't let Susan get near the road. Janice you're in charge."

"Bye Mother," Janice waved.

"Okay Steve. We need to remove this tire. It's gone flat." They struggled with the wheel on the Radio Flyer wagon atop the work bench.

"I think I need a wrench to get it off, Mike. Do you think it's too rusty?"

"Boy, it's on good," Steve grunted.

"Let's both pull on it." They both fell back as the screw broke loose.

"Good job, Steve. Now we need to find where the air is leaking and put a glue patch on it." Mike put water in a bucket and submerged the "faulty" wheel.

"There it is, Steve. Do you see the bubbles?"

"Yeah, that's quite a leak. Let's dry this off before I patch it."

"Yep, that looks good. That patch should last."

"We need to screw it back on the wagon."

Mike yelled, "Office girl, come here." Judy got up from her table where she was putting figures in a ledger, and walked to Janice and Nancy who were reattaching the wheel to the wagon.

"What's your name?"

"Pamela Sue," Judy answered. She always wanted to be Pamela Sue and do the girlie work while Janice and Nancy, being more tomboyish, pretended to be male workers and were mechanics, preachers, basketball players, or coaches.

"Pamela Sue, I need you to write up a bill for Cliff Hostetler. Charge him five dollars for fixing this tire," Mike said.

"Okay," Pamela Sue agreed, "but if your prices are so expensive, you're going to lose all your customers. When we're done playing garage can we play nurse? I found a great nurse cap. It's the white paper that holds the JELL-O powder inside the JELL-O box. I have a new invention to give shots. It's really good and it won't hurt—well, not much. I have pills and everything. It'll be like a regular doctor's office."

"Judy, pull me," Susan called, climbing into the wagon.

"It's my turn to choose," Nancy hollered. "You girls always get to pick. I want to play church and I'm the preacher. I'm going to have a revival meeting with an altar call like Rev. Light."

"Nancy, you just want to say hell and damnation," Judy whispered the words. "Mommy said those are bad words. We can't say them," Judy, the rule keeper, said smugly.

"Only preachers are allowed and I'm the preacher. We'll have a baptism too."

"I bapist, I bapist," four-year-old Susan begged, jumping out of the wagon.

"Okay Susie, you're old enough to go forward," Nancy agreed.

Judy squatted down to Susie, "Aren't you afraid to be dunked under water? You have to be dunked three times when you're baptized."

Susie's face fell. She wasn't so sure about this.

Janice, being more knowledgeable about spiritual matters said, "When you go forward to the altar, you have to repent your sins. Then you're saved by the blood and Jesus gives you rest. I think Susie's too young to be a sinner. She doesn't get drunk or gossip or curse. Adultery means you have to be an adult. If Jesus gives her rest, she could probably get a nap out of it."

Judy put her arms around Susie, "You don't want any of that bloody stuff, do you Susie? I think I'll stay in the church nursery with Susie when you all go forward."

"No! I repented for all of you. Now you have to repent when I'm preacher." Nancy stood, hands on her hips, turning to see Daddy's milk truck turning into the driveway. "No fair. You took all this time arguing with me and now Daddy's home and he'll put us to work. I'm not going to play garage or school or nurse anymore," she said, stomping to the truck to complain to Daddy.

Sauntering toward his daughters, Daddy called, "You girls sure made Nancy unhappy. What's Mommy doing? Judy, can you rustle up some lunch for us? I'm hungry."

They all went in the house, satisfied to be in the circle of their daddy. They looked in the refrigerator. "We're in luck, bacon. I hope Mommy isn't saving it for something. Judy, you fry it up. Nancy, you toast bread and set the table. Susie, you help me check the sweet corn, and Janice, you cut lettuce and slice tomatoes from the garden. I wonder when Mommy will be home," he muttered.

Dinner, as with most meals, was noisy. "I stopped at Pletcher's Sinclair Station to get gas on my way home. Johnnie was telling me about a kid who came in yesterday and stole soda and candy. Johnnie thought he was ten, about your age, Janice. The kid kicked Johnnie, told him to 'take a hike—no big deal, he only took soda and candy'. So girls, what do you think? It happened right here in New Paris."

A cacophony of voices, each with an opinion: "he kicked Johnnie," Nancy called out; "stealing is against the law and he sassed," Judy yelled; "he bad boy," Susie said; Janice thought for a minute, "you shouldn't steal, even if it's something little. Never talk back to an adult."

"You girls are very smart," Daddy nodded thoughtfully. "I can see you'd never do something like that. Nancy, you're right, Johnnie probably would have let him off if the kid hadn't fought back. Instead he called the police. Now the kid is in trouble. Judy and Janice are right about being sassy. You girls will be going to school soon. No matter what happens, you *never* talk back or get smart-mouthed to your teacher or any adult—it's 'Yes Sir, No mam'. If you think an adult is unfair, you tell Mommy and Daddy. Now Susie, you say he's a bad boy. Maybe so, but most bad boys are good kids who need someone to teach them. That's why we tell you girls to be friendly to them; they need friends. Janice, you're right, stealing is wrong, whether it's a soda or something big, like a car or money. Now do you all understand what I'm saying? In this family everyone does what is right and what is kind. Steffens never steal. Are we on it?" he asked, to solemn nods all around.

Daddy jumped up, "Now let's get busy. Janice, you're going in the field with me today. You're old enough to learn to drive the tractor. Go get a hat and long sleeves."

"Yea-a-a." Janice jumped up screaming. This was her dream.

"Judy, you make Mommy a nice sandwich and wrap it up. Put three pieces of bacon on it. Then you and Susie gather eggs and feed chickens. Put the eggs to soak so Mommy can clean them before the egg man comes tomorrow. She'll be home soon 'cause she has to take Nancy to Elkhart to the dentist. Get cleaned up and change your clothes, Nancy."

Eight-year-old Nancy's body wilted, her eyes on alert. Her day was ruined.

"Come here, Sweetie. Let me hold you. It won't be bad this time," his calloused hands were tender. "He's not going to pull teeth or put in wires. It's just a checkup, Mommy said. It shouldn't hurt this time."

Janice was sitting in front of Daddy on the tractor seat. "Do you think you're ready for this? It's a big responsibility, Janice. I'm not going to let you drive alone till I'm sure you're ready."

"Yes, I'm ready. You just have to show me what to do. Mommy says I'm a good learner."

"Yes, you are, but tractors and farm equipment can be dangerous. The most important thing is for you to be safe. If ever you're not sure if something is safe, stop the tractor. Nothing is worth the tractor rolling over on you."

"Are you trying to scare me?" Janice laughed.

"It's probably good if you're a little scared. Now you put your hands on the steering wheel and see how it feels when I turn. After a while, I'll let you drive and I'll watch. See, in a farm family everyone has to work. I think fieldwork can be your contribution. This will help pay for your college, Janice. Mommy and I have to start now to think about paying for college for all four of you. You girls will be somebody important. I don't really see Judy driving tractor. She'll probably milk cows. She's not as mechanical or outdoorsy as you. One thing is sure though, she'll be a good cook."

The afternoon wore on with Janice disking the field. "You can see that driving a tractor gets boring. I've known men who fell asleep driving; I've come close myself. The most important thing is to keep your focus. Something could happen at any time: you go over a bee's nest; you hit a big rock; or your disc gets caught on the fence. We'll go over all that. What it boils down to, Janice, is I'm not going to be with you, and I need to trust you to make the right decisions. You know I trust you to be kind to people. I trust you to tell the truth. I trust you not to steal, like that kid at Pletcher's gas station. In most things, you've proved you're trustworthy.

Now you're going to have to prove to me you can be trusted to drive the tractor and do the farm work," he ruffled her hair.

"I need lots of practice. I'll focus and be careful, but pretty soon you'll be able to trust me with the farm work."

It was a never-ending challenge for Helen to manage the domestic side of the family; something she hammered away at every day, but never felt like she pounded in the last nail. She made charts of rotating job assignments that got lost or forgotten after a few weeks. Sporadically, Walt or Helen would fly into a rage, using words like pig sty and living with maggots, launching an onslaught of scouring, mopping, vacuuming, and cleaning that became more apathetic as the day progressed. Everywhere she looked in the house, something needed to be done. But if she had to choose between nice kitchen cupboards and appliances, or piano and music lessons for the girls, well that explained their used and discarded kitchen cabinets, and the stove with one burner that didn't light. Adding red barn paint to old paint found in a closet, was *her* silly mistake that caused everyone to raise their eyebrows when they walked into the garish pink kitchen where there were always fresh garden flowers on the table.

The thing was, she liked what was lovely. Her big heart was captured by beauty and culture, though she didn't have a sophisticated eye, and the word "culture" wasn't in her vocabulary. It's as if she knew they were backcountry, and day in and day out she struggled to put a shine on them. She looked for ways to expose her family to the greater world.

Halloween was a big holiday in New Paris. Each girl went with friends to trick or treat, soaping windows if no one answered the door. The evening ended with a parade of kids in costume and a talent show at the high school gym. Helen determined the girls should honor the crowd by singing a Negro lullaby: "Sleep Kentucky Babe".

"But Mommy, we're not good singers," Judy spoke truthfully.

"Of course you are. Mrs. Reynolds is going to play the piano for you. I got the music from her. The words are sweet. It's what Negro people sing to put their babies to sleep. We'll practice till you get it."

"We're not Negroes. It won't look right," Janice stated the obvious, wanting no part of this.

"I have a plan for that. We'll burn cork till it's sooty, and make your faces black. Bright lipstick will make big red lips. You'll wear bandannas on your head and rock a doll while you sing. I have good ideas for outfits."

Now the girls were warming to the idea. "I'll put the soot on our faces," Janice volunteered.

"Lipstick, we're wearing lipstick? I get to put the lipstick on everyone," said Judy, the make-up girl.

The night of the talent show brought all of them to a state of nerves. They sure looked good though. The girls loved the way their black skin made their eyes and white teeth stand out.

"It's your turn next," Mother hustled them near the stage. "Sing loud. This big gym will muffle your voices. Mrs. Reynolds will nod when it's time to sing."

Their music teacher must have deemed this one of her worst gigs.

Skeeters am a hummin' on a honeysuckle vine.
Sleep Kentucky Babe.
Sandman am a comin' to this little coon of mine.
Sleep Kentucky Babe.
Silvery moon am shinin' on da
Heavens up above.
Bobolinks am pinin' for his little lady love.
You is mighty lucky
Babe of old Kentucky.
Close your eyes in sleep.
Fly away. Fly away Kentucky babe....

To their great surprise, they didn't win the talent show prize.

Another tradition Helen introduced was the eleven o'clock Christmas Eve candlelight service at the large, formal Methodist Church in Goshen. She warned the girls not to mention this at Yellow Creek or even tell Grandma Esther, "though I don't know what they should get upset about—after all, it's *not* Catholic." Walt drew the line here since his morning started at four o'clock, but the children dutifully traipsed after Helen, caught in the majesty of the soaring pipe organ, the liturgy, the refined choir, and the swell in their heart when they each lit a candle to welcome Baby Jesus. They listened in awe to Handel's "Hallelujah Chorus", humming the magnificent melody on the drive home, if not to perfection, certainly in joyful spirit. They all cozied up to the kitchen table for cocoa and cookies, eyes heavy, but with their own version of "visions of sugar plums dancing in their heads". They couldn't dally though, because Helen had to start wrapping presents—in newspaper of course.

The church was bedrock in the family. More than anything, it was important to Helen to give her children a spiritual foundation. Often in the fall after revivals, she went through a spasm of religious fervor, instituting nightly devotions. She was very motivated—this time it would work. They read from a devotional book, sang a hymn, took turns reading scripture, and prayed. Walt had had a long day and he went along to humor her, but he was tired. The kids, not used to being somber, squirmed and poked. The record of failure hung heavy. Eventually Helen would lose her temper—even get tearful, which really laid open the guilt. For a few more nights they would struggle through, until devotions slowly petered out—again. What Helen didn't realize, and what her children learned by osmosis, was she lived the Beatitudes every day. They just needed to watch her; she didn't need to drive it into them.

In fact, doctrinaire and evangelical didn't settle naturally on Walt and Helen. They liked a good sermon, and when Billy Graham became well-known in the 1950's they attended his tent meetings in South Bend. They weren't vocal in opposing those Christians who interpreted the Bible literally or insisted there was one way to salvation. It just wasn't *their* way. When foreign missionaries came to Yellow Creek on Sunday evening and took a free-will offering, Walt would grumble all the way home: "I hope you didn't write a check, Helen. If those native Africans want to dance to their rain god, we should let them be. Missionaries should get a *real* job." However, when one of Helen's relatives started a homeless shelter in Elkhart, they were loyal supporters. It was common for Walt to say, "Give me a check, Helen. Carl Groebe is going through a hard patch. His wife has been sick. I'm going to have him drive tractor for a while. He needs to feed his family."

They wanted their children to see and know the world, especially the beauty and culture of America. In 1953 they planned a trip to the American West. Walt now had two milk trucks and milked twenty cows twice a day—substitute workers needed to be found, a huge undertaking. They would be gone the month of August which was harvest season for farmers. The family of six piled into their 1949 Chevy, the trunk full of luggage, a camp stove, glass jars of canned beef, pans, plates and tableware, and a box of activities and games. This was the absolute in adventure, as if they were leaving for the moon. Grandma and Grandpa were there to see them off, a bag of treats for each girl. They visited several of the National Parks in the Southwest: Mesa Verde, Bryce, Zion, and Yosemite. They drove up Pikes Peak, stopping mid-way so the car wouldn't overheat. Helen had stories and books about American Indians and mountain animals. The days were filled with new sights: buffalo, bear, and elk; real Indians at an Indian Trading Post; and mountains and waterfalls. At lunch time Helen went to a grocery and bought bologna, a loaf of bread, and fruit, with the family eating at a roadside picnic table. In the evening they stopped at a cabin along the road. Out came the camp stove for a warm supper of noodles and beef with boiled potatoes, or whatever Helen pulled from the trunk. Some of the cabins were primitive: mice scurried around, and they had to clean away spider webs from the bare boards. Each day was a new venture with only a few hitches when Helen and Walt each blamed the other for misreading the map and driving over one hundred miles in the wrong direction, or when they left Judy at a gas station bathroom and didn't miss her until they were twenty miles down the road. The girls learned to know cousins when they spent a few days in California with Grandma Esther's sister Edith, and her husband Wilbur. Old Faithful Geyser, the animals in Yellow Stone Park, and Mount Rushmore were the high points of the return trip. They returned rejuvenated, informed, and proud Americans.

Having to use the privy was getting old and embarrassing, as most of their guests weren't countrified. Helen wanted two bathrooms, one downstairs between their bedroom and the laundry room and one upstairs.

"That's just asking for trouble. I know these girls; we'll have water running through the ceiling every few months. We would be fools to have an upstairs bathroom," Walt grumbled, silently thinking of the cost of it. The lone male in a house of women, he was determined to stand his ground on occasion. Unfortunately, Helen caved on that decision. They put the bathroom in the laundry room next to the kitchen with another door leading into the bedroom. The bathroom became grand central station; privacy was never figured in. Woe to the person who went in and locked both doors.

Even worse planning led them to put their filing system, keeper of all financial records, in a large wooden desk in the utility room with the washer and dryer. At any time, the large desktop held a pile of unread mail, receipts from Martin's Feed Mill, a load of unfolded laundry, a broken tea cup Helen intended to mend, junk mail circulars, old flashlight batteries, a dirty broken farm implement that needed to go to the welder, and a cooling pumpkin pie. As one might anticipate, this led to innumerable arguments between Walt and Helen, especially at tax time.

"Helen, I can't find the cancelled checks from January. We've got to get our taxes to the accountant by tomorrow for him to get done by the fifteenth."

"You shouldn't have waited to start till today."

"Why am *I* doing it anyway? *You're* supposed to keep track of this stuff," his frustration was mounting as he ruffled through shoe boxes of loose envelopes and drawers that were a catchall for anything official looking.

"Helen, get in here," he yelled. "I'm not going to spend all day looking for something you misfiled."

She came storming into the utility room, "You're not putting this on me. Those check stubs come in an envelope with your name on it," she squawked, sifting through the rubble on top of the desk.

"So, I don't do enough around here? I get up at four o'clock to milk, run the route, work in the field, and do the evening milking. Now I have to take care of the mail too?" He pulled receipts out of an envelope, "Look at this: six farm payment receipts from Weavers. I know you made a payment every month. What the heck did you do with the rest of the receipts?"

"Here's the January cancelled check stubs, right in front of your nose on the desk. I get blamed for everything." She moped.

"We've got to keep a better filing system. When you come home from making the farm payment, put those receipts together in an envelope. Every year when we do taxes, we go through the same thing. I'm sick of it," he bellowed.

That night they were both up till dawn, mad as hornets and hardly speaking, but working together to get their records organized. As they left the next day for the accountant's office, Walt would snuggle up to Helen, smooching and teasing, "Is my little brunette still mad at me? Come on, give me a kiss." Every year the same: disorder, fighting, working together, and making up.

* * * * *

"Okay Judy, here are the recipes. Get started because we need to take it to Grandma and Grandpa's back to school supper tonight."

"Do you think Marsha will be there? I hope Grandpa lets us ride Trixie." Eleven-year-old Judy loved cousin get-togethers and Grandma's picnic suppers.

"You girls really like to go to Grandma's since they moved to Milford, don't you? Their pony is quite a hit. Don't beg Grandpa to let you drive the pony cart; he's not comfortable with that. I think Marsha will come to Grandma's, but Aunt Louise said she can't ride Trixie. It would be nice if you took a book and read to Marsha. Rheumatic fever sure messed with her heart. Grandma's been taking care of her for weeks. She shouldn't have tried to have all of us for supper, but she wants to make this picnic a tradition. Be sure the cake is completely cool before you frost it," she said, adjusting her hat. "How do I look? This is an important meeting with the Chamber of Commerce officially making Goshen a Sundown Town, which means Negroes can't live in Goshen or even stay overnight. Years ago, Negroes lived in Goshen, but people sure are against it now. The group who host Fresh Air Children are speaking in opposition. Since we live outside city limits we can still have them, but Daddy and I think Negroes should be able to live wherever they want."

"You look nice, Mother. Why are you taking your coat?"

"Oh, just in case."

That night in bed, Walt and Helen were talking about the evening. "Earl and Esther found a good place. Just what they need, a little house with a few acres so they can have a few Herefords and the pony. They look more relaxed than they have in a long time," Walt said.

"I can't believe how they've changed," Helen smiled in the dark. "They have new friends at Bethany Church and they like the janitor job at the school. This move has been a shot in the arm for them," Helen's voice was drowsy. "Daddy said he and Mother are buying a television. We're the only ones without one now. I'm taking the girls to Mother's to see the "Miss America Pageant". They can get to bed late *one* night."

"I don't think it's just the girls who want to see Miss America," he chuckled. "I guess you realize the risk you're taking by letting them see those young ladies with fancy jewelry and beautiful gowns. Judy will decide she wants to dance instead of go to college," Walt's voice was serious.

"I don't think so. All she talks about is going to college to be a nurse."

"We need to encourage that," Walt said emphatically. "Everyone wanted to talk about "I Love Lucy" tonight. I've heard enough about Lucy. You don't want a television, do you, Helen?"

"No. I'm not going to raise my children with a television."

"I'm glad we agree on that," he said.

"I wish you wouldn't have said anything about Joseph McCarthy and the execution of the Rosenburgs. It sure got silent after that."

"McCarthy would have us believe there's a Commie behind every tree. He wants people to spy on their neighbors. I don't trust the guy," Walt's dander was up now.

"We don't want to start a family feud. You're not going to believe this," she lifted on her elbow and turned toward him, "After supper when we were cleaning the kitchen, I told my sisters I'm pregnant. Would you believe *all* my sisters are pregnant? We'll have babies within five months—how fun. Mother was ecstatic."

"My goodness, your family is growing. Let's see...that will be twenty-three total. That's quite a coincidence; you couldn't have planned that if you tried," he laughed. He pulled her into his arms, "How're you doing, Dearie?" his voice was tender.

"I'm asleep," she answered.

Never one to let a life lesson go wanting, Helen used her pregnancy as a teaching tool. She bought a book with caricature drawings, *How Babies Are Made,* to explain about the new baby: a baby began as a miracle between a husband and wife when the father planted a sperm seed into the mother's ova seed. They joined in the womb and grew for nine months until the baby was big enough to be born. A nice story, Helen was pleased with her modernity. It's just that her girls were a bit thick-headed on the subject of sex.

Janice and Judy retired to their bedroom. "Let's get the book out," Judy said. If there was anything in that big house meant to be concealed—be it candy, cough drops, Christmas presents, or intimate paraphernalia, those girls would find it. They pulled out Helen's hidden book, entitled *The Loving Couple's Marriage Manual*.

"This book doesn't have many pictures, just some stick drawings of men and women. That's not much help," Judy said, leafing through the book.

"It says here, 'Animal nature should not dominate your love, rather the higher instincts of the soul. Have no haste to brush the bloom from the fruit you covet—it will lose half its attraction at once. After all, the purpose of a woman's breast is to feed a baby, not pleasure her husband'," Janice read hesitantly. "Do you think animal nature means a man and woman do what the bull and cow do?"

"Probably something like that. They sure don't make this very clear. Are they saying the man sucks on the woman's breast like a baby? Now that's ridiculous," Judy grimaced, flipping more pages.

"Look what it says, Judy: 'The fact that a cow is a temperamental milker is not the sort of thing you spring on your husband after he already bought you'. I think we're right, it's like the cow and the bull. That's nasty—it couldn't be comfortable. One thing I know: Miriam Moore told me if the man accidently pees inside a woman, it will kill her."

"You'd really have to want a baby to risk that, wouldn't you, Janice? This book is boring. Let's get in our pajamas and pin-curl our hair."

"Did you have a good sleepover at Judianne's house?" Janice asked.

"I always love to go to her house. Same as when I go to Carol Jean's house on Sundays." These two girls were Judy's bosom buddies throughout childhood—one at school, one at church. "It's such a change: everything is quiet, orderly, and clean; no one raises their voice or argues; no one has jobs. Here, everything is dirty; the nap is worn off the carpet till it's threadbare. We don't have the normal things like Kleenex, just toilet paper. We don't have hand lotion."

"Yeah, it sure is ratty around here. I guess I'm used to it."

"Last week before the foot washing at communion, Mother yelled that I had to take the polish off my toenails. Well, how can you do it without polish remover? I sat in the car at church digging at my toenails till I was almost late. When we run out of toothpaste, Daddy says use baking soda. Yuk."

"Why don't you go to their houses more, not have them come here all the time," Janice suggested.

"That's what I try to do, Janice, but they just want to come here. You know how all the kids want to come here," Judy's voice raised in frustration. "I don't get it. We're just not suave." A prolific reader, Judy was always trying a new word.

Daddy called from the bottom of the stairway, "Judy, you forgot to kiss your mother good night."

"Gr-r-r!" Judy huffed, working herself into a head of steam. "Why does he always do that?"

"We all kiss both of them every night—we always have," Janice was uncertain why Judy was perturbed.

"It's just too embarrassing." Judy spoke rapid-fire in a shushed voice. "Do you know any other kid our age whose mother is *pregnant*? She just struts around all smiley with her stomach sticking out like she's *proud* of it. Usually her blouse top doesn't cover up that cut out hole in her skirt. Our family doesn't need more children; we already have more than most. It's disgusting."

"Don't you think it'd be fun if we get a little boy? They have such cute outfits: little bow ties and shirts. He could have a flat top haircut."

"With four girls, you think we're going to get a boy?" Judy harrumphed. "Look at Judianne's mother, Mrs. Kerlin: she has pretty curly auburn hair; she's tall and thin; and she always wears make-up and jewelry. Even around the house, her dresses are pretty and clean. Wouldn't you think Mother would see ladies like that and want to look that way too?" Judy couldn't understand her mother.

"Can you see Mother washing the milkers, working in the garden, and feeding the chickens in a pretty dress and jewelry? Come on, I'll go with you, even though I already kissed them," said Janice—always the reasonable diplomat.

"I might as well get it over with," Judy's face was hang-dog guilty after her outburst.

Walt thoroughly relished his family of hormonal females. Thus, his attempted nonchalance after Randall's birth, was exposed when he backed the milk truck into the car after returning from the hospital. Indeed, that little fellow never wanted for love or attention from the time he was born. Not wanting a tag along child, two years later, Steve was born. Walt figured he would be a millionaire if he had a dollar for every time someone said, "Finally got your boys, eh, Walt?" The older girls were in Junior High and High School when Randy and Steve were born. Those little dynamos jumped on the family merry-go-round, keeping the family young with their childish wonder and boyish exuberance. Even Judy was taken by them.

One would expect among diapers, sleepless nights, and baby food, the Steffen family might slow down, but that wasn't the way of it. Helen's girls were going to be well-rounded. The small New Paris High School included every willing student in clubs, choir, band, and drama. The country church bolstered any potential talent. Getting praise from adults they admired, led them to believe they could do anything. The girls had several 4-H projects and continued piano lessons with persistence and little talent. Janice picked up clarinet and Judy the flute, going to band and chorus competitions and marching in every holiday parade. As with every Indiana school, basketball was king. After every game, a disc jockey held a sock hop in the gym. As their church friends weren't allowed to dance, Janice and Judy were determined to attend, knowing that without a television to watch American Bandstand, they knew none of the dance moves.

Janice was stepping to the beat of "Yakety Yak" and "To Know Him Is to Love Him" when she looked far up in the gym bleachers to see her dad observing the action. He and Helen must have decided that their daughters faced little harm in spending a good part of the sock hop in a cluster of girls, so he never attended another dance. This did; however, give the girls cachet as they taught the Sunday School kids to dance, rolling back the rugs and dancing at church parties; one of several times the girls' behavior prompted a ministerial visit to Walt and Helen.

Helen also closely monitored the girls' efforts at kindness and inclusion, with attention to those children who were friendless or excluded to the fringes. The most common question after arriving home from school was "who were you friendly to today?" or "what kindness did you do?" Sometimes the girls tried to convince her *they* were the ones left out—she had little sympathy for that. She figured *they* could find their way. At church there was one unusual gal who was easily shuffled aside. The girls knew if they "stuck Ruth on the end of the pew", they'd hear it on the way home. In the same way, apology notes were de rigueur in the event their behavior wasn't exemplary: "I'm sorry my whispering interfered with your appreciation of the sermon," or "I'm sorry I said the cocoa you served at the Easter breakfast tasted like dish water."

Life on the farm was never humdrum or tedious. Each girl always had work to do: in the cow barn, in the field, feeding calves and chickens, herding cows, baling hay and straw, cleaning eggs, working in the garden and orchard, and canning and freezing food for the winter. Nancy probably did the least but not by choice. She spent enough time during her childhood at Riley Hospital, orthodontists, dentists, and various specialists and therapists, to get a college degree. Helen ran down every report of dentists who reconstructed the mouths of children with cleft palate, driving a far distance if necessary. There was a phase of blowing bubbles, wearing metal scaffolding at night, a period of pulling teeth and implanting bridges, braces with rubber bands, paraffin and wires. The inside of her mouth was mauled by countless devices. When Nancy couldn't be found, it was a sure bet she was running the long lane to the back of the farm—her method for relieving stress.

Janice and Judy were old enough to work for pay, babysitting for fifty cents an hour. They took turns working all day Saturday for a farm family: cleaning their large house; mowing the yard; making supper, and babysitting until the late night—all for three dollars. Some summers they were live-in babysitters, gone from home for the week. One summer they were volunteer Bible School teachers, traveling by Greyhound Bus as far away as New Jersey. Sue and Nan thought it unfortunate that Helen discovered reading enrichment workbooks when they were in elementary school. Every summer morning they spent an hour huddled over workbooks, with the intent to improve their reading comprehension. Around this time, all the siblings' names were shortened to one syllable: Jan, Jud, Nan, Sue, Ran, and Steve. They were too hurried to say a longer name.

There may have been a lot of yelling and threatening but there wasn't a lot of discipline. The girls were most often spanked for letting the cows' water tank run over. It was a matter of putting the hose in the tank, turning on the water, and turning it off when the tank was full—which was often forgotten. Too many days the barnyard looked like a swimming pool. One time the water went beyond the barnyard, down the hill about two blocks and into the creek—probably a few days running. Filling the water tank was done every day. Somehow no one ever thought to buy a timer, or set a reminder alert to turn off the water. Instead the girls were sometimes spanked, depending on Daddy's mood when he came home and found the barnyard afloat.

Around junior high age, each sibling opened a savings account. Though never receiving an allowance, money from outside jobs accumulated. The First National Bank in Goshen was an opulent marble building with burnished gold trim and mahogany wood "cages" for the prestigious and respected bank tellers. Earl Ulrey, the most esteemed teller, handled the Steffen finances, praising their accumulating college funds as he manually added the deposit to the little blue savings books.

Another highlight in the summer was hosting Fresh Air Children from Chicago. A few times it was more of a challenge than they wished, especially the two years the ten-year-old twins visited. Judy called Mrs.

Reynolds where Helen was waiting during Nancy and Sue's piano lessons.

"Mother, you need to go to the grocery before coming home. I can't handle these kids. They don't listen to me."

"I just got groceries yesterday," Helen pooh-poohed Judy's request. "Make bologna sandwiches for lunch."

"They got hungry this morning and made themselves sandwiches. The bologna is gone, and we have only four pieces of bread left. They ate two loaves before I even knew they were in the house. The rest of us can have tomato sandwiches but we don't have bre.... 'Sam, stop'," she yelled, dropping the phone then returning after a few minutes.

"What's going on?" Helen hollered.

"He's going to kill that chicken. He tied the chicken's feet together with a piece of long rope and fastened it to the seat of the bike. He's riding the bike lickety-split; the chicken is flying straight out behind him. Samella is chasing him, trying to grab the chicken. I couldn't catch him; he ignored me. He doesn't listen to me, Mother," Judy blubbered.

"He doesn't listen to me either, Honey. Those kids are only afraid of your dad—and he's never around. Glory be, I hope he doesn't kill himself. Don't worry about the chicken. We'll have it for supper; it won't lay eggs anymore. I was going to have Chef Boyardee Pizza, but we have only three boxes—sounds like that's not enough."

"Pizza, my favorite. Let's save it till they're gone." Pizza Pie was a new Italian dish; a favorite of all the family, and a rare treat.

"I'll be home as soon as I can. The girls' lessons are over. I'll stop at the store."

Occasionally when the girls argued and picked on each other, Walt made them get on the ground and fight it out. They thought they were brawny and tough: tumbling, hitting, and punching on each other. It never took them long to tire of the fuss and "give in". The first time Sam and Samella fought, the girls were stunned and in awe of the hard-hitting way inner city kids settled disputes.

"Cum' an git it ya' assole niggah," Samella leaned in and pounced, her eyes fiercely focused. "Skeered ain't cha?" She grabbed his shirt, tearing the pocket loose. Sam was down, Samella hammering his head with one hand, gouging his eye with the other, while spitting in his face. Blood splattered. Helen ran out of the house yelling, "You kids stop it. Stop it right now!"

Sam had rolled Samella: she kicking and pulling hanks of hair; he pummeling her eyes and bending her fingers backwards. "Shet up, ya ninny bitch. I gon' whoop yo ass."

Helen pranced helplessly around the tumbling twins, "Stan' back Missus. Ain't no place fer a lady." Grunt. Snort. Oomph. They clubbed and bashed in fast forward motion, buttons tore loose, Samella's lip split, blood running down her chin smeared Sam's hands. "Why don' cha give hit up, ya weenie?"

Samella saw her chance, "I gon' mash yo thang ta mush." In a split second she banged her knee into Sam's crotch with vicious accuracy. He crumpled to the ground, groaning and holding himself. Samella knew when to quit, all the girls running to the protection of the house.

"Ya jest wait. If'n I git cha, yo' dead meat," Sam yelled after them. The summer children from Chicago opened the world to the Steffens. While there were short memories of some children, Sam and Samella stories were oft repeated.

The Steffen sibling's best week of summer between first grade through high school was their week at the Brethren Church Camp. The kids stayed in primitive cabins and kept busy with typical camp activities. Mr. and Mrs. Schwalm, Camp Mack directors, had Indian heritage, and wore fringed buckskin clothes with headdress. Mrs. Schwalm had long braids down her back and at bedtime she sang a lullaby over the loudspeaker. For first-year campers this was an invitation for homesickness.

Dear Mommy and Daddy,

My cabin is Bide-A-Wee. I like the girls in my cabin. The food is good, especially the cinnamon toast. I got two treats at the camp store. Necco Wafers and a Sugar Daddy sucker. I put the sucker in my mouth after lights out and there were ants all over it. I had to wash it off. In crafts I'm making a pottery bowl. Swimming is my favorite class. I like the singing and stories each night at campfire. Judy, you said I'd get homesick. I'm not. I got a letter from Grandma Esther.

XOXO, Nancy

* * * * *

August 14, 1956

Dear Mother and Daddy,

Youth camp is a lot more fun than junior high. I hang out with the South Bend girls I met last year. There are lots of cute boys. I might have a boyfriend. I took a walk with Gene. He wrote in my autograph book:

2—cute
2—be
4—gotten

I easily passed the swim test. The lifeguard said I have a good dive. The South Bend girls and I get up for morning dip. That and 4-square is where you meet the cute boys. I'm bored with Brethren history. Every year we have to study the murals in the auditorium. In crafts I'm making you a macramé plant hanger, Mother. I got a letter from Grandma Esther. Having a great time.

Love, Jan

* * * * *

The household was the Wild West of a quirky family domicile. The Steffens were an anomaly of the priggish, stiff-necked 1950s. When conformity was the rule of the day, they contentedly lurched along by the seat of their pants.

"Don't make any noise, you kids," Helen giggled. "We want to surprise them."

The younger kids, excited by the novelty, skulked around the Andrew's home early on this Sunday morning, the older girls lagged doubtfully. Outside the bedroom window of their friends, they broke into joyous song: "Oh what a beautiful morning...Oh what a beautiful day"." Their voices carried through the clear morning air with fresh enthusiasm.

The curtain parted, and Ed in his pajamas, disheveled hair, and shocked expression took in the Steffens, singing their hearts out about the beautiful day. He was soon joined by the rest of his family, skeptical to be roused from sleep by song.

"Hurry Walt, let's get the camp stove fired up over beside the picnic table. You make the pancakes and I'll scramble the eggs. The sausage just needs to be warmed. You girls, get out the fruit and syrup, and set the table."

The Andrews, dressed and smiling, stumbled out of the house to join the breakfast fun. The older girls eyed their cool football-star sons with a sickly greeting. "This is a first—the most unusual party ever. Who would think of it besides Walt and Helen?" Glenna chuckled, throwing her arms around Helen.

Living in the country, the kids rode the school bus to New Paris. As they had barn chores in the morning, and Helen insisted on a warm breakfast, being ready when the bus came took some hustle and hitch-in-their-step to combobulate so early in the day. Don, the unflappable driver, was a study in droll patience as he boarded Jan and Judy, waiting at the end of the drive. Randy, coattails flying, came two minutes later. A tad behind came Nan, brush in her hair, rushing to catch the flyaway scarf she had dropped. Randy returned to the house to get his show-and-tell stuffed animal, then finally came Sue, ambling along in no particular hurry. As Don backed out the driveway, Helen came hollering and on a tear, holding out all five lunch boxes. The kids looked at each other, their heads drooping. Word had passed among them that the sandwich of the day was grated carrot. Helen was known for inventive sandwich ingredients when her larder showed empty: cottage cheese, or sliced potato with catsup were examples. The principal kept a running tab for the Steffen family to get cafeteria lunch tokens when lunches were forgotten, etc. Unfortunately, this day they would eat their carrot sandwich.

The bus driver's favorite Steffen story was the day Nan was hanging out the upstairs window, her head encumbered in three-inch pink sponge rollers, holding a towel across her chest, waving her arm to direct him to go on; while Helen was standing at the downstairs porch waving her arms and yelling, "Wait, Wait."

Helen was unflagging in her resolve to "do unto others". It was embedded in her daily routine, more than her family sometimes wished. The most popular, smart guy in Jan's high school class, was badly injured in a car accident. He was not close in Jan's circle of friends.

"Jan, I talked to Bryce's mother. He's home from the hospital. I'm going to make a banana cake for you to take them. I'll have it ready this afternoon when you get home from work."

"Mother, Bryce hardly knows who I am. Please, I don't want to take a cake. How embarrassing."

Walt chimed in, "Jan, why wouldn't you want to take him one of your mother's special banana cakes? Everybody loves them. Judy can go with you if you need moral support."

Now Judy had a horse in this race, "*I'm* not going. I don't know him at all."

"That's a good idea," Helen said. "You can go when Jan gets home." With both parents in cahoots, the girls knew they had no choice. Arguing would get them nowhere. As sometimes happened with Helen's cooking, the final product was less than perfect. This time, the three-layer cake wasn't completely cool when she frosted it.

"This is ridiculous. I don't see how I got sucked into this. They didn't even give me a chance to wash my hair," Judy griped, sitting in the passenger seat holding the cake while Jan drove.

"I can't believe they're making us do this. Do you think we can just give it to them at the door and leave?" Jan questioned.

"Oh no! The layers of cake are sliding. What am I going to do? I can't touch it; I'll mess up the frosting. I don't believe this. It's so like Mother to send us out with a cake that's falling apart," Judy said disgustedly.

"Oh Gee," Jan glanced over. "It looks like the frosting is melting and pooling around the bottom. You only need to keep it together a few more minutes till we get there. I'll be so glad when this is over," Jan mumbled.

"I'm going to have to use my fingers to stack the cake together, or it will fall off the plate when we carry it to the door." She poked and slid the cake, her fingers all sticky when Bryce's mother opened the door, making over the cake as if it were decorated by a French bakery chef. She took the girls to see Bryce, all their cheeks flushing pink, uncomfortable being in his bedroom, he in pajamas. His mother did her best to carry a one-way conversation until the girls could politely say good-bye.

"I wonder if they'll toss that cake," Judy wondered aloud.

"Why would they? The cake is good, it just looks bad," Jan said, relieved the visit was over.

"I can think of several reasons," Judy said.

In 1960, Helen enrolled part-time at Goshen College to complete her degree in education. She and Walt planned for her to teach when Steve started school—her salary becoming the children's college fund. Though her days were even more harried, she loved her classes, and her studies enlivened supper time discussions. Around this time, Walt sold the two milk can routes and bought a large refrigerated stainless-steel bulk milk truck. The business did well, and a few years later he hired a driver and bought a second bulk truck. With two trucks, he contracted to haul milk to a dairy in Ohio several days each week. On these nights, the girls did the evening milking and all the farm chores. Still a bit ragtag with plenty of hand-me-downs, no one would have noted the Steffens were moving up in the world. They watched every cent.

The 60's introduced the drug scene, juvenile delinquency, and "fast" teenagers. Surely all six of the children had behavior that could have maimed or killed. Throughout childhood, Walt and Helen left many decisions to the children, saying, "let your conscience be your guide", a dictum stronger than any curfew. God forbid that you be the girl to despoil the Steffen name. Without realizing, the girls looked out for each other, tracked the other's behavior, and watched each other's back. This lent an air of unique openness to the family. Woe to the girl who wanted secrets. After a date, Daddy had no qualm about asking, "Is he fast?" or "Did he kiss you?" The one telephone was in the center of the house, just outside the kitchen. It was a party line and everyone in the house could hear the conversation. It certainly put a choke hold on flirting.

Because there were so many girls, it wasn't unusual to have guys sniffing around, though a young man had to be pretty heroic to pursue one of the Steffens. Helen's eagle eye and Walt's friendly nosiness were not for the faint of heart. Helen's intent was to put a damper on one of her girls wearing a fuzzy, angora-wrapped class ring, indicating they were "going steady".

When the girls had a date they wanted to impress, they cleaned the house, made lemonade, and banished Randy and Steve to the woods, but they never knew what lunacy might happen. After returning from an evening out, Jan and Lowell, her date, were on the couch in the far corner of the living room—what passed for privacy. Randy came running through the room with underpants over his head, peering through the leg hole, yelling "I see London I see France. I see Jan's underpants." Later he stuck his head around the corner, and in a loud whisper said, "I don't know who you are, but you sure have big ears."

One Sunday afternoon the girls were in swimsuits, lying on blankets in the back yard with their Yellow Creek buddies. The transistor radio was tuned to WLS, they had oiled their skin to soak up the rays, and had a couple sultry Rook card games going.

"Joyce, is that scar on your leg where you broke your ankle when you fell through the ice at our creek last winter?" Judy asked.

"Yeah, I still have trouble bending it. Every time I come to the Steffens something bad happens. I'll probably get a sunburn today," Joyce grumbled.

"I know what you mean," Carol Jean asserted. "When I was here a few weeks ago we were doing chores, and Judy said it was a rule, if I spilled chicken feed, I'd have to eat it. Then she *accidently* spilled some."

"You didn't actually eat it, did you?" Melba asked.

"I ate a little," Carol Jean admitted.

"I didn't think you'd really do it," Judy confessed. "I helped you eat it though, didn't I, true-blue friend that I am."

"I'm surprised we didn't get sick," Carol Jean said.

"Nah, chickens eat it," Judy pooh-poohed.

"That's no worse than you did to me at Melba's sleep over," Jan grumbled, "waiting till I was asleep, then putting my hand in warm water so I peed in my sleeping bag." The girls laughed hilariously, remembering Jan's embarrassment.

"Hey Sharon, this is your trick; the Ace takes it."

"Oh, yeah," interrupting her crooning along with Pat Boone on the radio.

"Hey guys, I'm going to show you something that will crack you up. Judy, when are the folks getting home?" Jan asked.

"Not till milking time." Jan ran into the house.

"I know what she's going after: a condom," Judy said.

"A condom!" The girls chorused. "How do you even know your folks *have* condoms?"

"Because we snoop," Judy said matter-of-factly. "Doesn't everyone snoop on their parents?" Another chorus of "No's".

"You know, you two are a bad influence on us. We learn all our bad habits from you," Melba said.

"Oh sure," Judy said doubtfully, as they all gathered around Jan as she removed the foil from the condom.

"Won't your folks notice that you took it? My folks would kill me if I got in their stuff," Mary insisted.

"Mother is so busy since she started teaching, they're probably too tired to use a condom."

"Woo-Hoo, that sure is bigger than a Tampax. Ouch," the girls cackled, this forbidden activity causing raucous laughter.

"What's that gooey stuff?" Carol's nose puckered.

"All the better to poke you with, my dear," Mary said, her voice saucy. The girls rolled on the blanket, laughing at their risqué goings-on.

"Wait till you see this," Jan ran to the water spigot, adding water to the condom till it was a stretched blob of bouncing plastic. She threw it at Carol Jean who shrieked as water splashed in her face. Then it went to Sharon who refilled it—the girls chasing around the yard till they were wet and out of breath.

"Time out," Jan yelled as they all collapsed on the blanket. "They should make toys out of condoms. It's more fun than a balloon."

"We need to get rid of it, so the folks don't find it. Let's get some dry leaves and burn it on the trash pile." Judy went in for matches.

"I thought the guys might come by this afternoon. They knew we all came to Steffens," Melba said.

"They went fishing. I'm sure we'll cruise Bower's tonight," Joyce knew the whereabouts of Carl, her brother. "Hey Jan, what's with you and Dale?

You and Phil have been acting friendly lately. I'm sure Dale has noticed. Are you going to break up?"

Jan rolled to her back on the blanket. "Oh, I don't know," her voice was frustrated. "Dale and I aren't really serious; we just hang out together. Don't you think Phil livens up our youth group discussions? He's so smart and interesting. Poor Rev. Fike, he must get upset with our ungodly beliefs. I wouldn't mind going out with Phil though."

"You and Phil are more alike than you and Dale," Melba said. "You do realize if you break up with Dale, we're down to two convertibles to drive around Goshen and park at Bower's Drive-In. That's going to mess up our cruising. Just saying."

"I know. I thought of that. I wish there was another girl for Dale."

CHAPTER 44

High School and College

"We're not doing this again, so you'd better get it the way you want it," Walt said as he and Helen pored over home design magazines.

"Then I want the oven in a brick wall in my kitchen and nice walnut cabinets—like this picture," Helen nearly shivered with excitement.

"This is something I drew for the downstairs. What would you think of building out the two sides of the living room and adding a big picture window? That would update the front of the house."

"I like that a lot, Walt. I'm so excited. This is my dream house. We could put a fireplace in the dining room."

"I don't want us to skimp. We want it to be nice. I'm going to get all new Anderson Windows; they're the best. I've been asking around about construction companies. I believe an Amish contractor is best. I'm going to talk to them. You can trust the Amish to do a good job." That whole spring and summer the house was open to birds, raccoons, and mice during the remodeling project. The kids had to walk outdoors to get to the upstairs bedrooms. Now they mowed a larger lawn, had beautiful trees, and Helen's flower gardens. The farm changed from shabby to bucolic. By fall when renovation was complete, it felt like they moved to a new home.

Before the family got started in the school year, they took a vacation to Mackinaw Island and the Henry Ford Museum in Michigan—eight people in a 1954 Chevy. "Keep your eye on Steve. Something's not right about the way he moves," Helen whispered to Walt.

"You're right," Walt acknowledged that night. "It's like he can't control his movements. He's jerky. He doesn't seem to be in pain."

"Let's go home, Walt," Helen's voice was thick as she held back tears. After making arrangements to meet their family doctor, they started the long drive back to Goshen. Late that night Walt took Steve to the doctor's home, where they observed as he tried to walk and skip. After doing a physical exam and taking a blood test, Dr. Bosler agreed something was wrong. The next days held the tenor of dread as seven-year-old Steve's symptoms became more exaggerated. There was a rushed trip to a neurologist in South Bend, causing whispered clutches of conversations bordering on panic. Finally the doctors determined Steve had Sydenham's Chorea, an inflammation of the heart, formerly called St. Vitus' Dance, because the uncontrolled muscle movements looked like a perpetual dance. They suggested Steve earlier may have had unrecognized rheumatic fever, with the strep infection evolving to Chorea. Steve was put on penicillin and total bed rest, as the potential for permanent heart damage was significant. This diagnosis was a relief, as everyone had feared a brain tumor.

A hospital crib was put in the downstairs bedroom, padded to prevent bruising from banging his head and limbs against the side rails. Steve had to be fed and carried to the bathroom. He had elevated fever, enlarged painful joints, and fly-away jerking limbs and facial grimaces.

"There's no choice, Daddy. I have to help Helen like I helped Louise when Marsha was sick. She started this good teaching job; she can't take several months off until Steve gets better," Esther said.

"You're right, Mother. It's interesting how things have changed. Since so many young women are working, grandmothers are the back-up for child care. Sarah seemed old when she was sixty-five. That was the year she died. Here you are, Esther, at sixty-five taking care of a seven-year-old. You're going strong."

"I never thought about this being the age when my mother died. I'm thankful for my health. I'm like an old work horse; I keep plowing away."

Steve and Grandma settled into an easy rapport. Helen brought Steve his homework and library books. Grandma read stories and they played Uno and Yahtzee. She knotted comforters and wrote in her diary.

"Are you writing a book, Grandma?"

"I'm writing in my diary."

"What's a diary?"

"Every day you write what happened that day."

"What if you do something you don't want anyone to know about? Do you have to write your secrets?"

"It's up to you what you write. Hm-m-m... I guess I don't have any secrets to write about."

"If I wrote about something bad I did, Randy would read it and tattle, and I'd get in big trouble. Do you keep secrets from Grandpa?"

Grandma laughed, "Steve, you're as curious as *Curious George* in the book I just read. Grandpa and I are too old for secrets, and I don't write anything I wouldn't want people to know. You don't put a mouth on words you don't want splattered around. That stuff is better left unsaid."

"I need help going to the bathroom."

"Okay Steve. Put your arms around my neck and your legs around my hips. I'll lift you out of bed and carry you."

After returning from the bathroom, Steve said, "I'm going to call you Iron Woman. You're like a turtle, you have a hard shell. Are you made of iron?"

"For your information, young man, respectable grandmas wear foundation garments," Grandma chuckled.

"Is that why you move kind of slow? Does your iron get rusty?"

"Some days I do feel a little rusty. Now that's enough questions out of you. What should we have for lunch?"

Helen dived into teaching as would an Olympic athlete. She gave it her single-minded attention. She taught in a small country school whose families and teachers prized learning as much as she. She was always writing and directing a play, planning a history project, or organizing a field trip. Walt continued hauling milk from farms, transporting it to the Goshen Condensary and to Ohio.

The six children each marched more or less to the Steffen drumbeat: Jan was the responsible overseer of the siblings and settler of fractious squabbles. Judy detested milking cows and was dogged and goal oriented. Nan was easy-going and obedient, but with sass, and Sue was sick of the expectation that she measure up to her older sisters. As for Randy and Steve, the family favorites, everyone agreed they didn't have to work as hard as the girls and got fewer punishments. Still, each girl connived to outdo the others in spoiling the boys. With one family car, the logistical nightmare of this time was getting each kid home from after-school activities. On any day it wasn't unusual for at least one Steffen to wait in the dark on the steps of the locked up high school for Mother's pick up. This was a problem, because the girls needed to milk twenty-five cows, feed calves, and put down bedding straw after they got home.

The three older girls had jobs during summers, weekends, and occasionally, after school: Jan at Krogers, Judy at Dr. Bosler's office, and Nan at Kentucky Fried Chicken. One summer Nan won the prize by applying sixty-six places for a job. The money earned went for the occasional movie and meal at Bowers Drive-In, rarely clothes, and often into a saving's account.

While Daddy nosied about their dates: "Is this real romance or just puppy love?" Mother seemed to "get it" that high school years were fraught with a roller coaster of emotions between lay-awake drooling "luv" or agonizing, unrequited heartache.

Jan and Judy had returned from a summer of teaching Bible School at Brethren Churches, though they delighted in boys and other activities that had nothing to do with the Bible. "It sounds like you had a lot of free time," Helen commented, dishing out Cream of Wheat for the three of them on a Saturday morning.

"Oh, we did," Jan agreed. "We were at every church for two weeks, and we just taught Bible School in the mornings. There were always young kids from the church who took us to the swimming pool or cruising around. It was a blast."

"Hm-m-m. I was expecting it to be more rural. I thought you might get bored. No wonder you hardly had time to write letters," she teased.

"Everyone wanted to entertain us; we were never bored. In New Jersey we went to the beach and the board walk several times. In Jersey they have sandwiches called Hoagies that are so-o good," Judy thumped Jan's shoulder. "In Peru, this guy really had the hots for Jan. Did Jack say he'd come to see you, Jan? I bet he will. Peru is only about an hour from here."

"Well, Judy flipped over a guy named Joe in New Jersey. We were with this group of kids every day."

"Oh Mother, Joe is so cool. He has curly blonde hair, and he acts so mature. Jan's right, I fell pretty hard. He didn't see, but I cried when I kissed him good-bye," she dropped her eyes with this shy confession. "He's going to write to me."

A gentle smile played on Helen's lips, her eyes were thoughtful, "You girls learned a lot this summer; maybe not what I expected, but you were on your own and you handled it well. It was quite an accomplishment getting yourselves to New Jersey and back on the Greyhound Bus. I can tell you've grown and matured. Good for you. You're old enough to experience how it feels to love someone. That's good. These friendships will help you learn what you want in a life partner someday. You're young ladies now."

The early 1960's was the era of saddle shoes and rolled down bobby socks or, for dress, spike heels with nylon hose clipped to a garter belt. For school, the girls wore a starched crinoline under a poodle or squaw skirt. Hair was teased with a large comb and sprayed with Aqua Net Hairspray to hold its helmet-like shape. At the sock hop kids danced "the twist" and sang "I'm Sorry" along with Brenda Lee. While not fashion savvy, each sister had a couple "nice" dresses for school and dress-up. The summer style was pedal pushers. Though Helen seldom splurged at Lucille's Dress Shop for herself, nothing made her happier than buying one of her girls an outfit they desperately wanted. Special dresses, like formals, were bought in a thrift shop. It wasn't especially important the dress was liked, so long as it suited the purpose.

In 1960, Jan was the first to leave the nest, enrolling at Manchester College in Elementary Education. The farm and small-town ambiance stuck to each of the six children, none having the moxie to strike out at a large state university. All went to a small private college and graduated debt free.

* * * * *

Earl and Esther were returning home from the doctor's office. They were subdued, their thoughts mulling the doctor's words: "Earl, your heart is getting weaker."

"Well Mother, that wasn't what I wanted to hear: 'You're seventy-one and have the heart of an eighty-year-old'. At least it explains why I have sores on my legs and my feet are always cold. Doc says I have to cut back," he harrumphed. "He doesn't know anything about being a school janitor with kids making a mess of everything they do."

"I know how they are, Pop, but it's not good for you to stew about it. He said you worry like a harpy, whatever that is. Dear oh dear, I feel like we're sinking in quicksand." She was thoughtful, "I think the doctor was saying we need to make some changes. Nothing is more important than your health."

"Do you mean quit the school janitor job?" Earl sounded surprised.

"Daddy, I wonder if we should move back to Goshen, closer to the girls. We have all this lawn to mow and the care of the animals."

"But Mother, I thought you liked the country."

"I do, but at our age we can't work full-time and keep up a small farm. I know the girls would be relieved to have us closer. We would be nearer to the hospital where I volunteer. The grandchildren will visit more if we're closer to them."

He grimaced, anticipating the difficulties. "I hate to think about finding another house, packing up and moving. I'd probably need to find another job."

"Well, let's sleep on it. You know our fiftieth wedding anniversary is in November. I want more years with you, Daddy. We need to keep you healthy."

"Mother, you're my guardian angel; you take good care of me. You're usually right about these things."

In the summer they moved to a little house near Goshen College where Earl again got a custodian job. From the beginning they knew this new home was right. They were encircled by family who dropped by daily. The fifteen grandchildren loved when Grandma and Grandpa came to their ballgame, class play, or watched them show their animals at the 4-H fair. Always a gad about, Esther could hobnob to her heart's delight.

The joy of her heart was serving as a Gray Lady, caring for hospital and nursing home patients. Though elderly, she knew her life had purpose and meaning in her ministry to the ill, aged, and weary. She took the role seriously when asked to teach and mentor new recruits to the program. These senior years were likely her happiest. She mellowed, feeling bountifully blessed in serving others. This expressed her true nature.

During the move, Earl had discovered Louise's old bicycle. Believing exercise would be good for his heart, he began to ride most days, enjoying nature and making friends along the way. He often rode as much as twenty miles, accruing several thousand miles on his pedometer. As expected, his heart and circulatory problems improved significantly, and his worries and dark ruminations eased their rankle.

* * * * *

At the Steffen farm all the family were thrilled about the pending first marriage. Jan had followed to the letter the kick-start plan for her life: graduating college, marrying the long-suffering Lowell, and starting her teaching job in Kansas, all within the month of August 1963. She would support them while Lowell completed college.

Helen walked in from the mailbox, handing Jan an envelope. Jan showed her: "All A's for summer school," she said.

"Good for you, Jan. You have a great GPA, and you did it in three years."

"I'm glad I'm done. Were you nervous the day before you got married, Mother? I feel like...well, like I'm taking a huge leap and I don't know where I'll land."

"Honey, I think every bride is nervous. Something would be wrong if you weren't a little worried. Lowell is a good Brethren man. Your dad and I have always liked him. You'll be fine," Helen answered, as she put out sandwich fixings for lunch.

Walt heard her angst as he entered the kitchen, "Is our Jannie getting the marriage jitters?" he smiled, wrapping his arms around her. "If you and Lowell can't make it, I don't know who could. You're both good kids."

"We're certainly starting marriage on a shoestring. I hope Lowell has money to get us to Kansas."

"Don't worry about it, Jan. I'll talk to Lowell and we'll work it out. What time do I need to be at the rehearsal tonight?"

The rest of the siblings carried on with their game plans as well. Judy attended Goshen College, getting her B.S. in Nursing. She worked at Elkhart, the hospital where she trained, and after a year married Wayne, a co-worker. She worked as the Manchester College nurse while he received his Accounting Degree.

Nan joined Lowell and Jan in Kansas for two years at McPherson, a Brethren College. These were good years; Nan loved college and independence. She made good friends. Unfortunately, her doctors needed her to be in Indiana for several surgeries on her mouth. She left her friends and completed her B.A. in Social Work at Goshen College. Some individuals may have been embittered by on-going and invasive medical procedures. Nan's humor and insouciance blinded everyone to her personal struggles. Dating, following oral surgery, was actually hazardous to her health. One young man kissed her so ardently, not only was it excruciating, she was afraid the stitches would tear apart thousands of dollars of surgery. Her painful utterances were misinterpreted as ardor, causing the eager suitor to pummel away. When she was finally able to break loose, her mouth was a bloody, pulpy mess.

Then Nan met Ed, a young man much more to her liking. She shortly realized he had the Capital C on his forehead—anathema to Helen and Walt. The first several months Helen was hardly civil. Ed played the patient "weasel your way in" game. By the time they were engaged, Ed had joined the Church of the Brethren. That stilled the waves—after his baptismal immersion no one was higher than Ed in Helen's estimation, and the proud Brethren minister stuck a feather in his cap: he had plucked a Catholic for the Brethren fold.

Sue was probably least like Helen of any of the girls. While Helen was a hard-driving type, Sue saw no reason to hurry if you could stop and smell the roses. Though she tried, she had little inclination for academics—math and history fizzled in her head. It suited her quite nicely to lollygag through life. Sue's joy and focus in high school was singing, which was good as she was the only one in the family with a lovely singing voice. She played the piano and was in various choirs and singing groups.

She marched the Steffen path to college and after a year decided it was a waste of time and money. Unbeknownst to Walt and Helen, she committed to several months of research/service at the National Institutes of Health in Washington D.C. As she anticipated, this caused explosive, fulminating wrath. This was likely the first time any of the Steffens broke one of Walt and Helen's cardinal rules: college was a given. The family had never faced earthshaking rebellion. Only in hindsight could one see that Walt, Helen, and Sue set a precedent for settling conflict that besets every family who inevitably experiences honest and angry differences. This unspoken, yet set in stone rule, would give "the other" time, space, and gentleness; but differences could not be ignored or buried, they would be discussed and settled. As time passed, every member of the large extended family had the assurance of acceptance. Differences would never fray the years-long bond of Steffen unity.

While in service, Sue met Galen, a large teddy bear of a guy from the Shenandoah Valley in Virginia. His southern drawl and witticisms ("I'm as nervous as a whore in church") kept the family in stitches. After a spring wedding, they settled on his large family farm, milking hundreds of dairy cows and planting several hundred acres of crops. Their farm was a favored vacation destination for everyone who could claim to be relation. Sue still sings like a songbird.

In junior high, Randy and Steve did what all small-town Indiana boys did: bounce a basketball. Walt would get so riled during their games that someone had to go to keep him settled. The boys weren't as out of step with their peers as the girls had been; in the late sixties, Walt finally got a TV. Of course, there were limits as to how much they could watch, but Walt and Helen were never around to monitor.

They had farm chores: driving tractor, feeding calves, bedding down the loafing shed and mowing the large lawn. They were as bad as the girls in letting the water tank run over—a problem that after twenty-five years never found a solution.

Following their sisters' footsteps, Randy and Steve had no hesitation in rifling through drawers and purses. Anything found was fair game. One day when Cousin Don was visiting they found a whole silver-wrapped chocolate candy bar. Aha, the lodestone, mother of all treats. They wolfed it down and went about their play. That afternoon an unsettled flux seized their guts simultaneously with a liquid gaseous eruption that would have its way. The chocolate candy was Ex-lax.

* * * * *

"Woo-Hoo. Here he comes. I see him. Daddy, look, Daddy," Esther shouted, knocking her hat awry in her excitement. "You boys sure did a good job decorating his bike." Esther was so proud of Earl she almost lost her natural modest decorum during the Goshen Fourth of July parade.

"Grandpa, throw us some candy," yelled Steve.

There came Earl, dressed as Uncle Sam on his crepe paper and balloon decorated bicycle, his twinkling eyes and apple cheeks belying his seventy-seven years. Earl had gained some small fame as a long-distance biker, with requests to lead fundraising bike-a-thons and parades. Though meek and unpretentious, he felt shy pleasure in frequently seeing his picture in the Goshen News, contributing dollars to charity.

"Hey, Mother," his jolly smile swelled as he pulled off to the side.

"Daddy, is your knee bothering you? I brought you more water. Randy, get his empty bottle."

"The knee has a bit of a crink, but I'll ice it down tonight. I'm having a grand time. I hope I don't run out of candy."

"Are your gears holding up, Grandpa?" Randy asked.

"The bike is doing fine. I'd better get back in my place in the parade. Thanks for the water, Mother. See you later, boys."

"So, Grandma, what are you bringing for the picnic at Rosemary's?" Randy asked.

"I'm bringing the Phillips potato salad. I made a treat for your daddy this time. He raves over my pumpkin pie, so I made pie, even though it's not Thanksgiving."

"Oh, yum, I'm hungry already," Steve said.

Some of the most divisive years in U.S. history were in the early 1970's when Randy and Steve were in college. Manchester, the small Brethren school they attended, was pacifist. Though the Viet Nam War was winding down, anti-war sentiment was constant and vigorous. Daniel Ellsberg had released the Pentagon Papers, exposing misconceptions and untruths about the conduct of the war. This sparked demonstrations and occupation of buildings on college campuses everywhere.

In 1973 news broke about the Watergate break-in. White House officials were fired, and presidential tapes were released, eventually resulting in the Saturday Night Massacre. Two of Nixon's attorney generals resigned rather than fire the Watergate Special Prosecutor.

A counterculture was "in" on campus. Drugs were endemic. Dress harkened back to the hippie culture: long shaggy hair, polyester, and bell-bottom jeans. In Walt and Helen's opinion, the college environment was worrisome. They particularly didn't like the boys' long shaggy hair.

"I feel like I'm part of the mob," Steve laughed as he and Randy stealthily sneaked to the most secluded area in the cornfield.

"I know what you mean," Randy clutched the packet of seeds in his hands. "It's weird being out here in the dark. Flash the light ahead. We need to go in several rows to be sure Dad doesn't find the plants when they get tall."

"Did your friend tell you how to plant marijuana?" Steve asked.

"He said it's like any other plant, an inch or two deep—nothing to it. It'll be nice to have our own stash. Man, it gets expensive when you have to buy it."

"If this grows well we might have enough we can even make a little on it," Steve said as he dug a trench and dropped the seeds. By the way Ran, did you leave a pile of empty beer cans hidden in the barn? Dad asked me about it, and I don't think Mother left them," he chuckled at his humor.

"Oh, I meant to go back and get those. What did Dad say?"

"He said, 'I hope Randy's not getting in over his head. Booze can get a hold of you.' My guess is, he's a little concerned."

"Well, I don't think I have a problem more than any of the guys we hang out with," Randy grinned at Steve, "though they're probably not stellar role models. I guess we're done here. Grow, babies, grow," he said as they walked back to the house, the sun lighting the horizon.

That spring day, Earl and Esther were visiting friends who had a cottage on Fish Lake. They had roasted wieners for lunch and were sitting around the fire visiting and enjoying the weather. Earl slumped forward, his knees collapsing as the other three leaped forward and lowered him to the ground.

"Earl, Earl! What's wrong?" Esther's voice was panicky as she patted his cheeks. "Talk to me, Daddy."

Earl groaned, his eyes vacant, his body flaccid. "Earl, can you hear me?" John yelled into his ear.

"John, something bad has happened. He has heart trouble. Maybe he had a heart attack."

"Esther, we need to get him to a hospital. There aren't phones here at the lake. I'll bring my car close and we'll drive him to town. Elsie, you get a pillow and a blanket."

By the time the three lifted Earl into the back seat, he was unresponsive, saliva drooling from his mouth. He leaned against Esther's chest, her arms encircling him. "It's okay, Daddy. We're going to get help for you.... Just rest now.... You'll be okay...." She whispered the encouraging words she wanted him to hear—but doubted in her own panic. The ride seemed interminable. Once at the hospital he was hooked to machines. Tests were done. Elsie called each of the daughters on the pay phone and by the time the families had arrived, doctors determined he had had a stroke. They admitted him to the hospital.

Earl's life was never the same. His mobility and speech were compromised. His vision was damaged; no more could he ride the bicycle. His mental status changed; he was forgetful, disagreeable, and hard to please. In the months after the stroke, Esther missed her gentle, compliant husband.

He came into the kitchen where Esther was baking cookies. "I'm going to take a walk."

"I have a batch of cookies in the oven. If you wait a few minutes, I'll go with you," Esther answered. Earl grumbled and returned to the living room. Five minutes later, when Esther went to the living room, he was gone.

"Oh, my goodness, he left by himself," she mumbled as she hustled out the door, looking both ways. After rushing a few blocks, she hurried home and started searching with the car. She found him more than a mile from home.

"Where were you?" he said angrily, bursting into tears. "I got lost."

"Daddy, get in the car. We'll go home now." She guided him into the car.

"Why did you let me get lost?" he cried.

"It won't happen again, Daddy. You won't get lost again; I'll see to that. Let's go home and have a cookie," she said, drying his tears with her hanky and tucking him into the car.

He became fearful of leaving the house and being taken to a nursing home. One day he led her to the spare bedroom. "This is where I want to sleep," he said.

"Then we'll make up this bed and you'll sleep in here." After that, Esther "slept with one eye open" so she could hear him when he awakened and wandered around the house at night.

One morning she woke and went to the kitchen to start breakfast. She went to wake Earl and sensed something wrong. "It's time to wake up," she shook his shoulder. "Daddy, wake up," she shook him again. She lifted the blanket and rubbed his leg. It was cold. "Oh Daddy, this isn't right. I need help," she ran to the kitchen and called Erdene.

"Erdene, I can't wake up Daddy." She was dazed, "You need to come right away. I need help with Daddy." She went back to the bedroom, moving a chair to sit beside the bed. In minutes, Erdene and her husband, Howard, rushed into the room.

"Oh Mother," Erdene put her arm around Esther. "Howard, call Milo. Are you okay Mother? Let me pull up a chair." Within minutes, Milo Yoder, the family friend who was a funeral director, came into the bedroom.

Esther hurried to him, "Milo, I can't wake Daddy. Can you wake him up?" she cried tearfully. Milo took Esther in his arms and held her. "He's at peace now, Esther. He's happy now."

She looked at her dear soulmate of fifty-eight years. "He can't wake up, can he?" she mulled this in her mind as if a new idea. "You know, Milo, he hasn't been happy these last months. I would say something to him, and it didn't seem to register in his brain. He'd get so frustrated. You think he's happy now?"

"I know it, Esther. Earl was a good man. He's with the Lord."

"I'm glad, then. I'm glad he's happy. He gave *me* fifty-eight years of happiness."

"You and Daddy were good partners, Mother," Erdene said, holding her close.

The days became a blur—so many people, so many decisions, so much for Esther to do. When she returned home after the funeral, her daughters were concerned. Esther had never been alone.

"Things will be different, Mother," Rosemary said. "We'll take turns staying overnight until you're ready to be alone."

Esther was thoughtful, then she straightened her shoulders, "No, this is the time for me to start being alone," she said decisively. "You don't need to stay over. I'll get along by myself. I have my car, and when I get lonely, I'll get in the car and go. You girls don't need to worry about me."

* * * * *

When Steve and Randy had school breaks, they liked to go with their dad on the milk route. It was a time to bond; talk about whatever: religion, politics, girlfriends, or world news. This fall day, Steve had something on his mind.

"Dad, did you find anything growing in the cornfield?"

"Yes, Steve. There's corn in the cornfield," he stated the obvious. "We'll be ready to pick it in a few weeks."

"Did you spray insecticide on some tall weeds in the back corner?"

"I don't know what you're talking about, but whatever you and Randy are up to, I probably don't want any part of it. Colleges are like powder kegs now; anything can start a ruckus. You need to stay out of trouble. You know I'm not fond of your long hair, but in five years it will mean nothing. What's important is that you and Ran don't get in the kind of trouble you can't walk away from; that won't be forgotten in five years."

"I agree, Dad. There's lots of craziness on campus. A political group agitates and gets kids stirred up. Ran and I haven't gone to any demonstrations."

"What grade did you get on that research project on parenting? You know Steve, Mother was really quiet after reading your paper. I think your results hurt her feelings. Parents want to think they did a decent job raising their kids. I decided if she felt bad after reading it, I won't read it. I don't want to know all the mistakes I made."

"I was surprised at the results myself. If it made her feel bad, I wish I hadn't let her read it. I got an A on that paper. I really worked hard on it."

"So are you still going with that little gal from Illinois, the one with curly hair? I know you don't want my advice, but I'll tell you anyway: keep your pecker in your pants unless you want to live with that person for the next fifty years."

Steve smirked, "Well Dad, it's a good thing I came on the route today. You have a load of advice. I wish I had written down all your words of wisdom over the years. It would be interesting reading."

"I doubt that. I try not to give much advice. I figure I'm better off listening," he said.

"How's Grandma doing? I'm sure she's lonely. I stopped to see her yesterday and she wasn't home."

"She goes a lot. I'm glad you stopped; having grandkids visit is her favorite pastime. Yeah, she goes a lot. She's doing well."

CHAPTER 45

Heifer Project International

Esther observed the tiny waif asleep in her bed, her breath faint, her white hair sparse. She gasped, quickly setting down the meal tray. Could this be? The name on the tray said Edna Dierdorf.

Esther touched her shoulder, "Mrs. Dierdorf, I'm here to help with your lunch." The little lady startled awake. In the depths of her eyes, the fullness of her cheeks, and the wavy hair around her face, Esther could see the shadow of her beloved first grade teacher. Tears rushed to her eyes as she clasped the bony hand.

"Mrs. Dierdorf, were you ever a teacher? I think you taught me in first grade."

The tired eyes snapped to attention, her quiet voice was raspy, "Yes. I was a first-grade teacher for fifteen years. What is your name?"

"I was Esther Swihart. Mrs. Dierdorf, I never thought I'd see you again. You were my favorite teacher. I've loved you all these years."

"Yes. I remember you. A bright little girl you were. I believe I taught your sisters." The lady's mind seemed razor sharp.

"That would be Edith and Ruth. I understand you need help eating. Let me help you sit up so we can get started. You can't know how happy I am to see you again. I idolized you. I've had so many good memories of first grade."

Esther was an outstanding Gray Lady. In her later years she not only worked her scheduled hours, but became friends with several of her patients: visiting, taking treats, and being with them when they died. Hers was a life of mission. There weren't enough hours in her days.

Along with friends, Esther ate lunch and attended programs at Greencroft Senior Center near her home. There were always cookies and pies in her kitchen for the children and grandchildren who visited. She especially appreciated her close ties to her granddaughters, who trickled in with their bouncing babies and family news. Though the loss of Earl left an enduring void, her life was fulfilled and of worth.

Walt and Helen were soon to be empty nesters. Randy graduated college and in a lovely spring wedding married Vanessa. He got a job as field rep for a large dairy corporation; Vanessa was a home economics teacher in the local high school.

For years Walt and Helen had contributed to Heifer Project International (HPI), a charity started during WWII by Dan West, a Goshen acquaintance. American dairymen donated livestock to small farmers in third world countries who then grew their own herds, passing along newborn animals to start other budding farms. In this way Heifer Project seeded thousands of small farms across the world as well as providing meat and milk for poor families.

On this Saturday morning Walt and Helen were eating their normal breakfast of applesauce on toast with a glass of milk. He spoke as if needing care with his words, "I got this idea yesterday while working at the Heifer Project barn. Helen, we need to be making plans for our retirement. I've never thought it's enough to just give money to a good cause. We've mentioned we need to give ourselves—our time and our abilities. We should do something out of the ordinary that would be a stretch." He looked almost shy—not in the habit of expounding. "We've been given so much over the years. I thought yesterday, maybe it's time we start giving back: we have things paid for, we don't need money; the kids are well set; and we're young enough we don't have health problems."

Helen nodded, "You're right, we need a challenge. Do you mean something big, like go abroad? I'm only fifty-seven. I always figured I'd teach until I'm sixty when I get a better retirement package. Are you thinking of selling the bulk routes?"

"I think so, Helen. I haven't said anything to anyone; I'll do what you want. We'll get a good price for them." He went to the sink to rinse his saucer, "What we're doing would completely change. For the rest of our lives we'd be giving back."

"I'm with you on this, Walt. It makes me proud of you, and excited to think what it might be. I have no idea how we'll find the right job for us. I need some time to think about this—I assumed I had a few years to be with my kiddos."

At the Heifer Project spring banquet, Walt was surprised and honored to be recognized with the National Service Award. The goals of this organization meshed with Walt and Helen: feed poor people and help them start a small farm. They didn't have a missionary zeal to convert natives.

After the banquet Walt and Helen were surrounded by HPI executives. "Congratulations, Walt. We appreciate all your work for Heifer Project."

"Thank you," he said, shaking hands with them. "Helen and I want to make an appointment with you. We're heading into retirement and want to look into a long-term commitment of maybe a few years."

The two men looked at each other, their jaws dropping, "What a coincidence you mention that. We need to get you with the directors at Arkansas Headquarters. We have a huge project just getting off the ground. Let's set up a time next week."

* * * * *

It was the last day of the school year in 1978. Helen stood at the door of her room, hugging her fourth graders as she tried to control the lump in her throat and the tears filling her eyes. *This is it, the end of my twenty-two-year teaching career. Fourth graders were my love, wanting to please and not yet smart alecky. It was such a joy to follow them as they grew up, becoming successful citizens with families and careers. And to think I've taught the last eleven years without a single sick day, she thought with a smile.* She knew she couldn't go to her dear friend Glenna's room today; she would break down for sure.

She needed to go to 14th Street to see her mother and update her on the pandemonium in her life. Whew! Repeatedly she caught herself exhaling, as though short of breath when thinking about leaving her eighty-year-old mother. Esther had given her everything she had to give, believing in her, and making opportunities. She seemed healthy, but it weighed heavily that she may never see her again.

The two women sat in the living room surrounded by family photos through five generations, beginning with Sarah and Judd. She clasped her mother's hands, "Today was probably my last day being a teacher," her voice broke. "You and Daddy made it all possible," her eyes filled. "You let me live my dream all these years. And now Walt and I will be starting another dream. It's happened so fast Mother, I still can't believe it."

"Oh Helen. You're going to Africa for sure?"

"It's for sure. Walt is leaving next week to fly one-hundred-fifty Jersey cows to Africa. Seventy-five of them will stay in Kenya and Walt will take the rest to an island called Mafia, thirty miles off the coast of Tanzania. I brought you a map. See here, it's about halfway down the East Coast of Africa. You've heard of Zanzibar and Madagascar—it's between those two islands. Mafia Island is this dot in the ocean, fifteen miles long."

"You're going to live on an island?"

"Yes. There are twenty-five thousand Africans on Mafia. We'll be the only full-time white people. But listen, Mother," her voice broke in her intensity, "They've never had cows! The children have never had cow's milk to drink. If we're successful, think how we'll improve nutrition; and the calves that are born will start many little farms. It's a huge, expensive undertaking for Heifer Project. They don't know if American cows can adapt to Africa. It's a huge responsibility for Walt."

"Oh Helen...Oh Helen...Oh my DEAR," Esther mouthed the gravity.

"Imagine, our first flight on a big plane and it will be three days long. Walt will be in Africa five weeks to get the cows situated, then he'll come home and I need to be packed and ready to leave. Oh Mother, I just don't know. We prayed that God would have something for us, but honestly, we never dreamed of something of this magnitude. We have to speak Swahili, and they say it's the hardest language to learn...Oh Mother." Helen shook her head, overwhelmed with all the unknowns.

"How long will you be gone?" Esther asked.

"That's another thing; we'll be gone two years." Helen's composure dissolved, her shoulders shook. "I may never see you again, Mother."

"Now Helen, we're not going to think like that. If this is where God is sending you and Walt, we have to trust that He'll keep all of us safe. I believe He will. Now, how can I help? We've got work to do."

"I've got to clean out my classroom. I want to pack all my school supplies just in case I get to teach when we come home."

"I'll be at your house tomorrow morning at eight o'clock. I'll go to Krogers and get a bunch of boxes and packing tape."

Life in Goshen had long been provincial, slow-paced, well-churched, and highly moral. This was influenced by well-established small farm Amish, Mennonite and Brethren communities. The men who fought in WWII had little interest in world travel. Most Goshenites were happy to be ignorant of the dark African Continent. No one in Elkhart County jet-setted halfway around the world on an African safari, returning with elephant pictures and ivory figurines to hang on the wall. Ladies were interested in Tupperware, not handwoven foreign placemats.

Overnight this changed for the Steffen family. Their hale and hearty parents were now seen as fragile and vulnerable. Judy's intense concern spilled over in a phone call to Helen: "Mother, Dr. Meyer at the State Board of Health had a meeting today for all University Medical Center faculty. This is really important. You must take this seriously, write it down."

"Oh dear, what now?"

"There's a new disease called AIDS, Acquired Immune Deficiency Syndrome. It's very bad; there's no treatment or cure. It originated in Africa where people are dying by the thousands. In the U.S. it's only in California and New York, but he says in a few years it will be in every town in the nation. Mother, he almost sounded panicked about it, and doctors aren't like that. It spreads in the blood and by sexual contact. Apparently men in Africa have many sexual partners besides their wife, and they spread to all of them. They have all these orphaned children whose parents are sick and dying."

"Oh, Judy, do I want to hear this?" Helen asked, not needing one more thing.

"Mother, you *have* to hear it. It could save your life. It's spread through blood. Evidently they reuse needles and medical and dental instruments without sterilizing them—so any of these that break the skin can spread the virus. No one lives long with this disease, a few years at most. Mother, I'm going to do more research and send information, so you know how to protect yourself. This is scary stuff."

"Wouldn't you know a dreadful disease would break out just when we're going. We're getting everything medical and dental done now. I've never had so many tests and shots. Daddy and I are healthy and we won't take chances, but I guess it's good to know about this."

"It hasn't been in the news yet, Mother. The medical community is just now learning about it."

"Well don't tell Grandma about this."

Time ticked away. Decisions about overseeing the farm were made. All twenty-one Steffens: the siblings, spouses, and eight grandchildren had a weekend gathering at Camp Mack. This good-bye felt momentous. Sue and little Chris from Virginia stayed to close the farmhouse and box up necessities for Africa—for people *and* cows. It was time to leave.

CHAPTER 46

Mafia Island, Africa

Walt and Helen arrived on Mafia Island on a six-seater plane that crossed thirty miles of the Indian Ocean from Dar es Salam, Tanzania. Met by a shy, smiling driver in a Land Rover, they bumped over the potholed sandy path through the tiny village of Kilindoni, with its market, health clinic, church, phone operator, and two men operating sewing machines. Ragamuffin toddlers wearing only a shirt, scattered after the older children who wore U.S. flea market discards. The African women were a blaze of garish color, dressed in a blouse and large wraparound swath of material that covered all but their bare feet. Many ladies and older girls carried an infant swaddled in a sling. Everyone had short, nappy hair, some wearing a bandana. Life had come to a standstill; the natives were curious to see the new white people. For several miles, the path broke through coconut trees as far as the eye could see. The driver stopped and carried their suitcases into a brown, one-story house, then bowed his adieu.

Walt's arms encircled Helen, his fingers threading through her hair. "Welcome home, my dear. Are you worried what I got you in to?"

She gave him a quick kiss. "This will be our adventure—just the two of us. We have no one else to depend on." She broke away to explore their new home, "I know the first place I'll start: cleaning up dead bugs."

They walked through their cement home. It had a kitchen, living room, two bedrooms, and a bathroom with a toilet and shower. Each room had slatted windows which turned open, and screened openings near the ceiling for air circulation. This was one of few homes on the island that had electricity. The wood furniture was basic, just the essentials. Mosquito netting fell from the wall, crossing the beds.

"Better than I expected. I thought we'd have mud walls and a thatched roof," Helen said.

"That's what 95 percent of the islanders have," Walt answered. "They have community outhouses. We're royalty here. Do you want to go with me to check my cows? I want to get back soon; I expect Henry Stanley will come this evening. I don't want to miss him."

Mafia Island, covered with coconut trees, was controlled by Mafia Coconuts, Limited. All parts of the coconut were used, but the primary profit was from coconut oil which was exported in fifty-gallon metal drums. The executive of the British company was Henry Stanley, who divided his time between Mafia and England. Henry was the quintessential colonial overseer in his khaki safari shirt, shorts, and jungle helmet. He had power and connections: he was elite, respected, and feared because he hired 90 percent of the Africans on Mafia. Establishing the Heifer Project Dairy was beneficial to him; feeding the islanders was a perennial problem. His workers and their families would be healthier. Heifer Project, for its part, could not initiate the dairy without Henry's support and years of experience in Tanzania. When in Mafia, Henry lived with Maria, a young African lady. When he was off island, she was his "Girl Friday". If something was needed, one talked to Maria.

Only in retrospect could it be understood that Walt and Helen were the perfect couple to initiate the Mafia Dairy Project. They were the antithesis of the "Ugly American". They had no pretensions or arrogance; they recognized they were the ones needing to learn other ways of doing things. Their concerns were: how can we get this job done; how can we be a friend; and how can we assure that the project will continue after we're gone? While they had no illusions of grandeur, they wanted to leave their mark in Africa. This was especially true for Helen, who didn't have an assigned job. There were many days they were weary or homesick, when progress seemed futile. But they were irrepressible, refusing to succumb to discouragement.

Most islanders were Muslim. Walt and Helen's faith was expressed by their active participation in the small Christian church in Kilindoni. Certainly, they disagreed with aspects of the culture, but they were nonjudgmental of their neighbor man who had two wives, or of Henry who had a wife in England and a partner on the island. Africans' lives were not liberated; they had few options.

As a small farmer and milk hauler interacting daily with farmers, Walt had expertise with dairy cows. His intuition and problem-solving through the years stood him in good stead in Africa, where veterinarians weren't a phone call away. Two men, Malulu and Bange, spoke patch-together Swahili and English. Using hand motions, one and two word sentences, and an abundance of patience, the temporary "barn" they built out of rusty, cast-off coconut oil drums was make-do at best. They would milk cows by hand until milking equipment came from the U.S. The dairy needed to be operational by December when the heifers would have baby calves and cows would be milked twice daily.

Care of the herd was paramount and never ending. An ongoing focus was teaching the herdsman to observe for illness and injury as there were diseases in Africa unknown in the U.S. Each day the herd was driven to pasture on the nutritious grasses grown in the coconut groves. Twice weekly they were herded five miles to the long concrete dipping tanks. Each cow needed to swim through the pesticide-laced water to prevent bites by the tsetse fly. The fly carried trypanosomosis, or "sleeping sickness", a disease potentially fatal to animals and humans. Particularly during the rainy season, cows were subject to hoof rot, requiring the hoofs to be scrubbed and pasted with medicine. Snakes, spiders, and scorpions were ubiquitous, though bites weren't common if one took safety measures.

While Walt didn't have enough hours in the day, Helen was bored, literally to tears. Ali did the household tasks she ordinarily would do. Twice a day, six days a week, Ali walked six miles from his home to be their houseboy. He was devoted to Mama Helen. In fact, local knowledge suggested the best jobs on the island were those with the easygoing Americans who were kind, fair, and generous.

"Something is going to have to change around here. I can't live like this for two years," Helen sobbed to Walt. "We need to get rid of Ali. I can't stand having him *always around.*"

"Well Helen, there are things we can do, but we can't get rid of Ali. He has five children to feed."

"If I hear: 'Mama Helen, sit,' one more time, I'm going to hit him! Walt, you don't understand. There's nothing for me to do," she screeched.

"I thought this might be a problem. We have to find a way for you to meet some ladies. I see ladies and children walking to the village all the time."

"Oh Walt, I feel like an appendage. If I come to the barn, I'm in the way of you and the men; if I go to the market with Ali, I'm not needed; there's nothing to do at home. I'm just miserable."

"What would you like to do?"

"I'd like to wake up in the morning and have something to do that day. I'd give anything for a woman friend, even if we can't speak very much. I'm surprised how well Ali and I communicate. Since I have nothing to do, I've worked on my Swahili and I'm getting fairly good."

"The islanders are so poor, there has to be some way we can help. I'm going to talk to Maria. She knows the woman things going on. I was thinking, when the cows freshen, we could have you sell milk at the market, but that won't work either. You can't take a job from an African man."

"Don't tell Maria I was crying," Helen's voice was subdued. She'd run into many brick walls in her life; she could always surmount them, but finding a role for herself in Africa stymied her.

She knew the native ladies were too shy to come to her. She would have to brazen her way into their world. She asked Maria to buy bulk amounts of marked down polyester material on her next trip to Dar es Salaam on the mainland. She brought out a board game and played with the children, learning to know their mothers. She visited her neighbor ladies, taking a snack to share; they began to return the visits. She had Maria buy seeds, and she and Ali planted and tended a garden. In fall when twilight came earlier and the rains were starting, she suggested he make enough supper for both households, and return early to eat with his family. She went to the school, offering to teach English. A few students came to the house for weekly tutoring sessions.

When the material and sewing supplies arrived, Helen started sewing classes that continued the two years of their stay. She made several dress patterns and the ladies handstitched dresses for their daughters. In pictures of the children in Kilindoni, the boys were wearing tattered tee shirts and the little girls sashayed in their wear-forever polyester dresses. One of the classes even made a wedding dress for one of the ladies.

December 1978 was a bell weather month—the best of times and the worst of times. Randy's wife, Vanessa had given birth to Angela, their first child. It was hard for Walt and Helen to miss this momentous occasion. Steve, their youngest, had graduated college in May, and with his college friend Larry, planned a six-month trip through Europe, Africa, and India. Steve would spend six weeks on Mafia Island, the boost in the arm they needed. His carefree, lively humor lightened their everyday struggles. It was good to speak English with someone who understood them.

Walt began to notice some of the cows acting sickly: feverish, not eating well, and lacking energy. It was necessary to take daily rectal temperatures of each cow. They would soon deliver their calves—their health was essential. Blood samples were sent to veterinarians on the mainland who were unable to diagnose the disease. In one week, two cows died. Walt and Steve removed, bagged, and froze sections of all major organs, and had them flown to vets in Dar es Salaam. This was their worst nightmare, having the herd ill from an unknown disease. The blood tests indicated it wasn't sleeping sickness, confirming their procedure for dipping the cows in pesticide had been successful.

Walt experienced Africans' nonchalance regarding time, but everyone, from the herdsmen to the Tanzanian government, stepped up in this crisis. When Henry Stanley came to the barn, Walt insisted they immediately send vets from the mainland. Within a few days, three veterinarians working in Tanzania flew to Mafia: one from the United States, one from Great Britain, and one from East Germany. A representative from the U.S. Agency for International Development (U.S.A.I.D.) visited. Not only were Walt and Helen coping with sick cows, they were hosting these influential visitors. The three vets finally made the diagnosis: East Coast Fever. The disease was transmitted by ticks which bit the cows as they grazed in the tall grasses. Fortunately, there was medicine to prevent and treat this disease, and the cows slowly healed. They would need to be watchful.

When it rained it poured. This was the time Walt had his first bout with malaria, cycling between shivering chills and burning fever. "I need to check the heifer that didn't eat well this morning," Walt said to Steve after a rare afternoon nap.

"I hope you're not in a hurry; I can hardly walk. I told you I have jock itch. I've been using that fungus cream you gave me—it hasn't touched it. My whole ass is flaming red and burns like fire."

"Sorry it's not better, Steve. It's hard to get rid of fungus in the tropics. I told you not to wear underwear, didn't I? That's the only way I stay clear of it. I'll have Maria take you to the clinic for gentian violet. It's the strongest medicine they have here. Your whole ass will be purple, it stains everything it touches."

"You're saying I have to tell Maria my balls are on fire?" Steve said sheepishly. "If I go to the clinic, maybe I can get my yellow fever shot. The doctor in Goshen who gave it to me, wrote the date wrong on my medicine card, listing the month first instead of the day first. Tanzania customs think it's expired. They let me into the country, but they said they won't let me leave."

"Your mother will be upset by that, Steve. Before we left home, Judy told her about AIDS. It's a disease that can kill you. It's spread by blood on needles that haven't been sterilized. She was emphatic about not having dental work or getting an injection."

"Crap, Dad. What choice do I have? I believe I've heard of this AIDS disease."

The concern was exacerbated that night when Walt wasn't hungry, complaining of a splitting headache. He and Helen looked at each other knowingly. Though he took precautions, it was almost a given he would get malaria, as much time as he spent around cows. That night the bed shook with his shivering; the sheets were soaked with sweat. Helen changed the sheets and sponged him with a cool cloth. He was so sick he didn't notice her tears. She had never felt so despondent. She and Steve sat on either side of the bed, Steve holding Walt's hot calloused hand, overwhelmed by a disease that could so quickly strike down a strong, healthy man.

"I've never seen someone with malaria," she said, holding the cloth to his head. She startled as a small, harmless lizard scurried across the wall over the bed. "I hate those darn lizards," she said fiercely.

Steve's head jerked up, surprised at her first-ever "swear" word. "They do startle you when they run around the walls. I'm not used to them either." He knew her frustration and fear was directed at the lizard. This was no time to tease about her choice of words.

"Most of the natives get malaria. They treat it with a penicillin shot."

"My head, my head," Walt moaned, lost in his world of pain.

"The doctor from Dar will be here tomorrow for the weekly clinic. I've called for the Land Rover to be here by ten o'clock." Helen said.

"Is Dad going to get a penicillin shot?" Steve asked Helen.

"I have to get the shot, or I won't be good for anything. Even if I do, I can have malaria relapses. We'll just have to risk it." Walt's voice was shaky but definite.

The next morning at clinic the African doctor smiled, unperturbed by Walt's illness. "We fix. Penicillin shot. Another next week."

Helen explained to Maria, who interpreted to the doctor, about the disease called AIDS which was spread in Africa by unsterilized needles.

The doctor looked skeptical, "Ah-h yes, wasting disease. Mr. Steffen has malaria, not wasting disease." He showed Helen the reused needles soaking in liquid. "See, we sterilize needles."

"Are the needles cleaned and boiled?" Helen asked Maria.

"Is good," the doctor nodded vigorously.

This was Africa. All three knew when they came, there was risk involved. "Helen, we're getting nowhere here. I'll just have to trust I'll be okay. All those people waiting to see the doctor are sicker than me. We're taking too much time," Walt said.

"I guess if you're getting a shot, I'll get the one for yellow fever," Steve said, stepping up with his incorrectly dated medical card.

"Steve, we won't say anything to the kids at home about this. We have no choice. I'll leave and you can have him check your jock itch," Helen said softly.

"Walt was exhausted on the drive home, but his mind was busy as they discussed their experience. "It's interesting to me that everyone at the clinic today got free health care. Certainly, it isn't the quality we have in the U.S., but it's equal for everyone."

When they arrived home, they smelled the delicious aroma of Palau. This favorite African dish was reserved for special occasions due to expense and difficulty in obtaining all the ingredients. Ali, in his devotion and concern for Walt's health had walked all over the island to obtain beef, rice, vegetables, and spices, cooking the favorite meal that would tempt Walt to eat. Overcome by the morning's events, and Ali's kind expression of love, Helen rushed to hug him, "Oh Ali, twakupenda. We love you," her voice choked with emotion.

Walt continued with cycles of chills and fever until the next week when he got his second penicillin shot. Ali, Helen, and Steve were eating lunch in the kitchen when they heard Walt scream with more energy than he had shown in days.

"Steve, get in here," his voice was frantic. There was a loud crash, "Steve!"

Steve ran to the bedroom. "Oh shit, Oh shit. Dad, be careful!" he yelled. Walt had grabbed a barn boot and was chasing a giant brown hairy spider, the body the size of the palm of his hand with legs six inches long. Helen ran into the bedroom and screamed bloody murder. After one look at the spider, even Ali joined Helen outside. Steve and Walt, each with a boot, timidly chased that spider all over the room. They couldn't believe how fast it crawled and how it jumped from the wall when cornered, landing with a solid thump. Several times they hit it, thinking they surely killed it, only to have it stare with its evil eye and scamper away.

"I know we have big spiders here, but I've never seen anything like this. I think it's possessed!" In his weakened condition, Walt stopped to catch his breath.

"This just freaks me out. I know I'll have terrible nightmares," Steve's voice was shaking. "Is there pest spray here at the house?"

"Not now, but there sure will be—it's at the barn. We have to keep the spider in sight, or it'll hide in the house. I'm sure a bite would kill us, as big as it is."

Helen yelled in the kitchen door, "Are you okay? Did you kill it?"

"No, it's still here. Mother, come close the door into the living room. We need to keep it in the bedroom," Steve yelled.

"I heard it land on the floor; that's how I noticed it. I'm sure glad Helen wasn't here alone. Are you ready to give it another go?"

"Let's try to get it in a corner and both go after it. We can't let it squeeze into a place we can't get to. Dude, I can hardly stand to look at it."

They chased that spider for several more minutes until Steve's swat injured it and they were finally able to beat on it till it was dead. They put it in a bag, knotting it closed.

"It's gone. You can come in," Steve called to Helen and Ali.

"I'm almost afraid to come in. That spider has probably laid eggs all over the house. We'll have hundreds of huge hairy spiders hatching out. I can't stand it, Walt!" Helen, nearly berserk, was at the end of her senses. "I can put up with lizards crawling on the walls, birds flying in the house, scorpions in my shoes, and worms on the floor and in the maize meal. But I cannot live with spiders the size of a tennis racquet. There's a limit; this is it!"

"I'm with you on that, Mother. That totally grossed me out. There was something supernatural the way that spider looked at us and jumped and crawled away so fast. It made my skin crawl."

"I believe it just got into the house; I heard it land. It must have squeezed past the top screen near the ceiling and dropped to the floor. I'll get Malulu to come with the ladder and nail the screens tight. We'll spray around all the windows and doors. Steve you check every inch inside the house for spiders and eggs. By nighttime we'll all be able to go to sleep."

"Remember, Pauline and Len and Muriel and Milo are visiting this winter. Can you imagine the story Len would tell in Goshen if they'd see a spider like that?" Helen said, still wound tight as a tick.

"Mother, this is Africa. You knew it would be an adventure," Steve said, using a flashlight to check every drawer and dark cranny.

"I don't want people in Goshen to have a confrontation with a spider like we just had," Helen shivered. "I want them to go home with good memories." The truth for these three: for the rest of their lives, when the Mafia spider was mentioned, they blanched, shook their head in disbelief, and grabbed their gut.

* * * * *

"Oh, come in. What a treat to see all you girls together," Grandma's hands lifted to her cheeks in delight. Jan, Judy, Nan, and Sue sat on the sofa and floor around Grandma's chair. "Sue, you're here from Virginia."

"We're going to try to call Mother and Daddy tomorrow, so I drove here yesterday. We never know if the call will go through, but I so want to hear their voices; I've been homesick for them."

"Susie, so have I. Helen is good about sending the blue aerogrammes, but I miss her so much. Do you think they're doing okay?"

"They wouldn't tell us if they weren't. It's a good thing you taught Mother to make cottage cheese when she was a girl. I think the only dependable food they have is the milk from the cows. I know she hangs cottage cheese on the clothesline like you used to. The supply boat is supposed to come every two weeks, but it's erratic. She said the boat was caught in a bad storm and they had to throw all the food overboard to save the boat from sinking. They got a burlap sack of maize meal that was full of bugs—that was upsetting. I think they eat lots of dried beans. She talks about the natives not having enough food," Judy said.

"Grandma, the call is scheduled for tomorrow at ten in the morning. Mother and Daddy will be at the phone exchange in the village. But we must go through several international operators, each of which can disconnect the call. It can easily take an hour to place the call and sometimes we try a few times and have to give it up. There's no guarantee," Jan said.

Nan added, "The last time we called we had the best connection; there was no static. It seemed like they were in the same room. But after ten minutes the line went dead. Mother later wrote that the wind dropped a coconut on the telephone line, breaking it. The island didn't have phone service for several days."

"Girls, if I could just hear their voices—that would be such comfort. I pray for them often, but they seem so far away."

"We'll all pray for a good call tomorrow," Sue said. "How have you been, Grandma? Are you still going to the Senior Center for lunch?"

Grandma perked up and giggled like a seventeen-year-old, dipping her face behind her hand. "How have I been? I don't know if I should tell you," she blushed.

Nan teased her, "Grandma, I think you're holding out on us. Do you have something to tell? You're all antsy."

Grandma leaned forward as if divulging a secret. "Well girls, I think I have a boyfriend. It could even be serious. Can you believe, at my age?"

Sue chuckled, giving her a hug, "Why Grandma, you little dickens. You're never too old for a little hanky-pank. You're eighty-one aren't you?"

"I am, but I don't feel that old," she swished her hand as if her age was a moot issue.

"You're acting like a spring chicken, Grandma," Judy smiled.

"This nice man—Owen is his name, his wife died years ago—started sitting beside me at lunch at the Senior Center. Oh, the ladies started teasing me; he was so obvious. Well, the thing is, this lady named Bernice is chasing after Owen, and she won't give *me* the time of day." Grandma's voice was plucky and gossipy, her hands motioning dramatically. "Last week Bernice stopped to talk to Owen and when she left, he turned to me and said, 'That Bernice, she has a tongue like a shovel'." Grandma's laugh shimmered joyfully; her eyes widened at the audacity of such talk. "We've gone to church several times and he took me to the music programs at the Senior Center."

"Grandma, I definitely think Owen has the hots for you," Nancy grinned.

"W-h-a-t?" Grandma asked quizzically, as the girls cracked up laughing.

"We do have one problem; we're both as deaf as a doornail. Owen's even worse than me. But, in his favor, he likes to drive. He's a good driver and I'm comfortable riding with him. He has a nice car. And you all know how I like to go," she smiled.

"Oh yes, we know," the girls nodded unanimously.

"The other night we were talking, and I told him Erdene and Howard had just called from Cypress Gardens in Florida. I mentioned that I've never been to Florida. Then *he* said, 'I'd like to take you to Florida sometime, Esther'," she put her hand to her mouth and smiled coyly, her eyes twinkling. "That's why I said it might be getting serious."

"What do you think about remarriage? It's been several years since Grandpa died," Jan asked.

"I'm not sure, Jan. It seems kind of silly at my age. But I do get lonely. It's been nice to have a man's attention again. Grandpa always looked after me so well, and I miss that."

"If we get through to Mother tomorrow, you'll have to tell her what's happening with Owen," Sue said.

"She'll probably think she needs to come home from Africa and straighten me out," Grandma said soberly.

"She'll want you to be happy. That's what we all want," Nan hugged her.

"Do you want someone to come and get you? We'll have lunch after the phone call," Jan said as they stood to leave.

"Oh no, I'll drive. I'll see you in the morning."

* * * * *

By wintertime Mafia began to feel like home to the Steffens. Most mornings Helen put on her rain slicker and walked to the village, both to get exercise and to speak in Swahili with friends, Kamaria, Kesi, and Binti. One morning a large dog came out in the road ahead of her, barking ferociously, then charging toward her. There was nothing she could do but scream and bend forward, putting her arms up to ward off the attack. Fortunately the dog's owner heard her, soon pulling the dog off. She was frightened to death, oblivious to the man's apologies. She simpered on the way home, checking her wounds, knowing she could have been killed.

In checking for damage, she saw many bruises and scrapes, but few puncture bites. Helen was upset, assuming she would have to fly to Dar es Salaam for treatment. The next day they were hosting Charlie Burrwell, the CEO from Heifer Project, and John Baker from the World Bank. Gail Pate, a vet with U.S.A.I.D was already there for the meeting. She pulled herself together and walked to the barn where Walt and Gail were working.

The cows were forgotten as Gail tended her injuries. The man who owned the dog was waiting at their house, bumbling his apologies, and promising his dog was healthy and had the required shots. Gail had antibiotics for cows, suitable for Helen to take. If she went to a medical doctor in Dar she would likely be given injections with questionably sterile needles. They decided to rely on Gail's care and keep the incident quiet.

When hosting visitors, the Steffens often organized a forty-five-minute Land Rover ride to the Lodge, an upscale inn and restaurant on the coast which catered to wealthy tourists. Life was primitive in Tanzania and their visitors were happy to splurge on a beautiful beach where they could get a good European-style meal with a nice selection of wines and liquors. It was a festive party the next night. The cows were healthy and the dairy successful; the natives were guzzling all the milk they produced; and a little farm was starting with every baby calf given to a native farmer. There were high spirits and toasts of celebration. If anyone noticed their hosts seemed quieter than usual, they didn't mention it.

Walt and Helen counted the summer days until their oldest daughter's family came for a visit: Jan, Lowell, Matt—age ten, and Marcy—age six. They stored food, not wanting their children to suffer the food scarcity.

Jan and Helen were both tearful as Jan climbed out of the small plane and grabbed her in a big hug. It had been so-o long. There was much news to share. "Tell me about Grandma. What is she up to, Jan?"

"Oh, I wish you could see them, Mother. They both grin ear-to-ear. I think they're really happy. Their wedding was small, just your sisters and Owen's nephew. You know they went to Florida. They seem to be in good health. Grandma still writes in her diary and spends a lot of time with her Gray Lady duties. She's happy as long as she can go, and they *do* go."

"What does everyone think of Owen?"

"He's pleasant enough. He's so deaf, it's hard to have a conversation with him. He has managed to move into her house and have her wait on him hand and foot. Your sisters think he got a good deal."

"It seems like Mother thinks *she* got a good deal too, so there you go. What are all the kids up to?"

"You know how it is, everyone is crazy busy—especially with the warm weather. Lowell and I are glad we're teachers so we can travel this summer. Judy teaches oncology nursing and is busy with classes for her Doctorate, Wayne's still with the accounting firm in Indy. Nan helps Ed in his foundry making aluminum castings and calling on customers. I think they just got a big company that makes buttons. Galen and his brother are milking three hundred cows plus all the fieldwork. Sue's quite the entrepreneur with the travel business she's started. She just had a trip where a man had a heart attack on the bus. Randy always has some crisis with one of his farmers; he tells the funniest stories. Since Vanessa teaches Home Ecc, there are as many boys as girls in her classes. She lets them cook things like pizza. Some of her students do an internship in Goshen businesses. You know Steve just bought a house; we'll have to close the farmhouse when he moves out. He talks so much about his time here, and afterward, when he and Larry traveled. It's probably good we don't know everything about that trip. All the grandkids and babies are good—growing like weeds. We miss you and Daddy. It's not the same without you, but we're all staying close. Can you believe your time here is half over? How does that feel?"

"It's hard to believe. I think Walt worries the natives won't be ready to run it in a year. Everything takes longer in Africa. We thought the electric milkers would be here months ago. They keep saying, 'any day now'."

Walt walked into the kitchen, "We're going down to see the new barn. Do you want to come?"

"Come, Mommy. We're going to feed baby calves," Matt yelled.

"Let's go Jan. Maybe we'll see some of my friends. They're eager to meet you. These ladies are...so dear to me." There were stops along the way. Jan was surprised how relaxed the islanders were with Walt and Helen, like their own children and grandchildren.

"Here Matt, hold the bucket. Marcy, you can feed him capra cakes. He turned to Lowell, "This barn is going to work out well—much easier than milking them by hand in the corral. It's elevated with cement so is much cleaner. There are stanchions to keep the cows in place." Walt showed them around with pride. It was very basic by U.S. standards: covered but open-air, set up for electric milkers and a refrigerated milk tank.

The native ladies seemed very curious about Jan's hair, often touching it, then giggling. Several days later Jan and Helen were visiting Binti who was getting married in a few days. The sewing class had made her wedding dress and she was proudly showing it to Jan. Binti and Helen were speaking Swahili, caught up with hand motions. Helen finally understood, turning to Jan, "She wants you to style her hair for the wedding using my pink sponge hair rollers. I believe she thinks I can't do it with my crippled hand."

"Mother, I don't think those rollers will curl African hair. Do you care if she uses your rollers?"

"No, of course not, but I agree. I don't think it will work. I'm not sure what they put on their hair—probably don't want to know," she grinned.

"Tell her I'll be happy to do it, but I don't want her to be disappointed," Jan said. There was a long conversation with Binti smiling broadly, "She *really* wants you to style her hair," Helen responded.

The next Saturday, Lowell took a picture of Jan putting hair curlers in Binti's hair. "You're lucky, Lowell. It's unusual for Africans to let you take their picture. I have a hard time getting pictures of adults. I usually have to bribe them with something," Helen smiled.

Jan was pleased that afternoon when she took the curlers out of Binti's hair. She could coax it into curls—somewhat. Binti beamed! She was thrilled.

Many of the villagers came to the wedding. There was a short ceremony, music and dancing, and a meal: palau, cassava, pineapple, and cornbread. Everyone had a wonderful time. Lowell got good pictures, agreeing to send some to Binti. Each time her eyes found Jan, she smiled proudly. Jan realized that some things are the same the world over: women are particular about their hair and they want it special on their wedding day.

During the second year Helen was busy with many projects, often with the church women and children. At Christmas she translated carols and wrote the Christmas story in Swahili for a children's program. The children who practiced and the mothers who made costumes were totally consumed by this novel undertaking. An even bigger treat was the 250 Christmas cookies Helen baked in her oven, six cookies at a time. Her ladies' sewing classes were so popular a second class was started. She was amazed at their creativity, confident the ladies would meet to sew after her return to the U.S.

Helen knew she wanted to write about their life in Africa and document the accomplishments of Heifer Project. Part of each day was spent writing her children's book. In the evening she and Walt reviewed her work. By the time they returned to the U.S., she had the first handwritten draft of a manuscript.

Hallelujah! The shipment from the U.S. finally arrived. Now the dairy was a modern operation by African standards. Most important were the electric milk machines and the 400-gallon stainless tank to cool milk. Heifer Project had wisely filled the tank with valuable treasures: rubber boots, raincoats, potent antifungal cream, catsup, mustard, gum, and especially, alarm clocks. All these months, Walt had to go to the homes of the herdsmen to awaken them at five o'clock in the dark morning. Time was never a priority for the Africans, though they were never late getting to the barn after milking to get the free zip-lock bags of milk. There was never enough milk for everyone.

"I got an idea this afternoon, Helen. We should take a few days off and go to the mainland. When it's time for us to go home, we aren't going to want to take a safari; we'll be eager to get home. While we're here we need to see a little of Africa. I need to know if Malulu and Bange can run things without me. Henry Stanley is here now. If things get too bad, he can step in."

Helen jumped up and hugged Walt, peppering his face with kisses. "I never thought about *us* taking a vacation. I'd love that. If we go to Dar I need to get my tooth fixed. It's so sharp where it broke and I pad it with gum where it cuts my mouth, but it needs attention before it becomes an emergency. Henry can tell us a dentist used by Americans. Tell me when you want to go; I'll be ready."

Walt's trip idea was the perfect boost they needed. Maria scheduled their appointments and safari arrangements. They were gone five days, one of the few times they left the island during their stay. It was in their nature to be open to wonder, but the safari eclipsed their perception of God's creation. Seeing the animals close up in their own habitat, they marveled at their near-human behavior and the close interconnection between man and all things wild. Ahead of their time, they understood man's responsibility in caring for the environment.

The trip initiated their disengagement from Mafia. They would return home in two months. Their minds centered on tasks they wanted to complete. As the leave date counted down, Helen and Walt realized they felt the same as when they left the U.S two years earlier. Their hearts were one with their Mafia family; it would be difficult to leave them.

All the gift giving, good-byes, and tears, were put aside when Walt and Helen looked out the windows of their small plane flying into South Bend. "My goodness. Look at the crowd, Walt. There must be a hundred people. Do you think it's for us? Yes, I see my Mother. That must be Owen."

CHAPTER 47

Return from Mafia Island

"I can't believe you're really here," Esther said, holding Helen's hands the day after she returned home. "For two years I've prayed we would be together again; my prayers are answered. You're thin, but otherwise you look good."

"Walt and I both lost weight but our health is good. Sometimes food was scarce and there wasn't much variety, but we're well."

"I want to hear all about it," she smiled.

"I hardly know where to start. To be honest, it was harder than I thought it would be. I missed everyone here; that was the hardest part. In Africa everything is a struggle: you struggle to speak; you struggle to get food; you struggle when you walk somewhere; you struggle to stay safe—like not fall, or get bit, or eat bad food. Getting the simplest job done—just everyday living was an effort. I certainly understand poor people better now. All the struggle weighs on you. It's an undercurrent of stress you're not aware of, but you carry it around. We worried about the cows and dairy—that the project would be successful."

"And was it, Helen? I have wondered about that so much."

"Time will tell. It was a huge responsibility for Walt. There was always some catastrophe, but his ulcer never bled, so I think he took it in stride. Oh Mother, I wish you could see the children line up to get milk. We always ran out, but eventually there will be enough for everyone on the island. After two years, we believe so strongly in Heifer Project. They supported us in every way."

"Did you learn to know the people? Did you make friends? When I thought about you over there I wondered if you were lonely."

Helen's eyes spilled with tears; her sweet memories of leaving were fresh. "We have wonderful friends there. I miss them," she got a Kleenex to wipe her eyes. "It's so different; people here can't imagine. They have so little and live with so many hardships, yet they are the warmest, kindest, most generous people I know. They aren't spoiled by all our consumerism and living on a treadmill. Walt and I found it refreshing.

Here I am, blubbering on and on. Let's talk about your two years. You sure did surprise me," she grinned.

Esther lowered her eyes and dipped her chin, as if shy, "This seems backward: a mother telling her daughter about getting married," she chuckled. "I was lonely and Owen started paying attention to me. We both wanted companionship. I've enjoyed having a man in the house. We've sure been busy." She lowered her voice, though she knew Owen couldn't hear her in the next room. "I wish I wouldn't have agreed to sell my car though. Owen thought we didn't need two cars. But I want to go when I want to go. That was a mistake."

"Well Mother, buy a car."

"I don't think that would go over. He usually doesn't complain about taking me and he's easy to have around. We had a real nice trip to Florida with Ruth and Vail. I heard about all those places in Florida. Now I've been there too."

"Good for you. Has your health held up?"

"Oh, you know me. I wake up with all sorts of aches and pains. Owen and I have a litany every morning. Then off we go on another busy day," she chuckled. "Sometimes we walk to the Senior Center or I walk to Beth's. She's a good help and I enjoy seeing her children. All the grandchildren bring their little ones around. I never knew I would enjoy children so much at my age. Beth is typing my diaries. That's a big job—twenty years' worth."

"Steve gave us some good news when we got home: he and Julie Burkholder just got engaged. She was one of my fourth-grade students—one of the best students I've had. She's from a good farm family. Walt and I are thrilled. If I could have picked, she would have been my choice."

"Steve brought Julie to some of the family get-togethers. She's a nice girl. They'll be happy together. I've always had a soft spot for Steve since I took care of him when he was sick. You never knew what would come out of that boy's mouth," she laughed.

"I called Bob Gongwer, my principal at Union Center School. They don't have any job openings. I didn't think they would this late in the season. He said I can keep as busy as I want substitute teaching. We'll be too busy anyway. Everyone says they want to see our pictures."

"We're eager to see them too. Owen and I will be at your first program. We saw Jan's Mafia pictures. They're very interesting."

"Walt wants to work this afternoon to get our slides together. Heifer Project has already scheduled programs for us. I best be getting home. Can I pick up anything from the grocery for you?"

"No Helen. I think we're set."

Helen laughed, "I'm not sure I know how to shop anymore. Sue took me to the store and when I put a ten-pound bag of rice in the cart, she said, 'Mother, you and Daddy don't want ten-pounds of rice.' In Mafia I would have been overjoyed to get ten-pounds of rice."

Helen was busy substitute teaching and volunteering at the hospital while Walt worked at the Heifer Project farm. They showed their slides a few times each week to churches, service organizations, and clubs. Feeling she was getting pulled back into the frenzied pace of American life, she took courses at the college in calligraphy and oil painting. She was surprised how relaxing and enjoyable it was. When Steve and Julie were planning their wedding, they asked her to do the invitations. She didn't think of herself as an artist, but she had a new hobby she loved.

Helen's clubfoot had taken a beating for sixty-seven years. It was becoming painful and unsteady. The orthopedic surgeon was certain he could "build a new foot". She was in a cast with limited mobility for several months. The pain and physical therapy were difficult to endure. She still walked with a limp, but it was easier than it had ever been. During her rehabilitation she started painting greeting cards. They had a sweet appeal; unique artwork, and their message was simple. Many of her friends asked to buy her cards.

While incapacitated she hired an artist and prepared her African book for publication. Printed by a local press, the family celebrated with her, when at Christmas everyone got a copy of *Footprints in the Sand.* She could now add author to her credentials.

CHAPTER 48

Grandma Esther Interview

"Hello."

"Grandma? This is Randy."

"Randy! I'm glad you called." Her response to her grandchildren was always as if they were most important.

"Isn't this a special day? Are you busy celebrating?"

Grandma tittered coyly, "Oh Randy, I'm surprised you remembered—an old woman like me."

"How old are you, Grandma?"

"I'm eighty-five today. Can you imagine?"

"Grandma, we got you the best birthday gift ever. Vanessa had her baby. A little boy, Joshua. We'll call him Josh. Now you have someone in the family with your same birthday. We'll celebrate together."

"Randy, you and Vanessa couldn't have made me happier. Is everyone doing okay?"

"They're doing fine. We'll bring Angie and Nathan in a few days to show off their baby brother. You have a good birthday, Grandma. Don't get too wild. Bye now."

Esther went out in the kitchen. "That was Randy," she yelled. "Vanessa had her baby on my birthday. A little boy, Josh." She looked askance at Owen who was glugging down a big glass of water.

"You shouldn't drink Epsom Salt water every morning. I've never heard tell. It can't be good for you."

"I've been doing it for fifty years—still waiting for it to do its damage," Owen argued in his raspy voice.

Owen and Esther's lives were shrinking inward. He only drove locally to the Senior Center, church, and such. Esther was bothered by pain in her wrists and bursitis in her shoulder. She was no longer able to continue her Gray Lady duties. She had been honored with a ceremony celebrating her twenty years of service. She depended more on others: Beth washed her hair; Marsha trimmed her toenails; Rosemary took her to the grocery; Louise did the finances; and Erdene did the ironing and mending. Her family was in and out every day, bringing food and taking her and Owen to appointments. Year by year her independence had been chipped away. She knew there were days she was snappish and hard to please.

Judy had called from Indianapolis a few weeks before, requesting to interview her about her life and her mother Sarah's life. She was going to tape record their conversation, expected to take three days. This pleased Esther, but she couldn't imagine what she would talk about for three days. Her life hadn't seemed interesting.

The next day Esther and Judy were settled with a cup of coffee in Esther's kitchen. "Grandma, I appreciate your agreeing to talk to me. Let's begin with what your mother Sarah told you about her childhood with Uncle Levi and her life with Judd. I'm also interested in *your* childhood and marriage, and my mother Helen's childhood as *you* remember it. I believe life for the three of you had many struggles, and I want Lisa and Stephanie to know this heritage. I also plan to interview your sister Clara, and others in the family who agree talk to me."

"Judy, I'm glad you're doing this family history. I've been thinking about this since you called. I want to tell you the stories—I hope I don't disappoint you. I ask one thing: I don't want you to share it while I'm living. I don't want anyone to get upset with me."

"I agree with that, Grandma, and I promise to respect your wishes. Let's get started: did your mother tell you anything about her mother, Lucinda, and the cause of her death when Sarah was eight years old?"

"My mother was the best. I loved her so much. I always wanted to please her...." Esther told her stories for three days. She and Judy laughed, cried, and revered her tender confidences. Then the questions were over—the life story documented.

Esther reflected, "My life is nearly over. I wanted it to be worth something—to do some good. My work as a Gray Lady was something I could give. I knew I could never be a teacher, but there are other ways to help. Grandpa and I raised a good family. I know you're not supposed to be proud, but I'm proud of my family. I have so much love for every one of them."

"We all feel that," Judy said, clasping her hand.

"I just had to think of my great-granddaughters last night when they were all talking—Lisa and Stephanie, Marcy, Krista, Kelly, and Jennifer. They are young ladies now and have such different ideas because they've grown up in...well, you could almost say another world. And yet all your girls came and spent time with me. They made me feel like I was somebody; like I'm not out of the picture yet," she smiled through tears.

"Grandma, you're our legend! Even when you're no longer here, you'll be with us. I wish I could express how important you are to the family. If our children are doing well, it's because you taught your daughters, they taught us, and we've tried to teach our daughters. It all began with you."

"I think Judy, you've done something wonderful for me. I've been lifted out of a rut. You reminded me of the details of my life all these years. When you called to ask if I would talk to you, I thought, 'what in the world will I tell her'? But these last days I've remembered so much, and I value this time we've had."

"Grandma, it's meant everything to me. I feel a responsibility to share it in the way you would want."

"This is one thing I can say over and over: if I have wounded any soul today; if I have caused one person to go astray—I ask forgiveness. I don't want to hurt anyone; I want to love everyone. We look at people who do this or that, and we wonder. But we don't understand their situation. Maybe in their place, we wouldn't do any better. So I love people no matter, because I feel there's a reason for us not to know, and the good Lord will take care of these things. For that reason, all we need is His love."

Judy clasped her dear, aged grandmother to her heart, tears streaming. "You're my example of that, Grandma. I love you so much."

CHAPTER 49

Steffen Retirement

Life did not slow down in the 1980's Steffen household. Helen's Homespuns greeting cards "took off", requiring part of the living room be organized as workspace. Labor intensive, every card had a touch of original artwork. Helen celebrated when she sold one-thousand cards, then it was five thousand. Considerable time was spent designing new cards, making cards, and stocking card racks in stores around Goshen.

In addition, Walt and Helen were Deans of the yearly Camp Mack Family Camp, Delegates to the Brethren Annual Conference, on the Board of Heifer Project in Arkansas, and long-time Deacons at Yellow Creek Church. Their inclination was to help church families and others who were struggling: single mothers, the lonely, friendless, and elderly. They had favored charities. They often checked on Grandma and Owen. Grandma was ninety years old and limited because of carpel tunnel pain in both wrists. The couple's own children quick-stepped through busy lives. When the Steffen clan all gathered in the fall for the yearly weekend outing, Walt and Helen hurried off to church on Sunday to attend to those who "needed them", to the chagrin of their own children. For ten years they wintered in Tucson, Arizona with Mennonite Aid, living and working with several couples in a large guest house. The men rehabilitated inner-city homes while the ladies worked in food pantries and Head Start Preschools. As the same couples returned each winter, this group became devoted friends. A huge bonus of their winters in Tucson was reconnecting and spending time with Walt's sister Ann, and her husband Lester.

Elkhart County, with its 4-H, prosperous farms, and RV industry, was recognized as having one of the best fairs in the U.S.—the highpoint of the summer. An unexpected honor for Helen was her selection as Elkhart County Fair Senior Queen. Candidates were chosen by a sponsor to compete. It was a prestigious acknowledgment of accomplishment with parades, luncheons, and commendations. Helen had always kept a low profile, and Walt had always deflected attention. Now he was overjoyed for his "little brunette's" acclaim.

"Walt, I need help fastening my tiara and pinning the shoulder sash. Do I look okay? Compared to the young fair queen, I'm an old wrinkly relic."

"You look perfect. Just a minute." He returned to the bedroom with a beautiful arm bouquet of yellow roses. "You've been my queen for fifty-three years. I'm glad others are recognizing how special you are," he smiled, kissing her carefully.

"These are beautiful. I guess you knew I would wear yellow today. You outdid yourself."

"Jan helped. They're going to be at the lamb booth with Matt's lambs. She can't wait to see you. We'd better get going." They drove to the fairground, each lost in thought. "Now Helen, I'm going to stay on your left side except when you're handing out ribbons. Keep hold of my arm. I don't want you to trip on the uneven ground. You'll have to really watch your step. Okay, here we are. See the banner with your name? That's your golf cart."

"That fella looks familiar," Helen's brow furrowed.

"Hi, Mrs. Steffen," he smiled, extending his hand. "I'm your driver for this week. Do you recognize me? Think Jonesville School about forty-five years ago," his eyes twinkled.

Helen's jaw dropped, her eyes widened, "Chuck Grundy. I don't believe it."

"I'm sure you couldn't forget me. I was the one who put a frog in your desk and soap in the well. You made me pump it clear; it took all afternoon. I was such a brat. You had my dad come to school—embarrassed the heck out of me."

Helen reached up to give him a hug, "Look at you now, a member of the county fair board. I *told* your dad you'd get yourself straightened out."

"I'm a math teacher at Goshen High School. My wife and I have three children. My oldest, Ron, gave me nightmares just like I gave my folks," he chuckled.

"I'm proud of you, Chuck. You say I'll spend all week with you. What a treat."

"I asked to be your driver. You were my favorite teacher, so young and pretty. Here's your itinerary for today. It's chock full, we'd better get started."

"Chuck, this is my husband, Walt."

"Pleased to meetcha, Walt. You have a winner here," he said as they shook hands.

"I know," Walt smiled.

The week of the fair was a highlight for both of them. They were treated like royalty. Chuck drove Helen wherever ribbons were being handed out. The week was a blur of prize pies and homemade breads, champion calves and pigs, and 4-H dresses.

The next week they were eating breakfast, feeling a bit of a letdown.

"Remember, Judy is coming from Indianapolis today. She said she wanted to talk to us; it must be important. She's going to stop and see Grandma while she's here. We can leave to restock cards after she's gone."

When Judy came she seemed nervous. Her voice was shaking. "This is so hard for me. I know I'm going to disappoint you and that's the last thing I want. After fourteen years I believe I need to divorce Wayne. This is so huge, especially for the girls. I need to get your perspective. This makes me sad because I know it dishonors you," tears filled her eyes.

"Oh Judy, I'm so sorry," Helen said, surprise in her voice.

Walt was thoughtful, "This is becoming more common. You know Ed and Ruth got a divorce. I guess they're the only ones we know. The church opposes divorce; I think there's a scripture they quote, though that doesn't mean much to me. I think until we walk in others' footsteps we shouldn't judge."

"Are you sure about this, Judy? Is this Wayne's idea?"

"No, it's mine. He says I should get this crazy idea out of my head and let us get on with our lives. I think he believes, if he bullies me, I'll back down like I usually do. I know I'm too wimpy with him."

"Do the girls know about this?" Helen asked.

"No, not at all. How it affects the girls is what bothers me most. I made the decision to marry Wayne, so I need to accept the consequences. But Lisa and Stephanie are innocents in our problems; they'll be devastated. I just wanted good in their childhoods, not this. Wayne hasn't been working, so he's home with them. I hate to put them through it. I constantly wonder if they would be better growing up with divorced parents or parents in a bad marriage. That's my dilemma."

"I know you've been seeing a counselor. What does he advise?"

"Of course he won't tell me what to do, but I'm sure he thinks I need to be stronger; stand up for myself. I know it shouldn't continue as it is; we need to work on it."

"I'm sorry you have to go through this, Judy. We knew you and Wayne had some issues, but we didn't know it was this...desperate."

"I didn't want anyone to know. I'm embarrassed. I always thought if I had marital problems, I would work harder and solve them. I don't think that anymore. I've been losing weight, it's hard to focus at work, and I just found out I have an ulcer. That's what prompted me to do something—knowing it's affecting my health."

"I think we need to hear Wayne's side of the story. Not that we don't believe you, but there's always two sides to everything," Walt said.

"I wish you would. I know you'll have insights I've missed. You two have had such a good marriage, you've set a good example. I feel I've failed: you, the girls, the family, even Wayne. This isn't what he wants. It's November now. I told him last week that I want both of us to get counseling over the winter. If we aren't both working to make it better, by June when Lisa gets out of school, I'll file for divorce. Stephanie is only five, it will be even harder for her. That way they'll have the summer to heal a bit. In Indiana we have six months from the time of filing until the divorce is final. One year from now to make things right. I hope he'll agree to counseling, but he says he won't since I'm the one who needs it. Pray for us that we can work it out."

"Know that we support you, whatever you decide to do. We pray for all of you every day. It breaks our heart when our children aren't happy. In a few weeks we leave for Tucson. We'll spend the night in Indy and sit down and talk through this. You'll have our blessing whatever happens."

Tears slipped down Judy's cheeks. Grateful for their openminded concern, she wasn't sure she had the courage to do this without their approval. "Now I have to tell Grandma. This is the worst day of my life."

Indeed, it was a year later, on a beautiful day in October when Judy went to the attorney's office and signed papers dissolving her marriage. Afterward, Nancy took her to Eagle Creek Park where they sat on a bench beside the lake. Drifting fall leaves, endless blue sky, and gentle lapping water softened the blow of failure. Nancy provided the perfect solace and quiet musings. She promised they would loan Judy the money to pay her ex-husband his portion of the equity in their house. This assured that Lisa and Stephanie could stay in their home and return to their school.

All the siblings and in-laws pitched in, renovating the upstairs in Judy's home, allowing her to take in a female renter for a few years as a means to repay the loan. Ed was always available to fix a leak or teach Judy the importance of checking the oil in her big Chevrolet station wagon. Judy would find food in her pantry after Nan visited. Saturdays spent at the Children's Museum with Nan, Krista, and Kelly maintained Lisa and Stephanie's routine from happier times. Judy never appreciated things mechanical, necessitating gentle chiding when Ed found her car nearly empty of oil, again.

The hard-working siblings had built successful lives. This breach in Judy's family was an unanticipated pitfall that bonded them in their efforts to support her; each sibling found ways to help. It sealed the belief that all six would stick together—no one of them would walk alone. Misfortune to one imprinted on the others: barn fires that jeopardized livelihood, life-threatening illness, a needed kidney transplant, cancer, and accidents were met head-on—survived as a group. It's not that there were never words—they were Steffens after all. "Knock it off, you're a Steffen", was freely given and freely received. Their footprints followed the bloodline back to Sarah, Esther, and Helen—everyone pulling forward together. The tenor from this time set the tone for subsequent remarkable family cohesion.

CHAPTER 50

Walt and Esther

"Look Walt," Helen extended her left hand which was tremoring.

"Why does it shake like that? Can you make it stop?" Walt reached out to hold her hand.

"See, it stops when you hold it; moving my hand also makes it stop."

"I've seen other people whose hands shake. I guess when you're seventy-six these things happen. How long has it been doing this?"

"It just started. I can't control it. It doesn't hurt; I hope it's nothing. Mother's been complaining about pain in *her* hands, but I don't think they shake. She's given up knotting comforters. I've never been able to use my right hand, now my left hand shakes. I'm falling apart, Walt. Don't say anything to anybody; maybe it will go away."

It didn't go away. Over the next months the tremors occurred more often. Her only functional hand was no longer dependable to cut, chop, carry objects, or even hold the phone to her ear. When they told the children, Judy insisted she see the best neurologist in Indianapolis. His diagnosis was not what anyone wanted to hear: Parkinson's Disease. He said it was a disease with progressive deterioration. In some, the progress was rapid, in others, change occurred slowly. There was medicine to control the symptoms, though it had troublesome side effects. The goal was to balance the symptoms of PD with the side effects of the medicine.

Helen was determined this disease would not get the best of her. Learning her legs would become weak and unsteady, she bought a treadmill and set up an exercise regimen. Walt helped more in the kitchen; otherwise, she ignored the disease.

Around this time, Esther was scheduled for carpel tunnel surgery on both hands. Though surgery was risky on a ninety-five-year-old, she could no longer endure the pain and numbness. She would need to go to Greencroft assisted living after surgery, as both hands would be bandaged and nonfunctional. Helen and her sisters questioned if she would ever return to her home, believing Owen incapable of caring for himself without Esther's assistance. Though surgery was successful, Esther was overwhelmed by weeks of pain. She complained woefully to her daily visitors.

"Rosemary, you have to help me. I can't take this pain. I had no idea it could hurt so bad. Look how swollen my hands are."

Rosemary readjusted the pillows and ice bags. "Did you get your morning pain pill?"

"Yes, but it's not strong enough. I would never have had this surgery if I knew the pain would be this bad. I'm all by myself in this room. The nurses just come and go, bringing a pill or fixing the ice. When I move my head, I still get dizzy from the anesthesia. I worry about Owen...." Esther was unhappy and discouraged.

"Remember Mother, we didn't have a choice about having the surgery; you had too much nerve damage. At your age they must be careful how much pain medicine they give you. I'm going to stay and feed you lunch. Erdene will be in this afternoon. Helen is with Owen this morning. He's been quite forgetful; he forgets his medicine and loses his hearing aids. Yesterday they found his hearing aids in his denture cup. Louise is going to talk to his nephew about getting him a room in this same area where you are. That way you can spend time together."

Esther snapped to attention, "Owen will have a fit about that. He always said he wasn't going to throw his money away on a nursing home."

"We'll help him as much as we can, Mother, but I doubt it's safe for him to be alone. Next, he'll fall and break a hip."

Esther was thoughtful, "Rosemary, I bet I'll never get home again. This surgery has been too hard on me. I trust in the Lord, but I don't know why He keeps me alive. Ninety-five is too long to live."

"I know the pain wears you down and makes you discouraged, Mother. At your age it takes a long time for your hands to heal. But it will happen. Let's go down to the dining room and get you some ice cream. The more active you are, the sooner you'll be better."

"They do take good care of me here. I know I couldn't get along at home. I hope Owen listens to his nephew. He shouldn't be alone; he's too unsteady."

With Helen's diagnosis of Parkinson's, the couple realized they must move ahead with travel plans and settle their estate. By now the farm totaled 250 acres. Randy and Vanessa and Steve and Julie both built homes on farm property. The farmhouse was a hive of activity with seven of their grandchildren spending after-school hours with Walt and Helen.

In 1988 they took a month-long trip to Mafia Island, pleased to find the dairy running smoothly, small herds of cows scattered around the island, and plenty of milk sold in the village. They visited neighbors, church friends, and Henry Stanley and Maria. Other than children growing, they were surprised little had changed in eight years. For the remainder of the trip they took touristy excursions around Africa, Europe, and England. Finished with foreign travel, they returned to America, satisfied the dairy was successful.

Old age sidles into the elderly person's world so stealthily—like a buried secret that was always there but never confronted in the raw. In the normal day-to-day there were never enough hours—so much glittered and beckoned, calling one's name. One day you decided to end the day in the afternoon; soon that became the norm. Your vision became fickle; you decided it was easier to stay home at night. How did you get such a gut—belying your lunchtime salads, washing windows, mopping floors, and chasing grandchildren? There was the frustration that many body parts hurt and let you down—one day this, the next day that. Your brain balked when you tried to remember a friend's name. The most difficult to accept was what looked back when you gazed in the mirror: an inchoate startle that this happened while you were there and never saw it coming. From whence came the faded you, with webbed, blotchy skin, saggy jowls and errant hairs. Now the realization that you alone looked in the mirror and saw a spritely nineteen-year-old and a polished, confident forty-year-old. How could this be?

"Oh Helen, who would have thought I'd live this long?" Helen had returned Esther to her room in the nursing home after her ninety-eighth birthday party. "I keep thinking the good Lord will take me—and here I am."

"I know how you feel, Mother. In two weeks, I'll be seventy-eight. The years somehow slipped past and here I am, an old woman. I know you tire easily and have aches and pains, but your mind is still sharp. You're probably healthier than I am."

"It's because everyone in the family takes good care of me. Not a day goes by I don't see family. That's what keeps me going. I get such a kick out of the little ones who come in and make such a ruckus. I didn't think I'd outlive Owen, but now he's gone too. He didn't like the nursing home, so I'm glad he didn't linger."

"Walt thought Owen helped keep you alive. Looking after him kept you active and your mind occupied."

"That's probably right. He wasn't the easiest person to care for."

"You wondered why you're still here. It's because the family still needs you, Mother. We look to your example. You're still teaching us how to live."

"Thank you for saying that, Helen. It means a lot. Every day I pray I treat people kindly and don't complain, though I'm not always successful. I was miserable after that surgery, but it's good it was done. My hands are fine now."

"Your hands *are* good, aren't they? With this Parkinson's, my left hand is so shaky. I've decided to quit my greeting card business; I'm not satisfied with my artwork anymore. Mother, I sold 75,000 cards. Can you believe it? That little business was good for Walt and me. It helped fill our days and got us out and about."

"Everyone in Goshen knows your cards. They'll be missed. You've always accomplished so much in spite of great odds. You're *my* example, Helen."

* * * * *

Judy's mind was uneasy on the drive to Goshen. Though she was the "go-to" medical person in the family, her parents had never asked her to intervene in their health. Helen had called, convinced their family doctor was missing something with Walt. At seventy-seven years he was like an ox, strong and muscular. He was never ill, and still took no prescribed medicine. Helen said he was taking Advil a couple times a day, yet the pain seemed worse. It was uncomfortable for him to wear his pants buttoned. He was waking at night in pain.

"Okay Daddy, let's get to the bottom of this. Tell me where your pain is," she said as she palpated his abdomen. You think you've felt it at least three months? Dr. Rout gave you something for prostate, but it's not helping." After her examination, she agreed with Helen that something was wrong.

"I'm going to get appointments in Indianapolis for a gastro-enterologist and a urologist. They're good doctors. They'll work you into their schedules, I think. We'll figure this out."

A week later the Indianapolis gastroenterologist spent fifteen minutes with Walt. He called Judy into his office. "I don't have good news for you, Judy. I think your dad has either pancreatic cancer or cancer of the small intestine—maybe both. We'll get a cat scan this afternoon. Bring him back tomorrow and we'll know the answer. I'm so sorry to tell you this; your father is a nice man."

Struck by a thunder bolt, this news was incomprehensible. Anyone with this advanced cancer must have had symptoms for months. Her dad still looked healthy and kept to his normal activities. He just wasn't a complainer.

The next morning Judy went to her office and dialed in to the restricted line where radiologists dictate their findings: *This seventy-*

seven-year-old male has diffuse cancer throughout the abdomen originating in the pancreas. It has metastasized to the liver, the small bowel and multiple lymph nodes. "No, no! It's my daddy they're talking about," Judy screamed unknowingly, dropping the phone as if it burned her fingers. She knew she had heard a death sentence. In the family's sheltered world, they'd not known this depth of heartache.

That afternoon Doctor Calden told Walt, Helen, and Judy the horrific news. He was truthful: pancreatic cancer was a bad cancer. Because it had spread to other organs, the likelihood for cure was uncertain.

Walt was subdued, "Thank you for finding the cause of my pain. At least, now I know."

"Are you sure, Doctor? He hasn't seemed that sick," Helen spoke as in a trance.

"Yes, I'm sure, Mrs. Steffen. But we have options. I'd like you to see an oncologist. We can arrange this for tomorrow so you don't need to make another trip to Indianapolis. There's a new drug to treat pancreatic cancer. The oncologist can tell you about it and suggest if it has potential for you."

Judy's chest was bursting with desperation. She knew, and she knew Dr. Calden knew, the chances of this drug reversing her dad's cancer were almost nil. She also knew the drug had few side effects; it wouldn't make him even more miserable. After seeing the oncologist, Walt and Helen agreed to return the next week to start chemotherapy.

The return trip to Goshen was quiet, just occasional questions and mumblings. Their minds reeled, trying to process that their healthy, strong family patriarch was dying. Once home, they all sat around the kitchen table at the farm reviewing the previous days, finding slivers of hope and initiating plans for the weeks ahead. On medication that controlled his pain, Walt finally nodded off.

The siblings all went to Jan's house. Each found a quiet place where they could release pent-up shock and grief before they gathered in the living room. "I know he's going to die. There's nothing we can do about that. What I hate is that he'll have a difficult and painful death. That's just the way it is with pancreatic cancer," Judy said tearfully.

"How long do you think he'll live?" Steve asked.

"It's a guess, but probably through the summer."

"Mother won't be able to take care of him," Randy said.

"We'll take turns so one of us is with them all the time." In Jan's mind she was already blocking off weeks.

"I can't be in Virginia when Daddy is dying. Galen will understand I need to be here," Sue was the only one who lived a far distance.

Nan thought aloud, "Judy, you say he'll be in a lot of pain. Will *we* be able to take care of him at the farm?"

Steve nodded, "If I know Dad, he'll want to stay on the farm. We'll just have to find a way. He'll want to look out on his land and have the grandkids around."

"We'll be right there if they need us in a hurry." Julie said.

On into the night they talked, always circling back to the horrifying truth that their dad was dying.

A few days later Helen walked down the hall to Esther's room in the nursing home. One could hear the weight of the world in the slow drag of her foot. Tears came unbidden to her eyes as she clasped her mother's hand.

"Helen...what is it?" dread filled Esther's words.

"You know we took Walt to see a doctor in Indianapolis. He's very sick, Mother. He has cancer all through his abdomen." With her mother it was finally safe to release all the sadness, fear, and uncertainties of the previous days. Her tears were cleansing, bolstering her courage for the days ahead. "We'll take him back to Indianapolis next week to start the chemo. Oh Mother, pray that it heals him."

Esther's breath expelled as if forced from her chest. "You've known all these years I love that man," her voice crackled with watery tears. "It's just not right. He shouldn't go before me."

"Walt's very complacent. Yesterday he mowed that whole acre of lawn. It helped him think. We got our affairs in order a few years ago. More than anything, he's relieved to have something for the pain. It's hard for me not to feel angry at our family doctor who kept discounting his symptoms, but I know that gets us nowhere. The kids are taking care of things. It's good to have them around. He had a nice talk with Sue. He seems relaxed and accepting—not even sad. He told her this is as it should be; he's had a long, happy life. Much better he get cancer than a young farmer who has a family to raise. Our children are doing well; he's at peace about leaving us. Ron has been the best addition to our family—we all love him. He was here over the weekend helping Walt repair things around the farm. That man can fix anything. He and Judy are so happy together and he's good with Lisa and Stephanie. Mother, he fits into our family perfectly."

"I feel the same as you about Ron," Esther smiled. "He brought his Dad all the way from Indianapolis to visit me. They are such gentlemen. His dad was all decked out in a suit and tie, just to see me. Ron will take good care of Judy and the girls, I know it."

"Walt liked him from the beginning, and I've always said he's the best judge of character. I better go, Mother. We have lots of appointments this week, so I may not see you until the Sunday Mother's Day get-together."

"You tell Walt I love him and pray always for his healing. I pray for strength for you too, Helen. Don't worry about coming to see me. You take care of Walt."

The couple went to church as usual on Sunday. It seemed to Helen, Walt was more frail. A few days later he was admitted to the Indianapolis hospital for a medical work-up and to begin chemotherapy. In the hospital he was given intravenous morphine. They added a morphine skin patch which would take effect later that night.

It was decided Nan and Ed would spend the night in his room. Helen, Sue, and Jan stayed at Judy's house. Around two o'clock in the morning, Judy's phone shrilled in the quiet night.

"Mother, wake up," Judy jostled Helen from a deep sleep. Jan and Sue were instantly awake. Helen was groggy, "Is it morning?"

"No. It's about two in the morning. A chaplain from the hospital just called. She said we need to go to the hospital right away."

"What's wrong?" Helen asked, now alert.

"She didn't say, but I think we should hurry in case Daddy got worse." Helen washed her face and dressed with Jan and Sue's rushed assistance. Judy drove through the chill May night, running red lights as there was little traffic. A Catholic nun in her habit was waiting outside Walt's door.

"Your husband has passed to his eternal rest, Mrs. Steffen. He died about thirty minutes ago. Your daughter and her husband were with him."

Helen's hand flew to her mouth, her face crumpled. Never had this strong woman appeared so small and defenseless. "What happened?" she gasped. "He wasn't that sick. He mowed our lawn on Saturday. He was supposed to start chemo tomorrow."

"I'm not able to give you any medical information. In the morning you can talk to his doctor. If you like, I'll go in with your family and say a prayer."

"Thank you, that would be nice." Helen's mind was ablaze with questions and random thoughts—a meteoric splash in her brain. At the same time, she felt a hollowed-out void—she couldn't pull her thoughts together. She sensed a shadowy irony that a Catholic nun was praying for Walt at his death. She was drifting.... "In Jesus Holy Name, Amen."

The nun left the family to say their good-byes. Everyone was in a state of shock. This dear father who wanted so much for them, who taught them to be good people, who always stood up for them, who by example taught them to do for others—now gone. They only recently learned he was sick; they hadn't prepared for his imminent death. It would be awhile before the heft of it sunk in.

"Mother, we'll go out and let you have time with Dad. We'll be in the family lounge," Jan guided them out.

Helen's mind seemed to float: *I should be weeping. I just feel numb. Her lips formed a subtle smile. Anything I would say, I've said many times over the last fifty-six years. She lifted his thick calloused hand to her lips. Oh, Walt, this isn't what I wanted—I hoped to go before you. Now I'll be a burden for the kids.... We were good together, you and me. I'm thankful for every day of those years. There was never a time I didn't want to be with you.... There was never a time you didn't take care of me.... I think I pushed you too hard sometimes.... Before we got married you said what mattered was if you still knocked my socks off after fifty years.... Yes, you still knocked my socks off, Honey. Her hand reached her white hair.... No one will call me his little brunette anymore.*

Poor Nan and Ed somehow felt responsible, fearing the family would think they had failed in standing watch. Nan kept repeating: "Honestly, we didn't fall asleep. I had stood to walk a bit. I rubbed his feet and they moved. Not more than five minutes later I looked, and his chest wasn't moving. I stood up, motioned to Ed, and we saw he wasn't breathing. I can't believe I was sitting right beside his bed and didn't know he was dying." She kept repeating, "I don't understand how it happened."

Judy was quiet and thoughtful as she listened to Nan vent her misgivings. She led her into the hall. "I think I know what happened. It doesn't make any difference—you'd never be at fault for anything. I think they gave him too much morphine and it killed him. With an overdose, the respirations get slower and finally stop. They probably dosed him as they would other patients with end-stage cancer of the pancreas. But Dad was only taking Advil until two weeks ago—today was the first he had morphine. Remember they said the morphine patch would kick in at night? I think it did, and along with the IV morphine, he slowly quit breathing. I could be wrong, and we'll never know for sure, but Nan, what a blessing. This is the way it was supposed to be. It was God's plan for him. Daddy slipped away in his sleep and was spared months of pain and agony. We can remember him strong and vital. He would have hated being an invalid." The sisters embraced. Now the pieces fit together.

Helen wanted to stay in the farmhouse where she felt close to Walt and the grandchildren. Her only concession was to get locks on the doors. The children reluctantly agreed because Steve's family was just down the road. Also, Jan and Randy's families were in and out daily, feeding calves, mowing lawn, and keeping the house passably clean. As months went by it became apparent that Walt had compensated for Helen's progressive disabilities. Her perception of day and time were skewed. Her sense of taste and smell deteriorated, and she forgot to clean the refrigerator, sometimes eating spoiled food. Yet she resented when the children cleaned: "Jan, you don't need to clean my refrigerator and wash my clothes. I was going to do that this afternoon," was her constant refrain. She no longer understood basic math or could make change, at risk for setting herself to be scammed by a dishonest shopkeeper. The neurologist explained she had Lewy Body Dementia which sometimes occurred with Parkinson's. Ever-present was the familiar struggle between children and parent, balancing safety and independence—especially as she was unaware of her limitations.

Another difficulty for Helen was a side-effect of the Parkinson's medicine: hallucinations and delusions. She was afraid when she "saw" a man in the house, that "person" as real as her own children. She would wake in the night, not knowing what was real and what was a dream. It wasn't helpful for someone to tell her she was seeing an illusion.

Helen's world shrunk to self-care, family outings, church activities, and watercolor painting. After totaling her car, she was no longer allowed to drive. Despite this, her life was full: exercising, grandchildren's T-ball games, piano recitals, school programs, and dinners with family. She spent short periods of time with Sue and Galen in Virginia and wintery weeks in Florida with Judy and Ron.

She was with Jan and Lowell in Virginia after Christmas in 1996 when Sue got a phone call from Indiana. "Mother, Rosemary called. They don't want to ruin your vacation but they're suggesting you return home. Grandma Esther is slipping; they think she won't live much longer."

"I need to go. I want to be with her. Mother was hoping to make it to her one-hundredth birthday, but I guess she won't quite make it. She's tired—she doesn't want to linger."

"Let's get your things together. We'll leave in the morning," Jan said.

On December thirtieth Grandma Esther woke feeling uneasy, short of breath, and restless. When Beth visited in the morning, Grandma asked, "Beth, can you help me?"

"We'll be here with you, Grandma. Karen is coming in a bit. Would you like us to bring your sister Clara to see you today?"

"Yes, I'd like to see Clara." By lunch time Esther was no longer responsive. Throughout the day the family meandered into the nursing home, mingling in Esther's room or settling in the family lounge, reminiscing and telling "Grandma" stories. She was the beloved family matriarch; all the family wanted to be near. Her minister came. Clara, who would live to one hundred five years, came in the afternoon, situated in a place of honor at Esther's bedside.

As evening dimmed the horizon, Esther passed into the gentle night with all the family at her bedside. In the quiet, they heard Helen's limping foot slowly navigating the long hall to her room. Now all was well—everyone was here.

This moment of passing and quiet reflection felt auspicious. Esther had not only been the nucleus of the family, she symbolized the American Woman of the Twentieth Century during which the world changed immensely: from the wavering light of a candle to the light of nuclear energy; from a horse-drawn wagon to a space shuttle; from the general store to a mega-mall using credit cards and bar codes; from a wood-fired cookstove to a microwave; from a slab of bacon to draw infection, to antibiotics, contraceptive pills, and DNA sequencing; from walking to school to walking on the moon. These women of the century staunchly moved with history, and in their quiet and refined manner radiated their phosphorescent bloom onto the world—a heritage unequaled.

CHAPTER 51

Helen

Helen's heart thumped in her chest when she opened the letter from Greencroft Retirement Center.

She had been on their wait list to get an apartment; now one was available. As much as she hated to leave the farm, she knew it was time. Her heartbeat was irregular, Parkinson's caused instability, and though she'd never admit it, she realized her mind was failing. She had been alone at the farm for three years; she knew the children thought that was enough.

To leave the farm, her flowers, the baying calves, the songbirds, her porch swing, and the treasured possessions of her and Walt's life together gouged into her spirit. *This* good-bye felt like the *true* end of her life. Walt had hated the idea of a nursing home; she knew she'd never feel his closeness there. The remainder of her years would be back-peddling—just making do. What was hardest was facing the significance of this move: a further loss of independence and an inexorable step closer to death. It forced her to see her life slipping away.

It helped that she had friends at Greencroft. Her apartment was cozy; she had her own things. True to her nature she dived into her new home, signing up for physical therapy, exercise class, watercolor lessons, and game night. Church friends drove her to Yellow Creek on Sundays. The children visited daily, taking her to grandchildren's events. She planted and tended flowers outside her door. The days stretched to months, the months to years. She wasn't unhappy, it was that, in this period of her life, she had more limitations than even *her* foggy mind could ignore.

Randy always woke her in the morning and fixed her breakfast. Hazel, her Yellow Creek friend in the nursing home, accompanied her to lunch. Jan came every evening to make dinner. The sisters in Indianapolis helped with weekends.

Randy telephoned Jan, "I'm going to take Mother to see the doctor. When I came this morning, she couldn't speak right and what she says doesn't make sense. She's having trouble walking. She's upset. She knows something's wrong."

Being a school principal, Jan had a flexible schedule. "I'll come over, Ran. I guess she wasn't able to push the button on the alarm she wears."

The doctor examined her carefully. "You've had a mini stroke, Helen. This happens to elderly people and especially to those with atrial fib. I'll increase your medicine a bit. Does she forget to take her medicine?" he asked.

"She did. Now we give it to her. We don't miss medicine," Randy said.

"Usually with these mini strokes people recover somewhat but they tend to recur, so there's deterioration over time," the doctor advised.

"We'll need to get an aide to stay with her. She can't be alone, that's for sure. Do we need to move her to assisted living?" Jan asked.

"Let's wait a few days and see how she does. She has told me she wants to stay in her apartment." Helen's doctor was her friend and a strong advocate for her.

Randy laughed, "Yeah, we all know how she feels about that."

"Helen, when your mind clears a little, this would be a good time for you and your family to talk about medical directives. You need to get in writing what you want done in case of a medical emergency. For example, if you have a major stroke, do you want to be taken to the hospital? Do you want IV's started? The Greencroft nurses can help you with this, and I can answer questions as well."

Several days later Randy again called Jan, "Mother has fire in her belly this morning," he chuckled. "She wants to get rid of the nurse aides—says she doesn't need them. She's pretty much back to normal, which isn't great, but she thinks there's nothing wrong with her. She's definitely not going to voluntarily move to assisted living."

"Let's tell her we had to hire them by the month. We can let them go next week," Jan suggested. "We have a meeting about medical directives scheduled with the nurses next Thursday. Judy is writing a rough draft. She and Nan are coming from Indy Wednesday evening. Let's all eat at our house."

This was the trajectory of Helen's health: every three or four months she would have a mini stroke leaving her incapable of self-care for a few weeks. These strokes took their toll, it took longer for her to rebound, and she steadily lost ground. After one of the strokes the children realized that Helen could no longer participate in the decision to move to assisted living. She was no longer safe, and she potentially jeopardized other apartment residents. They were all there to put her in a wheelchair and move her across campus to assisted living. There wasn't a dry eye; the rhythm of her life was slowed yet again. She was utterly defeated, yet her shoulders were straight, a gritty determination in the set of her chin.

She was in assisted living for eight months. Friendly and compliant, she retained the essence of her previous eighty-four years. She gripped the wall railing, walking for exercise. Though she always knew her family, her brain was sometimes too damaged to live in the present. Increasingly she lived in her youth, conversing with friends of yore. If her children and friends searched and prodded, they retrieved a spark of the Helen that lurked and occasionally surfaced. The toddlers were not bothered, climbing on her lap and jabbering, not put off by her unusual conversations. They recognized her as she had been.

Her sister Rosemary was her devoted helper, kindness personified when Helen's behavior was strange. She visited every day, feeding her at lunch time. Hazel, Helen's dear friend from Yellow Creek and also a Greencroft resident spent time every day, feeding her supper and taking her to programs and church services. To the end she knew only love and support.

"You need to come right away. Your mother had a major stroke; she's only clinging to life. We're following her wishes not to hospitalize her or start intravenous medication to support her blood pressure." Each of the children were called by a nurse. By nightfall, all six were at Helen's bedside. Though not conscious, she had revived somewhat and was stable. Her grandson, Nathan, home from college, wanted to spend the night, so the sibs retreated to Jan's house to discuss funeral arrangements. It had been a long day.

It was peaceful for the six of them the next morning at Helen's bedside. Her room was cozy with soft music and comfortable chairs. The staff had set up a table with warm drinks and pastries. There was little change in her condition; she was still unresponsive. The nurses updated her condition and efficiently gave supportive care. Who would expect this little lady would draw so many to her bedside, bringing their memories and happy stories? Residents, staff, and doctors of the nursing home were attentive. Her church friends and ministers, sisters, cousins, nieces and nephews, remembered her calls to them each year on their birthday. Friends of the six children stopped by with a hug and gentle words. The care givers could have viewed the gathering of the children and the parade of visitors as a disruption, but they were grieving too. They wanted Helen to be encircled by those who loved her.

This was a unique bonding time for the siblings who weren't often all together for an extended time. These days took on an almost spiritual reverence. In the afternoon, a lovely lady with curly, auburn hair and an effervescent smile came into Helen's room. "My name is Carol. I love your little mother," she said. "Would it be okay if I sing to her? I often sang and she seemed to enjoy it." Unexpectedly the room was filled, the sound soaring down the hall with the most beautiful operatic soprano, "Nearer my God to Thee...." It seemed like a dream; otherworldly, that this professional voice would sing Helen to her rest. Carol was a volunteer who came several times each week to sing old-time melodies and hymns to the elderly residents.

The experience of these days felt foreign to Nancy and Judy who were "big city" women. In Indianapolis, the death of a parent would be a more private, circumspect affair. In this small-town culture, professionals, neighbors, and friends and family were integrated into the dying journey, demonstrating a community belief that it takes a village to bury one's parent. These days brought solace, overcoming the shadows around death, easing into the circle of life.

The third day after Helen's stroke her condition was unchanged, she was still comatose. She had not had food or water. "Sometimes we find our elderly patients fight death, believing they need to stay alive for some reason. Is it possible your mother needs your permission to die?" the chaplain asked. "You're a close family. Maybe she doesn't want to leave you," she said after spending time in Helen's room.

"I think it's possible Mother *is* fighting death. She sure isn't getting better," Jan said.

"We know Mother's a fighter. She fought for everything all her life. Why would she change now?" Sue smiled.

"It'll have to be Randy or Steve to tell her—you two are the only one's she's ever listened to," Nan teased, punching Ran.

"Go for it, Ran," Steve said, "I'll go with you."

"What am I supposed to say?" Randy asked.

"You can say the stroke left her brain too damaged to heal. We know she's tired. All her family will be okay. We love her and give her our permission to relax and slip away." Jan suggested.

"Let her know we're all here with her," Judy added.

"Okay, Steve, let's go talk to her. Then I need to go to work for a few hours."

Later that afternoon, Judy stepped up to the bed to check Helen's pulse, "Her breathing has changed. This is the way patients breathe just before death. Her pulse is too fast to count. We need to call Randy."

Twenty minutes later Randy rushed into her room to join the siblings sitting and lying on the bed, cradling Helen and tearfully saying good-bye, expressing gratitude to their mother and to each other. The six kids knew the bond they shared with each other and the spouses was rare, a treasure they couldn't assume or take for granted. They would be without parents now. It was up to them to live and pass along the decency and values Walt and Helen had instilled in them.

Judy wiped away tears, "Um-m, guys, I believe Mother isn't dying anymore." She laughed and then they all cracked up, bent double with emotional and uncontrollable raucous hilarity. "Her respirations were down to four a minute, definitely Cheyne Stokes. Now they're fourteen—that's normal."

"Up from the grave she arose," Ran cackled, singing an old Easter hymn.

"Uh, Mother, you have to make a decision here," Steve said with mock seriousness to Helen who lay in calm repose—one could almost detect a smile.

"I'm glad I hurried to get here," Ran was red-faced with pent-up emotion and laughter.

"Ran, what did you say to her when you gave her permission?" Sue teased. "Oh, wouldn't Mother have a hissy-fit if she heard us, hooting like banshees."

"Maybe she's faking all of this, just to get us together and spend time with her," Nan proposed.

Wonder of wonders, the next morning Helen seemed to revive. Her smile was sweet, she swallowed water dripped into her mouth and ate a little Cream of Wheat. She squeezed their hands on command and even murmured on the phone to Sue's daughter, Jennifer. This rebound seemed like a miracle—something only Helen could pull off.

Randy and Steve went back to work. Nan went to Indianapolis overnight. Judy cancelled her and Ron's flight to France. Their daughters and friends were already there, attending Stephanie and Jean Philippe's wedding reception. However, this recovery was short lived. She soon slipped deeper and deeper into a coma, seeming to rest comfortably.

The next day Helen again started Cheyne Stokes respirations, down to a few a minute. Her color was ashen. This time they waited "until they were sure" before calling Randy. Again, he rushed in to complete the circle of six and their dying mother.

"I don't know how she can go this long, hardly breathing and hardly a heartbeat," Judy said.

"Maybe you should give her permission again, Ran," Nan said, only half joking.

"I think she's going to do this her way," Steve said, with respect in his voice.

"Her heart must be so strong. She's had basically nothing to eat or drink for five days," Jan said.

As before, she slowly started breathing more regularly, settling into a peaceful "sleep".

"Foiled again," Judy grinned as they all moved from Helen's bed. This time it wasn't funny.

By Sunday, her organs were closing down. It was a long weary day. Believing she wouldn't live through the night, all six stayed at the nursing home, taking turns to be with her.

"Girls," Steve jostled them awake, "Come, it's time."

"What time is it?"

"Around one o'clock," Steve answered. Together they all slipped into her room. It was peaceful and quiet: no gasping breaths, no fight or struggle. She was done with this life and she did it her way.

When a life ends, emotion will percolate from the heart. However close or distant the tie, death goes not unheeded. Many feel desperate loss, some only a void. Others may feel anger; often there is relief from a struggle ended. In this room that early morning, a comforting peace settled—it was well with their souls.

"Well kids, we're on our own now," Randy said softly, his arm resting on Nan's shoulder.

"We know what they expect of us. They've been showing us all these years," Sue murmured.

"They left *their* mark—now it's our turn."

Steve cradled Mother's hand, "I can hear her say it: remember you're a Steffen."

Jan bent to kiss her mother's forehead, "We can do it, Mother. You won't be disappointed."

Their little mother who never quit trying, who wrote the book on "can do", had prepared them not only to fly, but to soar. No parent can give a greater gift. Their gratitude and pride in their mother suffused through each of them. They felt it as one: we must honor her.

They took this challenge to heart: to do right by her. To memorialize her with honor. While she was alive they hadn't noticed, but looking back on her life, what seeped to the surface was how she repeatedly surmounted hardship. That and the love story with Walt: either of the two alone might have been unimpressive, but the two together were a powerhouse. Such joy it was, imagining Helen, unencumbered by a diseased mind and a damaged body, dancing with Walt in Heaven.

The center of the flower arrangement on her casket was a pair of pink ballet slippers. For the first time she had pretty shoes—ribbons and lightness, allowing her to dance, to leap through the air, to move her body with ease.

At the memorial service, her granddaughters sang the following words:

Did you ever know that you're my hero
And everything I would like to be
I can fly higher than an eagle
'cause you are the wind beneath my wings.

Thank You, Thank You, Thank God for You....

And so, Lisa and Stephanie, my dear daughters. I honor my mother by telling her story, so your heritage can seep under your skin and into your soul. So you can pass it to Maya, Charlotte, Wyatt, and their children. Hear the voices of Sarah, Esther, and Helen. If you listen they will find you—because they *are* you. They are your essence, your sinew and your worth. They lift you up and march you forward, carry you if necessary, while you make your own story for *your* children to tell. A paean to generations of indomitable, honorable women.

Sarah

Esther

Helen

Acknowledgements

I am indebted to the following members of the extended Swihart family who shared memories so this story could come to print: Esther Swihart Phillips; Clara Swihart Gunderman and her daughter Ruth Evelyn Wilson; Noble, Ralph, Sara, and Becky Kendall; Marjorie Swihart and her daughter Barbara Smith; Erdene Phillips Mishler and her daughter Beth Filbrun; Rosemary Phillips Williams who also compiled the Swihart Family Genealogy and "Memories of my Parents", indispensable assets for my research. Rosemary's children, Linda Garber, and David Williams and his wife Jean, continue their mother's interest in family history and contributed stories and photographs. Dave's expertise about 1900's farming methods and implements was invaluable.

The staff at the Whitley County Historical Museum in Columbia City, IN. shared files, maps, photos, and 1800-1900's copies of area newspapers, leading me to Uncle Levi's log cabin and farmstead. Margaret Ott, the docent at the Noble County Historical Society in the old jail in Albion, IN "dug in" to help with my research. Rev. Craig Myers, pastor of the Blue River Church of the Brethren is a historian with interest in the Dunkard Brethren /German Baptist Church. He arranged an interview with Mrs. Ruby Sherman, a ninety-five-year-old member of his congregation, and kindly shared his historical expertise, memorabilia, and photos of Blue River Church of the Brethren. The librarians at the Goshen City Library assisted with microfiche newspaper records, books, and old maps.

My first readers slogged through the rough manuscript, giving perceptive feedback, and convincing me there was a "for real" story in my words. Family readers were my daughters, Lisa Miller and Stephanie Belieres, and my granddaughter Maya Belieres; Ron, my husband; and my siblings. I am most grateful to friends who were first readers: Patricia O'Brien and Jean Mumford of Venice, FL and Janette Yoder of Goshen, IN.

I am humbled by the generosity of my siblings: Jan Vanderveer, Nan Kerr, Sue Shank, Randy Steffen, and Steve Steffen in trusting me to crack open their lives for the world to chew on. While they are on this Earth—life is good. I am so proud and fortunate to be one of the six Steffens.

My dear and long-time friend, Lisa Plank, was the first to believe that my three ladies authentically embodied the times and culture of rural Indiana. She saw their heart. She has read and re-read, been on call for ongoing computer glitches, and shared her editing expertise. Her notes along the way will be forever treasured. Every author should have a Lisa.

At the beginning will always be Ron—my North Star, who let me bury in book for four years, who was patient beyond belief with every computer panic attack, who can parse the perfect word, and whose instinct always defaults to kindness.

SONGS

- "When Peace Like a River" (Page 11) Horatio G. Spafford 1873
- "Lord Jesus, I Long to be Perfectly Whole" (Page 43) James Nicholson 1871; William Fischer 1872
- "Tell Me Why the Stars Do Shine" (Page 91) Swiss-German folksong origin; Miriam Berg Collection, 1940's
- "Comin' Through the Rye" (Page 92) Robert Burns 1798
- "I'm But a Stranger Here" (Page 120) Arthur Sullivan 1872; Thomas Taylor 1836
- "Rock of Ages" (Page 119) Augustus Toplady 1776; Thomas Hastings 1880
- "Shall We Gather at the River?" (Page 121) Robert Lowry 1864
- "God Hath Not Promised Skies Always Blue" (Page 139) Annie J. Flint (lyrics) 1866
- "Whisper A Prayer in the Morning" (Page 164) anonymous
- "Softly and Tenderly, Jesus is Calling" (Page 179) Will Thompson 1880
- "Goshen (Buffalo) Gals, Won't You Come Out Tonight?" (Page 182) John Hodges 1844
- "Sleep Kentucky Babe" (Page 354) Negro Lullaby 1896. University Kentucky Research Center
- "You Are the Wind Beneath My Wings" (Page 430) Larry Henley and Jeff Sebar, Warner House of Music c 1982, 1989 (4 lines used)

CPSIA information can be obtained
at www.ICGtesting.com
Printed in the USA
LVHW111229240921
698556LV00007B/6

9 781506 910260